Issues in INTERNATIONAL BILINGUAL EDUCATION

The Role of the Vernacular

TOPICS IN LANGUAGE AND LINGUISTICS

Series Editors:
Albert Valdman and Thomas A. Sebeok
Indiana University, Bloomington, Indiana

ISSUES IN INTERNATIONAL BILINGUAL EDUCATION:
The Role of the Vernacular
Edited by Beverly Hartford, Albert Valdman, and Charles R. Foster

*I*ssues in
*I*NTERNATIONAL
BILINGUAL EDUCATION
The Role of the Vernacular

Edited by
BEVERLY HARTFORD
and
ALBERT VALDMAN
Indiana University
Bloomington, Indiana

and

CHARLES R. FOSTER
U.S. Department of Education
Washington, D.C.

LC
3715
·I83
1982

ST. JOSEPH'S UNIVERSITY   STX
LC3715.I83 1982
Issues in international bilingual educat

3 9353 00106 5661

196839

PLENUM PRESS • NEW YORK AND LONDON

Library of Congress Cataloging in Publication Data

Main entry under title:
Issues in international bilingual education.

   (Topics in language and linguistics)
   Bibliography: p.
   Includes index.
   1. Education, Bilingual—Addresses, essays, lectures. I. Valdman, Albert. II. Hart-
ford, Beverly. III. Foster, Charles R., 1927–
IV. Series.

| LC3715.I83 | 371.97 | 82-553 |
| ISBN 0-306-40998-4 | | AACR2 |

© 1982 Plenum Press, New York
A Division of Plenum Publishing Corporation
233 Spring Street, New York, N.Y. 10013

Printed in the United States of America

CONTRIBUTORS

Charles R. Foster, *U.S. Office of Bilingual Education and Minority Language Affairs*
Gerald L. Gold, *York University*
Phyllis L. Hagel, *Franklin Northeast Supervisory Union*
Beverly S. Hartford, *Indiana University*
Guy Héraud, *Université de Pau, France*
Rodolfo Jacobson, *University of Texas at San Antonio*
Braj B. Kachru, *University of Illinois*
Carolyn Kessler, *University of Texas at San Antonio*
John W. Oller, Jr., *University of New Mexico*
Christina Bratt Paulston, *University of Pittsburgh*
Shana Poplack, *University of Ottawa*
Mary Ellen Quinn, *Alamo Heights School District, San Antonio*
Isaura Santiago-Santiago, *Teachers College, Columbia University*
Muriel Saville-Troike, *Georgetown University and University of Illinois*
Merrill Swain, *Ontario Institute for Studies in Education*
Elizabeth Sherman Swing, *St. Joseph's University, Philadelphia*
Rudolph C. Troike, *University of Illinois*
Albert Valdman, *Indiana University*

ACKNOWLEDGEMENTS

We would like to thank all those who, directly and indirectly, have made this collection of papers on bilingual education possible. The idea for the book, and particularly its theme, came out of the conference on bilingual education held in November, 1980 at the Wingspread Conference Center in Racine, Wisconsin. Although this publication is not a compilation of the proceedings of the conference, the issues and results of research presented and discussed by forty internationally known scholars in bilingualism were invaluable to us in putting it together.

We particularly wish to thank Ms. Rita Goodman, the Johnson Foundation's Vice President for Programs. Her organizational skills and efficiency in handling the logistics made this conference one of the most pleasant and stimulating we have attended.

We would like to express our great appreciation to the three organizations that made the conference possible: to the Johnson Foundation for making the beautiful facilities of its Wingspread Conference Center available to us as well as providing travel support, to the Office of Bilingual Education and Minority Language Affairs of the U.S. Department of Education, and Indiana University for cosponsoring the conference. We are also grateful to the U.S. Department of Education and Indiana University for underwriting the cost of this publication. The ideas and opinions expressed in the papers, however, in no way represent those of the U.S. Department of Education or those of Indiana University.

Finally, we would like to thank Rogette Hector, Lois Kuter and Carol Wambold for their valuable assistance in preparing this collection of papers on bilingual education for publication. Without it, this volume may not have been realized.

CONTENTS

INTRODUCTION

CHRISTINA BRATT PAULSTON

There is an important difference between merely experimental and
genuine experiment. The one may be a feeling for novelty, the
other is rationally based on experience seeking a better way.
— Frank Lloyd Wright

Wright was talking about architecture, but the same difference can be
applied to analyzing the relationship between standard and vernacular
languages in bilingual education; surely we are also seeking a better way to
handle bilingual education based on experience.

How rationally based our efforts are, is another question. Works on this
and similar topics can at times become the scene for very emotional—and
very moving—presentations which sometimes are more utopian than
rational. One can perhaps call this a very 'rational' text, because so few of
the contributors are members of ethnic subordinate groups. Am I
suggesting that minority group members are less rational? Of course not. I
am suggesting that it is much easier to be calm, objective and scholarly
about the lot of others than about your own. The most salient feature about
the bilingual education of vernacular speaking groups is the social and
economic exploitation of its members by the dominant group. The papers
herein, treating bilingual education from a psychological perspective, agree
at least on the issue that an understanding of the social and economic
factors underlying bilingual education is crucial for understanding the
psychological studies on bilingualism.

But clearly there are many other issues one can raise about the role of vernacular languages in bilingual education. There is the deceptively simple question of linguistic description, which is a necessary element in bilingual education. Poplack's fine paper is incidentally an interesting comment on field methods courses and how much information is typically lacking from standard linguistic description. Her variationist approach to bilingualism, and particularly to the vernacular, is an impressive contribution to the documentation of the dual process of language maintenance and language shift. The process of language shift is comparatively easy to establish, but to document language maintenance in a bilingual shift situation is very tricky, and Poplack's attempt is both theoretically and methodologically interesting. For example, she demonstrates that variability in the vernacular could not be accounted for solely by the bilingualism or nonbilingualism of her subjects, nor by extended contact with English, but is based on what Labov calls 'inherent variability'.

Kachru's paper raised a number of other important linguistic issues to consider in the study of bilingualism. It is certainly clear that to be bilingual is a very variable condition. The theoretical problem at the heart of cross-cultural comparisons as to whether the 'bilingual' is to be defined from within the bilingual community or not is also raised here by Kachru. Are problems of language competence to be seen in terms of the individual or in terms of the speech community? I would argue for the latter, in terms of the speech community, because the socio-cultural-economic factors of the speech community are the ones that influence the particular conditions and constellations of characteristics in the individual. One of the phenomena Kachru looks at is code-/language-switching at various levels of possible linguistic analysis, demonstrating this individual/community interaction. He shows how sociolinguistic information such as setting, role, topic, influence the choice of code, and how, in the diglossic context of prestige forms vs. nonprestige forms, these factors influence code choice.

The Kessler/Quinn paper brings up the old question of language and thought from a psychological perspective. Even though it is clear that we are far from reaching any agreement on this problem, it still remains a viable question. Many of us do agree with Kessler/Quinn's paraphrase of Cummins 'that the critical question for research is not what effect bilingualism *per se* has on cognitive processes, but rather on identifying the conditions under which bilingualism facilitates or retards cognitive growth'. Their approach, which examines only one aspect of cognitive growth, divergent thinking and hypothesis formation, highlights the need to look at various areas of cognition, in order to discover as many areas of influence on cognitive growth by bilingualism as possible.

The paper by Swain partially does that. She sorts out for us which features of the Canadian immersion programs are salient for 'export', i.e., which aspects of the bilingual programs can be expected to be transferable and, equally important, those which are not. The paper is important in that it makes clear that the automatic success of the Canadian immersion programs cannot be expected, as is frequently claimed, by wholesale importation of the programs into a different social milieu.

Oller's paper makes clear how personal, subjective, and emotional issues in testing can become, in spite of the aura of objectivity that results from quantitative data. There are two issues we cannot afford to forget: 1) the disparity between the theoretical-technical issues in testing and the enormous impact of politics and the politics of testing on the entire process, and 2) (which is mostly ignored) the fact that testing is one of the major features within the schools which influences teaching and curricula the most.

Santiago-Santiago's paper continues Oller's conflictual approach and brings up an interesting issue that keeps surfacing in this volume, Carnoy's concept of schools as an instrument of social control to maintain existing policies. This is basically a neo-marxist perspective and although long common in Europe, one would not have heard such a notion in the United States ten years ago as frequently as one does today. The concept of the 'hidden curriculum' has become a household idea. Marxism saw conflict of interest only in terms of socio-economic class while neo-marxism adds the concept of ethnic groups and provides a viable alternative analysis and interpretation of the phenomena of bilingual education.

There are also papers on issues involving the implementation of bilingual education. From Santiago's rather abstract paper on curriculum, we turn to some of the minute details which are also necessary for bilingual education programs. Valdman painstakingly documents the importance of having a uniform orthography and how complicated a process the adoption of a spelling system can be, not only linguistically, but politically as well. Hagel's eminently sensible paper describes a practical-instrumental approach to bilingual education which once more makes it clear that children can learn two languages in school without problems, as long as the situation is free of conflict. It is a nice case study of teacher-parent cooperation.

I have problems with Jacobson's New Concurrent Approach; profound unease in fact. Most of what we know about language acquisition stresses the need to group the language into meaningful units and to separate the two codes in bilingual education. Jacobson deliberately introduces code-switching in the classroom and does so without convincing evidence to support this approach. Caveat emptor.

Interestingly enough, the Troikes' paper on teacher training deals with probably the most ideologically colored topic of the text. The paper emphasizes the political, social, and economic factors which influence bilingual education and, in turn, affect every dimension of teacher training. Their discussion of such issues as recruitment, determination of minimal competencies, and locating training sites, further underlines the view that teacher training tends to be profoundly ideological.

Gerald Gold's paper on Louisiana Creole/French gives us an interesting case study which serves admirably for comparison and contrast in identifying salient features in bilingual education programs. It is my own view that the best approach to a better understanding of bilingual education is to observe the same language and its role in different nations and cultures, and to examine the fate of different languages within the same nations. In short, to compare and contrast the dominant and vernacular languages in an effort to identify the causal variables. For that we need such papers as Gold's.

Another issue in international bilingual education is the relationship between language and nation. Europe is frequently said to adhere to the ideal of one language/one nation. Héraud's paper makes it clear that the actual situation is far from that ideal. Factors such as legislation, group size and prestige play a great part in the language policies of these nations. Iceland is probably the onlyl truly monolingual country in Europe, and that is a result of its geographic isolation. Swing documents, in a case study of the Belgian situation, how very complicated multilingualism within a nation can become. Her admirable paper points up the importance of national economy and politics on national language policy and, in Belgium, the consequent suppression of individual needs and desires in favor of the overriding importance of the territorial group.

And finally, Foster gives us a brief and straightforward picture of bilingual education in the United States. His brief history and discussion of official attitudes towards bilingual education and civil rights offer support for his claim that there is a growing awareness in our schools that the United States, as Europe, is not monolingual and that our school system should reflect that fact. We are, little by little, finding 'a better way' to deal with this issue.

The papers in this volume are concerned with understanding better the role of vernacular languages in bilingual education on an international scale. By sharing experiences, we can only hope that Frank Lloyd Wright's quip, when asked which he considered his greatest building, applies equally well to works on bilingual education: 'The next one, young Johnson, always the next one.'

BILINGUALISM AND THE VERNACULAR

SHANA POPLACK

THE VERNACULAR/STANDARD DISTINCTION

It is well known that any large, socially complex speech community will be linguistically differentiated not only along geographical dimensions, as studied by traditional and modern dialectologists, but also according to sociodemographic characteristics of speakers and the contextual features of situations and activities.

The functioning of a hierarchical social system generates simplifications and stereotypes about the linguistic and other behavior of its members at various levels of the hierarchy. The distinction between vernacular and standard is one such simplification. It obscures a number of distinctions, including those between the spoken and written language, informal and formal speech styles, varieties characteristic of working-class speakers and those of bourgeois speakers, naturally acquired versus educated or literary speech, regionalisms and metropolitan varieties, colloquial and 'correct' speech, current usage and that codified in grammars and dictionaries.

The work of Labov (1966, 1968, 1970, 1972a, 1972b) is an important milestone in the demonstration of the systematicity of the vernacular and in debunking the supposed communicative superiority of the standard. To arrive at these conclusions, Labov had to resolve the methodological problem of observing the vernacular freed from the hypercorrectively distorting effects of a normatively imposed standard.

Without denying the importance of the Observer's Paradox and the technology developed by Gumperz (1964), Labov (1970), and others to circumvent it, it is also true that the vernacular, in the sense of ordinary, every-day language, not only differs from speaker to speaker and from context to context, but the situations in which it is unaffected by influences from one or more standard(s), even in the absence of the observer, may be quite rare. This immediately leads to two problems inherent in the idea of isolating the vernacular. First, there are any number of vernaculars in a single speech community, each situation involving linguistic patterns at least marginally different from the next. Second, there can be no unitary standard for the spoken language, at least in any objective, well-defined sense. The written forms of a language do not coincide with upper class speech, nor with that of prestige centers, nor with the speech behavior of literary or learned persons. Norms of formality, correctness and grammaticality are only occasionally reflected in anyone's performance.

Indeed, the standard may be seen as some idealized set of features which do not completely characterize any real situation, though they may be reflected in different proportions in different linguistic varieties, and whose importance is their contrast with features of one or more vernaculars, informal or colloquial, minority or accented, regional or rural, working-class, etc. Note that these varieties are identified with sociological rather than linguistic labels. It is the ill-defined and idealized nature of the standard which is crucial, since it permits the grouping together of all the diverse varieties of upper-class, learned, conventional speech against all other vernaculars, and perpetuates the notion that the distinction is primarily of linguistic origin when it is really a socially-motivated contrast.

We reformulate the problem of isolating the vernacular, then, as one of describing the speech patterns of a community, as opposed to examining the ideas, intuitions and attitudes which constitute the standard.

METHODOLOGICAL CONSIDERATIONS

Labov (1966) has demonstrated the prevalence of categorical perception in the characterization of linguistic phenomena. Whereas individuals may perform with subtle quantitative differences from situation to situation, both as speakers and as listeners, the subtlety of these differences is not readily accessible to conscious intuition. Many such differences are not remarked at all, while those that are, are exaggerated to the status of categorical occurrences. Indeed, this is a major mechanism leading to the stereotypes mentioned earlier. The problem of categorical perception affects not only methodologies which appeal primarily to native speakers' intuitions, it is also a defect of analyses based on casual observations, even over long periods of time, or collections of examples and anecdotes.

This leaves systematic empirical observation of speech in context as the only reliable way to gather information on the vernacular. Because of the multiplicity of vernaculars, i.e. the variability of the vernacular from one context to the next, and because of the quantity of data necessary to characterize adequately even a few of the important patterns observed, this approach leads to masses of data. To account for these data, an analytic framework is needed which is capable of reflecting the range of differences between contexts in concise and accurate terms. This is the motivation for the development of variation theory.

The internal differentiation of a speech community is not one of some structure or usage being present in one context and absent in a closely related one. Rather it is a case of more or less. In a given situation a speaker uses the available sentence structures in a certain proportion, she chooses appropriate lexical items with specific frequencies, and applies phonological reduction rules at a certain rate. In a somewhat different situation all the frequencies and rates will be slightly different and the differences will tend to be systematic from speaker to speaker. Of course, in very different contexts there may be some more categorical distinctions, but these are relatively rare. A combination of several quantitative changes suffices to make one speech pattern very different from another. To document the differences then, careful counts must be made of various usage patterns, taking into account not only the occurrence of given phenomena, but also every time they did not occur when they might have.

To incorporate the results of these analyses into a theory of linguistic variation, sociolinguists have proposed a number of ways of generalizing the structures of formal linguistics to account for speech performance. These include probabilistic grammars, implicational scales, variable rules, and probabilized lexicons, among others.

While the statistical analysis may be integrated into the linguistic description, it also provides the basis for correlation of community speech behavior with extralinguistic factors. Correlations of frequencies with sociodemographic factors provide clear indices of the linguistic stratification of a community, and the comparison of quantitative results from one situation to another provides an objective taxonomy of linguistically relevant distinctions and similarities among social contexts.

THE SOCIAL IMPLICATIONS OF THE RESEARCH FRAMEWORK

Studies of minority or stigmatized dialects using qualitative or unsystematic methodologies have done a great deal to contribute to the existing ideologies shared by speakers, observers, and all too often, academics, about vernaculars, in particular urban vernaculars. Thus, in a study of the pronunciation of English in New York City, Hubbell (cited in

Labov 1966:36) concludes that 'the pronunciation of a very large number of New Yorkers exhibits a pattern. . . that might most accurately be described as the complete absence of any pattern'. Joseph Matluck says of Puerto Rico that there are few norms of standard language, as Puerto Ricans do not recognize the necessity for them. Because of this, there is no linguistic consciousness whatsoever in the schools, without which it is impossible to fight the pressure of English and the progressive deterioration of Spanish syntax on the Island (1961:342).

Examples such as these could be multiplied for all dialects spoken by any population large or visible enough to attract the attention of researchers. More distressing is that these 'findings' about language, particularly those spoken by minorities, are then translated into appreciations shared by the public and the speakers themselves. It is well-known and no cause for surprise that New Yorkers, Blacks, Hispanics, Montreal French speakers, etc. have a high index of linguistic insecurity.

Misdirected educational policies, bias in employment and social situations, which are all too often the lot of monolingual speakers of vernaculars, are compounded in the case of bilingual individuals and communities. Bilinguals have two languages to contend with, and in urban United States settings, they are generally both considered nonstandard varieties. Whereas the monolingual's vernacular may be characterized as degenerate, there is an added dimension to the study of the bilingual's vernacular: the effects of the contact situation. In a well-established tradition of studies in bilingualism, researchers have claimed over and over that the presence of this or that feature is due to contact and convergence with the language of the majority. To exemplify with Spanish speakers in the United States, prime targets for this sort of study, it has been claimed that their Spanish is losing its gender system (Barkin 1980), that it is losing the subjunctive (Floyd 1979) and other tense/mood distinctions (Klein 1976), that through the intermediary of code-switching Spanish syntax is gradually being replaced by English syntax (Urciuoli 1980), that borrowings are impoverishing the language and the culture (Matluck 1961; Varo 1971) —all purportedly due to contact with English.

Systematic quantitative analysis of monolingual vernaculars has succeeded in discovering regularity and stability where other methodologies could only detect randomness and deterioration. Thus Labov's work on Black English in New York City (1968, 1972b) was replicated in other urban centers (e.g. Mitchell-Kernan 1969; Wolfram 1969; Legum et al. 1971; Baugh 1979). Studies on Montreal French (e.g. G. Sankoff and Vincent 1977) are comparable with quantitative studies of other varieties (Pohl 1975; Ashby 1976). Early work on Caribbean dialects of Spanish (Ma and Herasimchuk 1968) has been replicated again and again by later studies (e.g. Cedergren 1973; Terrell 1975, 1979a, b).

This tradition of scientific investigation of the spoken language has had relatively little impact on bilingual studies. The kinds of stereotypes and bias which have been at least in part dismantled by monolingual vernacular studies are still widely held with respect to bilingual communities.

A VARIATIONIST APPROACH TO BILINGUALISM

To exemplify the role of systematic investigation of linguistic variation in bilingual studies, we examine in ensuing sections the notion of convergence, as it applies to various aspects of Puerto Rican Spanish spoken in East Harlem, New York. Bilingualism has been said to be the major determinant of linguistic convergence, which usually involves the lexicon, but may also affect the grammar. In fact, language contact can cause such far-reaching changes as to modify the structural type of a language (Weinreich 1953; Gumperz and Wilson 1971).

The studies described below focus on the linguistic aspects of an interdisciplinary study of language use on a block in El Barrio, perhaps the oldest, and until recently, the largest Puerto Rican community outside of Puerto Rico (Language Policy Task Force 1980).

Over three years of participant observation of 102nd Street (Pedraza 1979) has indicated that although there are certain interactional norms which guide language choice, and which are instrumental in maintaining Spanish, neither Spanish nor English is used exclusively in any setting. This lack of functional separation of the two languages is at least in part responsible for the widespread use of code-switching as a norm of interaction on 102nd Street.

In addition to the participant observation, a detailed language attitude questionnaire was administered to 91 speakers representative of the different social networks on the block (Attinasi 1979). Among the results which conern us here was a near consensus on the attitudes that Spanish is not well regarded by the American community at large, but that it should nevertheless be kept alive in the Puerto Rican community in New York.

Most respondents claimed to speak 'good Spanish' regardless of their reported language dominance. Indeed, when asked to rate their Spanish competence on a seven point scale, the majority rated themselves as 'perfect' or 'excellent'. 'Good Spanish' was described in a variety of ways, with the most frequently recurring characterizations being good vocabulary and pronunciation. Very few speakers pointed to grammatical correctness as an identifying feature of 'good Spanish'. When asked who could be considered to speak Spanish well, most respondents cited older people, who in this community are mainly Spanish-dominant speakers. This pattern of responses indicates a strong awareness of a Puerto Rican Spanish norm, distinct from that of Castilian Spanish. As we shall see, however, it is precisely the areas of vocabulary and pronunciation in which Puerto Rican Spanish speech most diverges from other dialects.

Given the particular configuration of use of both Spanish and English in this stable bilingual community just described, the positive attitudes expressed by speakers towards both, and the generally negative attitudes of noncommunity members towards language varieties used by Puerto Ricans in New York, we may now turn to some properly linguistic questions. What sorts of changes, if any, come about when two languages are in contact, a situation which has been hypothesized to accelerate, or even cause, linguistic change? In the case of the 'mother tongue' or Spanish, in particular, it has been claimed that lack of exposure to a 'standard' caused by transplanting this language and culture into a new environment, must with time, cause the language to diverge farther and farther from the standard until communication with monolingual speakers is endangered.

To address these issues, the sociolinguistic component of our research has examined the morphophonological, syntactic and semantic levels of linguistic structure. The studies reported here were drawn from data collected from a sample of 20 speakers interviewed on the block. These were chosen on the basis of their representativeness with regard to several parameters, including age, sex, participation in key social networks, age of arrival to the United States, age of acquisition of English, and most importantly, present reported and observed bilingual ability. About half of the speakers may be characterized as balanced bilinguals; the remainder are Spanish-dominant.[1] The sample was constructed in this way under the assumption that influence from English would be more apparent in the speech of those who report and are observed to use it as much as Spanish.[2]

We now review the findings of a series of quantitative studies of language use in a bilingual setting, which all point most strikingly to a single result— the integrity of the Spanish language at its deeper levels despite constant contact with English and purported lack of exposure to the 'standard'.

Variable Concord in Plural Marking

The first problem area we discuss is the variable deletion of plural markers (s) and (n).

Standard Spanish marks the plural redundantly across the noun phrase onto each determiner, noun and adjective in the constituent. Plurality is then repeated in the verb phrase, where the verb must agree with its subject in person and number, as in (1).

1. *Tu sabes, los doctores trataron—sin operarla, a ver si la podian arreglar.* 'You know, the doctors tried to—without operating, to see if they could fix her up.' (02/12)[3]

This results in a great deal of redundancy in the sentence. Moreover, almost every sentence or its context also contains non-inflectional indicators of plurality—morphological, lexical, syntactic and semantic—so that redundancy is even greater than would appear from the surface.

In a study of some 2,500 sentences consisting of an overt or deleted noun phrase and a verb phrase (Poplack 1980a), we sought to answer two types of questions. The first concerns the nature of patterns of plural marking at the sentence level, and the second, the effects on these patterns of long-term contact with English.

Although English also has a concord rule for plural marking, it is characterized by a lesser amount of surface inflection than the Spanish rule. As may be seen in the translation of (1), English only marks plurality inflectionally on the noun. The standard English and Spanish marking sequences may be schematized as in (2). But because both (s) and (n) are subject to deletion, we could also theoretically obtain, for a Spanish noun phrase with two components, any of the eight sequences listed in (2c), after deletion has applied.

2a. Standard Spanish marking sequence: SSN[4] (*Los doctores trataron.*)
2b. Standard English marking sequence: ØSØ (The doctors tried.)
2c. Possible Spanish marking sequences after deletion has applied:

S S N	S S Ø
S Ø N	S Ø Ø
Ø Ø N	Ø Ø Ø
Ø S N	Ø S Ø

In contrast to other studies which have examined these segments in isolation (e.g. Cedergren 1973; Terrell 1979a, b; López-Morales 1980; Alba 1980), we decided to study the interaction between (s) and (n) deletion processes in the same sentence, since plural concord in Spanish is really a sentence level phenomenon. The study was undertaken to see whether marker deletion in the noun phrase and marker deletion in the verb phrase specifically constrained each other, or whether the noun phrase and the verb phrase acted independently, subject only to an overall functional constraint against ambiguity.

Given the differences just mentioned between Spanish and English in both amount and place of plural marking, were we to find that balanced bilinguals deleted markers overall more frequently than Spanish-dominant

Table 1. *Proportion of deleted and retained plural markers on determiners, nouns and verbs for bilingual and Spanish-dominant speakers.*

BILINGUAL						SPANISH-DOMINANT					
Determiner		Noun		Verb		Determiner		Noun		Verb	
Ø	S	Ø	S	Ø	N	Ø	S	Ø	S	Ø	N
.492	.508	.787	.213	.079	.921	.294	.706	.690	.310	.090	.910

speakers and/or that the sequence of such marking as is present in surface structure resembles the English schema (ØSØ), we might hypothesize that these results are due to influence from and convergence with English.

As Table 1 shows, however, this is not the case. Though bilinguals delete more from determiners (.492 vs. .294), they also delete more from nouns, and less from verbs, compared to the Spanish-dominant speakers. In both of these latter cases, this is the opposite of what we would expect from English influence.

We also note from Table 1 that in the noun phrase most plural inflections are deleted. Indeed, in only 39% of all noun phrases was plurality conveyed inflectionally at any site: determiner, adjective, or noun. Although these deletion rates might seem rather high, they are in fact fairly common for Caribbean dialects of Spanish, when compared with the quantitative studies of Cedergren in Panama (1973), of Terrell in Cuba (1979a) and the Dominican Republic (1979b). They are actually lower than the rates found for a functionally monolingual Puerto Rican community in Philadelphia (Poplack 1979a). Verbs, on the other hand, *are* inflected with one or another phonetic variant of (n) 93% of the time, showing a tendency in Puerto Rican Spanish to mark the plural on the verb and not in the noun phrase, the opposite of what is required for English.

We may next ask whether the verbal plural markers are retained in the same sentences in which the nominal plural markers are lost. Table 2 shows that the opposite effect prevails. It is true that a large proportion of verbal markers is retained (about 86-88%) when markers are deleted from the noun phrase, but this simply reflects the fact that (n) deletion is not very advanced as a phonological process. Indeed, a significantly greater percentage of verbal (n) is retained when the markers are also retained in the noun phrase.[5]

Table 2. *Percentage of deleted verbal* (n) *for different marking patterns in the noun phrase.*

Noun Phrase Marking Pattern	% Deleted Verbal (n)	N
ØØ	14%	(13/91)
Ø	12	(27/233)
Total for uninflected NPs	12	(40/324)
SØ	7	(8/114)
S S	7	(5/67)
S	6	(5/90)
ØS	23	(3/13)
Total for inflected NPs	7	(21/284)

We may term this a concord effect. It is a weak quantitative version of the categorical normative agreement rule. Moreover, the rule of concord works independently of the fact that a sentence is semantically plural, i.e. either to delete markers or to retain them.

Is there any difference between Spanish-dominant and bilingual speakers? Table 3 gives the observed frequencies and proportions of plural marking sequences in Spanish, along with expected proportions for each group. The expected values are calculated from the information in Table 2, under the hypothesis that deletion at any given position is statistically independent of deletion in any other.

We note first that the differences between observed and expected values depend on whether or not local concord obtains in the noun phrase. For those sequences containing local concord (marked with an asterisk), we observe more sentences than would be expected under the hypothesis that marking in each slot proceeds independently of any other. Where there is no local concord we observe less than would be expected. This indicates that marking of the two components in the noun phrase does not proceed independently.

While there are distinctions between Spanish-dominant and bilingual speakers, these are consequences of differences in predicted values for the two groups, i.e. differences in overall deletion rates for each grammatical category. What are the consequences of the dissimilarities between the two groups? We saw from Table 2 that bilingual speakers show a greater overall tendency to delete markers from both determiners and nouns than the Spanish-dominant speakers and a lesser tendency to delete from verbs. This

Table 3. *Proportions of various plural marking patterns on the sentence level, as observed and as predicted under the null hypothesis of no concord and no functional compensation.*

Marking Patterns for: 2-slot Noun Phrase		BILINGUAL			SPANISH-DOMINANT		
NP	VERB	N	OBS	EXP	N	OBS	EXP
*ØØ	N	54	(.391)	.357	57	(.218)	.185
S Ø	N	49	(.355)	.368	102	(.389)	.443
*S S	N	18	(.130)	.100	68	(.259)	.199
*ØØ	Ø	9	(.065)	.031	8	(.031)	.018
ØS	N	4	(.029)	.096	10	(.038)	.083
S Ø	Ø	2	(.014)	.031	8	(.031)	.044
*S S	Ø	1	(.007)	.009	7	(.027)	.010
ØS	Ø	1	(.007)	.008	2	(.008)	.008
1-slot Noun Phrase							
Ø	N	98	(.705)	.725	186	(.635)	.628
S	N	32	(.230)	.196	82	(.280)	.282
Ø	Ø	6	(.043)	.062	22	(.075)	.062
S	Ø	3	(.022)	.017	3	(.010)	.028

leads to different preferences between the two groups for the three most important sequences at the top of the Table. Spanish-dominant speakers prefer marking on the determiner, deleting from the noun and marking on the verb (S Ø N), followed by the standard marking sequence SSN, and then by marking on the verb alone (ØØN). Bilinguals favor verbal marking alone, then marking on the determiner and the verb, and finally, the standard full concord form.

Now, if one result has emerged consistently from different quantitative studies of (s) deletion in Caribbean dialects of Spanish and Brazilian Portuguese, it is that determiners, or elements in the first position in the string, are most conservative with regard to marker retention (Ma and Herasimchuk 1968; Cedergren 1973; Terrell 1975; Guy and Braga 1976; Scherre 1978), although by no means does retention operate categorically here, even in functionally monolingual communities (Poplack 1980b). The behavior of the bilinguals may be explained by the fact that they have generalized the deletion rule, which operates most frequently in nouns and adjectives, to a category, determiner, where its operation has been comparatively infrequent. The differences between expected and observed frequencies are the same for Spanish-dominant and bilingual speakers, indicating that aside from overall deletion rates the two groups behave similarly. In particularly, the differences in pattern frequencies cannot be attributed to influence from English; none of the sequences involved is cognate with English. Patterns which would resemble English sequences ØSØ (The doctors tried.) and SØ (Doctors tried.) are almost nonexistent, representing less than 1% of the Spanish data for both groups.

Of course, standard English is not the only influence on Puerto Rican speech. It has been observed in this community (Pedraza 1979) and shown in others (Wolfram 1974; Poplack 1978a), that Black English may also influence Puerto Rican speech. The concord rule in Black English is also variable, largely due to -s deletion and hypercorrect -s reinsertion on both nouns and verbs. However, the outcomes of these processes are not directly comparable. Black English hypercorrect -s insertion does not necessarily function as a plural marker, but rather results in neutralization to third person singular on verbs, and neutralization of the singular/plural distinctions in nouns. The only attested instances of hypercorrect -s insertion in Puerto Rican Spanish verbs, which may be considered analogous to Black English -s insertion, serve, in contrast, to reinforce rather than neutralize the singular/plural distinction.

Thus we see that while reorganization has clearly taken place with regard to the standard Spanish rule for plural marking, we have no reason to attribute it to influence from English. It is due rather to an old and widespread process of phonological weakening and deletion of syllable-final (s)—first attested in Spain in the 16th century (Lapesa 1965), and to the elimination of inflectional, but not other types of redundancy from the sentence. This is made possible because 1) the Spanish verb (unlike the English verb) carries information as to person, number and tense, 2) inflections *are* generally retained on these verbs, and 3) a large amount of noninflectional redundancy remains in the discourse.

Social and Syntactic Functions of Code-Switching

Another area of study concerns code-switching, or the alternation of two languages within a single discourse, sentence or constituent, as in (3).

3. But I used to eat the *bofe,* the brain. And then they stopped selling it because *tenían, este, le encontraron que tenía* [they had, uh, they found out that it had] worms. I used to make some *bofe! Despues yo hacía uno d'esos* [then I would make one of those] concoctions: The garlic *con cebolla, y hacía un mojo, y yo dejaba que se curara eso* [with onion, and I'd make a sauce, and I'd let that sit] for a couple of hours. Then you be drinking and eating that shit. Wooh! It's like eating anchovies when you're drinking. Delicious! (04/101)

Code-switching has been observed by Pedraza (1979) to function as a widespread mode of communication on the block. Educators and intellectuals (Varo 1971; de Granda 1968; LaFontaine 1975) have seen such language mixture to constitute evidence of the disintegration of Puerto Rican Spanish language and culture, although community members themselves recognize its existence and do not view it negatively.

An early pilot study of a single balanced bilingual speaker observed to be one of the most prolific code-switchers on the block (Poplack 1978b), provided quantitative empirical evidence that first, code-switching is governed by functional or pragmatic constraints, as had already been noted anecdotally in the literature (Gumperz 1971, 1976; McClure 1977; Valdés-Fallis 1976, 1978). We found that the occurrence of code-switching is affected by both the ethnicity of the interlocutor and the formality of the speech situation, such that it is more frequent when speaking with another Puerto Rican, and in informal speech styles.

Aside from the extralinguistic constraints, we wanted to account for the syntactic distribution of switch points. Most of the literature on code-switching is only tenuously related to empirical research, and almost none of it is based on systematic analysis of a large corpus of natural speech. Nevertheless many theories of syntactic constraints on code-switching have been presented. Scholars who have proposed such constraints include Gumperz (1976), Hasselmo (1972, 1979), Timm (1975, 1978), Wentz (1977), McClure (n.d.), and Gingràs (1974). Most of the constraints derived in an ad hoc way from the linguist's own intuitions or from acceptability judgements.

In the 400 switches analyzed from the balanced bilingual speaker, we found exceptions to every one, which led us to posit two more general constraints which hold very strictly for these data as well as the data published in other studies, though they had not been formally enunciated as such in the literature.[6]

The first, the *free morpheme constraint,* prohibits a switch from occurring between a bound morpheme and a lexical form unless the latter has been phonologically integrated into the language of the former. This excludes switches like (4a), which in fact are not attested, but *not* forms like (4b), although we consider this an instance of monolingual Spanish speech, and not a code-switch.

4a. *RUN-*eando* [ɹʌn-e'ando] 'running
4b. *jangueando* [haŋge'ando] 'hanging out'

The second, the *equivalence constraint,* states that the order of sentence constituents immediately adjacent to and on both sides of the switch point must be grammatical with respect to both languages involved simultaneously. This requires some specification: the local cogrammaticality or equivalence of the two languages in the vicinity of the switch holds as long as the order of two sentence elements, one before and one after the switch, is not excluded in either language. This is illustrated in Figure 1, where the dotted lines indicate permissible switch points and the arrows indicate ways in which constituents from two languages map onto each other. The speaker's actual utterance is reproduced in (C).

A. Eng   I | told him | that | so that | he | would bring it | fast.

B. Sp   (Yo) | le   dije | eso | pa' que | (él) | la trajera | ligero.

C. CS   I   told him   that | pa' que la trajera ligero. (04/73)

Figure 1. *Permissible code-switching points.*

Operation of the syntactic constraints permits only code-switched utterances which, when translated into either language, are grammatical by both L_1 and L_2 standards, and indicate a large degree of competence in both.

To ascertain whether these results were merely the artifact of having studied a balanced bilingual, a larger study was undertaken including both Spanish-dominant and balanced bilingual speakers (Poplack 1979). Analysis of almost 2,000 switches confirmed that these constraints were upheld by even the nonfluent bilinguals in the sample.

Speakers were found to engage in at least three types of code-switching, each one characterized by switches of different levels of constituents, and each one reflecting different degrees of bilingual ability. These are exemplified in (5).

5a. **'Tag'-like Switch:**
Vendía arroz 'n shit. 'He sold rice and all.' (03/24)
Ave Maria, which English? 'Oh God, which English?' (08/436)

5b. **Sentential Switch:**
It's on the radio. *A mi se me olvida la estación.* I'm gonna serve you another one, right? 'I forget which station.' (08/187)

5c. **Intra-sentential Switch:**
Si tu eres puertorriqueño, your father's a Puerto Rican, you should at least *de vez en cuando,* you know, *hablar español.* 'If you're Puerto Rican, your father's a Puerto Rican, you should at least sometimes, you know, speak Spanish.' (34/25)

(5a) shows a switch of a tag or interjection, freely moveable constituents which can be inserted almost anywhere in discourse without fear of violating a grammatical rule of either language. This type of segment may be switched into L_2 with only minimal knowledge of the grammar of that language. Next on the scale are full sentences or larger segments, which require much more knowledge of L_2 to produce (5b), although hypothetically, not as much as is required by the third category, intra-sentential switches (5c). In order to produce this latter sort of switch, the speaker must know enough about the grammar of each language and the way they interact to avoid ungrammatical utterances.

Figure 2 displays our finding that nonfluent bilinguals are able to code-switch frequently, and still maintain grammaticality in both languages by favoring tag-switching, the type requiring least skill, while the balanced bilinguals favor the sentential or intra-sentential type, which we had hypothesized to require most skill. (Each line on the graph represents a speaker.) The figure shows that reported language ability (which in all cases but four corresponds to observed ability) is an excellent indicator of code-switching patterns. Figure (2a) shows that most of those who report that they know, feel more comfortable in, and use more Spanish than English, tend to switch into L_2 by means of tag-like constructions, sometimes to the practical exclusion of sentential or intra-sentential switches. Those who claim to be bilingual, on the other hand, show a reversal (2b). They favor large amounts of the switches hypothesized to require most knowledge of both languages, sentential and intra-sentential switches.

The few exceptions to these patterns are represented by the dotted lines on the graphs. These are precisely the cases where ethnographic observation and linguistic analysis were previously found to conflict with self-report, because the speakers either underrated or overrated their ability in English. The studies provide evidence that rather than representing a debasement of linguistic skill, code-switching is actually a suggestive indicator of bilingual competence.

Linguistic performance constrained in this way must be based on simultaneous access to the grammatical rules of both languages, raising the question of the existence and nature of code-switching grammar.

We thus attempted to describe formally how the code-switching constraints determine the way the two monolingual grammars may be combined in generating discourse containing code-switches (Sankoff and Poplack 1980). As the code-switching constraints operate on the surface syntax of a sentence, we adopted a formalism based on direct generation of surface phrase structures by a context-free grammar (having shown that switched items are in no way constrained to be of the same language as the

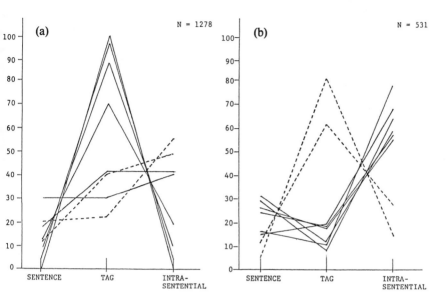

Figure 2. *Percentages of switch types for Spanish-dominant and bilingual speakers.* (a) *Percentage of switch types for reported Spanish-dominant speakers.* (b) *Percentage of switch types for reported bilingual speakers.*

elements which may be adjacent to them in deep structure, but rather, if at all, by their surface neighbors). We then probabilized the rules of the grammar so that it could account for the quantitative patterning evident in the data. An important conclusion drawn from this part of the exercise is that even in portions of discourse in close proximity to one or more switches, the speaker strictly maintained both qualitative and quantitative distinctions between Spanish and English grammars. Whenever a stretch of discourse, e.g. a sentence or constituent, could be clearly identified as monolingual, the rules of the appropriate monolingual grammar, and their associated probabilities, were exclusively at play. The analysis of code-switching has deep implications for grammatical theory, as it points to ways in which two languages can reconcile, but not change, their differences, to result in a mode of communication widely functional as monolingual speech.

The evidence we have presented for the syntactic integrity of Spanish and English grammars, even when they are being used sequentially and simultaneously, bolsters other arguments for nonconvergence of Spanish and English in the Puerto Rican speech community.

Verb Usage

In a quantitative semantic analysis of tense, mood, and aspect in the
entire Puerto Rican Spanish verbal paradigm, and again involving both
Spanish-dominant and balanced bilingual speakers (Pousada and Poplack
1979), we compared the ranges of meaning covered by verb forms for the
two groups, with those prescribed in normative Spanish grammars. Our
goal was to examine the extent, if any, to which the Puerto Rican Spanish
verb system has diverged from the standard, by ascertaining whether the
semantic fields, or ranges of meaning, covered by verb forms were being
extended or restricted, and in what direction: specifically, were some forms
being extended to cover semantic fields of others which have fallen into
disuse within the Puerto Rican Spanish system, or is there adaptation to
specifically English semantic fields? To do this we first distinguished
absolute from extended uses of verb forms. An example of the former
would be use of the present progressive to convey ongoing action in present
time. Examples of extended uses are given in (6). A construction line (6a)
was assumed to result from transference from English, because the present
progressive occurred with a verb of perception, which in standard Spanish
categorically requires the simple present. On the other hand, (6b),
exemplifying use of the present to convey action in future time, is a
perfectly acceptable extension of the uses of the Spanish simple present.

6a. *Yo no estoy viendo eso.* 'I'm not seeing that.' (002/314)
6b. *Mañana voy a Caguas.* 'Tomorrow I'm going to Caguas.'

We then compared the rank distribution of the verbal forms in the speech
of our sample with the Puerto Rican Spanish standard as represented by the
written speech of a prominent Puerto Rican author, then with a sample of
15th century Spanish, with a sample of modern Andalusian Spanish, and
finally, with the New York City English of a monolingual.

The results indicated, first, that there were virtually no instances of verbs
being used in an ungrammatical or idiosyncratic way. Extended uses not
attested in prescriptive grammars constituted less than 1% of the 9,000
verbs studied. Table 4 shows that of the 26 verb forms originally studied,
there are only three inflected forms which are quantitatively important: the
present, which represents half the data, followed by the preterite, and then
the imperfect. All other inflected forms individually represent 3% or less of
the data.

When we examine how these verb forms are distributed to convey the
semantic fields of {PRESENT}, {PAST} and {FUTURE}, we find that the
preferred way of expressing present reference is through use of the simple
present, while preterite and imperfect forms are generally used to express

Table 2. *Verb distribution in vernacular and standard Puerto Rican Spanish.*

| | Vernacular Puerto Rican Spanish | | | | | | Standard PRS | |
| | Spanish Dominants | | Bilinguals | | All Speakers | | | |
	N	%	N	%	N	%	N	%
INDICATIVE								
present	3231	49.5	1078	50.2	4309	49.6	133	49.3
preterite	904	13.8	324	15.1	1228	14.1	25	9.3
imperfect	543	8.3	148	6.9	691	8.0	15	5.6
present perfect	143	2.2	43	2.0	186	2.1	6	1.1
conditional	49	0.8	14	0.7	63	0.7	10	3.7
preterite perfect	22	0.3	5	0.2	27	0.3	2	0.7
future	12	0.2	3	0.1	15	0.2	5	1.9
preterite anterior	0	0.0	1	0.0	1	0.0	0	0.0
future perfect	-		-		-		-	
preterite conditional	-		-		-		-	
PERIPHRASTIC								
present modal + infinitive	245	3.8	78	3.6	323	3.7	12	4.4
present periphrastic future	158	2.4	43	2.0	201	2.3	4	1.5
imperfect modal + infinitive	23	0.4	16	0.7	39	0.4	0	0.0
preterite modal + infinitive	15	0.2	6	0.3	21	0.2	1	0.4
imperfect periphrastic future	4	0.1	4	0.2	8	0.1	0	0.0
PROGRESSIVE								
present progressive	135	2.1	54	2.5	189	2.2	2	0.7
imperfect progressive	26	0.4	5	0.2	31	0.4	0	0.0
preterite progressive	6	0.1	3	0.1	9	0.1	0	0.0
SUBJUNCTIVE								
present subjunctive	257	3.9	51	2.4	309	3.5	7	2.6
imperfect subjunctive	71	2.0	10	0.5	81	0.9	2	0.7
preterite perfect subjunctive	4	0.1	2	0.1	6	0.1	0	0.0
present perfect subjunctive	1	0.0	1	0.0	2	0.0	1	0.4
future subjunctive	-		-		-		-	
future perfect subjunctive	-		-		-		-	
imperative	173	2.6	82	3.8	255	2.9	0	0.0
infinitive	510	7.8	176	8.2	686	7.9	45	16.7
TOTALS	6532		2147		8679		270	

reference, and that the periphrastic and simple present are also the preferred ways of expressing future time. This explains how Puerto Rican Spanish expresses past, present and future reference by means of a basic present ~ past tense distinction: the present has been extended to cover the semantic fields of the future form, which is used only rarely, and not necessarily to convey futurity. (In fact, one third of the attested future forms were used for present reference.) These findings are in keeping with studies on Spanish in the Southwest (Floyd 1978), which although not quantitative, repeatedly indicate that these three verb forms are the most productive, maintaining their usual functions as well as expanding to include those of other forms.

Table 4 also shows strikingly little difference between what we are calling 'standard' Puerto Rican Spanish and that of the East Harlem sample, despite the fact that the standard material was extracted from a written text. Statistical tests on these figures showed that the most significant differences between the two data sources are in the area of past tense forms—the East Harlem speakers used more due to their more informal speech style, which contained many narratives of personal experience requiring verb forms in the past tense. The standard also shows significantly more of the inflected conditional and future forms. Use of the conditional is probably an aspect of learned or academic speech, and the future, as in other languages such as French and English, may be largely reserved as a marker of formal speech performance.

The Table also shows that there is remarkably little difference between the Spanish-dominant and bilingual speakers, despite the fact that the latter could be hypothesized to be more under the influence of English. In fact, the most startling aspect of these findings is their great regularity. Log-likelihood tests based on these figures show that the only significant area of difference is in use of the subjunctive, which the bilinguals use somewhat less than the Spanish-dominant speakers. Now just this tendency has been hypothesized (e.g. de Granda 1968) to be due to influence from English, which has lexicalized or lost most of the distinctions expressed by the subjunctive. Although this possibility cannot be overruled, no conclusive evidence in its favor has yet been presented. In fact, the Table shows that 'standard' Puerto Rican Spanish is characterized by subjunctive usage closer to that of the bilinguals than to the Spanish-dominant speakers. These results, then, cannot be considered evidence for any significant degree of convergence of vernacular Puerto Rican Spanish towards English.

Figure 3 correlates the rank order of inflected verb form frequencies among the East Harlem speakers and *La Celestina*, a 15th century Spanish picaresque novel.

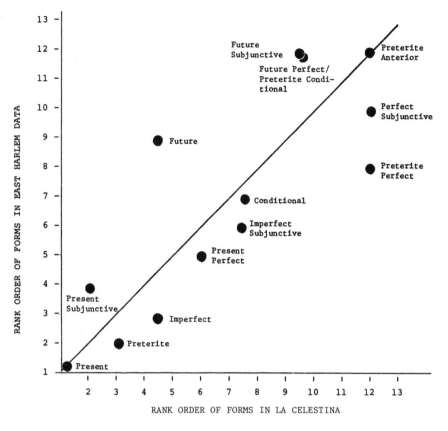

Figure 3. *Rank order of inflected verb form frequencies in East Harlem data versus order in La Celestina.*

Points lying near the diagonal represent forms of relatively equal importance in each corpus. Strikingly enough, Figure 3 shows that the relative ranking of verb form usage has remained basically unchanged since the 15th century.

The only real exception is in use of the inflected future, which had much greater importance in the 15th century than today. Indeed, this form has practically been replaced by the periphrastic future in vernacular Puerto Rican Spanish. As may be seen in (7), the rank correlation of these figures is .85, indicating a strong similarity in the distribution of verb forms.

7. Rank correlations of verb form usage.

East Harlem — 15th century Spanish	.85
East Harlem — modern Andalusian Spanish	.79
East Harlem — English	.53
Andalusian — English	.57

When compared with a corpus of English verb forms, in contrast, we find that their distribution is significantly different for every verb form but one; that is, influence from English does not appear to have affected these core areas of the Spanish language. The correlations in (7) summarize this lack of influence.

Indeed, in our study of East Harlem, the only factor which was found to differentiate verb usage in any significant way was the speech situation in which the form was uttered. Different speech situations were shown to favor different proportions of verbal forms, providing yet another example of the inherent stylistic variation which characterizes natural language.

Thus we see that the only significant change in the system, decrease in use of the inflected future, is intrasystemic: it is the result of the extension of the present periphrastic and simple present forms to convey futurity. This process is widespread in other Romance languages as well as in English.

The example given in (6a), *Yo no estoy viendo eso,* is one of only three in the entire corpus. The evidence thus is against convergence with English. Such conclusions were not drawn from qualitative studies of verb usage in other varieties of United States Spanish (cited in Floyd 1978; Bills 1975). However those studies have concentrated on supposed deviations from the standard, without quantitative study of the standard itself.

Lexical Borrowing

The lexicon is one area in which language contact has had clear influence on Puerto Rican Spanish. Systematic study of the introduction and incorporation of English loanwords into Puerto Rican Spanish (Poplack, Sankoff, and Pousada 1980) indicates first, that borrowings from English are used largely in areas of modern urban culture, for which no traditional Spanish usage existed—though there are now, of course, neologisms and calques in modern metropolitan and other prestigious Spanish varieties. In this sense, borrowings represent an expansion of the lexical resources of the community, rather than a suppression of Spanish vocabulary.

Second, despite the fact that many speakers command an English phonology which is quite distinct from their Spanish, the loanwords which are used with any frequency are rapidly Hispanicized, so that no systematic perturbation of phonological processes or syllabic patterns internal to Spanish can be detected. Indeed, statistical tests prove that frequency of use is clearly a determinant of the degree of phonological integration of a loanword.

Third, words of English origin tend to take on very specific and normal Spanish grammatical functions. In examining several hundred borrowed nouns in natural speech, we found that in virtually every case where Spanish syntax required the presence of a determiner, the loanword was so accompanied (Poplack and Pousada 1980). In those contexts from which a determiner is usually omitted, the loanword had none.

Fourth, the rules for gender assignment to Spanish nouns apply rigorously to loanwords. The well-defined criteria depending on word-final segments operate consistently, even for words which show two alternative paths of phonological integration (e.g. *el suéter, la suera* 'sweater'; *el hambérguer, la hamberga* 'hamburger').

In summary, the addition of new words from English to the Puerto Rican vocabulary is seen to have little effect on the existing lexical stock, and no effect on the phonological, morphological and syntactic patterns of Spanish.

DISCUSSION

We have argued that the vernacular/standard distinction contrasts two epistemologically incommensurable concepts, neither of which have been well characterized. The standard is an idealization not tied to systematically observed behavior, and the vernacular has been attested to by anecdote. In the reality studied within the variationist paradigm, there are only vernaculars, upper-class vernacular vs. lower-class vernacular, formal vs. colloquial, etc. The abstract notion of the standard has often been used to show that the language of socially dominated groups is incorrect and inferior. In the case of many bilingual minorities in the United States the vernacular/standard distinction cuts two ways. The English of these minorities, insofar as it may be characterized by community-wide features, is considered deviant. And their language of origin differs, of course, from any abstract standard, so that it too is considered aberrant. The role of the linguist in this situation has often been to invoke the easiest type of explanation for developments in local varieties (i.e. convergence with English), and thus lend scientific authority to negative attitudes toward the minority language.

A systematic variationist study of the speech community is an effective way to avoid stereotypes and assumptions about the standard. The deviant forms cited by researchers on Chicano and Puerto Rican Spanish are also present in our data, but the studies reported here show that when apparent deviations are placed within the context of the entire system, they are seen to constitute only a minuscule portion of the total verbal output. This leads us to confirm that emphasis on anomalies in multilingual situations on the part of researchers, educators, and intellectuals, is merely stereotyping due to the phenomenon of categorical perception, whereby deviation from a norm may be seen as far more prominent than its negligible frequency would warrant.

These studies raise serious questions about the theory of language convergence in contact situations. It is clear that the Puerto Rican Spanish spoken in El Barrio has been influenced by English, but this influence is most evident in the lexicon. However, the grammar of Spanish, which has been shown by our ethnographic and attitudinal studies to serve a wide range of communicative functions, has been extraordinarily resistant to influence from the grammar of English; this despite the economic and political dominance of the English-speaking community.

The evidence of Gumperz and Wilson (1971) for the convergence of Urdu, Marathi and Kanada, in Kupwar, India, must be due to a greater time scale, or to very different historical and cultural contexts, perhaps reflecting a restricted functioning of one or more of the codes involved, which as has been shown in preceding sections, is not the case here. Other cases of putative language convergence may simply reflect an uninformed purism, or nonquantitative methodology, or a preoccupation with borrowing of noncore vocabulary. More dangerous than the linguistic outcomes of contact to a vigorous and thriving Spanish, at least in this instance, are those who would restrict its usage from schools, government, and other institutions, and purists who stigmatize the expanded expressive repertoire of bilingual speakers in a linguistically complex milieu.

NOTES

*The analyses reported here are part of a research project on Intergenerational Perspectives on Bilingualism supported by the National Institute of Education under NIE-G-78-0091 and the Ford Foundation.

[1] This characterization was made on the basis of observed frequency of usage combined with self-report of the language that 'feels most comfortable' and is used most frequently in a series of domains. We shall see that the resulting assessment generally corresponds to the linguistic assessment of language capability.

[2] Of course, influence from English may be expected to be most apparent in the speech of those who are 'English-dominant'. These speakers were not included in the present sample because they simply did not produce enough Spanish to compare quantitatively with the others. Two possible outcomes of the contact situation may be hypothesized for their Spanish:

(1) such Spanish as they do speak may undergo restructuring so as to approximate English structures; that is, it may converge with English, (2) the Spanish language *in toto* may gradually disappear from the repertoire of these speakers, and be retained only for emblematic purposes (e.g. through insertion of Spanish words or idiomatic expressions into English), in which case the grammar of the language would remain unaffected. Our ethnographic observations of language use in this community may be interpreted in favor of the second possibility, but we have no linguistic evidence with which to substantiate either hypothesis at the moment.

[3] Numbers in parentheses are speaker identification codes.

[4] 'S' and 'N' refer to any phonetic realization of the variables (s) and (n) respectively, other than phonetic zero.

[5] Note that this behavior holds when the subject noun phrase precedes the verb, the canonical sentence structure in Spanish, but not when it follows. There is no significant difference in verbal deletion rates between inflected and uninflected noun phrases when these are postposed.

[6] The general validity of these constraints has been observed independently in the literature by e.g. Jacobson (1976), Lipski (1978), and Pfaff (1979). However, none of these scholars has specifically incorporated them into their analyses.

[7] The data on early modern Castilian Spanish were provided by a frequency analysis of verb usage in *La Celestina* by Criado del Val (1966).

THE BILINGUAL'S LINGUISTIC REPERTOIRE

BRAJ B. KACHRU

INTRODUCTION

Recent research on bilingualism,[1] especially during the last two decades, has significantly contributed to our understanding of two rather neglected areas of this topic: the neurolinguistic study of a bilingual's brain (Paradis 1979), and formal and functional analyses of the linguistic (or verbal) repertoire of a speaker of a language (Kachru 1981; Wald 1974).

The focus on the functional aspects of bilingualism has shown that, functionally (and formally), bilingualism does not invariably entail 'the native-like control' of two languages (Bloomfield 1933:56). Nor is it necessarily an 'alternate' use of two or more languages (Weinreich 1953:1). The bilingual's (or plurilingual's, if we prefer this term) use of languages may also be viewed from the perspective of possessing a linguistic or verbal repertoire functional within a specific societal network (Gumperz and Hernandez-Ch. 1971). The focus on the repertoire—within the context of the speech community—leads to a functional realism of our understanding of a bilingual's use of languages.

The terms 'linguistic repertoire', 'code repertoire', and 'verbal repertoire' are used more or less identically to refer to the total range of codes which members of a speech community have available for their linguistic interaction.[2] But no speaker necessarily controls all the codes which constitute the verbal repertoire of a speech community. Each code in the repertoire has markers[3] (clues[4]) which provide various types of identities essential for understanding how individuals function in a wider societal context: for example, class (Robinson 1979), caste (Brown and Levinson 1979; Giles 1979), religion and ethnicity (Kachru 1973; Miranda 1978a, b), sex (Smith 1979), and region (Allen and Underwood 1971). In this sense then the concept 'linguistic repertoire' is not restricted to a bilingual's or a multilingual's competence in distinct 'languages'; it may also be used to refer to the repertoire of styles and registers, or dialects. Thus this concept applies both to a monolingual and to a bilingual, though the constituents (or the set) which comprise the repertoire are not necessarily identical. Functionally, both a monolingual and a bilingual can be distinguished on the basis of *code range, code confusion, code-extension, code-switch,* and *code-mix.* The differences between the two are in the types of choices made, their linguistic characteristics and the contextual meanings. Gumperz (1968:381) refers to this similarity when he points out that 'in many multilingual societies the choice of one language over another has the same signification as the selection among lexical alternates in linguistically homogeneous societies.'

The monolingual's repertoire will not be discussed here. Rather, this study is concerned with some linguistic aspects of code repertoire within the broad framework of three approaches to the study of language in societal context. One might use the following cover terms to identify these approaches: 'context of situation' (Kachru 1980a; Mitchell 1978); 'ethnography of communication' (Hymes 1962, 1964, and 1974); and 'linguistic repertoire' (Gumperz and Hernandez-Ch. 1971). These three approaches have been chosen because they share some underlying assumptions about language and its function in society. For example, they emphasize (a) the study of language in functionally determined contexts, (b) the heterogeneity and variation in codes as a characteristic of a speech community, and (c) the relationship between the structure of code and the structure of social context.

Within the framework of such approaches, this paper discusses the following six aspects related to a bilingual's repertoire of codes and their functional implications. First, the concept of repertoire of codes is viewed in terms of a *functional hierarchy,* which is related to the 'context of situation' in terms of what I have earlier called *contextual units* (Kachru 1966, 1980a), participants, etc. Second, the role of language *shift, switch,* or *alteration* is considered within the total repertoire range of a bilingual as a member of a speech community. Third, a formal and functional distinction is suggested for separating the linguistic strategies of *switch* and *mix.* Fourth, the process of 'mixing' is shown to be not a random but a rule-governed process, with constraints on 'mixing' the units of two or more codes. Fifth, the effects of repertoire range, and the process of *switch* and *mix* are studied in a wider context, that of initiating structural changes in the linguistic systems of a language at various linguistic levels. Finally, in a minor digression, I have listed some of the educational implications of code repertoire, code hierarchy, and code-mixing.

VERNACULAR, CODE REPERTOIRE, AND CODE HIERARCHY

I shall use the term 'code repertoire' in roughtly the same sense in which the terms 'verbal repertoire', 'linguistic repertoire', and 'communicative repertoire' have been used in earlier literature (Gumperz 1964, 1972:20; Hymes 1972:xxxiv).

Code repertoire refers to the total range of codes available to a bilingual, including his or her *vernacular*. A vernacular is defined here, for the lack of a better term, as the mother tongue (or L_1). One need not distinguish the use of the term 'vernacular' from that of literary (or formal) language used in literature or the school system. Actually, the dichotomy is not so neat; the status of a vernacular and the use of this term varies from one bilingual context to another, and the attitudinal responses to 'What is a vernacular?' are not identical in all contexts. European scholars have generally used this term to refer to all the modern South Asian or African languages, in a sense distinguishing these from the classical languages and the 'prestigious' (literary) Western languages. In such a use, 'vernacular' becomes a cover term, on the one hand for Bengali, Tamil, or standard Hindi (Khariboli), and on the other hand for Magahi, Maithili, or varieties of Kashmiri. These cases are not identical in terms of their literary traditions, functions, and the native speakers' attitudes toward them. Therefore, the use of such a cover term must be redefined with reference to each speech community.[5]

The set which comprises the repertoire range is also not identical in all bilingual contexts. Consider, for example, the following possibilities which might be included in the 'repertoire range': (a) dialects or 'styles' of a language (Gumperz 1964); (b) a variety of distinct languages, from a closely related language family to a not-so-closely related family (Annamalai 1971, 1978; Kachru 1978a, 1978b); and (c) languages from two distinct language families (e.g. Sanskrit and Tamil).

The *code hierarchy* is essentially determined on the basis of function, that is, in terms of what a particular code accomplishes for the user in terms of status, identity, mobility, advancement. It may also depend on the attitude of a caste, class, or society at large toward a code. Such pragmatic considerations determine the functional allocation of vernaculars or other codes in the bilingual's repertoire. Therefore, the attitude toward a code and its ranking on the code hierarchy are not necessarily permanent. Consider the emerging dialect conflict in the so-called Hindi area, which is the result of postindependence reconsiderations of the dialect speakers (such as of Maithili and Rajasthani) toward Khariboli Hindi (see Y. Kachru and Bhatia 1978).

DIMENSIONS OF CODE REPERTOIRE

The code types which constitute a code repertoire of a bilingual may be identified in terms of their formal features and the functional domains. In formal terms, generally two devices are used: *foregrounding* and *neutralization* (or *backgrounding*).[6] The term 'foregrounding' is used here in the Prague School sense, referring to the use of language in such a way that the formal devices attract attention. The attempt, then, is to *deautomize* language use, (Fried 1972:125). This then entails 'conscious' use of phonological, grammatical, and lexical devices. The *registral function* may be marked by a specific type of lexicalization. In India, for example, Persianization has traditionally been used for the legal and court registers in the Hindi, Kashmiri, Kannada, or Telugu areas. On the other hand, the process of Englishization is evident in the registers of science, technology, and the social sciences.

The *style function* is a dimension of 'register classification' (Halliday et. al. 1964:92-3). It refers to the relations among the participants, and thus characterizes a formally determined choice. Again considering the Indian situation, the style function may be identified by choosing a 'high code' from the available codes, e.g. high Hindi (Sanskritization), and Persianization, or by Englishization. The presence or absence of the 'high code' marks styles such as *grānthika* 'classical' and *vyāvahārika* 'colloquial' in Telugu, and *sādhu bhāṣā* 'literary' and *calit bhāṣā* 'colloquial' in Bengali.

The *identity function* establishes an 'in-group' relationship, a village identity (e.g. by switching to Magahī, Maithilī, or Braj [see Gumperz 1964]), a religious identity (see Dil 1972; Kachru 1973), a caste identity, or an elitist identity.

'Neutralization' is a device for not drawing attention to some of above-discussed 'identities'. It is a linguistic strategy to 'unload' a linguistic item from its traditional, cultural, and emotional connotations by avoiding its use and choosing an item from another code. The borrowed item has referential meaning, but no cultural connotations in the context of the specific culture. Thus a borrowed item is used not because it fills a 'lexical gap', but because for the user it has certain neutrality and specificity.

In Tamil, as Annamalai (1978) shows, one function of code-mixing with English is to avoid revealing social, regional, or caste identity. The user avoids lexical items from the vernacular because they carry such connotations. For example, because Tamil kinship terms *maccaan* and *attimbeer* are associated with caste connotations, one tends instead to use the English 'brother-in-law'. The same is true of the lexical item *saadam,* which is Sanskritist or *sooru* 'purist'; English 'rice' has no such connotations. The lexical items for 'wife' also are not so innocent, *manaivi* is formal and *peṇḍaaṭṭi* is colloquial, but English 'wife' has no such style identification.

Neutralization may also be used for establishing a linguistic identity to convey the idea that 'I am one of you.' The participants in a speech act know that this linguistic device is artificial, and they use it as a means of accommodation. Let me illustrate the switch of this type from Kashmiri, in which traditionally two religious varieties have been recognized, i.e. Hindu Kashmiri and Muslim Kashmiri (Grierson 1911) or Sanskritized and Persianized (Kachru 1973:7-11).

Set 1	Set 2	Gloss
athɨ pɔthrun	athɨ čhalun	'to wash hands'
khɔdā	bagvān	'God'
patīlɨ	bohgun	'cooking vessel'
kəhvɨ	čāy	'tea'
nāṭɨ	neni	'meat' (lamb)
āb	pōn'	'water'
yēzārɨ	pɔ̆jāmɨ	'pajama, trousers'

Almost all of these lexical items are intelligible to speakers of both varieties.[7] The users of the above two sets can be marked as Muslims (set 1) or Hindus (set 2). In many situations a lexical switch takes place to deemphasize the religious separation. Neutralization, then, is a linguistic attempt to achieve 'accommodation', and 'almost ingroupness'. Note, however, that even when a lexical switch is made one may clearly retain the 'separateness' at the phonetic level. 'Phonetic switches' seem more difficult to accomplish than lexical switches. Some phonetic 'markers' of two religious groups are given below. In these examples the first phonetic markers refer to 'Hindu Kashmiri' and the second to 'Muslim Kashmiri'.

1. central vowel → front vowel (e.g. *rɨkh* → *rikh* 'line'; *tɨkh* → *tikh* 'run')
2. high central vowel → low central vowel (e.g. *gə̃ṭh* → *gã̄ṭh* 'eagle'; *dəh* → *dah* 'ten')
3. central vowel → back vowel (e.g. *māĭ* → *mōĭ* 'mother')
4. initial back vowel → central vowel (e.g. *ōlav* → *əlav* 'potatoes')
5. v → ph (e.g. *hohvur* → *hohphur* 'wife's parents')
6. initial Cr → C' (e.g. *brōr* → *b'ōr* 'cat', *krūr* → *k'ūr* 'well')
7. r → ṛ (e.g. *gur* → *guṛ* 'house'; *yor* → *yoṛ* 'here')

The phonetic 'accommodation' is, however, acquired by those who want to switch to the 'urban/educated' variety of Kashmiri. (See Elias-Olivares 1976:182 for a Chicano example; see also Scotton 1976.)

In functional terms, the bilingual's codes may be viewed either as *inclusive* or *exclusive*. The inclusive codes are 'free access' codes, and conscious efforts may be made to increase the number of their users. Such codes may be termed, for example, *national language, official language, lingua franca, koine,* or *creole.* These codes generally cut across language and/or dialect boundaries. The use of such a code may be sought for nationhood, educational status, political unification (e.g. the case of Hindi in India, Swahili in parts of Africa, English in nonnative contexts). The exclusive codes tend to have a restricted membership. These may be termed 'limited access' codes, and they mark an 'in-group identity'. Such codes are used for *trade, secrecy, caste, religion,* and *initiation* (Halliday 1978). The membership of each type is not necessarily mutually exclusive. In a sense, the literary codes have the characteristics of restricted codes. For example, Sanskrit has traditionally been a literary code and by and large an 'exclusive code'. The dichotomies, therefore, do not always provide a clear picture.

It seems that in bilingual communities—and even in monolingual communities—attitudes toward codes (generally termed 'language attitudes') are based both on the formal and functional characteristics of a code. On the basis of these attitudes loyalty toward a code is expressed. Consider, for example, the use of the following attitude-marking terms toward various types of codes:

a. *aesthetic/unaesthetic:* The attitude toward Italian in Europe, or toward Bengali, Tamil, and Punjabi in India. (Note the use of 'musical' in this context.) In India, Bengali is considered 'musical' and 'melodious', and Tamil and Punjabi 'harsh'.

b. *correct/incorrect:* The dichotomy of literary/nonliterary. This refers to the mixing of style, e.g. 'formal' vs. 'informal'. One is therefore not expected to use contracted forms in formal English.

c. *cultivated/uncultivated:* In terms of the literary traditions.

d. *developed/undeveloped:* English vs. Indian languages; Tamil/ Bengali vs. Hindi (see also *c* and *g*).

e. *dialect/nondialect:* Attitude shown in both the mediums, i.e. written and spoken.

f. *educated/uneducated:* See Quirk's (1960) analysis of 'Educated British English'.

g. *effective/ineffective:* Attitude toward English (or French) in South Asia, Africa (justification: register range).

h. *primitive/nonprimitive:* An attitude which developed with colonization.

i. *proper/improper:* Languages of rituals or liturgy, e.g. Sanskrit or Latin.

j. *religious/nonreligious:* Attitude common in South Asia, for example, toward Sanskrit and Arabic.
k. *regional/nonregional:* Essentially based on phonology, lexis (see also *e*).
l. *sacred/nonsacred:* Arabic for the Muslim world and Sanskrit for Hindus (see also *j*).
m. *slang/nonslang.*
n. *standard/nonstandard.*
o. *u/non-u:* A dichotomy based on class, *u* (upper class) and *non-u* (lower class). A. C. Ross provided the illustrations and Nancy Mitford made it popular.
p. *vigorous/nonvigorous:* Attitude toward literary forms; for example, Urdu is considered 'vigorous' and suitable for 'forceful' poetry as opposed to Hindi which is considered suitable for *bhakti* 'devotional' poetry.

The attitudes toward codes have serious linguistic implications. To a large extent, the concept of code-standardization is based on 'language attitude', and such attitudes are indirectly responsible for the rise of academies (e.g. in Italy in 1600; France, 1635; Spain, 1713; Sweden, 1739). In a number of bilingual contexts one task of such academies is *code purification,* a linguistic activity aimed at curtailing linguistic change.

CODE ALTERATION

In the literature a variety of terms have been used to describe types of code alteration, so terminological 'untangling' is not easy (Baker 1980). It has, however, been shown that out of the total code repertoire the bilingual tends to make two types of code alterations, termed here *code-switching* and *code-mixing.* The strategy of switching tends to be used, for example, as an aside for explanation for establishing communicative 'intimacy', or as a bond of identity. Formally, such switches result in embedding one or more sentences in a verbal interaction. Consider the following two examples from the written texts of Nigerian English and Hindi.

1. 'Good! See you later.' Joseph always put on an impressive manner when speaking on the telephone. He never spoke Igbo or Pidgin English at such moments. When he hung up he told his colleagues: 'That na my brother. Just return from overseas. B.A. (Honours) Classics.' He always preferred the fiction of Classics to the truth of English. It sounded more impressive.

'What department he de work?'

'Secretary to the Scholarship Board.'

''E go make plenty money there. Every student who wan' go England go de see am for Rouse.'

''E no be like dat,' said Joseph.

'Him na gentleman.'

'No fit take bribe.'

'Na so', said the other in disbelief.

(Chinua Achebe, *No Longer at Ease,* 1960)

2. [Standard Hindi] maĩ sab samajhtā hũ. tum bhī khannā kī tarah bahas karne lage ho. maĩ sātvẽ aur navẽ kā pharak samajhtā hũ. [switch to Awadhi] hamkā ab prinspalī kare na sikhāv bhaiyā. jonū hukum hai, tonū cuppe [switch to English] kari auṭ [switch] karo, samjhyo nāhī.   (Srilal Shukla, *Rāgdarbārī,* 1968:31).

[Kharibolī; standard Hindi] I understand everything. You also have started arguing like Khanna. I understand the difference between seven and nine. [switch to Awadhi] Don't teach me, dear, how to be a principal. Whatever is the order you carry it out quietly. Do you understand or not?

In (1), the West African novelist Chinua Achebe switches from English to pidgin; the contextual appropriateness of the text is maintained. In (2), the switch is from Kharibolī (standard Hindi) to a dialect (Awadhī). There is also a sprinkling of English lexical items to convey the effect of authority (*principal, carryout*). In switching, then, the units from another code are essentially sentences which are preserved with a clear function in the discourse. Code alteration of this type indicates the bilingual's facility with several codes, and their use in appropriate contexts with relation to the participants, setting, and for specific effect (e.g. the use of Awadhī in the above). Further, consider the following interaction in a typical educated Kashmiri family:

A. Hello, how are you, Kaul Sahib?

B. *vāray mahrā* [Kashmiri]
   'well, sir'

A. *vəliv bihiv* [Kashmiri]
   'come in (hon.), sit down (hon.)'

A. *zarā cāy lānā, bhāī* [to a servant, in Hindustani]
   'some tea bring, brother' [mode of address]
   I will be back in a minute.

In these five sentences three codes are represented (English, Kashmiri, Hindustani), but each unit is a complete utterance in a specific code. The switching is at the intrasentential level, and becomes meaningful within the context of 'greetings'. If understood in that specific context, there is a cohesiveness in the text.

Another example entails a slightly different use of switching:

(On the telephone) When will you come?
(To his wife) *me dītav kāgaz pensali*
         [Kashmiri: 'Please give me some paper and a pencil.']
(On the telephone) What is your address?
(To his children) *šōr mat karo bhaī, zara čup karo.*
         [Hindustani: 'Don't make noise, keep quiet.]
(To his wife) *talay yim kar nāvukh tshɔpi*
         [Kashmiri: 'Please keep them quiet.']
(On the telephone) All right, I will write to you. Thank you.

One should add here that the speaker could have used only English but instead chose to use three different codes. We still understand very little about such switches by bilinguals, especially when there is one *shared code* between the participants in a speech event and no *status* or *identity* questions seem to be involved.

The functional attitudinal dependence of such switches—versus the one discussed above—is illustrated by Gumperz (1964) in the code repertoire of a typical villager in Khalapur. Khalapur, a small town 80 miles north of Delhi, has a population of about 3,000. The profile of the population's code repertoire is as follows. The local dialect is used for 'local relations' and as a code of identity by the educated people. The standard language, Hindi, is used as a symbol of status and for commerce, etc. The other varieties of the local dialect are *moṭibolī* 'rough/coarse dialect', *sāf bolī* 'refined/pure dialect' the market style, and the oratorical style. The 'linguistic bounds' are marked by the appropriate choice of the code from this code repertoire. There are formal differences which mark the local varieties from standard Hindi, but I shall not discuss these here.[8]

In Kashmir such context-dependent code switches may entail a switch from Kashmiri to one or more other languages, such as Urdu, Hindi, Panjabi, English, Persian, Arabic, or Sanskrit. On paper, such a situation appears rather complicated, but in actual interaction, given the appropriate role and situation, this is a normal verbal strategy used in multilingual contexts. In fact, in traditionally bilingual societies, a mark of an educated or cultivated speaker of a language is to have this competence in switching. Creative writers have made very effective use of such strategies, as we saw in the examples from Achebe and Shukla.

In terms of linguistic units, 'mixing' entails transfer of the units of code *a* into code *b* at intersentential and intrasentential levels, and thus '...developing a new restricted—or not-so-restricted—code of linguistic interaction' (Kachru 1978a:79, 1978b; Sridhar 1978; Warie 1978). It seems that a user of such a code functions, at least, in a disystem. The resultant code then has formal cohesion and functional expectancy with reference to a context.

In such a situation there is an 'absorbing' code and an 'absorbed' code. The absorbed code is assimilated in the system of the 'absorbing' code. There is rarely a situation in which the user of such a mixed code can not identify the 'absorbing' and 'absorbed' codes. The transferred units may be morphemes, words, phrases, clauses, sentences, and what are traditionally called 'idioms'.

At the lexical level, then, such 'mixing' may result in having a choice of several *lexical sets* which function in identical contexts. The choice of a particular set may be made for functional, attitudinal, or registral reasons. Consider, for example, the following lexical sets available to a Hindi bilingual.

Set 1 (Sanskritization)	Set 2 (Persianization)	Set 3 (Englishization)	Gloss
āgyā denā	ijāzat denā	permission denā	'to grant permission'
parikšā denā	imtihān denā	examination denā	'to take an examination'
krodhit honā	gussā honā	angrī honā	'to be angry'

A code-mixed variety, as mentioned elsewhere (Kachru 1978a, 1978b), often acquires a new name which refers to its hybrid characteristics. The name may be attitudinally derogatory (as in the case of Tex-Mex [Gumperz 1970]), or not so derogatory, e.g. Bazār Hindi (Apte 1974), Englañol (Nash 1977), Hinglish (Kachru 1979), Singlish (Fernando 1977), Spanglish (Nash 1977).

The devices of 'switching' and 'mixing' have traditionally been used for stylistic effects in literature. In Sanskrit, the switch to Prakrit was specifically used for women, the nonelite, and clowns. In Indian poetry, *bhāṣā sankar* 'language mixture' is an accepted linguistic device for stylistic effects and was used successfully by the Hindi poet Amir Khusru (12th century) and the Kashmiri poet Parmānanda (1791-1874), to name just two. The use of such a device in literature is discussed in Kachru (1981a), Pillai (1974), and Timm (1975).

Code Alteration and Speaker-Hearer

Code-switching refers to the alteration in which the speech event does not necessarily require that the speaker and hearer share identical code repertoires. The user may be bilingual and the receiver a monolingual.

On the other hand, in code-mixing, the codes used and the attitudinal reactions to the codes are shared both by the speaker and hearer.

Hypotheses for 'Mixing'

The main hypotheses for explaining the phenomenon of mixing are as follows:

1. *'Borrowing' hypothesis.* This hypothesis treats 'mixing' (or switching) as a manifestation of what has been traditionally termed 'borrowing' (Baker 1980:4-5; Gumperz and Hernandes-Ch. 1971:320). It seems that it is difficult to explain mixing as merely borrowing (Kachru 1978a). First, the items borrowed in mixing are not necessarily motivated by the 'lexical gaps' in the 'mixer's' L_1, although traditionally that is considered one of the main arguments in favor of borrowing. Second, the absorbed items are not restricted to one unit, for example, a lexical item; 'borrowing' extends to phrases, clauses, and sentences. In addition, collocations and idioms are 'absorbed'. Third, 'mixing' provides parallel lexical sets which are marked for register, style, or for identity functions, as illustrated by the parallel sets in Hindi or Kashmiri. Furthermore, as Pfaff (1979:195) has said, 'The use of borrowing does not presuppose bilingual competence since "borrowing" may occur in the speech of those with only monolingual competence.' Bautista (1975:85) argues that 'the term "code-switching" is not appropriately applied to the instances of the use of loanwords, for instance, lexical items from lexicon L_2 in L_1 utterances. Although there is a branching into the lexicon of L_2, there does not seem to be a switch in code or linguistic system—the linguistic system is still that of L_1.' (See also Leap 1973, esp. p. 286).

2. *Pidgin hypothesis.* The pidgin hypothesis as an underlying motivation for 'mixing' certainly does not apply to 'educated mixing'. Pidgins are characterized by their restricted functional range, structural simplicity, and inability to express abstract ideas (Kachru 1978a:110-11). The users of pidgins generally do not share a mutually intelligible code of communication, so a pidgin is the only code of communication available to them. In contrast, users of 'mixed' codes generally share mutually intelligible codes and use a mixed variety for various functional, attitudinal, and sociocultural reasons.

3. *Distinct code hypothesis.* The code-mixed texts clearly show formal cohesion and functional dependency (Kachru 1978b:31), despite the fact that constituent features of the resultant code are from two or more codes. The cohesiveness is the result of certain types of lexicalization and pattern symmetry (adjustment). The contextual appropriateness of a code-mixed text is the result of such lexicalization (e.g. Persianization, Englishization, or Sanskritization in South Asia). Extended borrowing is only one

component. The appropriateness (or *expectancy*) of a code-mixed text must be judged within the context of situation. (See also Kachru 1978b:29-31).

This view is not necessarily in conflict with the preoccupation of linguists with the notion of 'a language' and its description. The vital question is: When do we know that we have a *new* code? Ferguson asserts that 'linguists, by and large, have put that problem aside' (1978:98). But one is still compelled to consider how one code can be separated from another code. Ferguson provides three criteria for 'delineating' the 'natural unit' of language, i.e. *autonomy, stability,* and *functional range.* *Autonomy* refers to the 'structural' and functional distinctiveness of a code in comparison to other codes. *Stability* is the degree of internal variation, and the *functional range* is 'the degree of restriction in semantic range'. It might be useful to apply these criteria to the code-mixed varieties, too.

Toward a Typology of Repertoire Types

At present, we have very limited cross-linguistic and cross-cultural empirical data on the types of code alteration. These are some of the possibilities in the repertoire range of a bilingual:

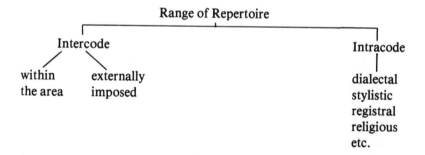

It seems that the more intercode mixing there is, the more structural 'conflicts' are possible which might create problems of cohesion in code-mixed texts (Bautista 1975; Gingrás 1974). Let us consider some of the typical situations discussed in literature.

1. Chicano situation (Elías-Olivares 1976):

Code-Switching

| Standard Spanish | Popular Spanish | Español Mixtureado | caló | | Chicano English | Standard English |

In this situation the repertoire range comprises standard varieties of both Spanish and English, and other 'mixed' or 'not-so-mixed' codes which have distinct functional roles.

2. North Indian rural situation (e.g. Srivastava et al. 1978; see also Gumperz 1964 for the situation in Khalapur):

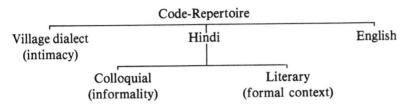

This presents the range of a typical educated Hindi speaker from a village of the *madhya deša* (Hindi-speaking belt). The range comprises the village dialect, the colloquial and literary varieties of Hindi, and English. In a number of cases Sanskrit may be used as a language of religion. The switching and mixing may take place in all these codes, depending on the participants and the context.

3. Indian urban situation (Gujarati businessmen in Bombay)
(Pandit 1972, 1977):

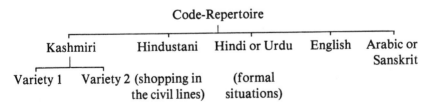

4. Kashmiri situation:

Code-Repertoire

| Kashmiri | Hindustani | Hindi or Urdu | English | Arabic or Sanskrit |

| Variety 1 | Variety 2 (shopping in the civil lines) | (formal situations) | | |

The last two situations (3 and 4) differ basically in the range and types of codes a person has available. The situation 3 is not very extensive, though it is also not very restricted. It is an impressive example of functional multilingualism, further seen to a lesser degree in the repertoire range of an educated Kashmiri (situation 4).

Pandit (1972, 1977) shows that a Gujarati businessman in Bombay has the following functional repertoire range:
- (a) Gujarati (with family members for identity and as a family language);
- (b) Katchi (as a trade language);
- (c) Marathi (with servants in the business and with peddlers);
- (d) Bazār Hindi (with milkmen who are generally from Uttar Pradesh, the Hindi-speaking region);
- (e) English (used in interstate commerce, trade, correspondence, etc.). The situation of an educated Kashmiri is not much different from situation (3).

What, then, is the function of the vernacular in the above repertoire range? This question presupposes that we have a widely accepted and well-motivated definition of what we mean by the term 'vernacular'. As we know, that is not the case. It is even not clear that such a term is useful for providing a classification of various code types. But that is another story.

It has been suggested that a vernacular may be identified as a code with which one feels close identity, emotional attachment, and which one uses in intimate contexts. The problem is that this definition can not be generalized. In terms of a hierarchy of prestige, a code immediately next to the code one is using is generally termed a vernacular. It is an attitudinally loaded concept. An English educated Hindi speaker considers Hindi a vernacular (so did the European scholars), a Kharibolī (standard Hindi) speaker thinks of a dialect (e.g. Awadhī, Braj) as a vernacular. A speaker of a dialect of Hindi considers the rural varieties as vernaculars. As I mentioned earlier, the distinction between literary vs. nonliterary does not seem to apply in this context. In the above Gujarati situation, for example, the functional allocation of code types seems to be more important than of the vernacular vs. nonvernacular distinction. It is, however, clear that functionally restricted codes seem to be labelled 'vernaculars'.

MANIFESTATIONS OF 'MIXING'

The manifestations of 'mixing' range from the use of lexical items to units up to a sentence or more, and embedding of idioms from other codes. Kachru (1978a; 1978b) shows how this process works with reference to Hindi and English.[9] The borrowing code makes the use of 'mixing' in such a way that the resultant text has both formal cohesiveness and functional appropriateness. In fact, it is due to such cohesiveness and appropriateness that such codes are functionally relevant in bilingual situations. Consider, for example, the following illustrations in which 'mixing' is not restricted to only one unit.

1. *ṭank* [tank] *va reḍār* [radar] *prāpt karne kī bhī yōjnā*
'tank and radar procure do of also scheme'
2. *sarkas* [circus] *aur numāyiš yahā̃ phēl* [fail] *haĩ*
'circus and exhibition here fail are'
3. *purānī hai tō kyā huā, phāin* [fine] *to hai.* But I do not like Rajesh Khanna
'old is what happened fine however is. But I do not like Rajesh Khanna.'
4. *aur maĩ parivartan ghar se šuru karū̃gā kyū̃ki* charity begins at home.
'and I change home from begin will do because charity begins at home.'
5. akṭing *vekṭing maĩ kyā jānū̃ re*
'acting and the like I what should know hey'
6. mujhe is bat mẽ bilkul *doubt* nahī̃ hai, *rather I am sure* ki *this year* B. Sc. *examination* ke *results* bahut kharāb haĩ. kuch to *examiners* ne *strictness* kī aur kuch papers bhī aise *out of way* āye ki *students* to *unexpected questions* ko *paper* mẽ *set* dekh kar *hall* kī *ceiling* hī *watch* karte rah gaye. itnā *failure* to *last three or four years* mẽ kabhī huā hi na thā abkī *admission* mẽ bhī *difficulty* uṭhānī paṛegī. *Last year* bhī *in spite of all attempts* kuch *applicants* ke *admission almost impossible* ho gaye the. *After a great stir registar* ko *move* kiyā jā sakā, jisse kuch *seats* kā *extra arrangement* kiyā gayā. (Bhatia 1967:55)

The English rendering of the above illustration (6) is as follows. The italicized items are present in both texts.

I have no *doubt* in this matter, *rather I am sure* that *this year* the *B.Sc. examination results* are very bad. To some extent the *examiners* used *strictness* and the *papers* also were *out of the way.* On seeing *unexpected questions set* in the *papers* the *students* kept *watch*(ing) the *ceiling* of the *hall.* This much [high percentage of] *failure* had not taken place in the *last three or four years.* This time, too, we will have to face *difficulty* in *admission. Last year,* too, *in spite of all attempts, admission* of some *applicants* became *almost impossible. After a great stir* the *registrar* could be move(d), which helped in making *extra arrangement*(s) for some additional *seats* [places, openings].

In the above illustrations we find the following types of units from English mixed with Hindi: (a) a noun phrase (in 1); (b) a hybrid noun phrase (in 2); (c) a sentence (in 3); (d) an idiom (in 4); (e) reduplication (in 5);

and (f) an extreme case of code-mixing with English, with appropriate cohesion within the text (in 6). In the last text, out of 113 lexical items, counting both content words and function words, 44 percent are from English.

We now have a large number of studies which show that the device of 'mixing' is used almost in all bilingual contexts and is not specific to any particular bilingual society. The following examples of code-mixing represent several language families in a variety of cultural contexts.

Ansre (1971) provides examples from West African languages:

1. *Mele* very sorry, *gake mena* every conceivable opportunity -*i hafi wò* let-*m* down (Ewe).
   'I am very sorry, but I gave him every conceivable opportunity and yet he let me down.'
2. *Se wɔbɛ*-report *wo ma me bio a mebe*- dismiss *wo* without further warning. (Twi)
   'If you are reported to me again I shall dismiss you without further warning.'
3. *Ne* phoneme *nye* minimal phonological unit *eye* morpheme *nye* minimal grammatical unit, *lo, ekena* lexeme *anye* minimal lexical unit. (Ewe)
   'If the phoneme is the minimal phonological unit and the morpheme is the minimal grammatical unit, then lexeme will be the minimal lexical unit.'

Bautista (1977) gives '...instances of language 1 NPs [Tagalog] appearing as subjects and complements in language 2 [English] units.' Consider the following illustrations.

1. *Dito po sa atin* ... *ang intensyon po talaga ng tinatawag na* national parks is to set aside an original area *na tinatawag po natig may magandang tanawin*
2. *Ang* family planning *po dito* is really the most crucial at the moment.
3. They are given *ivong tinatawag na* academic appointments.

Warie (1977) considers the case of contact of Thai and English:

...*khɔ̂ɔkhwvan cam kìaw kàp* income effect *kɔ̂ɔkhǐi wâa man pen bùak sàmɔ̌ɔpay čên nay kɔɔ-ra-nii kìawakàp khɔ̌ɔŋleew* inferior goods *nán* income effect *àat pen lóp dây.*

'...things to remember about income effect is that it is not always positive, for example in case of inferior goods, the income effect can be negative.'

Nash has discussed 'language mixture' in Puerto Rico and gives the following examples of what she terms 'midstream code switching' (1977:214):

1. Buy your home in Levittown Lakes, *donde la buena vida comienza.*
2. *Yo y mi* Winston-*porque* Winstons taste good like a cigarette should;
3. If the boss calls, *digale que no estoy.*

One may add to this list studies such as Annamalai (1978), Gingràs (1974), Jacobsen (1978), Lawton (1980), Lindholm and Padilla (1978), McClure (1977), Pfaff (1976), Poplack (1981), Sridhar (1978), Valdes-Fallis (1978), and Zentella (1978).

CONSTRAINTS ON 'MIXING'

A number of language-specific studies have shown that the receiving code does not mix units from another code without certain formal constraints. Code-mixing is clearly a rule-governed and function-dependent phenomenon; in terms of function in some multilingual situations it is almost a sign of language dependency.

There seems to be a range between acceptable 'code-mixing' and what may be termed 'odd-mixing'. On the basis of the types of 'mixing', one notices a cline on which the code-mixed varieties (within a variety) may be marked. There is, on the one hand, 'educated' code-mixing (e.g. registral, or style-specific) and, on the other hand, the type which is characteristic of codes such as *butler English* (or *butler Hindustani*), and what are called *boxwallah* varieties in Indian English (Kachru 1980c).

We lack any study which gives us a typology of constraints found across such codes. In what may be termed 'educated' code-mixing with English by Hindi-Urdu speakers, the following constraints are found, but at this stage of empirical research one has to make generalizations with reservations.

1. Rank shift constraint:
   (a) **merā skūl* which is in *bosṭan bilkul acchā nahī̃ hai*
       'My school which is in Boston is not at all good.'
In this case the rank shift clause cannot be from English.

2. Conjunction constraint: the conjunctions 'and', 'or', etc. from English are not used to conjoin nonEnglish NP's or VP's.

(a) *pustak* and *čābī bhī lānā*
   'book and key also bring'

On the other hand, conjoining two sentences from two codes is acceptable.

(b) *čāy jaldī piyo* and let us go
   'tea quick drink...'

(c) You must eat some food *aur dūdh bhī pīna*
   '...and drink some milk, too.'

As I have said earlier (Kachru 1978a:40), if the code-mixing in a language has been assimilated, this constraint is not applicable, for example, Persian and Sanskrit conjunction markers in Kashmiri.

3. Determiner constraint:

(a) *maĩ five *sundar laṛkiyõ ko jāntā hũ*
                                    (numeral)
   'I five beautiful girls know.'

(b) *āp that *makān kī bāt kar rahē haĩ?*
                                    (demonstrative)
   'You (hon.) that house of talk doing are.'
   'Are you talking of that house?'

4. Complementizer constraint:

(a) *maĩ sočtā hũ* that *ham ko jānā hogā*
   'I thinking am that we going will be.'
   'I think that we will have to go.'

For a discussion on other languages see, for example, Annamalai (1971); Bautista (1975); Gingras (1974); Pfaff (1979); Poplack (1981); Sridhar (1978); Timm (1975); McClure and Wentz (1976).

'Constraints' and 'Cohesiveness'

The syntactic constraints provide only part of the picture. One must extend the concept of 'cohesiveness' (or 'integration') both to formal cohesiveness and to contextual appropriateness. Cohesiveness refers to 'the integration of the units of another code into the systems of the receiving code, and organizing the units from two codes into a semantic relationship' (Kachru 1978b:112-113). 'Semantic relationship' entails *integrating* the L_2 items in such a way that the contextual appropriateness is maintained without 'violating' the rules of formal cohesion. As is well known, this is achieved by various means, e.g.

1. the use of productive grammatical processes of L_1 to nativize the items of L_2. Consider the following examples of Hindi:

Number: *filmẽ* 'films'; *ajensiyã* 'agencies'; *moṭarẽ* 'motors'.

Gender: *māsṭarin* (f) 'master'.

Abstract nouns: *ḍāctarī* from 'doctor'; *aphsarī* from 'an officer'.
(see also Pandharipande 1979).

2. the use of syntactic 'equivalence' (Annamalai 1971; Sridhar and Sridhar 1980).

CONVERGENCE OF CODES AND CODE CHANGE

It is evident that 'mixing' and 'switching' are a consequence of code contact or convergence. In earlier literature (Clyne 1972; Weinreich 1953) a number of examples illustrate the impact of language contact on language change. The contact has two manifestations: first, in terms of the extension (or addition) of the verbal repertoire of bilinguals; second, in terms of the structural changes initiated at one or more levels of language.

An extended code normally acquires a label which may in some cases indicate the processes involved in developing the code, for example, the case of the so-called Hindi area and Nagpur in central India. In the Hindi area the code repertoire includes the following, among others:

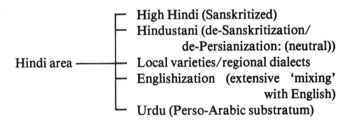

```
                 ┌─ High Hindi (Sanskritized)
                 ├─ Hindustani (de-Sanskritization/
                 │              de-Persianization: (neutral))
Hindi area ──────┼─ Local varieties/regional dialects
                 ├─ Englishization (extensive 'mixing'
                 │                       with English)
                 └─ Urdu (Perso-Arabic substratum)
```

One can recategorize these on a different dimension with refrence to function, using terms such as *formal, informal,* and *register-specific.* The Nagpur situation is not identical to that in the Hindi area (Pandharipande 1980). Nagpur has a bilingual speech community *within* the borders of Maharashtra (the Marathi-speaking state of India), and parts of the state border on the Hindi dialect area. The result is that some syntactic features in Nagpur Marathi (NM) are shared with Hindi and not with the standard variety, Puṇerī Marathi (PM). The situation is somewhat as follows:

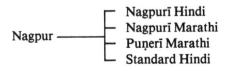

```
              ┌─ Nagpurī Hindi
              ├─ Nagpurī Marathi
Nagpur ───────┼─ Puṇerī Marathi
              └─ Standard Hindi
```

NM is the language of *bahujan samāj* 'the majority of the people'. In informal situations NM and NH are used, and in the formal situations the switch is to PM and Standard Hindi. In creative literature, NM is used primarily for local color, for marking character-types, and for informal conversation. In formal or what the newspaper editors consider 'serious situations' NM is not used, since, as one editor commented, 'the readers' opinion about the news is affected by the type of language used in the newspapers' (Pandharipande 1980:32). Therefore, some lexical borrowing and loan shifts are used from NH, but 'syntactic constructions which reveal the influence of Hindi on Marathi are rarely found in the newspapers.'

The contexts for structural changes, especially syntactic, are not always identical. Let us consider the following cases. First, two language families influence each other and thus, over a period of time, contribute to the development of a language *area* comprising various language families (Emeneau 1956; Masica 1976). In this situation the change either is initiated in a *contact area,* or the contact is indirect (Gumperz and Wilson 1971; Nadkarni 1975; Sridhar 1978). Second, two speech communities have lived together using two codes, and the linguistic implication is the development of two distinct varieties of *contacting* languages. In Nagpur, NM and NH are the result of such contact. Third, there may be a contact with an 'imposed' language associated with elitism, power, administration, mobility, advancement, and access. The cases of Persian and English in South Asia provide good examples of this (Kachru in press).

We shall not consider the influence of language contact at all linguistic levels, since a large body of literature on this topic discusses the implications of such contact in phonology and lexis. However, we still have limited evidence for the influence of such contact on syntax, especially in Asian and African bilingual contexts, one reason being that syntax is generally resistant to such change. The following case studies will illustrate the point.

In Dravidian languages, as Sridhar says, 'the influence of Indo-Aryan is least pronounced on the level of syntax' (1978:204). There are, however, several traces in 'modes of compounding', which are not typically Dravidian in structure since the determiner is placed 'before the determined and are probably due to the influence of Sanskrit', (e.g. *yathāśakti* 'according to one's ability'), the passive construction (e.g. 'the door was opened by the girl'), which is 'also likely to have developed under the influence of Sanskrit, a tendency further reinforced by the influence of English', and finally, 'the clausal mode of relative clause formation' (Sridhar 1978:204; Nadkarni 1975).

On the other hand, the Nagpur situation has two faces, one deeply influencing Marathi, and the other deeply influencing Hindi at all linguistic levels. However, both these varieties remain attitudinally low on the language hierarchy. Despite such an attitude, the 'transfer' in syntax is present both in NM and NH, as shown in Pandharipande (1979). I will present a few examples from both varieties. NM has several syntactic features which it does not share with PM but which it does share with Standard Hindi (or NH). The following are illustrative.

1. Progressive construction:
   (a) PM: *ti   gāṇā mhaṇat   āhe*
              she song say-prog. is
              'She is singing a song.'
   (b) NM: *ti   gāṇā mhaṇūn rāhilī   āhe*
              she song say   prog. is
              'She is singing a song.'
   (c) Hindi: *vah gānā gā   rahī   hai*
              she song sing prog.   is
              'She is singing a song.'

Note that in PM, the progressive aspect of a verb is indicated by adding /t/ to the verb stem, which is followed by the relevant form of the verb *as-ṇe* 'to be' (Damle 1911, quoted in Pandharipande 1979).

2. Negation:
   (a) PM: *āmhī udyā   mumbailā zāṇār nāhī*
              we   tomorrow Bombay to will go not
              'We will not go to Bombay tomorrow.'
   (b) NM: *āmhī udyā   mumbailā nāhī zāū*
                                        zāṇār nāhī
              we   tomorrow Bombay to will not go
                                        will go not
              'We will not go to Bombay tomorrow.'
   (c) Hindi: *ham kal   bambaī nahī̃ jāẽge*
              we tomorrow Bombay not   will go
              'We will not go to Bombay tomorrow.'

Note that, in (b) above, NM allows both constructions (i.e. PM-type and H-type), but the H-type (c) seems to be preferred. Further evidence for the preference for H-type constructions is the NM speakers' use of another type of negative construction. In PM, the verb *pāhije* 'to want' when negated is deleted and replaced by *nako* 'to not want'. Consider the following:

(a) PM: *malā cahā pāhije*
          I-dat. tea   want
          'I want tea.'
(b)   *malā cahā nako*
          I-dat. tea   do not want
          'I do not want tea.'
(c) NM: *malā cahā nako* (or)
          malā cahā nāhī pāhije
          I-dat. tea   do not want
          'I do not want tea.'
(d) Hindi: *mujhe cāy cāhiye*
          I-dat. tea   want
          'I want tea.'
          mujhe cāy nahī̃ cāhiye
          I-dat. tea   not   want
          'I do not want tea.'

In NM, then, the variation is a result of the extended code repertoire, as compared to PM.

On the other hand, as Pandharipande (1979) has shown, NH clearly has syntactic transfers from Marathi. Consider the following examples:

1. Conditional sentence:
   (a) NH: (*agar*) *vah āyā rahtā to māĩ usse   milā rahtā*
             if   he   came aux. then I   he-with met aux.
             'If he would come, I would meet him.'
   (b) Hindi: (*agar*) *vah ātā   to   māĩ usse   miltā*
             If   he   came then I   he-with meet
             'If he would come, I would meet him.'
2. Coercive causative:
   (a) NH: *māĩ ne uskō   kām karnekō lagāyā*
             I   Ag. he-dat. work to do   made

In Hindi this construction is not possible.

3. Quotative construction:
   (a) NH: *māĩ āũga karke bol rahā   thā*
             I   will come thus say prog. aux.
             'He said that he would come.' ('"I will come," thus he said.') (See also Y. Kachru 1979).

4. Have-to construction:
   (a) NH: *mujhe bambaī jānekā*   *hai*
               I-dat. Bombay go-possessive is
               'I have to go to Bombay.'
   (b) Hindi: *mujhe bambaī jānā hai*
               I-dat. Bombay to go aux.
               'I have to go to Bombay.'

The next case is that of the Englishization of South Asian and African languages. The switching and mixing with English has contributed to syntactic innovations as well. Kachru (1979) discusses some of the processes of Englishization with reference to Hindi. It is claimed that, among other processes, the following may be attributed to the Englishization of Hindi syntax: (a) the tendency in some registers of Hindi, especially in creative writing and the newspaper register, to use SVO word order of English, as opposed to the preferred SOV word order (see also Mishra 1963:175-77)[10]; (b) the introduction of indirect speech which was not traditionally used in Hindi, e.g., *šyām ne kahā ki voh čāy piyegā,* as opposed to *šyām ne kahā ki maĩ čāy piyũgā* 'Shyam said that he will drink tea' as opposed to 'Shyam said "I will drink tea"'; (c) the use of impersonal constructions in the Hindi newspaper register which initially started as translation 'equivalents' of constructions such as 'it is said', 'it has been heard', (*kahā jātā hai, sunā gayā hai*); (d) the use of passivization with an agent ('by'; Hindi *dwārā* or *zəriye*), e.g., *yah nāṭak šekspiyar dwārā likhā gayā hai* 'This play has been written by Shakespeare'; (e) the development of post-head modifier *jō* 'who', although there is no agreement on whether this construction is due to the influence of English (Tiwari 1966:293) or Persian (Guru 1962:530-31), e.g., *vah amrīkī jō gaṛī mẽ hai merā dost hai* 'The American who is sitting in the car is my friend'; and (f) the development of the parenthetical clause in Hindi, considered by some to be due to the influence of English, although others treat it as a typical Indo-Aryan construction (Tiwari 1966:297-98). The number of examples at various levels can be multiplied, as can the sources responsible for the influence. However, the important point to recognize is the far-reaching linguistic significance of code alteration in syntax.

CODE REPERTOIRE AND LINGUISTIC DESCRIPTION

Let me now revert to the bilingual's code repertoire within the context of a linguistic description. The centrality of variation within a code, and its implications for synchronic and diachronic descriptions, have been

convincingly demonstrated by Labov (1966, 1972b) and other 'variation-
ists'. But equally exciting and at the same time more complex questions
have yet to be faced by linguists. As Ferguson (1978:101) puts it: 'What goes
on in a speech community that uses—let us say—four languages?' In other
words, can one write a grammar of bilinguals' complex linguistic roles?
After all, that is how bilinguals use languages for *living,* and in their use of
codes they always show an awareness and concern for *appropriateness.*
Those who have observed how traditional multilingual societies work with
their code repertoire have clearly seen that the codes function as 'one
system' with formally and functionally definable subsystems. The challenge
is, to quote Ferguson again, to 'try the job of writing grammars of such
complex systems' (1978:104). This statement will surely cause jitters,
because the task is enormous and methodologically complex, as Ferguson
admits: 'I know it is hard enough to write grammars, anyway, and what I
am suggesting makes it even harder. But I still think this is the job of the
linguist.' This is a call to take the next step from Gumperz' and Hymes'
notion of 'linguistic (or verbal) repertoire'. The aim is to build this concept
into a linguistic description, and to structure the exponents of such
repertoire. There are, as Ferguson mentions, several fragmentary attempts
already available; Denison (1968), Scollon (forthcoming), Trudgill
(1976-77). This new demand may entail taking a new theoretical and
methodological direction, perhaps within the existing theoretical frameworks which have shown concern for accounting for such formal
complexity in linguistic behavior.

The complexity of the task is obvious, as is the desirability for such
descriptions of bilinguals' code repertoire. This is perhaps the only way to
establish meaningful relationships between the formal and functional
apsects of the bilingual's linguistic interaction.

One need not go too far to see that, functionally, code repertoire is used
as 'one system' of linguistic behavior by bilinguals or multilinguals. One
notices this in classrooms with bilingual or bidialectal children, in creative
writing where such verbal strategies are constantly exploited for their
stylistic effect or for distinguishing various character types, and in the
personal interaction of the members of bilingual communities in
performing their roles as parents, husbands, buyers, sellers, and as
participants in other social and religious interactions. The task, then, is to
account for this linguistic reality.

IMPLICATIONS

As indicated earlier, I shall use this digression merely to list some of the areas in which our better understanding of the role of vernacular in a bilingual's code repertoire has serious implications. The range of such implications is far-reaching, and a complete picture is not possible without more interdisciplinary and cross-cultural research. Consider areas listed below which are illustrative and not exhaustive:

(a) Literacy planning
(b) School instruction
(c) Curriculum development
(d) Codes in professions and their intelligibility
(e) Code modernization
(f) Code and media
(g) Attitude toward codes
(h) Codes as markers of 'styles' and 'registers'

Theoretical and empirical research in some of these areas has already been initiated, but it still is limited and restricted to selected parts of the world (Cazden et al. 1972; Cicourel et al. 1974; Ferguson and Heath 1981; Freed 1978; Heath 1978; Hymes 1977; Robinson 1978; Sinclair and Coulthard 1975; Srivastava et al. 1978; Valdes-Fallis 1978; and Tough 1977).

CONCLUSION

In recent years we have collected substantial data to prove that speech communities—monolingual or multilingual—are not homogeneous users of single codes. A speech community tends to use a network of codes which are functionally allocated in terms of their societal uses. The type and range of such codes, however, vary from one community to another. Contextually, the codes alternate in several dimensions, e.g. status, sex, region, setting, age. And each context has its formal exponents which mark the context specification of a code. In some contemporary approaches to language description, such as Labov, Hymes, Halliday, Firth, and Gumperz, to name just a few, understanding of such societal functions of codes has become pivotal. However, one can not deny that some paradigms of linguistics still continue to treat such societal and functional concerns as marginal or secondary. In these approaches, there is not only hesitation to go into these areas, but even a clear indifference toward developing such concerns for linguistics. In this respect, Hymes (1972:xi) has described the attitude of linguists well when he says '...some linguists whether in disgust, disdain, despair, or some combination of matters, saying that the present state of linguistic theory is so confused that linguists can tell teachers nothing useful at all.'

However, one cannot deny that concepts like contextualization, functionalism, ethnography of communication, and pragmatics have increasingly been used in linguistic descriptions and the pedagogical concerns of linguists, as for example, in the work of Candlin (1980), Gumperz (1970), Halliday (1970, 1973), Kachru (1980b), Munby (1978), Paulston (1971), Widdowson (1978), and Wilkins (1978). The internal (structural) organization of a bilingual's codes is better understood now than it was only two decades ago. The result is that code-mixing and code-switching are now seriously studied in terms of their formal constituents and constraints, and their functional and pragmatic uses. It is true that the attitudinal reactions to some mixed varieties of codes have not yet changed, for example, toward Tex Mex, Bazār Hindustani (Kalkatiyā Hindi; Bambaiyā Hindi) or Nāgpurī Marathi. Reference to these or some other varieties are still made in a pejorative sense, even tending to indicate some type of 'linguistic deprivation'.

On the basis of the last two decades of empirical research we can now give less ambiguous answers to questions such as the following: (a) What is meant by the functional allocation of codes? (b) What are the processes which result in code-mixing? (c) What constraints separate 'code-mixing' from what may be termed 'odd-mixing'? and (e) What are the functional and attitudinal criteria for establishing hierarchies of codes? The change may be slow; language habits are slow to change and least prone to legislation. But they do change. During the last thirty to forty years there has been a clear change toward the caste dialects in the South of India, toward the Received Pronunciation in the English-speaking world, some discernible change toward what is termed the Black dialect in America, and toward the nonnative varieties of English (Kachru 1982). What is more important, we have begun to take seriously the 'socially realistic' linguistic frameworks and their methodology (Kachru 1980a, 1981). That, in itself, is a sign of new awareness and a new direction.

Another important question is how linguists'—or educators'—under-standings of the formal and functional characteristics of bilingual speech communities has been related to the bilingual/bidialectal educational system. This is, of course, a double-edged sword, with a pedagogical side and a linguistic side. An applied theoretician must accept a planner's role with ramifications which touch upon more than one discipline. And one therefore, treads on many sensitive toes. That makes applied linguistics (or its subfield 'educational linguistics') a difficult area to work in. Its methodology has yet to be sharpened and its concerns highlighted. But there is no doubt that the underlying theoretical framework must be based upon a paradigm concerned with 'socially realistic linguistics'.

Concern about such an approach to a bilingual speech community, and its educational ramifications, is not restricted to the U.S. context. It is a pervasive concern with international implications. In a restricted sense one might see it as Coballes-Vega (1979) sees it in the context of the Chicano and Puerto Rican children in Chicago, or as Warie (1978) sees it with reference to the Thai-speaking speech community. But the concern is larger, very vital, and with significant implications in education. After all, most speech communities in the world are not monolingual. A majority of language users have multicodes of communication, whether we see such codes in terms of 'bidialectism', 'bilingualism', or 'plurilingualism'.

Another significant phenomenon of our times is that one code functions across such linguistic and cultural pluralism: the English language. In functional terms, bilingualism in English is historically unprecedented, and provides the first example of the role of a natural language as an almost universal language. Out of 363 million speakers of English, only 73.3 percent are native speakers. The non-native users of English contribute toward its further role-extension and actual expansion. But we still have far to go to understand the pragmatics of nonnative varieties of English (see Kachru 1980b, 1980c, and 1982). The professions which train teachers of English for various parts of the world, and other supporting agencies, have so far shown indifference to such issues and concerns.

In understanding the role of English in a nonnative English user's linguistic repertoire, the need is to recognize three types of clines. First, the range of *Englishes* which such a user commands can vary from pidgin English to what may be termed a 'standard' variety of English. Second, such varieties are used in different roles for *intranational* or *international* functions. Third, there is a relationship between the variety and the participant in a linguistic interaction. This, then, is an attempt toward the contextualization of *Englishes* within a context of situation. Through such contextualization the underlying reasons for the acculturation or nativization of English in Asia or Africa will be understood. I shall not elaborate on this point here, since studies on this topic have just been published or are forthcoming; for example, Smith (1980), Kachru (1980b, 1982, and in press), Kachru and Quirk (1980), and Bailey and Görlach (in press).

This paper has merely attempted to highlight some of the manifestations of code repertoire, its theoretical implications, and its relevance to our understanding of various societal, educational, and literary concerns. This is only a fragment of the uninvestigated linguistic 'iceberg'. A significant part of it has yet to be uncovered.

NOTES

[1] This paper incorporates several ideas and illustrations—either modified or without modification—presented earlier in Kachru (1978a; 1978b). I have used 'bilingualism' as a cover term to include the concepts of 'multilingualism' and 'plurilingualism'.

[2] Hymes (1972:xxxiv) also uses the term 'communicative repertoire' in this context.

[3] See Scherer and Giles (1979:xii): '. . . the term "marker" should be taken in a fairly general sense to mean speech cues that potentially provide the reader with information concerning the sender's biological, psychological, and social characteristics.'

[4] See Trudgill (1974:14).

[5] The term is primarily used to refer to a 'language' or a 'dialect' spoken by the people of a particular country or district. It is generally a native or indigenous 'language' or a 'dialect' (see *OED*). A vernacular is traditionally distinguished from the literary language.

[6] It has been suggested, for example, by Christina Paulston (personal communication) that in this context the term 'backgrounding' may be more appropriate.

[7] However, there are other lexical items which are not necessarily mutually intelligible since these are register-restricted.

[8] The main differences between the local dialect and the standard variety are, e.g., retroflex vs. nonretroflex /n/ and /ṇ/, /l/ and /ḷ/; retroflex flap /ṛ/ and retroflex stop /ḍ/; diphthongs with an upglide *uī, aī, oī; s* and *š, ø;* consonant gemination in medial position *loṭṭā* ' jug' > *loṭā;* differences in inflectional endings; and the infinitive suffix (*bōlnā > bōlaṇ* 'to speak'). There are also substantial lexical differences.

[9] A partial list of such studies on several other Western and non-Western languages is given in Kachru (1978a, 1978b).

[10] A detailed discussion is given in Kachru (1979). See also Tiwari (1966:290;305).

COGNITIVE DEVELOPMENT
IN BILINGUAL ENVIRONMENTS

CAROLYN KESSLER and MARY ELLEN QUINN

In spite of extensive resources committed to bilingual education for programmatic implementation in the United States over the last decade, very little basic research has focused on fundamental questions relating to an understanding of the bilingual child. From the psycholinguistic viewpoint, cognitive development and language development are intimately related, as indicated in the vast body of psycholinguistic research that has emerged in recent years. Although studies focusing on first language development and relationships to cognitive functioning have given insights into general developmental aspects of young children, they leave open the question of the special issue concerning the young child who from language onset is simultaneously developing in two languages or who is undergoing the encoding of a second language in the childhood years. To meet the needs of these children more adequately with educationally sound bilingual programs in the school setting and to understand more completely the interactions with the bilingual environments in which these children participate, much more extensive empirical research is needed on the relationships between cognitive and language development in bilingual children from a developmental psycholinguistic viewpoint and, in turn, on the interaction of these relationships with educational programs.

This paper reviews relationships between cognitive functioning and bilingualism as indicated in the relatively few empirical studies currently available. It examines cognitive and linguistic interdependence in the context of educational programs and in the context of theoretical perspectives on cognitive development. Particular attention is given here to the interaction of cognitive and linguistic development as exhibited in a science education program conducted by Kessler and Quinn (1979, 1980a, 1980b). With this empirical base, together with that provided by other studies of cognition and bilingualism, this paper attempts to forge a coherent conceptual framework for addressing the interrelationships between aspects of cognitive functioning, bilingualism, and educational programs for children.

BILINGUALISM

Any study involving the variable of bilingualism is confronted with the problem of defining bilingualism. A sociolinguistic view is taken by Weinreich (1953) who broadly defines bilingualism as the alternate use of two languages. From a psycholinguistic perspective, Haugen (1956:6) sees bilingualism as the ability 'to produce complete and meaningful utterances in two languages'. Together, these definitions give a psychosociolinguistic definition used here. Bilingualism, then, in its broad sense is seen as the alternate use of two languages, either vernacular or standard varieties, manifested in complete and meaningful utterances in each of the languages. This still leaves open issues regarding assessment of the two languages as well as the relationship of the two languages in the bilingual individual, particularly with reference to age of acquisition of the two languages and relative proficiency in each.

In looking at interrelationships between cognitive functioning and bilingualism, of particular relevance are the notions of child bilingualism, balanced bilingualism, and subtractive and additive bilingualism.

From a psycholinguistic point of view, an issue of critical concern in the study of child bilinguals is that of the developmental sequence in the acquisition of the two languages. The simultaneous acquisition of two linguistic codes from the onset of language acquisition, a phenomenon also referred to as first language bilingualism (Swain 1972), defines a different situation from that of the successive acquisition of two languages. Following McLaughling (1978), the position is taken here that the child who is introduced to a second language before age 3 simultaneously acquires two languages. The introduction of a second language after age 3 defines successive acquisition in which one language follows the other. As an operational definition in examining cognitive consequences of bilingualism in children, both groups taken together represent child bilingualism. More specifically, child bilinguals are those children who are engaged in the process of acquisition of two languages no later than the elementary school years.

The notion of balanced bilingualism is surrounded with considerable ambiguity in the literature. Lambert, Havelka, and Gardner (1959) intended the term to be applied to native language proficiency in both languages of the bilingual individual. This state is distinguished from language dominance in which the bilingual is more competent in one language than in the other. Current definitions in federal guidelines for children of limited English proficiency use the concept of balanced bilingualism to apply to children who may, in fact, be developmental in both languages and, consequently, not be characteristic of the variety of balanced bilingualism described above. Duncan and De Avila (1979) obviate the distinction by using the term 'late language learner' for the child still developmental in both languages and 'proficient bilingual' for the polar opposite.

As Weinreich (1953) points out, many factors may affect the degree of proficiency of an individual's two languages, including age of acquisition, order of acquisition, opportunity for communication, and social function, among other variables. As a result, a crucial variable in the relationships between bilingualism and cognitive functioning is the degree of proficiency in both languages. Among researchers who have argued for consideration of this issue are Lambert (1977), Segalowitz and Gatbonton (1977), and Duncan and De Avila (1979).

Lambert (1977) has suggested that the consequences of bilingualism may be dependent on the dominance relationship of the bilingual's two languages. He makes a distinction between additive bilingualism, characterized by the acquisition of two socially prestigious languages, and subtractive bilingualism, characterized by the replacement of one language by another. Relatively few research studies have examined the effects of these types of bilingualism on cognitive functioning, yet these are varieties of bilingualism commonly found in school settings. Examples of subtractive bilingualism can be found in members of ethnic minority groups in the United States, perhaps most recently with Vietnamese speakers and other Indochinese minorities for whom the acquisition of English is beginning to result in the gradual loss of the first language.

The basic notion of child bilingualism, balanced bilingualism, and language dominance, additive and subtractive bilingualism all have direct consequences on the study of interrelationships between cognitive development and the child's encoding of two language systems, whether they be vernacular or standard systems.

COGNITIVE PROCESSES

Cognition in its broad sense refers to perceiving or knowing, embracing processes which are more general than those strictly associated with linguistic functioning. An aspect of cognition particularly studied in regard to bilingual children is that of cognitive style. As Kagan, Moss, and Sigel (1973) explain, the term refers to stable individual preferences in mode of perceptual organization and conceptual categorization of the external environment. In enumerating essential characteristics, Witkin, Moore, Goodenough, and Cox (1977) point out that cognitive styles are concerned with the form rather than the content of cognitive activity. When defined in terms of processes, they are then seen as individual variations in how one perceives, thinks, solves problems, learns, and relates to others. Among cognitive styles identified as particularly relevant for bilingual and second language studies are field independence/dependence, cognitive flexibility, and divergent thinking.

The field independence/dependence concept of Witkin and his colleagues has been extensively studied and has had wide applications to educational settings. Field independence characterizes an analytic style of perception, a general ability to overcome embedding contexts in perception on tasks requiring that part of an organized field be separated from the larger field (Witkin and Goodenough 1977). Some children, in other words, characteristically analyze and differentiate the stimulus field, labeling subparts of the whole. This perceptual disembedding ability appears to be related to a similar ability in problem-solving. In opposition to this tendency is field dependence, a tendency to categorize a relatively undifferentiated stimulus. As Witkin et al. (1977) explain, field independent individuals are more likely than field dependent persons to analyze a perceptual field when the field is inherently organized and to impose structure when the field lacks organization. The notion of field independence is particularly germane to studies of cognitive functioning and second language acquisition where the learner must differentiate and organize linguistic rules from a background of complex language input without explicit focus on the linguistic rules and structures of the second language. Among studies showing field independence to be positively correlated with successful second language acquisition are those of Naiman, Froehlich, Stern, and Tadesco (1978) for secondary school students and Genesee and Hamayan (1980) for young primary grade children.

Another cognitive style relevant to bilingualism is that of cognitive flexibility. A significant variable in a number of studies, it is, however, a term that lacks some precision in the literature. Peal and Lambert (1962) use it in relationship to performance on measures of general reasoning.

Ben-Zeev (1972) sees cognitive flexibility as ease in the manipulation of linguistic structures, skill at auditory reorganization of verbal material, and advanced performance on Piagetian tests of concrete operational thinking. Balkan (1970) views cognitive flexibility as perceptual and verbal set changing abilities. In whatever perspective cognitive flexibility is defined, evidence indicates that it is a salient feature in the cognitive/bilingual interface.

A special type of cognitive flexibility reflecting a fertile imagination and ability to generate rapidly a wide variety of possible solutions to a problem is that of divergent thinking (Guilford 1956). Some researchers see this process as an index of creativity. However, as Lambert (1977) points out, creativity is probably best viewed as a cognitive ability distinct from divergent thinking.

CONSEQUENCES OF BILINGUALISM ON COGNITIVE FUNCTIONING: RESEARCH EVIDENCE

Investigations of the effect of child bilingualism on cognitive functioning span most of the twentieth century. During this period positions have moved from a largely negative view towards effects of bilingualism on cognitive functioning to a consistently more positive one. Research of the 1920s and 1930s generally reflects negative consequences. In the movement of the pendulum from negative to positive, Macnamara (1970:33) expresses a neutral position in that 'it seems unlikely that bilingualism should have any effect upon the development of the basic, common, cognitive structures.' The accumulating body of research conducted over the past two decades, however, points more and more consistently to positive cognitive consequences of bilingualism, especially as they relate to aspects of cognitive flexibility.

Studies Showing Negative Consequences

The development of standardized measures of intelligence in the 1920s gave researchers a new tool for assessing the effects of bilingualism on intellectual processes. Early studies in the United States showed that bilingual children scored lower on intelligence tests than monolinguals. Both Graham (1925) and Mead (1927), for example, tested children of immigrants generally from a low socioeconomic level. These and other studies, such as that of Saer (1923) in Wales, confounded the socioeconomic and linguistic proficiency variables, testing children in a standard variety of English at an early stage in their English language development. No studies took into account the nature of the first language, vernacular or standard, nor the possibility that the children's English was a vernacular rather than standard variety.

Reviewing 32 studies carried out in the United States, Arsenian (1937) found that 60 percent concluded that bilingualism has strong negative effects on intellectual processes. Of the remainder, 30 percent reported the intellectual handicap attributed to bilingualism to be a minor one. Only 10 percent found no adverse effects due to bilingualism. In reviewing the literature, both Darcy (1953, 1963) and Jensen (1962) point out the difficulty in generalizing findings in the research as a result of differing definitions of bilingualism and methodological procedures involving sampling and analysis of data. Peal and Lambert (1962) also in their review specifically cite methodological defects in failing to control for socio-economic level and degree of linguistic proficiency in the bilingual's two languages. Cummins (1976) observes that in a large number of studies the negative effects of bilingualism on cognitive processes are seen primarily in the areas of verbal and academic achievement, relating directly to an inadequate level of language proficiency in the bilingual subjects.

A recent study of Mexican-American bilingual children conducted by Brown, Fournier, and Moyer (1977) using a battery of Piagetian task tests concluded that bilingualism leads to a negative developmental lag. Like the earlier studies, this one also failed to control for level of linguistic proficiency. Furthermore, the tests given in both oral and written form presented a separate set of issues for children with low reading ability. Neither in this nor in the earlier studies using standardized intelligence tests is consideration given to the fact that all tests were administered in the standard language, a confounding variable when used with children who were, in all probability, vernacular speakers.

In commenting on deficiencies in studies of cognitive and bilingual relationships, Ulibarri (1972) points out that even recent studies frequently do not account for such factors as the child's lack of experiential background, acculturation problems, the attitudes of the child, and cultural conflict. As Schumann (1978) explains in his model of second language acquisition, psycho-social variables are critical in the process of becoming bilingual. These variables were largely ignored in the earlier studies. A critical variable, however, not considered in any of the studies is that of language variety, vernacular or standard, used in the various assessment procedures.

Studies Showing Positive Consequences

Since the early 1960s an increasing number of studies have shown the positive consequences of bilingualism on intellectual functioning. Working with matched monolingual and bilingual 10-year-old children in six middle-class French schools in Montreal, Peal and Lambert (1962), in a benchmark study, concluded that bilingual children have a greater cognitive flexibility and a more diversified set of mental abilities than monolingual children. In their cross-sectional study controlling for age and socio-economic level, Peal and Lambert also controlled for degree of bilingualism by using French-English bilingual children who had attained a balanced high level of proficiency in both languages. Of particular significance in their study is the evidence that bilinguals outperformed monolinguals on measures of verbal intelligence as well as nonverbal measures. Analyzing a battery of tests, they found that bilingual children significantly outperformed monolinguals on such factors as cognitive flexibility, concept formation, picture completion and figure manipulation. Their results indicating that bilingualism may have positive consequences on the structure and flexibility of thought have since found further confirmations from many parts of the world.

Balkan (1970), in a study conducted in Switzerland, found that balanced bilinguals significantly outperformed a matched monolingual group on cognitive flexibility. Within the bilingual group, Balkan further found that bilinguals who had learned both languages before age four were superior to those who had successively acquired the second language after age four.

Evidence that bilinguals may analyze language more intensively than monolinguals comes from studies by Ben-Zeev (1972) working with Hebrew-English bilinguals and Ianco-Worrall (1972) studying Afrikaans-English bilingual children in South Africa. Ben-Zeev found that bilinguals are capable at an earlier age than monolinguals of separating the meaning of a word from its sound. In addition to demonstrating a more flexible manipulation of the linguistic code, the bilinguals in Ben-Zeev's study gave evidence also of more advanced levels in concrete operational thinking. Ianco-Worrall found that bilingualism in early childhood accelerates the analytical ability to separate sound and meaning.

In a study of young bilinguals in a preschool Head Start program in the United States, Feldman and Shen (1971) found bilingual children outperformed monolinguals on a Piagetian object constancy test. These tasks make use of various transformations on different common objects such as a paper plate or cup. Even though their study presents evidence generally supportive of cognitive advantages for bilingual children, results are weakened by questionable methodological procedures for identifying bilingual children. A similar problem is observable in a study by Liedtke and Nelson (1968) comparing bilingual and monolingual children. Using a test on concepts of linear measurement, they found that the concept of measurement was at a more advanced state in the bilinguals. From this, they concluded that the bilinguals were more adept at concept formation.

Although many of the recent studies deal with child bilinguals, there is also accumulating evidence that bilingualism which results as a product of school programs providing second language acquisition opportunities, such as the immersion bilingual education programs in Canada, may positively affect certain cognitive processes. Bruck, Lambert, and Tucker (1973) working with French-English bilingual children in a pilot class of the St. Lambert project found that bilinguals performed on measures of divergent thinking at a significantly higher level than monolinguals at grades three, five, and six. Using data from the pilot and follow-up classes in the St. Lambert project, Scott (1973) studied the effect of bilingualism on divergent thinking. Results show that children who had become functionally bilingual through an immersion program for bilingual schooling scored substantially higher than the monolingual controls equated for IQ and socioeconomic level. Furthermore, Scott hypothesizes that bilingualism can both influence and be influenced by divergent thinking. In other words, divergent thinking has a causal relationship to facilitating functional bilingualism.

Also studying relationships with bilingualism and divergent thinking, Landry (1974) found that sixth grade children who had attained considerable proficiency in a second language through an on-going school program performed better than monolingual children on the verbal and figural parts of the *Torrance Tests of Creative Thinking*. However, children in grades one and four with much less exposure to a second language instructional program did not do better than monolingual controls when given the test in their second language, suggesting that the degree of proficiency in the two languages is a critical variable.

Cummins and Gulutsan (1974) tested sixth grade bilingual and monolingual children in western Canada on a task in which the subjects within a given time limit were to enumerate as many uses as possible for an object named by the experimenter. Controlling for SES, age, and sex, they found that bilinguals outperformed monolinguals on measures of nonverbal and verbal ability, including a measure of divergent thinking seen in a measure of verbal originality. Similar results were reported earlier in a study of bilingual children in Singapore conducted by Torrance, Gowan, Wu, and Aliotti (1970) who found higher levels of originality and elaboration on measures of divergent thinking. Elaboration of structural detail was also found to be a characteristic of the 7 to 9-year-old Spanish-English bilingual children from a low SES studied by Ben-Zeev (1977). Cummins (1978) further found in studying Irish-English bilingual children in Ireland and Ukrainian-English bilingual children in Canada that bilingualism promoted an analytic orientation to linguistic input, a result of actually functioning fluently in two languages.

In a cross-cultural study, Bain and Yu (1978) investigated three different samples of bilingual children in western Europe: 1) French-Alsatian speakers, 2) German-English speakers, 3) English-French Canadian bilingual children living overseas in Europe. In all cases bilingual groups performed significantly better than comparable monolingual groups on tasks drawing on cognitive flexibility.

Controlling for relative linguistic proficiency as well as socioeconomic level, De Avila and Duncan (1979) studied nearly 300 children in grades one and three in the United States and Mexico on measures of cognitive functioning. Comparing bilingual children who were fully proficient in two languages with children fully competent in one language, De Avila and Duncan found a cognitive advantage for bilingual children on both Piagetian-type conservation tests and Witkin-type cognitive style measure of field independence/dependence.

In a cross-sectional study of four Hispanic groups totalling 202 Spanish-English bilingual children—urban Mexican-American, rural Mexican-American, Puerto Rican-American, and Cuban-American—Duncan and De Avila (1979) investigated the relationship between the degree of bilingualism and cognitive functioning. Groups were categorized ranging from proficient bilinguals to late language learners with low proficiency in both languages. Their findings indicate that increasing proficiency in two languages predicts higher scores on measures of perceptual disembedding or field independence/dependence.

In summary, the majority of the studies of the past two decades have consistently reported positive cognitive consequences associated with bilingualism. Utilizing methodological procedures which are more tightly controlled for linguistic proficiency and relevant personal or background characteristics such as socioeconomic level, age, and sex, the recent studies provide a substantial body of empirical evidence to counter the negative findings of the earlier studies of this century. Although most of the recent studies have focused on balanced or additive bilinguals, a few have examined the effects of a nonbalanced bilingualism such as that, for example, of Genesee, Tucker, and Lambert (1975) or of Duncan and De Avila cited above. Even here, under certain conditions which Cummins (1979) describes, positive outcomes can be observed. The theoretical issue that arises, then, revolves on how to account for the positive effects of bilingualism on cognitive functioning.

COGNITIVE AND LINGUISTIC INTERDEPENDENCE

Each bilingual learning environment has its own uniqueness and as such presents difficulties in generalizing effects from one situation to another. In reconciling disparities in research findings, Cummins (1976) argues that the critical question for research is not what effect bilingualism *per se* has on cognitive processes but rather on identifying the conditions under which bilingualism facilitates or retards cognitive growth. As he points out, a critical variable differentiating recent studies from the older ones of this century is that the bilingual subjects of recent investigations probably differ substantially from those of the earlier ones in the level of linguistic proficiency attained through the bilingual learning situation. The emphasis in recent studies on ensuring that the bilingual subjects were balanced bilinguals at a high level of proficiency is a significant difference from pre-1960s studies. A majority of the early studies were carried out with minority language children whose acquisition of the second language resulted in subtractive bilingualism in which the first language was gradually replaced by a more prestigious second language. These studies, as seen in the literature reviewed here, reported a negative relationship between bilingualism and aspects of cognitive functioning. Conversely, those studies conducted in an additive situation have reported various cognitive advantages associated with bilingualism. In particular, a positive advantage has frequently been reported between bilingualism and both cognitive flexibility and divergent thinking. Others have shown that bilingualism seems to promote an analytic orientation to language.

To provide a theoretical framework for studying the developmental interrelationships between language and cognitive functioning in the bilingual child, Cummins (1979) presents two hypotheses. The first, the threshold hypothesis (Cummins 1976, 1978, 1979), is concerned with the cognitive and academic consequences of different patterns of bilingual abilities. The second, the developmental interdependence hypothesis (Cummins 1978, 1979), addresses functional interdependence between the development of the first and second langauges.

The Threshold Hypothesis

Observing that some of the positive effects of bilingualism may depend on the degree of bilingualism attained, Cummins hypothesizes that there may be threshold levels of linguistic competence that bilingual children must attain both in order to avoid negative cognitive consequences and to experience the potentially positive effects of bilingualism on cognitive functioning. For Cummins (1978) linguistic competence refers to the ability to make effective use of the cognitive functions of language. More specifically, it is to use language effectively as an instrument of thought and to represent the thinking processes by means of language. The threshold hypothesis claims that those aspects of bilingualism which exert positive influences on cognitive functioning are unlikely to come into effect until the child has attained a certain minimum or threshold level of linguistic competence in two languages. Conversely, if a child attains only a very low level of linguistic competence in either of the two developing languages, interaction with the environment through that language will be impoverished with resultant negative consequences.

In presenting the threshold hypothesis, Cummins (1979) further makes the claim that there may be two threshold levels, a lower one sufficient to avoid any negative cognitive effects and a higher one which might be necessary for accelerated cognitive growth. This form of the hypothesis appears to be most consistent with available data such as the findings from a longitudinal study conducted by Barik and Swain (1976) with French-English bilingual children in Ottawa and Toronto immersion programs and those from a study conducted by Cummins and Mulcahy (1978) with Ukrainian-English bilingual children in Canada. In the Duncan and De Avila (1979) study of Hispanic children, findings on performance on the *Children's Embedded Figures Test* also showed that a threshold level of L_1/L_2 competence is required before positive effects of cognitive functioning can be observed.

The threshold itself is not defined in absolute terms since it undoubtedly varies with the level of cognitive development and the academic demands the child experiences. Furthermore, the threshold level of bilingual competence is, as Cummins (1976:23) explains, 'an intervening rather than a basic causal variable in accounting for the cognitive growth of bilinguals'. The actual attaining of the threshold is determined by more fundamental psycho-social factors.

The Developmental Interdependence Hypothesis

The developmental interdependence hypothesis addresses the issue of how the bilingual's two languages are related to one another. It also addresses the types of bilingual learning environments that lead to additive or subtractive forms of bilingualism.

Cummins (1979), in proposing a developmental interdependence hypothesis, argues that the development of second language competence is a function of the level of the child's first language competence already attained at the time when intensive exposure to the second language begins. Applied to home-school language switch programs, intensive exposure to a second language as in the Canadian immersion programs is likely to lead to high levels of L_2 competence at no expense to L_1 competence when the child's first language has already been adequately developed. An initially high level of competence in the first language is a determining factor in the development of high levels of proficiency in the second language. On the other hand, when L_1 is poorly developed, intensive exposure to a second language impedes further development of the first language and, in turn, places a limit on L_2 development.

The basic notions of the developmental interdependence hypothesis, which points to an interaction between the level of competence the child has developed in the first language and the language of instruction, were expressed by Toukomaa and Skutnabb-Kangas (1977). The hypothesis was strongly supported in their findings from a study of Finnish migrant children in Sweden who were being schooled in Swedish (Skutnabb-Kangas and Toukomaa 1976). They found that the extent to which Finnish, the first language, had been developed prior to the onset of Swedish, the second language, was closely related to the degree of Swedish acquisition the children attained. Older children who migrated at age 10, for example, maintained a high level of Finnish and achieved a level of Swedish as a second language comparable to their monolingual Swedish peers. Younger children who migrated, however, at age 7 or 8 and who were, consequently, at a lower level of development in Finnish experienced considerably more difficulty in learning Swedish.

If, as research indicates, the level of linguistic proficiency in the bilingual's two languages is a critical variable in the consequences of bilingualism for cognitive functioning, the hypotheses presented by Cummins are crucial for generalizing across bilingual environments to predict outcomes for cognitive functioning in the bilingual child. Not only do the theshold hypothesis and developmental interdependence hypothesis suggest that linguistic competence is important in understanding the dynamics of the bilingual child's interaction with the educational environment but also that linguistic and cognitive interactions play a critical role within the educational setting. Empirical evidence for the interplay of these factors can be seen in the report by Skutnabb-Kangas and Toukomaa (1976). In school subjects such as science, which requires an abstract mode of thought, bilingual children educated in a second language with a good level of development of their first language succeed significantly better than children who do not have adequate development of the first language. This type of dynamic interaction between certain cognitive processes, as those tapped in science problems, and level of linguistic proficiency raises issues regarding specific relationships between language and cognitive development.

PERSPECTIVES ON COGNITIVE DEVELOPMENT

Universals in Cognitive Development

One explanation of the hypothesis that bilingualism can have positive consequences for the development of cognitive processes can be found in the theory of cognitive development presented by Piaget (1970). Although Piaget has not specifically addressed the issue of bilingualism, his position on cognitive development and its relationship to language development has implications for an understanding of the effects of bilingualism. Furthermore, even though Piaget takes a conservative position on the relationship between language and cognition, that position does not seem to deny that bilingualism represents an enriched form of experience capable of exerting a positive influence on cognitive development.

According to Piaget, the development of cognition can be categorized into a series of stages, the order of which is invariant. Furthermore, these stages are universal, available to all normal individuals in all cultures. They are neither entirely biologically determined nor a product of the environment but, rather, are constructed or created by children as they actively try to understand the world.

The objective at each stage of cognitive development is the attainment of a state of cognitive equilibrium. The child's attempt to introduce consistency or equilibrium into the developing cognitive system plays a major role in motivating progress through the various stages. Experience, then, is only a partial explanation of the series of stages since what a child learns from any given experience is a function of the developmental level of the child at that time. Cognitive equilibrium for the child results from the dynamic interplay of the processes of assimilation and accommodation. As Piaget (1952) explains, assimilation is the incorporation of new elements of experience into an internal system. Accommodation, on the other hand, refers to modifications of the same system as a result of one or more assimilations. It is a process of adaptation to the demands of the environment, involving the incorporation of these demands into existing mental structures. Equilibrium is consequently reached when the processes of assimilation and accommodation reach a state of balance, with a final state of equilibrium reached at the state of formal operations. These interrelated processes are then seen as making cognitive development possible, processes which are, in Piagetian theory, universally operative.

Beyond Universals

The acquisition of a first language is a universal achievement, a developmental phenomenon achieved by all normal individuals in all cultures. Bilingualism or the acquisition of a second language, on the other hand, is a nonuniversal achievement. As Feldman (1980) suggests, however, universal and nonuniversal domains share a sufficient number of attributes that both may be considered as developmental. He further proposes that these nonuniversal domains may also be conceptualized as consisting of a series of levels, similar to universal stages, mastered in an invariant sequence. A distinguishing feature of nonuniversal achievements is that they tend to require some form of instruction or facilitating conditions for their acquisition.

A differentiating factor between universal and nonuniversal advances is that of specific environmental conditions. Those required for universal attainments are more pervasive and effective than the environmental conditions for nonuniversal achievements. Again, this is illustrated with first language acquisition for which environmental conditions occur universally and effectively. Bilingualism, however, requires specific conditions which are nonuniversal. But in acquiring a second language or achieving bilingualism, individuals pass through qualitatively different levels of development, experiencing again the conflicts of the equilibrium process that entered into the universal achievements found in first language development.

The question then arises as to what effect this 'second time around' or reapplication of underlying cognitive functioning associated with the acquisition of more than one language may have on observable cognitive processes. Research to date suggests that there are positive consequences for cognitive flexibility, cognitive-perceptual performance, and divergent thinking. If this is the case, an educational program which utilizes an inquiry approach with its emphasis on problem-solving situations should indicate particularly positive consequences for bilingual children. The processes of inquiry give a critical role to divergent thinking and draw on the ability to formulate hypotheses in problem-solving situations. It may be predicted that bilingual children, given a program of instruction or intervention of the type necessary for the development of nonuniversal achievements may excel monolingual peers who have experienced the underlying cognitive processes utilized in divergent thinking to a lesser degree.

INTERACTIONS OF COGNITIVE DEVELOPMENT
AND BILINGUALISM
WITH AN EDUCATIONAL PROGRAM IN SCIENCE

Contemporary models of science education with their focus on inquiry provide an especially appropriate type of educational program for examining cognitive and linguistic interaction. Such programs give a critical role to divergent thinking and the ability to formulate hypotheses in problem-solving situations. To solve problems students must select and order varied types of information or data, making use of concepts that they know. Inquiry addresses itself primarily to using concepts, only secondarily to learning them, although, of course, the end product of the inquiry process may be the development of new ideas or concepts. An instructional program in science, concerned with making students more effective inquirers, necessarily makes use of cognitive processes involved in problem-solving.

In asking if these abilities can be taught, researchers have investigated the effects of instruction on various processes utilized in science problem-solving activities. Quinn (1971) and Quinn and George (1975) have shown that students can be taught to form scientific hypotheses of increasingly high quality through the use of problem-oriented filmloops which tap divergent thinking processes. Pouler and Wright (1980) have also shown that hypothesis-forming behaviors can be taught effectively as part of normal classroom instruction by providing students with criteria of acceptable hypotheses and differential reinforcements. Wright (1978) has shown that intensive instruction, through an event that creates a discrepancy between the observer's expectations and the information received, leads to an increased capacity for problem-solving. These and other studies (Salomon 1970) have suggested that hypothesizing skills can be enhanced by various forms of intensive instruction.

None of these studies, however, takes into account the linguistically different child, in particular, the large number of bilingual children in schools throughout the United States.

The framework for studying the interactive relationships between cognitive development and bilingualism with an instructional program in science is set forth in Quinn's (1971) study. Defining an hypothesis as a testable explanation of an empirical relationship among variables in a given problem situation, she evaluated a method for teaching hypothesis formation to sixth-grade children in two different socio-economic settings. Findings from four groups of monolingual sixth-graders in Philadelphia, Pennsylvania, indicated that the formulation of scientific hypotheses can be taught, that the quality of the hypotheses elicited can be measured, and that a significant difference (p < .001) exists between the quality of hypotheses generated by students who received instruction in hypothesis formation and those who did not. Using a control and an experimental group from an upper middle class suburban socio-economic level, where standard English is the norm, and a control and an experimental group from a lower working class urban socio-economic level, where vernacular varieties of English prevail, Quinn further found that the cognitive processes tapped in formulating scientific hypotheses function independently of socio-economic level.

This study and those discussed here in examining the interactive effects of cognitive development and bilingualism focus on the cognitive process of divergent thinking in the context of an inquiry-based instructional program in science and the complexity of the language used to express scientific hypotheses. In a study of monolingual English-speaking children, Quinn and Kessler (1976) found that the psycholinguistic abilities of children reflected in the syntactic complexity of written language as measured by the Botel, Dawkins, and Granowsky formula (1973) are affected positively and significantly by formal instruction in the process of hypothesizing solutions to science problems. Findings suggest that this positive correlation is also independent of socio-economic variables (Kessler and Quinn 1977). In regard to bilingual children, Kessler (1971) concluded that certain aspects of the bilingual's two languages are not encoded separately but, rather, derive from common underlying structures. Results of these studies argue for the unifying role of Piaget's equilibration model in the acquisition of both cognitive and linguistic structures.

Study of Subtractive Bilinguals

Holding the socio-economic variable constant, Kessler and Quinn (1979) examined the relationship between nonbalanced, subtractive bilingualism and monolingualism in the context of ability to formulate scientific hypotheses and the ability to express these hypotheses in writing. All procedures were conducted in English, the second language for the bilinguals.

Children participating in this study were 28 sixth-grade students in an intact classroom of a school in a low socio-economic area of South Philadelphia. Of the subjects, 14 were monolingual English speakers and 14 were Italian-English bilinguals in the process of replacing their first language, a nonstandard Italian dialect, with their second language, English. The two groups were matched not only for SES, age, and grade level, but also for IQ as measured by the *Otis Quick-Scoring Mental Ability Test, Beta, Form FM*. The mean IQ for monolinguals was 101.4 and for bilinguals, 101.9. All were students in the same school and the same classroom. Although the bilinguals had acquired one of the vernacular varieties of Italian characteristic of southern Italy as young children, they had never used it in their formal schooling, reserving use primarily for close relatives and certain other adults. By grade six they were dominant in English and gave evidence of being equal or superior to their monolingual peers in reading English as measured by scores on *The Pupil Series, Diagnostic Reading Test.* The mean score for monolinguals was 52.2 and for bilinguals, 56.4.

Instructed as a group in an intact classroom, the children were given a series of 12 science inquiry film sessions and 6 discussion sessions, each 40 minutes in length and all conducted by the same teacher. Each film session utilized a 3-minute film loop of the *Inquiry Development Program in Physical Science* developed by Suchman (1962). The physical science problem presented in the film sets up a discrepant event for the student, leading to inquiry and seeking an explanation to resolve the discrepancy. In serving as the source of data to explain the observed event, the teacher invites questions from the students to which the response is either *yes* or *no.* Problem presentation sessions ended with students writing as many hypotheses as possible in a rigorously controlled 12-minute period. All hypotheses generated by each student were then scored on two criteria: Quinn's Hypothesis Quality Scale (1971) and the Syntactic Complexity Formula developed by Botel, Dawkins, and Granowsky (1973).

In the follow-up discussion sessions students critiqued which questions were effective and why as they were guided by the teacher through an analysis of the problem, determination of the facts gathered, and assessment of the quality of their hypotheses. Children were shown how to make use of their observations and inferences to generate hypotheses of higher quality as measured on Quinn's scale. The scale uses a 0 to 5 range for scoring each hypothesis with *0* given for no explanation, *1* for a non-scientific explanation, *2* for a partial scientific explanation, *3* for a scientific explanation relating at least two variables in general or nonspecific terms, *4* for a precise scientific explanation using a qualification and/or quantification of the variables, and *5* for an explicit statement of a test for a precise scientific explanation.

Derived from transformational-generative grammar, the Botel, Dawkins, and Granowsky measure of syntactic complexity was selected from among others because of the theoretical basis on which it was developed and because of the ease with which it can be used by the nonlinguist. Syntactic structures are assigned weighted scores ranging from 0 to 3. Simple sentences as 'I hit the ball' are given *0,* for example, while clauses used as subjects are given a score of *3* as in 'What it might do is fall down.' Syntactic complexity, then, is a function of specific structures rather than sentence length.

Table 1. *Mean scores for subtractive bilinguals and monolinguals matched for socio-economic level.*

VARIABLE	MONOLINGUALS (N = 14)	SUBTRACTIVE BILINGUALS (N = 14)
Hypothesis quality	41.29	48.07
Syntactic complexity	79.50	84.21
I.Q.	101.36	101.93
Reading	52.21	56.36

Comparative relationships between subtractive bilinguals and monolinguals given the same experimental treatment are shown in Table 1.

Differences in the means for hypothesis quality and syntactic complexity were found to be significant at the 0.01 level.

Findings from this study of children matched for socio-economic level but differing on the linguistic variable of monolingualism and bilingualism suggest that bilingualism, even in the nonbalanced, subtractive form, has positive consequences for aspects of cognitive functioning and linguistic development. From this, it was then predicted that additive bilingualism should exert an even greater positive effect on the process of divergent thinking utilized in hypothesis formation and on related language processes and that this should be observable across socio-economic levels.

Study of Additive Bilingualism

Subjects for this investigation (Kessler and Quinn, 1980b) were sixth-grade 11-year-olds in four intact classrooms, two monolingual English-speaking classes with 32 children in each and two Spanish-English bilingual classes with 30 children in each. One control and one experimental group of monolinguals were from an affluent suburb of Philadelphia, all from an upper middle class SES and all in the same school. The control and experimental groups of additive bilinguals were Mexican-American children in the same school in the lowest socio-economic area of San Antonio, Texas. According to demographic information available from census data, the additive bilinguals were from a considerably lower socio-economic group than the subtractive bilinguals in Philadelphia and both groups were much lower than the monolingual English-speakers.

Replicating the procedure used in the study of subtractive bilingualism, Mexican-American children exhibiting additive bilingualism in Spanish and

English were compared with monolingual English-speaking children of the same age and grade level. The Mexican-American children were double additive bilinguals in that during the school years they had added standard English and standard Spanish to their linguistic repertoire without loss of their first language, a vernacular Spanish regional to South Texas. In the very low socio-economic neighborhood, or barrio, where they lived, vernacular Spanish functions as the language of the home and the community.

Language proficiency tests designed by the school district and administered in Spanish and English at entry to kindergarten had identified the children as Spanish dominant with little or no proficiency in English. As a result, they were placed in a bilingual education program for grades K-3. The transitional bilingual program utilized Spanish, in a combination of both standard and vernacular, in teaching content areas, and standard English for a portion of the language arts curriculum as well as some of the content. Subsequently, the children were exited from the bilingual program and placed in an all-English school program. By grade six, all instruction was in English, the second language, but vernacular Spanish continued to function in peer interactions, in the home and community. Because the bilingual program in which they had participated taught literacy skills first in standard Spanish and only later in English, the children were literate in both Spanish and English.

The same teacher who conducted the experimental treatment for the subtractive bilinguals also conducted that for the additive bilinguals and the monolingual group, which provides a control, consequently, on the teacher variable as well as the actual procedure for all groups. Other variables controlled in the additive bilingual/monolingual study, in addition to experimental treatment, were age and grade level of the subjects. Variables were in linguistic proficiency, monolingualism vs. additive bilingualism, and socio-economic levels with monolinguals at a very high SES and bilinguals at a very low SES. Because the study with monolinguals at different socio-econmic levels had shown SES not to be a significant variable (Quinn 1971; Kessler and Quinn 1977), differences in hypothesizing ability and language complexity between monolinguals and bilinguals could be attributed to the type of linguistic proficiency the children exhibited.

In addition to SES, age, and grade level, the monolingual control and experimental groups were matched on IQ as measured by the *Otis Quick-Scoring Mental Ability Test, Beta, Form FM;* reading scores as measured by Part III of the *Pupil Progress Series, Diagnostic Reading Test;* and overall grade-point averages. The control and experimental bilingual groups in addition to SES, age, and grade level, were matched on mathematics scores, science scores, and reading scores, all as measured by the *Comprehensive Test of Basic Skills,* Level 2, Form S.

Table 2. *Experimental design.*

GROUP	SEQUENCE OF PROCEDURES		
	1	2	3
Control Group	Covariable Test	Criterion Variable Test	Treatment
Experimental or Treatment Group	Covariable Test	Treatment	Criterion Variable Test

Table 2 outlines the experimental design, which utilized the same treatment as that for the study of the effects of subtractive bilingualism.

Both control and experimental groups were given the treatment in order to minimize any negative effects of intervention in the regular school curriculum by giving only one class specialized instruction in science. The experimental design, however, reverses the order of treatment and the criterion variable test. In effect, then, a pretest, posttest situation results.

Mean scores for control and experimental groups on the two variables of quality of scientific hypotheses formulated and syntactic complexity of the written language to express them are given in Table 3.

Although both experimental groups profited from instruction in formulating scientific hypotheses, the bilingual groups exhibited far higher gains, both in quality of hypotheses and in language complexity. The difference in means between the control and experimental groups for both monolinguals and bilinguals is significant at the 0.001 level when analysis of covariance is performed with reading grade equivalent used as covariant. Furthermore, Pearson product moment correlation coefficients for interactions between hypothesis quality and language quality shows a high positive correlation (p < .001).

Table 3. *Mean scores for control and experimental groups.*

GROUP	N	HYPOTHESIS QUALITY	SYNTACTIC COMPLEXITY
Monolingual control group	32	25.4	52.6
Bilingual control group	30	29.5	39.6
Monolingual experimental group	32	53.3	130.0
Bilingual experimental group	30	176.0	181.8

Results of this study of additive bilingualism indicate that bilingual children proficient in both of their languages in the sense that they use each and are literate in each as a result of participation in a bilingual education program outperform monolingual peers when given the same instruction by the same teacher in formulating scientific hypotheses. Not only do they exhibit superior performance on tasks which require aspects of divergent thinking but also they manifest a level of syntactic complexity in their second language higher than that of the monolinguals in expressing their solutions to science problems.

In summary, both subtractive and additive bilinguals exhibit positive consequences of bilingualism on aspects of cognitive functioning with the degree dependent on the level of relative linguistic proficiency in the bilingual's two languages. Bilingualism, even in its nonbalanced subtractive form, appears to interact positively with an inquiry-based educational program utilizing problem-solving situations. Bilingualism, in an additive form, appears to enhance the cognitive consequences related to divergent thinking and the related consequences for language complexity. While also benefiting from the same type of instructional program, monolinguals do not appear to make gains in the same degree as bilinguals, particularly additive bilinguals. These results argue, then, in favor of the threshold hypothesis proposed by Cummins. The additive bilinguals may be viewed as having reached, or perhaps surpassed, that threshold level in both languages which yields positive cognitive consequences attributable to bilingualism. The subtractive bilinguals, while experiencing positive gains, may be taken as representative of a lower point of bilingual linguistic proficiency on the language development continuum, possibly just at or nearly at the threshold level where positive effects become evident.

DISEQUILIBRIUM AS A FACTOR IN INTERACTIONS

In the Piagetian sense, one may view instruction in the generation of hypotheses as an effort to facilitate the learner's movement to a higher cognitive level of inquiry (Feldman 1980). In Piaget's theory, discrepant events, such as those presented in science problems, assume a critical function in establishing the type of internal conflict necessary for intellectual development.

The sixth-grade preadolescent 11-year-olds participating in the study of cognitive consequences of bilingualism presented here represent, according to the Piagetian stages of cognitive development, a transitional stage between concrete operations and formal operational thought. According to Piaget and Inhelder (1969), the development of formal operations begins in the preoperational period, roughly about age 5, continues through the concrete operational period between ages 7 and 11, and ends in the formal operational period between approximately ages 12 and 15. Children in the concrete operational stage understand qualitative but not quantitative relationships whereas those in formal thought are described as understanding both qualitative and quantitative relationships and as having some notion of the relevant theoretical constructs. From about age 5 children's problem-solving strategies are rule-governed, with the rules progressing from less complex to more complex with age. Stages in cognitive development, neither biologically nor environmentally determined, are constructed or created by children as they actively attempt to understand the world about them. Cognitive development, in the Piagetian sense, occurs in the coordinated presence of something to act on, such as a science problem, and someone to do the acting. Furthermore, Piaget's theory attributed an increasingly important role to language in implementing abstract thought in the stages of concrete operational thought and formal operations, stages characteristically represented by the 11-year-olds in these studies.

The role of internal conceptual conflict in cognitive development, as Piaget (1970) explains, is crucial to the position underlying this study that conceptual conflict, which triggers the processes of assimilation and accommodation needed for cognitive development, is stronger for the bilingual child than for the monolingual. This dynamic interaction between the two processes is seen as the fundamental mechanism needed for cognitive developmental change. Structures are likely to change when they are in disequilibrium, when the balance between assimilation and accommodation is upset. This then facilitates the cognitive activity needed to restore equilibrium.

In going beyond universals in cognitive development, described in Piagetian theory, Feldman (1980) expands the notion of disequilibrium, identifying three aspects that are relevant to nonuniversal changes: 1) external disequilibrium, 2) internal disequilibrium, 3) affective disequilibrium or the 'energetic parameter' or disequilibrium. For the nonuniversal achievements observed in the study of interactive effects between cognitive processes and linguistic development in the context of an instructional program in science, these aspects of disequilibrium appear to have particular relevance.

External Disequilibrium

The external event which sets up an internal disequilibrium is very central to cognitive reorganization and development. Science problem-solving situations, where the emphasis is upon both the quantity and quality of output, provide the type of discrepant events that set up disequilibrium. Such problems provide an external disequilibrium in the sense that the source of the discrepancy is external to the child. Science problems which set up this type of discrepant event draw on the interplay between a child's existing cognitive system and experience. When the child confronts and tries to cope with the event, disequilibrium occurs. If, however, the event provides too much discrepancy to process, the child simply may not respond. The critical point is that a problem must fall between what the child knows and what the child can deal with. In other words, there must be an optimal discrepancy between the child's developmental level and the nature of the problem. External disequilibrium rests on experiences sufficiently discrepant to trigger restructuring processes in the child's cognitive system.

Science problems of the type utilized in the instructional program for monolingual and bilingual sixth-graders apparently were at an optimal level of discrepancy and, therefore, provided an experience which required thinking skills characteristic of a more advanced developmental stage. As the children interacted with these problems, evidence from the quality of the hypotheses generated indicates that cognitive restructuring was taking place and that this process favored bilingual children.

Internal Disequilibrium

The achievement by the treatment groups in learning to formulate better scientific hypotheses and, concominantly, to draw on increasingly complex language structures resulted from responses by the individual children to perceived problems needing solution. These achievements observed for the experimental groups are creative in the sense that they could not have been totally taught even though opportunity to realize advancements was provided through interaction with an instructional program. No effort was made, for example, to teach the children to use increasingly complex language. This type of creativity, which takes into account nonuniversal advances, draws on the same equilibration processes which Piaget describes for general cognitive development and which appear to be more fully operative in some respects for bilingual children.

In contrast to external disequilibrium, internal disequilibrium is associated directly with the child's own intellectual organization. According to Feldman (1980), it reflects a kind of contradiction or competition among the child's alternatives for dealing with experiences. Unlike external disequilibrium, which draws on environmental discrepancy, internal disequilibrium arises from discrepancies or inconsistencies within the child's internal system.

In this view, one might consider bilingualism as a source of internal disequilibrium in that it provides the child with a certain kind of alternative for dealing with experience. In terms of the child's internal system, the availability of competing linguistic codes provides a potential for setting up internal disequilibrium, serving as a possible impetus for the bilingual child to build new cognitive systems at higher levels. Furthermore, for the additive bilingual the likelihood of moving back and forth between competing systems is greater than that for the subtractive bilingual. This may result in an enhancement of the internal disequilibrium that generates cognitive restructuring. Internal disequilibrium may also be a factor in accounting for the high correlation between the quality of scientific hypotheses generated and the linguistic complexity for expressing them. Both surface manifestations may be drawing on similar underlying processes of competition within the child's cognitive/linguistic internal system.

Affective Disequilibrium

The child must not only be cognitively ready to act on the discrepant event that sets up external disequilibrium triggering internal disequilibrium but also must, as Langer (1969:30) puts it, 'feel that something is wrong', which he terms the 'energetic parameter'. The affective character of disequilibrium, then, also enters into the process of cognitive advancement. Once the child realizes that something doesn't quite fit, affective disequilibrium may enter into the relative interactions involving the equilibration process as the child tries to make it fit.

Science problems dealing with the physical world around the child at a level in tune with the child's internal disequilibrium may engage features of affective disequilibrium at an optimal level. Problems, such as those presented on the film loops used in this study, apparently were at the level where participants in the experimental groups could 'feel that something was wrong'. In fact, a critical part of the procedure was the role of the teacher in ascertaining that all of the children recognized the problem presented on the film loop. From that starting point, they generated hypotheses to 'make things fit'. Affectively, science questions may engage the language and cognitive systems, triggering brain mechanisms that facilitate their interaction for positive development in both areas.

IMPLICATIONS FOR RESEARCH
AND EDUCATIONAL PROGRAMS

The nonuniversal achievement of bilingualism appears, through mounting empirical evidence, to have positive consequences for the bilingual child, enhancing universal aspects of cognitive functioning available to all normal children. Furthermore, studies suggest that the consequences of bilingualism on cognitive functioning are related to the degree of linguistic proficiency in the bilingual's two languages. In support of Cummins' threshold hypothesis, positive effects can be seen once the bilingual reaches a certain level of linguistic proficiency, not necessarily a balance between the two languages, however. Much further research is needed in examining the linguistic nature of the threshold, specifying more fully the level needed to overcome negative consequences of the type observed in many of the earlier studies of this century and the level needed for realizing highly significant positive gains.

Since nonuniversal achievements require some type of intervention, research issues remain regarding the most efficient and successful types of intervention programs for facilitating the development of bilingualism in the child. Even though research of the past decade has brought considerable insight into the nature of the second language acquisition process, much remains to be investigated in regard to the acquisition of two languages in first language bilinguals and pre-school and school age second language learners. More understanding is needed regarding differences between the simultaneous acquisition of two languages and the successive acquisition of a second language in childhood. Research to date has not differentiated these children, generally including both types of bilinguals in samples of children who have access to two linguistic codes. Not only is this a methodological consideration but also it is a theoretical one in that the two types of bilingual development may have some distinguishing characteristics not yet observed. This, of course, related to the age of bilingual acquisition, an area in need of further consideration. In large measure, the positive consequences of bilingualism on cognitive functioning observed for children relate to the later elementary school years. The consequences of bilingualism for children in early childhood and the primary school years are largely lacking empirical study.

Positive findings from the research on the interaction with a science inquiry program, cognitive functioning, and bilingualism suggest one area of needed research, raising the issue regarding the effect of similar types of programs in other components of the school curriculum. The degree to which positive gains in one area of the curriculum affects achievement in other content areas of the educational program needs extensive investigation. In general, the educational as well as the environmental conditions which give rise to qualitative shifts in the levels of cognitive and language functioning require further study. Little is yet known about the interaction between educational treatment and the child input factors in bilingual programs.

Questions can also be raised regarding the maintenance of positive consequences of bilingualism. A number of the post-1960 studies reviewed here observe that children are cognitively enriched once they have reached a certain degree of linguistic proficiency in two languages. Under what conditions can this be maintained and under what conditions it is lost are areas largely unexplored.

The focus of this paper on cognitive and linguistic variables interacting with school programs has not included the social variables for which other research evidence indicates a highly significant interaction. A full understanding of the relationships between cognitive development and language functioning in bilingual environments necessarily must include the relevant psycho-social variables, such as those articulated by Schumann (1978). Potential effects of child bilingualism may be critically dependent on the social significance and the function of the child's two languages. How these variables interact with cognitive functioning is not yet clear.

Theoretical issues remain unanswered regarding the relationship between bilingualism and aspects of cognitive processes. Scott (1973), for example, argues that bilingualism both influences and is influenced by divergent thinking. She hypothesizes a causal relationship between divergent thinking and functional bilingualism with one facilitating the other. Cummins (1976), on the other hand, sees bilingual language development in terms of the threshold level of linguistic competence as an intervening rather than a basic causal variable accounting for cognitive development. As Cummins (1979) points out, and as the research reported here supports, educational achievement and cognitive development are a function of the type of linguistic competence in two languages that the child brings to the educational program. This, of course, argues for instruction in the first language even after the primary grades in order to develop a cognitively and academically beneficial form of additive bilingualism (Cummins 1980). For children whose first language cognitive/academic language proficiency is better developed, second language cognitive/academic proficiency is manifested more rapidly than for younger learners since the proficiency from the first language is available for use in the second language. This may be a significant factor in the superior performance of additive bilinguals whose first language has been more fully developed through well-implemented bilingual programs.

Because educators and others working with bilingual children have not fully understood interactions between cognitive development and bilingualism, bilingual children have in many cases been diagnosed as handicapped and placed in compensatory education programs of various types. Research results, however, on the positive consequences of bilingualism, suggest that it would be more in the interest of the child to be placed in a well-organized bilingual program where the positive interactions of cognitive functioning and language development can be facilitated.

In summary, the post-1960 research results reviewed here indicate that bilingualism in children can accelerate the development of verbal and nonverbal abilities. Positive interactions between aspects of cognitive functioning, such as divergent thinking, and bilingualism in the context of certain types of school programs suggest that the bilingual child not only has achieved universal types of development described in Piagetian theory but has gone further along the universal-to-unique continuum. This added nonuniversal achievement accomplished by bilingual children indicates an enrichment, often first provided in the home and community setting, that can be facilitated in the school setting and lead to a fuller realization of the human potential.

IMMERSION EDUCATION: APPLICABILITY FOR NONVERNACULAR TEACHING TO VERNACULAR SPEAKERS

MERRILL SWAIN

INTRODUCTION

Immersion education has been hailed in Canada as an innovative and effective method of second language teaching (e.g. Barik and Swain 1975; Stern 1978; Tucker 1980). However, in a recent article on 'The Importation of Bilingual Education Models', Mackey (1978) states that: 'In most parts of the world, education in a language other than that of the home (in America, called "immersion") has long been the only type available—even the only sort of education possible' (5). And in the same article, writing about African education, he suggests that 'To presume, therefore, to introduce immersion education in Africa as an innovative contribution from America is to display a profound ignorance of the history and development of African education—if not to risk being accused of neocolonialism' (4).

Although I could not agree more with Mackey's general argument that one cannot simply import a successful model of bilingual education from one situation and introduce it in a new situation, I am not convinced that there are not some innovative elements—both in structure and in process—in what Canadians refer to as immersion education. Mackey, for example, in the same article, suggests that 'What is now possible—and this is the new dimension—is...bilingualism through schooling in both the mother tongue and another tongue' (5). Immersion education, as practised by Canadians, incorporates this dimension. Thus, one of the purposes of this paper is to describe immersion education as it is understood by Canadian educators, and to discuss the applicability of its importation to other settings, specifically to that of vernacular speakers learning a nonvernacular language. The nonvernacular could be the standard dialect of the vernacular or a second language.

A second purpose of this paper is to suggest that by opposing immersion education against other forms of second language instruction, an unfortunate dichotomy related to the methodology of second language teaching is established. On the one hand, immersion programs have been described as providing a setting that resembles a natural language acquisition setting in some important respects, including the opportunity to use the second language for real communication about a wide variety of topics (e.g. Harley and Swain 1978). That is, the appropriate teaching methodology is simply to teach about subject content using the second language, thus providing the essential language input for acquisition to occur. On the other hand, other programs of second language instruction have been described as 'grammar-oriented'; that is, the focus is on teaching *about* the language based on the assumption that knowledge of language form will be directly accessible for language use. Within this context, other oppositions have been established: grammar-translation versus direct method; cognitive code versus audio-lingual; and so forth. These dichotomies, useful as they may be as a general label, gloss over the fact that each method incorporates some of the other, and that indeed they are but two ends of long continua. The same is the case, it will be argued, for the distinction made between immersion and other second language programs.

CANADIAN IMMERSION EDUCATION

In this section, the significant characteristics of primary French immersion programs in Canada will be described in terms of background, structure, methodology (process), and outcomes. Each of these needs to be considered in determining the applicability of the immersion model for nonvernacular instruction. The focus of the discussion is on primary level programs because it is most likely to be at this level that vernacular speakers would be introduced to second language instruction or some form of bilingual education.

(i) Background
It is probably the case that most major changes in an educational system derive from pressures external to it. The development of French immersion programs in Canada is no exception. The first French immersion class in the

public sector began in 1965 in St. Lambert, a suburb of Montreal, as a result of pressure from a group of English-speaking parents whose common concern was that the level of French attained by students in a traditional French as a second language (FSL) program would not be sufficient to meet their children's needs in a community and country that was increasingly emphasizing the importance of French as a *langue de traveil* (Lambert and Tucker 1972). French immersion programs spread across Canada, from communities with significant portions of French speakers to unilingual English communities, pressured by similar groups of parents. The parents were actively interested in their children's education, relentless in their search for documentation supporting immersion, and articulate in expressing their demands.

The parents and their children are part of the dominant, majority group in Canada. Learning a second language does not pose a threat to their sense of personal or cultural identity, nor to the maintenance of their mother tongue, although parents wanted to be assured that the development of their children's English language skills would not suffer. Indeed, these parents wanted their children to learn a second language as long as it was not at the expense of mother tongue literacy skills or academic achievement. Furthermore the second language to be learned, French, is one of Canada's two official languages. To be bilingual in English and French in Canada opens up job opportunities and social contacts otherwise closed. In addition, French is an important international language and the official language of approximately 30 countries in the world (Commissioner of Official Languages 1980).

Once an immersion program is established in a community, it still remains an optional program. Participation in the program is voluntary, and parents can always choose to enroll their children in the regular English program in the same school or in another school in the same community.

These characteristics—parental pressure and involvement in program initiation and implementation, majority group membership of participants, positive attitudes towards the target language, and the possibility of choice between mother tongue education or bilingual education—have played a significant role in the success of French immersion programs in Canada.

At least some of these characteristics may not be present among vernacular-speaking populations. Consider, for example, Francophones in Ontario who in their community are a minority group, and who speak a nonstandard dialect of French. In a survey conducted by Mougeon, Brent-Palmer, Belanger, and Cichocki (1980) it was shown that in no such community do all students or their parents speak 'mostly or always' in French in any of a number of communicative situations. Furthermore, in one community where the concentration of Francophones is particularly low (Pembrooke), less than 50% of the Francophone parents responded that they used French 'mostly or always' with their children. If such figures can be taken to reflect parental attitudes towards the acquisition and maintenance of French by their children, then they suggest, at best, an ambivalence. Indeed, in this community, specific aspects of standard French (e.g. the use of reflexive pronouns with pronominal verbs) were not acquired by some students even by the end of Grade 12, in spite of their having attended a Francophone school, and although they were acquired by students by the beginning of their schooling in Ontario communities where the Francophone population formed a significant majority. As Mougeon, et al. point out: 'The inability of French-language schooling to reverse assimilation processes in Franco-Ontarian minority localities is probably in part the result of the fact that such assimilation depends mostly on factors which lie outside the school and over which the school has little or no influence' (145). In this case, the minority group status of the participants and their apparent ambivalence towards acquiring standard French are at least two factors present in the Franco-Ontarian situation which are not found amongst the Anglophone participants in French immersion programs.

(ii) Structure

The structure of French immersion programs consists of several features which are frequently overlooked by those who wish to argue that the Canadian French immersion experience 'proves' that children can successfully be educated in a second language. One important feature is that all children who enter the program at the primary level do so with the same level of target language skills—none. This is in contrast to the situation—which in the United States is often referred to as 'immersion'—where children who are to learn the target language are mixed together with other children who are native speakers of the target language—a situation for the learner which we have referred to as 'submersion', not immersion (e.g. Swain 1978a). Rather than begin on an equal footing with all other classmates as regards the language of instruction, the submerged children find themselves in a necessarily handicapped position which can do little to enhance any sense of self-esteem or permit equality of learning opportunities. The Canadian immersion program is, then, initially a segregated one; that is the learners of the target language are separated from native speakers at least until their linguistic skills are sufficient to permit them to learn academic content on a par with native speakers.[1] In fact, the immersion program is not only initially segregated, but in most cases remains segregated due, once again, to forces beyond the control of the school system.

A second feature of the Canadian French immersion programs is that the teachers are bilingual in the child's home language and the target language. Although the teachers only speak the target language in class, they make considerable use of the children's home language in the sense that they understand everything the children say to them. Thus, as should be the case in any classroom, the teacher accepts and starts from the existing language and interests of the children. This is in stark contrast to a situation in which the teacher does not understand the children's home language, and of necessity must follow a preestablished curriculum that may relate neither to the children's interests or first language abilities. We will return to this point in the next section, as it has obvious methodological implications.

A third feature of the Canadian immersion programs is that the home language is incorporated into the curriculum. In the primary level program, English literacy skills are taught usually from grade three on, and at later grade levels it is also used as a medium of instruction for specific academic subjects. The two languages continue to serve as languages of instruction throughout schooling. In the case of French immersion programs, English is introduced to ensure that the students develop English literacy skills comparable with their unilingually English-educated counterparts. As was pointed out before, parents wanted their children to learn French, but not at the expense of mother tongue development.

The fact that Canadian immersion programs include instruction in both the mother tongue and the second language is, as Mackey (1978) pointed out, a new dimension, and is different from what has typically been referred to as 'immersion' in the United States which has involved instruction only in the second language. But once again, the background characteristics of the Canadian immersion program are important to keep in mind in considering its potential success in another setting. In the Canadian immersion program, there has never been any ambivalence in attitudes towards the importance of mother tongue development. Parents and educators have insisted that the English language skills of the early immersion students be closely monitored. In some cases, unconvinced that their children's English would not suffer when French was the sole language of instruction in the early grades, parents insisted that English also be part of the curriculum at the initial stages, or even that French immersion not be introduced until later grades (Swain 1978b). Furthermore, unlike in some languages, there is no shortage of English materials for instructional purposes, nor is there any shortage of qualified English teachers.

Immersion education then, as it is practised by Canadian educators, assumes a homogeneous student population with respect to knowledge of the target language, uses teachers who are bilingual in the home (vernacular) language and the target language, and uses both home and target languages as languages of instruction in order to ensure mother tongue maintenance. The Canadian immersion model, therefore, seems particularly suited to vernacular speakers who want to maintain and develop their own language while also learning a second dialect or second language. When the second language or dialect should be introduced into the curriculum, however, will be discussed below in the section on outcomes.

(iii) Methodology

Immersion education has frequently been described as one in which the second language is acquired in much the same way as a child acquires a first language, through extensive exposure to and use of the target language in real communicative situations. In its methodology, it has been contrasted with formal techniques which provide specific instruction about the target language per se. There are at least two issues that need to be raised with respect to these descriptions: first is there accuracy; and second is the relative effectiveness of each methodology.

Let us turn first, then, to examine the accuracy of the description of immersion education methodology and in so doing, be more explicit about what actually occurs in an immersion class. Immersion education began in Canada with the idea that through the exclusive use of French by the teachers to communicate with their students, the second language would be acquired incidentally—incidental to learning about the content of what was being communicated. The focus of the teachers has been to get the content across to their students and to respond to the content of what their students are saying, no matter how they are saying it, nor in what language it is being said. Here the importance of being able to understand the child's home language is highlighted. Were the teacher not able to understand the child's language, there could be no meaningful discourse, a crucial element in language acquisition. As Macnamara (1972) has pointed out, knowledge of what is likely to be said given the situation will enable the child to guess correctly what the utterance means. This implies that the adult must say the kinds of things the child expects to hear. If the teachers do not understand the child's home language, then there is little likelihood that they will be able to respond relevantly to the child's questions or statements.

The initial focus, then, in immersion methodology is to develop target language comprehension skills. I think it is sometimes forgotten that comprehension is a skill separate from production. In natural language acquisition, comprehension precedes (and exceeds) production. Indeed one might characterize the process as production flowing from comprehension. Thus, although the 'direct method' of second language instruction has in common with immersion instruction the insistence on the use of the target language by the teacher, the two differ in that the former requires the students to produce target language utterances immediately. Doing so severely increases the demands placed on the learners and forces them, at least initially, to reproduce meaningless sounds.

Although the initial focus in immersion is on developing comprehension skills, it would be inappropriate to suggest that this is accomplished by 'just talking' to the students. Specific instructional techniques are used. Key lexical items are taught in the context of trying to convey a real message through the use of pictures, gestures, and other body language cues. The initial emphasis is on teaching relevant vocabulary, so that when it is used in the natural flow of speech, the general content of what is being expressed can be understood. In methodology, this is comparable to other communicative instructional approaches which emphasize the development of comprehension skills first and which use similar techniques such as Asher's (1969) *Total Physical Response* or Terrell's (1977, 1980) *Natural Approach*.

Immersion education has been characterized as not incorporating any explicit instruction about the second language. This characterization is derived from the description of immersion as focussing on conveying content rather than on the form in which content is conveyed. However, as has already been noted, focussing on content involves the explicit teaching of vocabulary—in context though, not as isolated lists of words to be memorized. Similarly, grammar is 'taught', not as isolated rules into which words are plugged, but as a means of making use of words to communicate more effectively. This is largely accomplished through the use of implicit, covert correction by teachers in student-teacher interaction in a way similar to that which occurs when native speakers interact with nonnative speakers (see, for example, Hatch 1979; Krashen 1980) or adults with children (see, for example, Snow and Ferguson 1977). The explicit teaching of grammar and structure, however, is also incorporated into the curriculum.

In a study of the teaching of listening and speaking French in primary immersion classes undertaken by Ireland, Gunnell, and Santerre (1980), the strategies and techniques used by immersion teachers were identified. Ireland et al.'s analysis was based on observations and tape-recordings of 71 visits to immersion classes from the kindergarten to grade 6 level. Their data show that as the children get older, the teacher's speech includes more explicit reference to, and instruction about, grammatical and structural points. Two categories of teacher speech and one of student speech are of particular interest here. The first category, 'teacher asks grammar questions', includes such examples as: *'En grammaire, a quoi ca sert le participe passe?' 'Est-ce cheveux est masculin ou feminin?'* and *'Quand on parle d'une proposition subordonnee qu'est qu'on veut dire?'* The second category, 'teacher gives grammatical explanations', includes explicit information or explanations given about syntactic categories, analysis or rules. The third category, 'students take part in grammar exercises', includes situations where the students given definitions of grammatical terminology, identify and analyze grammatical units (sentences, verbs, nouns, adjectives, etc.), state rules, and produce grammatical forms in contextual isolation (e.g. conjugate verbs; transpose singular nouns to plural, past tense to future, masculine to feminine, etc.).

In kindergarten through grade 2, less than 2% of the teachers' speech includes asking grammar questions, and less than .1% includes giving grammar explanations. Similarly less than 3% of the students' speech includes taking part in grammar exercises. From grade 3 on, however, the situation changes. There is an increase from grade to grade in the percentage of speech included in each category. Grammar explanations constitute approximately 3% of the teachers' speech in grade 3 and 7% in grade 6, while grammar questions constitute approximately 5% in grade 3 and 22% in grade 6. Similarly oral grammar exercises constitute approximately 6% of the students' speech in grade 3 and approximately 30% in grade 6. For the most part, grammar is dealt with in these ways in specific lessons, rather than when the lesson is focussed on teaching academic content.[2] Thus immersion education incorporates instruction both implicitly and explicitly.

It has been suggested, then, that immersion education incorporates basic components of structural and communicative approaches to second language instruction. The key differences between early immersion education and most other second language instructional programs would appear to be two-fold: time provided and sequencing of input.

Second language instruction is typically offered in schools through daily periods of relatively short duration, whereas immersion education, by definition, occupies more than 50% of the school day. One would expect on this basis alone that the second language performance of immersion students would be superior; and indeed, the research evidence confirms this (e.g. Barik and Swain 1975, 1976). Were the second language program to be offered for similar periods of time, the second language performance of the students might be superior, but the content learned by the immersion student would have been lost to the language student. This type of intensive language-focussed program has sometimes been referred to as 'immersion', but certainly does not reflect the methodology of Canadian immersion programs.

The second factor, the sequencing of second language input, may or may not be of significance, but until further data are available, its significance is certainly debatable. On the one hand, early immersion begins with a virtually unplanned sequence. Teachers and children interact, with the language the teachers use being innocent of intentional simplifications. Their language is simplified in a way natural to that of adults talking with children and nonnative speakers. Stern (1980) has referred to this as a nonanalytical approach. On the other hand, most second language instructional programs work from a predefined syllabus. The syllabus is sequenced according to a higher-order constraint such as grammatical simplicity (based on linguistic analysis) or functional need (based on sociolinguistic analysis). Stern (1980) has referred to this as an analytical approach. As we have seen, immersion incorporates the explicit teaching of grammar at a later stage (or initially, in the case of late immersion programs) where the sequencing is presumably based on the grammatical inadequacies of the students. And frequently, analytical programs become more communicatively oriented as learners become more advanced, although even then the sequencing of input may be controlled (e.g. ESP courses).

The question of whether the sequencing of second language input makes a difference to target language competence breaks down into two separate questions. The first question asks whether the sequence of analytical to nonanalytical (communicative) instructional techniques leads to equivalent results over time as the sequence of nonanalytical to analytical. As part of this question, one also needs to ask whether the age at which a learner begins influences the impact of either sequence. There are no data which directly address this issue. The second question asks whether the sequencing of input per se makes a difference to target language competence.

With respect to the second question, Felix (1980) has recently reported on a study concerned with the effects of formal instruction on second language acquisition. In his study, the target language output of high-school students in Germany beginning their study of English was observed for a period of eight months. The students followed an audiolingual program in which the input was highly controlled and structured. The students were exposed to English only during classroom hours. Felix found that the students' utterances showed many structural features which are known to characterize first language acquisition and untutored second language acquisition. The students, however, were continuously forced to produce structures for which they were not yet ready according to the order observed in untutored environments. In these instances, the students used two basic strategies. Either they produced utterances similar to those found in early stages of untutored learning, or they randomly selected any one structure from a finite repertoire. This study suggests that sequencing of input cannot overcome the natural tendencies of a learner to acquire language in a developmental order, which according to Krashen (1979) can best be served by the provision of an 'acquisition rich' environment.

In another study recently completed, Bialystok (in preparation) investigated the grammatical performance of intermediate and advanced ESL learners on several tasks which varied along a dimension of formal/grammatical to informal/communicative. Her data reveal that accuracy on the formal/grammatical tasks does not predict accuracy on the informal/communicative tasks. In other words, although students had the relevant knowledge to complete successfully the grammatical tasks, they could not use this knowledge when the task demands required focussing on content. These findings are consistent with Krashen's monitor model (1979) which suggests that rules which are taught and learned serve only to monitor the acquired system. Furthermore the monitor is used only under restricted circumstances: when the learner is focussed on form rather than on content, and when the learner has the time to apply it.

Bialystok (1980) formulates the issue in a somewhat different way. She argues that the learner has two different sources of linguistic knowledge: explicit and implicit (analyzed/unanalyzed). Depending on the task faced by the learner, different combinations of each will be required. Learners' performance on a particular task will depend on the degree to which each knowledge source is acquired/learned, and the automaticity with which it can be assessed.

Although the two formulations differ somewhat, they both agree that knowledge of grammatical rules does not mean it can be used in a communicative setting. They differ in the way in which the knowledge of grammatical rules is used: Krashen suggests as a monitor; Bialystok suggests as one source of knowledge which must be combined with other knowledge sources. Both, however, would agree that the sequencing of grammatical input plays little role in the communicative abilities of the learner except as it serves the established communicative system. (See also, the literature reviewed in Canale and Swain (1980) that suggests that grammatical instruction is not sufficient for the development of communicative abilities.)

Thus, it would appear that the particular sequence of input taught is largely irrelevant as learners will make what they can of the input data to construct their own target language system. Furthermore, rules they may learn in the course of instruction are not necessarily applied in situations of actual language use. This is not to say that teaching about the target language is ineffective. It is, however, to say that its effectiveness is likely to be limited to developing that which it was intended to develop—knowledge about the language rather than the ability to be able to use it.

To summarize, it has been suggested that immersion education incorporates the methodological approaches of both structural (analytical) and communicative (nonanalytical) second language instructional programs.

The initial emphasis in Canadian immersion education is on developing comprehension skills, and the major emphasis is on communication rather than form which contrasts with many second language instructional approaches where the initial emphasis is on developing production skills, and the major emphasis is on form rather than communication. There is no inherent reason, of course, why the relative emphasis of immersion education cannot be incorporated into second language instructional programs. Indeed, this is precisely what has been done in the *Natural Approach* (Terrell 1977, 1980). The relative effectiveness in the long run of either approach is not known. There is evidence to suggest, however, that learners move towards target language proficiency in a developmental sequence that defies input otherwise sequenced, and that they cannot automatically apply known rules to situations of actual language use. Furthermore, in comparing immersion with other second language instructional approaches, one needs to remember that in immersion education, not only are target language skills being developed, but students are learning content material as well.

The actual results of Canadian immersion programs will be outlined in the next section. But at this point, it seems worthwhile to ask whether immersion methodology as described above can be successfully used with vernacular speakers. Day (1979) reports on a study of kindergarten to grade 3 speakers of a low prestige, creolized language, Hawaii Creole English (HCE). The children had no formal English language program. There was no instruction in learning to speak English. Day states, 'I did not believe that such a program would work. This belief is based on the assumption that only those children motivated to do so will. . . [speak]. . .in standard English, since speaking the socially accepted variety in a speech community is a matter of personal identification' (301). Instead the teachers used standard English, accepting the children's use of HCE in school. Two oral sentence repetition tests were given, one in HCE and the other in standard English, either 8 or 20 months apart. The results indicate significant increases in the scores on both tests. The main conclusion of this investigation is that HCE-speaking children can acquire standard English without losing fluency in HCE, and without a formal English program.

This study is interesting as the immersion approach was used precisely because it was considered ineffective to force the children to use standard English, suggesting that the choice of methodology should rely on considerations related to the psychological well-being of the child. Immersion methodology, whether applied in a second language classroom, or to the entire school day, seems to have far greater scope in this regard by providing a supportive environment in which the child's own language is accepted.

(iv) Outcomes

The linguistic and academic outcomes of primary French immersion programs have been relatively consistent across Canada (for reviews, see for example Swain 1974, 1978b; Genesee 1979). In this section, the results from a number of evaluations of French immersion programs will be summarized with respect to mother tongue and second language development as well as achievement in academic content taught in the second language.

The learning of content material has been measured over the years through the use of standardized tests in mathematics, and from approximately grade five, through the use of standardized tests in science and social studies. It should be noted that the tests of content mastery were written in English, thus potentially handicapping the immersion students who had been taught the subject material in French. Almost without exception, the immersion students perform as well as their unilingually educated peers on both computational and problem-solving tasks in mathematics. Additionally, the immersion students demonstrate equivalent performance to their comparison groups in science and social studies (e.g. Tucker 1975; Barik and Swain 1978).

The English language skills of the early immersion students have been monitored over the years and across programs using a variety of techniques ranging from standardized tests measuring vocabulary knowledge, reading comprehension, punctuation, spelling, and grammar to the measurement of communicative abilities and sensitivity to the needs of the listener (Genesee, Tucker, and Lambert 1975) to global and detailed scoring of stories written (Swain 1975; Genesee and Stanley 1976) and told (Edwards and Smyth 1976) by the students.

The results show that the primary French immersion students do not do as well as their unilingually educated peers through to the end of grade one. This is not particularly surprising as they have had no formal instruction in English. One exception to the inferior performance of the immersion children at this grade level is that they were found to be, in their oral communicative skills, more sensitive to the needs of the listener than were children educated in their native language. Genesee, Tucker, and Lambert (1975) suggest that these findings may be related to the immersion children's experience in school which 'may have made them more aware of possible difficulties in communicating as well as providing them with some experience in coping with such difficulties' (1013).

Through to the end of grade three the immersion students continue to have some difficulty with such technical skills as spelling, punctuation and capitalization. But by the end of grade four, the immersion students and their English-educated peers perform equivalently. This appears to be the case even if English is not introduced into the curriculum until grade three, or even grade four. By the end of grade five the immersion students, in some instances, out-perform their comparison groups on several aspects of measured English skills, for example, reading comprehension and vocabulary knowledge.

As with English, the French language skills of the primary immersion students have been monitored through a variety of tests and techniques. The results reveal consistently superior performance of the immersion students relative to students taking daily periods of French as a second language (FSL) instruction. Furthermore, after six or seven years in an immersion program, students perform on the average at least as well as 50% of native French-speaking students who served as the norming population for the standardized test employed. Their performance in the areas of listening and reading approaches native-like levels; whereas in the areas of speaking and writing, many differences between immersion and francophone students still remain (see, for example, Spilka 1976; Harley and Swain 1977; Lepicq 1980).

For example, in a detailed study of the verb system used by several grade five students, while interacting with an adult interviewer, Harley and Swain (1978) concluded that, in general, the immersion children may be said to be operating with simpler and grammatically less redundant verb systems than native speakers of the same age. They tend to lack forms for which grammatically less complex alternative means of conveying the appropriate meaning exist. The forms and rules that they have mastered appeared to be those that are the most generalized in the target verb system (for example, the first conjugation -er verb pattern). In the area of verb syntax, it appears that where French has a more complex system than English (for example, in the form and placement of object pronouns), the immersion children tend to opt for a simple pattern that approximates the one that they are already familiar with in their mother tongue.

Lepicq (1980) asked francophone peers and adults (unilingual and bilingual) to judge the spoken French of grade 5 immersion children after listening to a 10-15 minute tape-recording of a child interacting with an adult. Although there were some differences among the groups of judges, they all judged the speech of the immersion children to be quite acceptable. Furthermore, acceptability was significantly correlated with comprehensibility. Two other findings of interest emerged from Lepicq's study. First, the data reveal that different criteria of acceptability are used when nonnative speakers are judged than when native speakers are judged. Secondly, psycho-social judgements of the learners such as confidence in oneself, willingness to communicate, etc. affect judgements of acceptability independent of the linguistic characteristics of the speech used. These are relevant points to keep in mind when considering the importance of attaining native-like speech patterns.

It is perhaps surprising that after six or seven years, the speech of the immersion students is not native-like. This does not seem to be due, however, to a lack of grammatical knowledge which, as indicated by their performance on tests of French achievement intended for francophones, is about average. It may be that the lack of opportunity to use the language in the upper grade levels is in part responsible. As with most classes at this level, much of the classroom time is taken up with teacher talk. As one immersion student told me recently, 'History is the only subject where we get any chance to talk.' He went on to talk about what happens when he uses French: 'I understand everything anyone says to me, and I can hear in my head how I should sound when I talk, but it never comes out that way. Maybe I shouldn't talk so fast.' (Immersion student, personal communication, November, 1980).

The difference between the speech of the immersion students and their francophone counterparts may also in part be accounted for by their lack of interaction with native French-speaking peers. In the French immersion classroom, the students are for the most part exposed, in any one year, to only one native French-speaking model; namely, the teacher. Otherwise the spoken French they hear is largely that of their nonnative French-speaking classmates—all of whom have the same first language—in interaction with the teacher or each other. Once the children have reached a point in their second language development where they can make themselves understood by their teacher and classmates, there is no strong social incentive to develop further towards native speaker norms.

These same problems—lack of opportunity to use the target language, whether in or out of class—may also be present for some vernacular speaking groups. Vernacular speakers may not have the opportunity to use the target language out of class either because it is not spoken in the community (e.g. Standard Spanish in Southwestern United States, Standard French in Ontario), or because of the social isolation their own vernacular causes them (e.g. some Franco-Ontarians prefer to remain silent or speak English when they come in contact with standard French speakers, due to their own linguistic insecurity). There is no reason to think, however, if immersion students can be taken as an example, that instruction about the target language will cure these ills.

The academic and first language results must be considered in their context, that of children who in all likelihood would succeed in school (Paulston 1975) and who live in homes and communities where English is the only language used. Furthermore, their vernacular is the accepted standard language so that introduction of it into the school program is not only expected but highly valued. This is in contrast to many vernacular speakers whose language is a low prestige, not educationally valued language. Additionally many vernacular speakers in the United States, whose home language is a minority language or a low prestige dialect of the standard language, are not expected to succeed in school. If *all* the structural and methodological features of immersion education described above were present, would that be enough to overcome the lack of background characteristics thought to be significant to the success of French immersion? Perhaps, in some instances. But not in all.

The situations where it seems least likely to succeed have two characteristics: the vernacular is not valued by its own members, and the target language is that of the majority group. Under these circumstances immersion education is unlikely to lead to bidialectalism, but rather to rapid assimilation. Under these circumstances, if one wants to achieve results similar to immersion education in Canada, education must start with the vernacular to overcome the overwhelming use of the majority language in the environment. This may lead to bilingualism, but will it lead to improved school performance?

In a longitudinal study undertaken in England, Wells (1979) found that oral language production skills of preschoolers are only weakly related to the later acquisition of reading skills in school and to general success in school. What is interesting is that the nature of the interaction which took place between caretaker and child appeared to be a good predictor of success in school, including reading. It appears that the extent to which parents accept and develop children's verbal initiations, that is, the extent to which meaning is negotiated in constructing a shared reality is an important predictor of reading attainment, and of general success in school.

Smith (1978) claims that a prerequisite for learning to read is being read to. According to Smith, being read to provides children with the basic insights necessary for being able to read—that is, that print is meaningful, and that the printed text is different in form from the spoken language.

If parents are ambivalent about their own language, feeling they speak an inferior dialect, they may be reluctant to use it with their child (Cummins 1980). They may not read to their child. They may not interact with their child to 'negotiate meaning'. Thus the children may arrive at school without the linguistic skills essential as the basis for the literacy demands that school will place on them. (It should be pointed out that this reasoning is largely speculation, and that data concerning the actual nature of preschool parent-child interaction in the home of minority language groups are sorely needed.) Presumably early schooling could incorporate these aspects of language usage into the curriculum, and it seems most efficient to do this in a language the children already know (see also Cummins 1980; Swain 1981).

SUMMARY AND CONCLUSIONS

The characteristics of primary immersion education as it is understood by Canadian educators have been outlined in order that the practicability of using immersion for the teaching of a nonvernacular language to vernacular speakers may be more accurately assessed. It has been suggested that immersion is best suited to vernacular speakers who wish to maintain their home language. When this is not the case, immersion seems an inappropriate model to use.

It was suggested that immersion methodology, where emphasis is initially placed on comprehension rather than production and on content rather than form, is more appropriate to use with young children, because it values and respects the language children bring with them to school, and does not force them to produce language which is foreign and meaningless to them. It permits the development of the target language in ways natural to first language acquisition. Although grammar is explicitly taught and practised in the later grade levels, the spoken and written French of the students is different from native speakers. Several reasons were suggested for why this might be, including the lack of opportunity to use the target language in or out of class. Limited opportunities for use might also face vernacular speakers in some communities. Teaching about the language does not appear to provide a solution if it cannot be accompanied with opportunities for use.

Finally, it was suggested that even if the structural and methodological aspects of immersion were present, the results of French immersion education which include learning a second language with no detrimental effects on mother tongue development or academic achievement, were unlikely to yield similar positive results for vernacular speakers who do not strongly value their own language and for whom the target language is the language of their environment. To obtain results similar to immersion education, initial and continuing education in the mother tongue is required.

This paper also appeared in *SSLA*. 1981. 4.1:1-17.

NOTES

[1] I have frequently suggested in writing (e.g. Swain 1978b) and in public meetings that immersion students should be integrated with Francophones after several years of French immersion education. Immersion students from Quebec have commented on the need for additional contact with Francophones in order to reduce interethnic tension (Blake, Lambert, Sidoti, and Wolfe n.d.). Sometimes this is not possible, however, because the Francophone population is nonexistent in the community where the immersion program is offered. As often as not though, the suggestion has been greeted with cries of 'linguistic genocide' by members of the Francophone section of a community on the grounds that to implement such a suggestion would only hasten the already rapidly occurring assimilation. It is interesting to note, however, that in some communities where no Francophone school exists, some Francophone parents are enrolling their children in French immersion programs as 'the only possible way of having my children educated in French' (parents from Manitoba, personal communication, 1979).

[2] The extent to which the grammar explicitly taught is linked to the difficulties encountered by the students has not been studied in early immersion programs. Making this link seems essential if the grammatical instruction is to be maximally useful.

EVALUATION AND TESTING
IN VERNACULAR LANGUAGES

JOHN W. OLLER, JR.

Educators have long suffered from what may be called *psychometrosis*—a generalized uneasiness about tests. As John Upshur (1969) once noted, '"Test" is a four letter word.' Educators worry about tests for many reasons. Some of their worries are well founded. Tests are often misused and persons subjected to them are thereby abused. Tests may sometimes be unfair and result in inappropriate evaluations that lead to incorrect judgments about students, teachers, and even whole educational systems. However, for all the potential damage of testing, the dangers of not testing are even more ominous. No one tries to run a business without some method of determining whether or not he is turning a profit. No one but a test pilot would think of getting into an untried model of an aircraft. Strangely, however, many educators seem to be willing to conduct school business without bothering to do sufficient evaluation. Questions such as, 'Are the students benefitting from the curriculum?' are shunted aside with vague remarks about 'political realities', 'the infinitely many and varied factors that enter into school performance', and 'the uncontrollable socio-economic variables', etc. All of this argumentation is offered by clever administrators and bureaucrats who are trying to continue to dodge the issue: they are making excuses for not having done the sensible sorts of testing and evaluation that are essential to the whole process of education. Perhaps some of them are sincere pedagogues who have merely been deceived into thinking that their psychometrosis is entirely reasonable—sufficiently so as to make flying blind and without instruments a rational alternative. Indeed, many educators seem to think it is the only alternative.

I would like to argue in this paper that psychometrosis is a disease propagated primarily by fear and ignorance and that its only cure is a better grounding in testing theory, research, and practice. There are many issues in connection with the treatment of institutionalized psychometrosis that must be handled gingerly and with tender diplomacy, but there are others that must simply be done away with by frontal assault. For instance, there is a common confusion among many U.S. bureaucrats involved in the bilingual education movement concerning what are often termed 'political realities' and what may be called 'empirical issues'. While it is true that the former may be manipulated by voting, or by some other method of political maneuvering, the latter cannot be decided by power plays or opinion polls. Empirical issues including questions such as, 'Are the students profiting from the curriculum?' cannot be decided by vote. For educators in a free society to argue that reasonable empirical evidence cannot be obtained on such questions is preposterous.

Nowhere, in my judgment, has the smokescreen of bureaucratic malarky been thicker than in the area of American educational programs in vernacular languages. In many instances public monies have been invested by the millions in programs where little or no attention was paid to the need for systematic testing and evaluation (Oller 1974). There are known instances where instruction in a vernacular language has been offered to children who were monolingual speakers of the majority variety of English (Teitelbaum 1976). Had this been done in the name of second language instruction it might have been justified, but when it was done ostensibly to make the curriculum more accessible to children who already knew the vernacular language in question, it became a ludicrous misuse of public funds. The persons most apt to suffer are the very minority children the programs were supposed to help.

A crucial part of the progressive resolution of this sort of problem must be an adequate program to evaluate proficiency in the majority language as well as in the vernacular languages. An approach to such a program of evaluation and testing cannot be based on endless discussions of 'political and socio-economic realities', but rather must be founded in sound reasoning and careful research. While it is true that political and socio-economic issues must certainly be taken into account in regard to educational policies, discussions of such matters are no substitute for careful research on precisely those issues as well as others. This paper will concentrate on the empirical questions pertaining to evaluation and testing in educational programs that serve vernacular language populations. Three questions will be addressed: (1) What can we measure with tests? (2) How can we best evaluate the prerequisite skills as well as the desired outcomes of educational programs? (3) When should systematic testing be done?

Finally, a number of unresolved researchable questions will be briefly discussed.

WHAT CAN BE TESTED?

Contrary to a lot of unfounded speculation about the difficulties of reliable and valid language testing, language proficiency (as a psychometric construct) can probably be measured as well or better than any other psychological capacity that is commonly discussed by educators. Insofar as the construct, that is, the theoretical entity, 'language proficiency' can be defined in relation to school tasks, it can be tested quite reliably and validly. This is not to say that any single completely adequate test or testing technique exists, but rather that many combinations of tests and testing procedures are known on the basis of solid research to produce highly reliable and valid indices of language proficiency. Evidence on this issue can be found in great abundance in the published literature. For instance, see Carroll (1980a), as well as Oller and Perkins (1980), Oller (1979), and their references. (This is not to say that there are no unresolved problems in language testing. See the section below, Remaining Research Questions.)

It is a widely accepted and well demonstrated fact that a certain level of language proficiency is a prerequisite to the accessibility of educational programs. Not only is proficiency in the language of instruction a prerequisite to the intelligibility of the instruction itself (see Freedle and Carroll 1972), but the advancement of the learner's capacity to express and comprehend propositions within a given area of the curriculum is often the principal aim of instruction and also its only measurable outcome (Oller and Streiff in press). In fact, it is possible to argue, and there is considerable evidence in support of the contention, that so-called 'intelligence', 'achievement', and even 'personality' tests may sometimes measure deep aspects of language proficiency more than anything else. Gunnarsson (1978), for example, shows that items drawn from tests aimed at constructs of 'IQ', or specific areas of 'achievement' (e.g. reading or arithmetic), or even 'personality' variables may often resemble items in tests aimed at language proficiency so much that they are for practical purposes indistinguishable. Therefore, on the basis of this and other evidence, we may conclude that tests aimed at constructs other than language proficiency may often be measuring language proficiency to a much greater extent than intended. Not only is language proficiency one of the most measurable of psychological constructs, but it may also be a principal factor in many tests that are intended to measure something else.

It is not argued that only language proficiency can be tested, but it is argued that educators everywhere should be made aware of the pervasive importance of language proficiency in the tests, and also across the entire school curriculum. Moreover, the importance of language proficiency to the accessibility of the curriculum itself can be translated into a mandate for testing in vernacular languages as well as in whatever the dominant variety (or varieties) may be. A crucial problem in the U.S. is to determine the relatively proficiencies of children who use one or more language varieties other than a standard variety of English. This needs to be done both in the standard variety *and* in the vernacular(s). Traditionally American bilingual programs have stressed 'dominance' testing in relation to a five point 'balance' scale. A child is judged to be at the center of the scale if he performs equally well in the majority language and in the vernacular on some test or evaluative procedure (sometimes a questionnaire filled out by a parent or teacher or even by the child himself). If the child is monolingual in the vernacular he falls at one extreme of the scale, and if he is monolingual in the majority language he falls at the opposite extreme. Between the midpoint and the extreme ends of the scale, the child may fall toward the vernacular side if his performance is better in the vernacular than in the majority language, and he may fall toward the majority language side if his performance is better in the majority language. Such a dominance scale is explicitly defined as part of the now famous (in the U.S. at least) 'Lau remedies' (Linguistic Reporter 1975:1). However, this sort of scale is, by itself, quite inadequate (Zirkel 1974).

What is required in addition to some measure of 'dominance' or 'degree of balance' between the majority language and the vernacular is a meaningful measure of proficiency both in the majority language and in the vernacular. That is, at least two proficiency scales are required. In spite of the fact that norm-referenced scales have fallen on hard times in the educational press, it is essential that some normative criterion be at least implicitly defined in order for a proficiency scale to be interpretable (and 'interpretability' has been suggested by one influential psychometrician, Robert Ebel [1972], as a criterion of greater importance even than 'reliability' and 'validity'). Since the very process of language acquisition in an important sense is one of progressively approximating some socially defined norm (i.e. internalizing the grammatical system underlying the performance of a social group), it makes sense for language proficiency measurement to be referenced against the criterion of that group norm. If a child is going to have to compete with monolingual speakers of Spanish in a given educational setting at a certain grade level, it makes sense to define the requisite level of Spanish proficiency with reference to the normative criterion of typical native speakers at that level. As Carroll (1980a) points out, it is a rather arbitrary matter whether one chooses to regard a scale defined in this way as 'norm-referenced' or 'criterion-referenced'. In an important sense such a scale is both.

Given roughly equivalent (and therefore comparable) proficiency scales in the majority language and one or more vernaculars, it will be possible to make much more meaningful judgments concerning the performance of individual children than would be possible in terms of only a 'balance' or 'dominance' scale. (Of course, the balance scale information obtainable from proficiency scales—though the reverse is not true.) For instance, consider the case of a child who is above the established norms both in the vernacular and in the majority language. It might well be argued that this 'balanced' child could be expected to benefit from instruction in either language. But consider another 'balanced' child whose performance in both languages falls near the bottom of the respective distributions. In this instance, the child might be expected to have trouble no matter which language is selected for instruction. (For more on such cases, see the discussion of language disorders and bilinguals below.) The sort of case which would establish a clear preference for instruction in either the vernacular or majority language would be where the child reveals a clearcut dominance favoring one or the other language system, and furthermore reveals a below norm score (or preferably, scores) in the weaker language. In such cases, it would be sensible to argue for the presentation of curricular material in the stronger language. In cases, however, where the imbalance does not involve a below norm score in either language, it would seem to be a moot point as to whether one language or the other should be selected for instructional programming.

Although there has been little research of the required type, the research that has been done (see Oller 1979:74-104 and references given there) supports considerable optimism both concerning the possibility of devising appropriate tests and also of setting criteria for the equating of scales across languages. Furthermore, the technology for resolving the remaining practical problems has existed for a number of years now (Carroll 1980a). As many observers have noted, the stubborn problem of fully satisfactory validity will never be resolved, but there is no reason in principle why the highly valid techniques already in existence cannot continue to be improved.

One of the problems that thwarts the development of valid tests in the vernacular language (Valdman, personal communication) is the often hypothesized claim that users of the vernacular may fail to reveal their true ability under many ordinary testing conditions. For instance, the speakers of the vernacular language may be illiterate in the language, or worse yet, it may be an unwritten language. Therefore, some sort of oral testing would be required. However, even in oral test situations, like the Foreign Service

Institute procedure, the vernacular language may be socially stigmatized and be placed at a disadvantage.

The research of Labov (1976) reveals some telling weaknesses of standardized testing procedures as applied in the case of inner city Blacks. Clearly his criticisms could be generalized to many testing procedures. However, it must be said that there are certain very real disadvantages to presenting a curriculum in a language that does not already possess the extensive literature of major world languages. Moreover, if a language is not regarded by its own users as suitable for the formal settings of student-teacher interactions, it will be necessary to find some way of changing those societal attitudes that prevent the free use of the vernacular in formal settings at school (Spolsky and Irvine 1980), or it will be necessary to deformalize the interactional business of education. Neither of these goals seems easily attainable. On the other hand, there seems to be no insurmountable obstacle in the path of valid vernacular language testing. The problem is simply to define suitable testing procedures. It is imperative to avoid the unnaturalness of certain testing procedures as well as the undesirable presuppositions associated with the much despised tradition of 'deprivation' and 'deficit' theories about nonmajority cultures. Of course, the problem of unnatural testing procedures also needs to be resolved in the case of majority language testing.

HOW CAN SKILLS AND OUTCOMES BEST BE EVALUATED?

At this juncture we come rather naturally to our second question: just how can valid testing be done? The research on specific testing procedures such as cloze, dictation, oral interview, narrative tasks, spontaneous speech samples, essays, and the like is far too extensive to be reviewed here. However, a few rough guidelines may be stated, and certain naturalness criteria elaborated more fully elsewhere may be summarized (see Oller 1979:1-73). Tasks that conform faithfully to ordinary discourse processing requirements and which can easily be quantified are among the best language testing procedures. It is difficult if not impossible to formulate hard and fast rules concerning what to do or not to do, but some examples may prove useful.

A typical error of considerable importance is to ask the examinee to do something that appears to be unreasonably bizarre. (The fact that people will do bizarre things is not doubted, but it is argued that there are levels of bizarreness that are intolerble to many people, especially in tests.) For instance, consider a task where a child is asked to name an object that an adult interviewer is holding in his hand. As Labov (1976 and elsewhere) has shown, many intelligent children refuse to participate in such nonsense because they know first that the adult knows what the object is, and further that the adult knows that the child knows what the object is called. The child does not have to be perversely uncooperative to consider the game he is asked to play unreasonable. A similar strangeness arises in narrative tasks where an adult tells a child a story and then asks the child to tell it back. The youngster knows that the adult already knows the story. Therefore, it seems strange to tell it back in all its detail. Admittedly, some children will perform such a task with great enthusiasm, but this should not influence us to judge harshly the child who sees the silliness of the whole thing and cannot believe that an adult would really want him to do it. Another example violating constraints on ordinary communication is the writing task where the teacher (also the reader) asks the students to write about facts that are already well known to the teacher—much better known to the teacher than to the student.

In each of these cases the bizarreness of the tasks can be reduced or largely removed by creating more realistic communication problems. For instance, instead of asking the child to name objects plainly visible to the adult-tester, the objects may be placed in a bag which the adult cannot see into and the question might be, 'What do you see in the bag?' Or, in the case of story-retelling, the child may be asked to tell the story to someone who, as far as the child knows, has not heard it. Or, in the case of the essay task, the student may be asked to write about some aspect of a topic for which he has information not already available to the teacher.

Concerning the evaluation of language proficiency in general, still more global criteria can be stated. Discourse normally exhibits properties of meaningfulness and temporal development. Propositions which are asserted or implied are never just plopped down out of nowhere without any pragmatic motivation or without antecedents or successors. Utterances or surrogates of utterance forms are normally used to express propositional meanings that are systematically linked to meaningful events in a temporally ordered stream of experience. Language tests which meet the naturalness constraints of meaningfulness and temporal development generally work better than those which do not. This is demonstrated in item analysis statistics, reliability indices, and validity estimates. In fact, it appears to be generally true that testing procedures which require the deep level processing of propositional values which are inferentially associated with the stream of experience work considerably better than procedures aimed at the surface elements of spoken and/or written forms. Testing procedures that seek to assess the examinee's ability to process propositional values at a deep level may be termed 'pragmatic' procedures, while those aimed at surface forms may be termed 'discrete point' procedures.

Dramatic evidence of the superiority of pragmatic procedures over discrete point methods comes from two studies of the diagnosis of language disorders in children. Damico and Oller (1980) found that teachers trained to look for certain pragmatic difficulties (e.g. lack of topic maintenance, use of unspecified referring terms, and the like) referred a greater number of children later judged to have genuine 'language disorders' than did teachers trained to look for deviations in discrete points of surface structure (e.g. deletion of tense markers, plural morphemes, and the like). Also, teachers who were trained to look for the more traditionally recognized surface deviations apparently failed to identify more cases where real problems existed. That is, they made a greater number of false alarms, and they overlooked a greater number of real problems than the teachers trained to look for pragmatic difficulties.

In another study more directly relevant to the interests of education in vernacular languages, Damico, Oller, and Storey (1980) showed that pragmatic criteria are also superior to discrete point criteria for diagnosing language disorders in bilingual children. In the past the bilingual child has endured a kind of double jeopardy with respect to language disorders. Because of the use of surface criteria as a basis for diagnosis, the bilingual who is merely weak in the majority language is apt to be incorrectly diagnosed as language disordered, and the child who has genuine problems is apt to be overlooked for the same reason. Granted that certain neurological and other disorders do in fact occur in a small percentage of monolingual cases, we should expect the distribution of disorders in bilinguals to be similar.

Out of thousands of children in the Albuquerque public school system who come from a background where some language other than English is used, ten speakers of New Mexican Spanish were referred for diagnosis. (Criteria for initial selection are described in greater detail in Damico, Oller, and Storey 1980.) After extensive samples of speech were collected in both Spanish and English, they were evaluated according to both pragmatic and discrete point criteria. As expected, some of the children appeared to be perfectly normal according to the pragmatic criteria while others appeared to have genuine language problems which could be expected to interfere with school progress. The surface oriented criteria for diagnosis, however, resulted in a quite different classification. Three of the ten who were classified as 'language disordered' by the pragmatic criteria were classified as normal by the discrete point criteria, and one of the three children classified as normal by the pragmatic criteria would have been classed as 'disordered' by the discrete point criteria.

To test the validity of the two procedures of classification, pre- and post-test scores on language and achievement were examined for all ten children. It was predicted that the children classified as normal by the pragmatic criteria would make substantial gains in both language and achievement scores while children classified as 'disordered' by the pragmatic criteria would exhibit little or no gain either in language or achievement scores. It was also predicted that the surface deviations indicated by discrete point criteria would prove to be relatively less strongly correlated with growth in either language skills or other subject matter. Both of these predictions proved correct. The children identified as normal by the pragmatic criteria made normal gains in every case, and in all instances those identified as normal (by the pragmatic criteria) made greater gains than any of the children identified as having genuine language disorders. However, the discrete point criteria worked less well, as was expected. For instance, the subject who made the greatest gain in achievement (as indicated by the Peabody Individual Achievement Tests, pre and post) also exhibited the largest number of surface deviations. Moreover, the three subjects who made the fewest errors by the discrete point criteria were all judged to have genuine language problems by the pragmatic criteria and they made little gain in achievement (7.3 percentage points on the average as compared with an average of 32.4 for normals) and they actually fell a half a standard deviation on the Myklebust Pupil Rating Scale which was used pre and post to assess growth in language skills. The normals averaged a gain of 2.4 standard deviation units on the same scale.

On the basis of all of the foregoing it seems reasonable to conclude that pragmatic criteria are not only superior for the assessment of language development in normals, but also for the diagnosis of disorders in abnormal cases. The use of pragmatic criteria places the emphasis on meaning rather than on surface form. However, surface form is not neglected, merely relegated to its properly less significant role.

WHEN SHOULD TESTING BE DONE?

Unfortunately testing is often regarded as a kind of addendum to the curriculum. It is seen as an adjunct that is something over and above the curriculum rather than an integral part of it. However, this should not be so. The answer to the question, 'When should testing be done?', ought to be 'Before, during, and after instruction'. Testing should be done throughout. It is necessary to inform the curricular efforts from the beginning. How can we know whether instruction should be delivered in the majority language or in a vernacular unless prior information is available about the client population? And, how can we know what the distribution of skills is in the client population without some reliable and valid indices of language proficiency? Therefore, tests are clearly necessary before instruction is offered.

Testing is also necessary during instruction. Unless the teacher in the classroom is constantly probing comprehension and seeking evidence of the productive utilization of concepts by students, how will it be possible to know how to pace the instruction? Communication in general depends for its effectiveness on feedback systems which imply regulatory corrections. Thus testing during instruction is essential.

Finally, testing needs to be done after the fact. In order to document progress, to inform the whole educational process, it is necessary to keep some meaningful records of growth rates for the pupils in the system. There needs to be a basis to compare alternative methods of instruction—e.g. delivery of the curriculum in the vernacular versus delivery in the majority language possibly supplemented by instruction in the majority language as a second language system, or instruction in the vernacular itself possibly supplemented by delivery of curriculum in the vernacular, etc. Educators are often leary of such comparisons between methods, and not without reason. However, if testing is valid, and if the curricular options are clearly distinct, there hardly seems to be any rational basis for supposing that meaningful (i.e. measurably reliable) differences will not emerge.

It is sometimes argued by bureaucrats posing as educators that the most important outcomes of 'bilingual programs' in particular are intrinsically immeasurable. They will claim that 'The children enjoy school more', but that this is an 'affective' outcome that is not accessible to measurement. Admittedly, such an outcome may be more difficult to measure than, say, 'arithmetic skills' or any number of other so-called 'cognitive' outcomes, but to say that a construct such as 'enjoying school' or 'being happy in class' is intrinsically inaccessible to measurement is to throw in the towel much too soon. More than that, such a move is more apt to be due to sublimated psychometrosis rather than any knowledge of psychometrics.

If the children in a certain program like school better, this should be reflected in attendance, in overall performance, and above all in the observable atmosphere of the classroom. I see no reason to believe that sensitive teachers and other observers could not be trained to reliably rate the 'positiveness' of the classroom climate. There is, to the contrary, much evidence that experienced observers, or even ordinarily intelligent humans (not necessarily adults even!) can tell the difference between a school setting in which the children appear to be happy and one in which they appear to be unhappy. However, it is difficult to conceive of an argument for 'affective' outcomes which will justify their being promoted above the importance of associated 'cognitive' outcomes. It can be argued that children who do better will also feel better, and conversely that children who feel better will also do better, but who can feel good about failing to learn to read, write, and do arithmetic? It is especially hard to do so when you know that the purpose of schooling is to teach you such things. On the other hand, who can feel bad about success in learning to read, write, and do arithmetic? Success in such things, contrary to a lot of popular press, is not necessarily inimical to the proper interest that educators have in children's feelings. Furthermore, no amount of tenderness will sufficiently compensate the child who has been robbed of the opportunity to become functionally literate.

REMAINING RESEARCH QUESTIONS

In the previous sections, I have tried to concentrate on what I believe are relatively uncontroversial conclusions that can be drawn from existing theory, research and practice in testing. In this section the emphasis shifts to areas of doubt and controversy. Here we will consider somewhat further the nature of language proficiency, its relation to intelligence and other areas of the curriculum, and the advantages of instruction in the vernacular language of the school clientele.

Until recent decades, especially the 1970's, it was popular to regard language proficiency as a collection of capacities which were more or less autonomous. This view was due in a large part to the claims of structural linguists who saw the phonology of a language as something clearly distinct from its morphology and syntax, and phonology and syntax at least as more or less independent of lexicon. Further, literacy skills appeared to be quite different from what have recently been termed 'oracy' skills, just as 'productive' skills appeared to be separable from 'receptive' skills. All of these divisions were justified by the same analytical logic that was so appealing in the early days of Bloomfieldian structuralism. Even later, with the advent of Noam Chomsky's transformational theory, the componential approach seemed to be sustained by linguistic theory.

A problem for the component oriented, analytical approach began to appear on the horizon in the early 1970's when it was found that many tests aimed at the supposedly distinct components posited by analytical theories were more strongly correlated than expected. Why, for example, should a listening task such as taking dictation correlate very strongly with a reading task? Or an oral interview? Or an essay writing task? The strength of observed correlations led to the postulation of a deep communality across the skills of listening, speaking, reading, and writing, as well as a nonsummative interaction between the components of phonology, morphology, syntax, and lexicon. In what now appears to have been an over-reaction against the analytical (discrete point) theories of the 1950's and 1960's, it was suggested (Oller 1976, and the Appendix to Oller 1979) that perhaps a single global factor would prove adequate to explain all of the reliable variance in a great many tests of radically different types. This extreme position was convincingly refuted by Bachman and Palmer (1980), and was effectively countered by arguments from Upshur and Homburg (1980) and Carroll (1980b).

Nevertheless, evidence for a strong general factor (though not an exhaustive solitary one) still remains (Farhady 1980). How to explain that general factor remains a matter of controversy. It was argued at one point (Oller and Hinofotis 1980) that claims for the divisibility of language proficiency into multiple factors and claims for a general factor of language proficiency were mutually exclusive. As Upshur and Homburg (1980), however, have shown, multiple specific factors and a general factor are simply different ways of looking at the same phenomena. Both may be more or less correct views. The problem then becomes one of determining which way of viewing language proficiency works best for certain purposes. The evidence now shows that there are both global and componential aspects to language proficiency (and it might be better to say 'proficiencies'). The perfect theory of the right mix of general and specific components, however, has not been found—and probably will never be agreed on.

Related to the problem of characterizing the components of language proficiency and their interactions is the matter of where language proficiency leaves off and knowledge of a different sort, or capacity of a different sort begins. Cummins (1979, 1980) has argued that at least some subset of language abilities—namely, basic interpersonal communication skills (BICS)—are quite independent of a general factor of 'intelligence' which he believes is strongly correlated with another subset of language abilities—cognitive/academic language proficiency (CALP). Cummins identifies CALP with the general factor of language proficiency observed in many of the studies reported in Oller and Perkins (1980) and elsewhere. However, he contends that BICS must be autonomous and separate from CALP since all normals possess BICS in roughly the same degree. Of course the distinction is hardly above dispute, and there is at present no conclusive experimental evidence to support it. It is also worth mentioning that classical theories offer many other analytical schemes. For my own part, I believe that it may be much more difficult than theorists have often claimed to distinguish language abilities from knowledge and intelligence, insofar as any of these constructs can be defined at all.

A final controversial issue to be considered is the evidence for and against instruction in vernacular languages. From a logical point of view, there is little or no defense for offering instruction to children in a language that they cannot understand. This strong argument, however, is mitigated by evidence (especially from the Canadian experience so well represented in other papers in this volume; especially, Swain) showing that ordinary children are able to overcome the initial problem of an unknown language by simply learning it in the process of struggling through the business of life at school. In fact, the Canadian experience with second language immersion programs suggests that delivery of instruction in vernacular languages may be a luxury at best. If the Canadian findings could be generalized, one might be tempted to conclude that instruction in a nonvernacular language more or less incidentally results in the acquisition of that language with no detrimental side effects.

On the other hand, there is the history of failure of monolingual (nonvernacular) educational programs especially in the American Southwest. It has been hoped by proponents of bilingual programming—or in some cases initial monolingual programming in the vernacular language—that it would be possible to enhance the likelihood of success at school for historically oppressed minorities. Evidence that bilingual programming is accomplishing this, however, is difficult to come by. Perhaps, some have argued, the problem is not so much whether the curriculum is presented through the medium of the vernacular or majority language, but whether or not school success and school related skills are valued by the minority culture in question. A child who comes from an illiterate background may have precious little encouragement to read books at home. Changing the language of instruction may not alter this unfortunate fact. Moreover, in those cases where instruction through the medium of the vernacular has been provided to children who are already dominant in the majority language, the minority child has simply had an additional burden thrust upon him—or so it would seem.

An exceptionally useful and encouraging study by Rosier and Holm (1980) will allow us to conclude on an optimistic note.[1] Holm and others have been working at Rock Point on the Navajo Reservation for some years now in a vernacular language program. Evidence on reading tests reveals that children at Rock Point outperform comparable groups of children at BIA schools elsewhere. Since the Rock Point students are taught to read first in Navajo, the vernacular, the fact that on standardized tests of reading comprehension in English, they eventually surpass children taught to read initially in English suggests that there is a genuine advantage to instructional delivery in the vernacular language. Vorih and Rosier (1978) discuss some of the evidence not only for cognitive benefits, but for affective advantages as well. According to results obtained in 1975, children at Rock Point surpass their peers who are taught only in English by the second grade and continue to advance their lead from there on. By the sixth grade, Rock Point children have advanced their lead over children taught in monolingual BIA programs to 2.04 grade levels in total reading scores. The Rock Point children thus achieved levels comparable to monolingual counterparts in the mainstream English-speaking population while the Native Americans at other BIA schools were about two grade levels below the norm. Observers who visit the Rock Point school often comment that the children are more 'involved' and that they create far fewer 'discipline problems' (Vorih and Rosier 1978:268). Perhaps it is indeed true, as many have believed for a very long time, that presentation and utilization of the vernacular language and culture in a favorable light is the best way to ensure success at school—especially for children whose language and culture may have been stereotypically stigmatized due to socio-political oppression.

At any rate, a great deal more careful testing and evaluation is needed. It is particularly requisite that both cognitive and affective measurement be developed and employed in the case of vernacular language programs due to the special costs of such programs. While not all programs can be expected to appear in a good light if careful evaluation is done, the demonstration of ineffectiveness is sometimes as informative as evidence of success. Besides, there already exists positive evidence from such programs as the Rock Point experiment. Vorih and Rosier (1978:269) write:

> Research as well as impressionistic evidence indicates that language, self-image, and cognitive development are all closely related and interdependent. The children at Rock Point perform better than do their peers taught in monolingual English programs, and yet their horizons have been broadened and their self-image heightened by their Navajo language development.

There is, therefore, reason for optimism. However, in the final analysis optimistic hopes for vernacular language programs need to be supported empirically through careful testing and evaluation.

NOTES

[1] Unfortunately, I have not been able to obtain a copy of the Rosier and Holm (1980) report in time to include the most up-to-date findings in this paper. Therefore, rather than rely on second hand information, I refer below to the earlier published report by Vorih and Rosier (1978). I understand from colleagues, however, especially Stephen W. Rose here at UNM, that the more recent publication only strengthens the earlier findings.

THIRD WORLD VERNACULAR/BI-MULTILINGUAL CURRICULA ISSUES

ISAURA SANTIAGO SANTIAGO

There is significant international educational activity that is receiving little attention in the curriculum theory and planning literature. This is the effort of Third World nations to design educational curricula that will more effectively meet the educational needs of their societies and of children and adults who, through a variety of social, political, and economic mechanisms, have previously been denied access to public education or have been afforded limited opportunity for participation because of their membership in vernacular language groups.

This paper will focus on the nature and scope of the challenge Third World nations are facing in designing educational systems to meet their linguistic, social, and economic realities and needs in the context of a changing world. The paper will show that:

1. All Third World nations, and highly industrialized nations as well, face complex national and educational language policy issues;
2. Language of instruction policy is one of these issues;
3. Policy governing the extent to which the vernacular language is introduced as a medium or subject of instruction varies from country to country as a function of many social, political, and economic factors;
4. Changing the language of instruction is not enough, other curriculum components must also be reformed if humanistic and development goals are to be reached;

113

5. The literature on vernacular/bi-multilingual education is replete with identified problems and needs related to implementation. However, many nations are having difficulty allocating the diverse resources needed for planning and implementing linguistically, culturally, and pedagogically sound curricula;

6. There is little evidence that nations that have changed language of instruction policy and/or practice to provide for instruction in the vernacular have consistently given attention to broader, more deeply rooted issues related to other aspects of the curriculum;

7. There is a critical need for research and development on local, national, and international levels.

The paper concludes by arguing that changes in language of instruction policy probably require concomitant reform in other aspects of the curriculum and that public officials, language planners, and the education establishment would do well to unite in early efforts to prepare for this complex social, political, and economic undertaking. These efforts should be accompanied by thoughtful documentation from a descriptive, ethnographic, formative, and summative evaluation perspective. In the final analysis, the potential impact of vernacular language instruction is directly related to the extent to which governments are prepared to challenge historical dogmas and premises about education and to address those that relate to administrative realities, psychological assumptions, and political prejudices.

Vernacular Language Education

The term 'vernacular language' is often used in lieu of the terms 'mother tongue', 'first language', and 'native language'. Within the context of this discussion, a key qualification is inherent in the use of the term. This is explicit in the United Nations Educational Scientific and Cultural Organization (UNESCO 1953:46) definition: 'a language which is the mother tongue of a group which is socially or politically dominated by another group speaking a different language.' A language is not considered a vernacular in one country if it is the official language in another country. 'Vernacular languages', as used here, span a variety of language forms; these include standard languages, dialects, and language varieties for which there exist no standard orthography or written form. It is communication and everyday speech in students' homes and immediate environments.

Of course, in many Third World countries vernacular language speakers are numerically a majority but often form part of economic and social minorities. In Haiti, Creole is spoken by the majority, but French, the language of the colonial experience, is still the language of prestige and government. Yet changes are taking place; a standardized orthography has recently been developed and instituted as the language of instruction (Valdman 1975; Foster 1980). In Paraguay, Guarani is the language of the majority, yet Spanish is the official language. Here, too, since 1973 Guarani has been accepted as a language of instruction (Rubin 1978). On three major continents, Asia, Latin America, and Africa, language planning agencies have engaged in similar efforts. The need for this level of activity is based on the fact that, taken to the extreme, the use as a medium of instruction in public education of a vernacular or a variety of language different from that used by students is almost a universal (Cheavens 1957; Ferguson 1978). But the focus of this discussion is on 'marked' vernaculars, that is, as defined by Fishman (1976) a language of less repute than the 'unmarked' language that may be either the regional/national language or language(s) of wider communication and prestige.

In nations where changes have occurred, in a number of instances, the result of the demand for vernacular language recognition has elevated the vernacular language to national recognition and official status. Far more frequently (because of the more frequent occurrence of vernacular diversity within nations in the Third World) the outcome has been that speakers of nonstate languages are taught two languages (often the case in Latin America) or three languages (often the case in India and Africa)—their vernacular and/or dialect or regional language, and the national language(s) to varying extents and for varying spans of their educational experience. Hence, reference to bilingual or multilingual education in the literature is not synonymous with vernacular language education. Bilingual education often takes place without vernacular language education.

The term 'bilingual education' refers to systems in which two languages, often the vernacular or 'marked' language, and a second language, often the national/regional language or the unmarked language, are both used as media of instruction. Here, too, there is variation since in some cases the vernacular is admitted as a subject of instruction with or without its use as a medium of instruction. For the purpose of this discussion, vernacular language education and bilingual/multilingual education are used interchangeably. Zierer (1977) describes many of the variety of combinations of the social and educational use of two or more languages, which are too numerous to discuss here. Lewis (1978b) offers a perspective on the international dimensions of bilingualism in education.

Linguistic Heterogeneity Around the World

Linguistic heterogeneity of one form or another is an internal reality today in all nations. Most sociolinguists agree that language diversity has been an historical constant, though the ways in which groups of people and nations have responded to this reality have varied. Most have suggested, however, that bilingualism, and in many cases multilingualism, on the part of individuals has historically been one of the outcomes, while eradication of languages has been another. The true extent of these phenomena is not known, nor is there a complete understanding by linguists, sociolinguists, or psycholinguists of all the variables involved in the acquisition and maintenance of individual, group, or national language diversity, and of the consequences of such diversity. Much less is known about the total context in which these take place.

Nonetheless, language planning is taking place throughout the world on local and national levels, and it is affecting many aspects of life. Nowhere are the complexity, scope, and conflicts of such planning more evident than in education, but neither is there more potential in any other sector (Heath 1978).

The complexity becomes more evident when one considers that in India some 80 languages are used as media of instruction at different stages of education, not to mention the many dialects and vernaculars (Khubchandani 1978a,b). In Mexico, there are at least 55 recorded languages and at least twice that number of Indian vernaculars (Heath 1972; Suarez 1978). In many countries of Latin America Indian vernaculars are numerous, but in too many cases little is known about them (Suarez 1978). UNESCO reported in 1953 there were at least 369 languages in Africa (each of which may relate to a group of vernaculars or a single vernacular) in former British territories alone. There are hundreds more in the rest of the continent (Houis 1976). Similarly, numerous vernaculars are spoken in Asia (Barnes 1978; Fincker 1978) and Southeast Asia (Lester 1974).

In many Third World countries, large numbers of children have no access at all to primary schooling. The disparities within particular countries is more distressing. In Colombia, one of the more advanced of the less-developed countries, nearly 60 percent of the rural schools offer no more than the first two grades of primary school; only 6 percent have the facilities to offer the four-year primary sequence. In Kenya, about 80-85 percent of the relevant age children in the more advanced Central Province attend primary school; but in other districts and provinces, the rate may be as low as 35 percent. In Mexico, the percentage of the population that has completed four or more years of schooling is strikingly higher in the Federal District (Mexico City)—60.6%—than in the rural states such as Chiapas (11.3%), Guerrero (9.18%), and Oaxala (11.9%) (Harbison 1975:541).

Recognition of the international concern with vernacular language education is evident in the UN General Assembly's charge to UNESCO to consider the question. UNESCO held a conference in 1951 on vernacular languages in education. The scope of the problem is delineated in the preface to the conference report (1953:6): 'We have, then, the fact that over one-half of the world's population is illiterate and that a large proportion of the children of school-age are not in school or are learning through a tongue which is not their own. We have the proposition that education is best carried on through the mother tongue of the pupil. But we have too the fact that between the proposition and its realization many complex and difficult questions arise.'

In 1976, the General Conference of UNESCO called another meeting of experts on language teaching in a bi- or plurilingual and multilingual environment. In 1977 representatives of 22 nations attended as well as experts from many international organizations. Once again, they considered the question of education in the vernacular, but this time they realistically considered the complexities of linguistic heterogeneity and avoided prescribing uniform solutions. Experts attending the meeting identified many issues, among them (UNESCO 1977:4):

1. Organizing language teaching in plurilingual contexts is a complex undertaking, and its success is conditioned by a variety of linguistic, social, education, economic, geographical, religious, psychological, historical, political, ideological, and administrative factors;
2. Therefore, a model that functions satisfactorily in one context may not be transferred to another context;
3. The problem of mother-tongue teaching, particularly in connection with literacy, was considered of primary importance within the overall development policy of a given plurilingual country.

Despite social, economic, and political pressures on an international level toward the use of 'world languages' (English, French, and Russian) during this century, increasing numbers of standard national languages (often the outgrowth of national language planning efforts) have emerged in the past three decades (Fishman 1969). There has also been an increasing awareness and cultivation of vernacular languages around the world. Fishman (1976:49) predicts that there is very good reason to believe that this trend will continue and that the use of vernaculars in education will increase, particularly in the early grades. The 1970's alone have seen numerous changes in national language policies and/or language of instruction policies in many countries, including Peru, Mexico, Spain, and the Phillippines, to name just a few.

Clearly the challenge of responding to linguistic diversity is felt by both highly industrialized and less industrially developed nations. Lewis (1980) has contributed much to our understanding, from both a historical and sociolinguistic perspective of bilingualism and bilingual education in the

U.S., Europe, and Russia. Through a comparative analysis, Lewis' study emphasizes the need to look at each country's context on its own terms, while including historical, external, institutional, behavioral, and community variables. Furthermore, he emphasizes the need to view linguistic diversity within a nation as one aspect of larger social diversities that may be associated with a group's linguistic differences. Groups in a country may differ, he suggests, in ethnicity, levels of economic development, social structure, access to or quality of education received, race, religion, degree of political participation, and patterns of family life. He concludes that in the Soviet Union, Europe, and the U.S. these variables have interacted and made bilingualism a desirable or at least a necessary element of their system of education—if only as a transitional process leading to the use of the national language. He asserts (1980:321): 'Among the most important of these societal variables are the type of linguistic community, the historical development of bilingualism and bilingual education in such communities, population change arising from conquest, colonization, and other forms of migration as well as urbanization, levels of social and industrial development associated with the process of modernization, attitudes to the vernaculars and their place in education, and finally beliefs about the cultures with which the languages are associated and about how close or necessary that association is or should be in the system of education.'

Studies of bilingualism and bilingual education in Third World nations of this substance and scope are needed to assist the work of language planners in these nations where 'the lion's share of language planning ventures are currently underway and will continue in the foreseeable future' (Fishman 1972:29). Irrespective of the need for research, in the final analysis the persistence and survival of vernacular languages in many national contexts, and in many cases the number and variety of languages involved, present an unavoidable problem that Third World nations must address in designing educational systems (Ferguson 1978; Fishman et al. 1968; Fishman 1969).

While making decisions about the language of instruction there is a need to focus on education from a broader perspective—the curriculum. There is no comparative international treatment of bilingual or vernacular language curriculum except on language criterion, and these only tell what languages are used, for how many hours in the week, and for a span of how many years at school, the language competency goal for participants, and in some instances the subjects taught in each language. The literature over-whelmingly documents that this is the only dimension on which curriculum reform has occurred. Yet curriculum includes the what, when, how, and what we educate for (Kliebard 1977)—not only in what language educational experiences are provided.

Few would disagree that there is growing evidence that educational language planning and comprehensive curriculum planning are isolated processes. The underlying assumption that surfaces from country to country is that changing the language of instruction requires no other substantive curricula reform (except, in some cases, perhaps some limited, if not vague, commitment to increasing participants' 'knowledge' of the history or culture of the minority group involved).

The key to the success of vernacular language education and bilingual education in the Third World may be whether these nations are able to integrate their social and broader based national language policy planning efforts with educational planning. If they can, true curriculum reform would occur. The possibility of schools playing a role in solving problems of social and economic inequity may increase as a result. Such thinking may lead to meaningful questions about what is being taught, when educational experiences are being provided, toward what social ends, how educational experiences are provided or facilitated, and who or what is facilitating learning (individual teachers, other social institutions, or other mechanisms).

Social and Economic Context of
Third World Vernacular Language Curriculum Reform

There are a number of factors that should be considered when analyzing the nature and scope of vernacular language curriculum issues in the Third World. At the risk of oversimplification and perhaps distortion, there are some trends in public education in the Third World that impact on many nations, though to varying degrees and certainly not on all nations at the same historical moment.

The latter half of the twentieth century found developing nations facing similar problems in responding to socioeconomic conditions and in designing educational systems. 'Nationhood' included struggling with deeply rooted concerns and questions of nationalism and development. A number of countries based a decade of orchestrated national efforts on a number of false assumptions. One assumption centered on the relationship between language and nationalism, another on the relationship between education and development.

The assumption about language and nationalism is that common language is a necessary and sufficient criterion of nationalism. Fishman (1972) asserts that while it could not be effectively argued that language does play a role, it has certainly been the view of modern nationalist movements that it is a major criterion (Ansre 1970; Obina 1979). This has led to increased efforts to impose languages of wider communication—both imported and indigenous. As Fishman (1972:80-1) reports: 'Although some vernaculars have gained a level of recognition since independence that they never had in colonial days, the positions of English and French, on the one hand, and of Hindi, Urdu, Malay, Indonesian, and Filipino, on the other hand, are definite signs of the continued stress of South and Southeast Asian language planning.'

In many nations, then, the processes of modernization and unification and the central symbols of nationalism do not incorporate vernaculars alone, but advocate the use of two or more languages. Exceptions aside, new African and Asian states did not come about as a result of nationality (re)formation and intensification, nor did statehood follow nationality lines. In addition, countries including many language and culture groups have not split up, and existing boundaries (though they may divide ethnolinguistic groups) have, by and large, remained intact.

If language has not been the cause of nation formation, it certainly has been used to achieve the feelings of nationalism that many feel are necessary for nation-building and development. The elite of many nations felt compelled to learn vernaculars so that they could communicate with the largely illiterate masses. They may not have realized that many of these populations spoke social, regional, and experiential variations of a vernacular or that the vernacular was not suitable for modern political exchange and exhortation. Nevertheless, in an effort to bridge the gap between the people and themselves, the new elites grasped upon the vernacular as a tool to unify, activate, and educate the growing heterogeneous urban and literacy-dependent labor force. Many leaders, commented Fishman (1972:43), were 'dependent upon vernacular literacy, if not upon vernacular education, in order to secure the modern political-operational stability and participation without which ultimate sociocultural integration cannot come to pass.'

Illich (1979) analyzed the historical, military, and economic role the vernacular has played within the context of social structure. While focusing on vernacular values and education, he warns against the neocolonialist role played by vernacular languages and values in the educational systems of many new nations—echoing the warnings of the UNESCO 1977 meetings quoted earlier.

It is clear then that the use of the vernacular in many multilingual states involved identifying one or more of many vernaculars that became a medium of instruction, for example Hindi in India and Filipino in the Philippines. However, this does not mean that children were being taught in their own vernacular in all schools. In very many cases, India, for instance (Khubchandani 1977), the number of languages involved requires very complex language planning efforts, recognition of local vernaculars is still a challenge faced by social and economic planners in many nations, and often at the root of internal conflicts are demands for greater access to education.

Demand for vernacular language education may be a function of a group's marginality in a nation. Indian tribes and indigenous hamlets in isolated regions of Latin American countries are often quite marginal to the national language and culture. At times this is a result not only of the demography of the country but the length and the historical causes of the isolation and the country's economic and political history and ideology. Isolation and the relatively small size and large degree of marginality of a group induce it to design its own institutions and/or mechanisms to address educational needs. When the national culture intrudes on these isolated communities, what happens to the group's own institutions is unclear.

On the other hand, there are those who fear vernacular language education when it is used to decrease the social isolation of groups. Some fear that if their children do enter a public educational system and succeed in it, rather than return to their rural towns they will move to urban settings where they can earn money with their new skills. All people in a rural village of India, for instance, do not view education as a means for social change (Goel and Saini 1972).

The second assumption that many new nations—in an exhaustive drive to industrialize—based their development plans on was the notion that there is a direct link between education and development. In fact, in the 1960's education came to be considered a vital prerequisite for economic development (Sheffield 1974). Consequently, nations spent vast sums on education. Educational systems became major sources of employment, they consumed major portions of the national budget, and they generated major bureaucracies within government.

This assumption also led nations to perceive education as an industry, and they therefore implemented mass production approaches, stressing uniformity, centralized control, and bureaucratic systems, with little provision for local input to educational decision-making. In the 1960's education was increasingly stressed in development plans, and Western nations included education in aid strategies (Ward 1974). New technologies were seen as panaceas (Sweeney 1975). Extensive investments were made in universities.

By the end of the decade, however, a variety of factors raised serious questions about these naive assumptions, and schools came under attack and were called upon to respond to a host of social problems. These included the growing underemployment of school leavers, rapid urban migration, the failure of agricultural productivity to keep pace with population growth, the widening gap between small urban elites and the vast majority of the rural populations, and the rising cost of education relative to other sectors (Carnoy 1974; Coombs 1968, 1974; Harbison 1975; Sheffield 1975; Sweeney 1975; Ward 1974).

Furthermore, to the extent that economic development was successful, its byproduct, together with rising inflation, has been an increase in the gap between the haves and the have-nots. Discussion of the issue of education in the vernacular, then, is often coupled with broader issues of equity.

Despite these problems and the overall inability of the schools to meet expectations, increases in the demand for education by vernacular language groups were often caused by the fact that they saw growing numbers of indigenous group members in more affluent conditions. Lewis (1980) relates that the pressure for vernacular and often bilingual education in most African countries did not become apparent until a significant proportion of the native populations had succeeded in advancing economically and socially. By then a thread was drawn between education and mobility—between reality and Western myths.

Yet, as Ward (1974:565) notes: 'Where basic education was provided (and it did grow substantially), it was in the form of elementary schools for young people, usually the first cycle of the inherited colonial systems left more or less intact.' All in all, the role of schools and education in Third World nations have not substantially deviated from the Western models imposed on many during the colonial experience.

Yet, Western models have not been successful in educating Hispanic and Black minorities in the West. Ogbu (1974), in an impressive ethnography of education in an urban area of the United States, concludes that without massive social change, the schools will not bring about equity. The under-achievement of minority children in public schools is a result of urbanization and subordination. Blacks, he suggests, have internalized the social order and have adapted accordingly—achieving won't make a difference in the social outcomes so why try to achieve?

For the Third World few models have offered hope. Among these were the Cuban experience in eliminating illiteracy (Kozol 1978) and the work of other revolutionaries, such as Freire (1972, 1978) and Illich (1972), who called for radical changes in society and schooling—but there is little evidence that these models have had substantial impact in the Third World. Yet, the roots of their analyses of the role of education as oppressor is nowhere more apparent than in the insidious ties between the Third World and industrialized nations with respect to education.

Industrialized nations, particularly the former colonial powers, have played a substantial role in the substance and scope of education in the Third World. A variety of formal and informal transactions and a network of relationships among nations, institutions, and individuals across national lines have resulted in what some term 'neocolonialism', that is, industrialized nations have maintained influence over Third World nations through new forms of dependency. This is evident not only in the fact, alluded to above, that new nation states, once free of colonial rule, maintained the educational systems imposed on them by their colonizers and based on foreign values, goals, and methods. These systems were not only maintained but expanded. In turn, many nations have continued to extend their dependency by looking to the industrialized powers for guidance, books, journals, curricula, technology, and research agendas.

While some might feel that this is normal (Altbach 1977) because the West has the money, brain trusts, and technology for progress, one must question, given the current crisis, at what price? Many suggest that Western models are simply inappropriate when transplanted to other societies (Freire 1978; Illich 1972; Mackey 1978; UNESCO 1977). The study supported by the International Association for the Evaluation of Educational Achievement (1976) raises important questions in this regard. Among the 21 educational systems studied, the most important differences observed in all the results are between the majority of the countries and the four developing nations included. Achievement levels in all the systems studied were notably lower in the poorer nations. However, the factors that appeared to predict achievement within each country were different. In developing nations the proportion of achievement variance accounted for by in-school variables, compared to the proportion accounted for by home background variables, is much greater in the developing than in the developed nations (Passow et al. 1976; Peaker 1976). This probably suggests that different educational programs and strategies are needed in each context.

However, the reality is that neocolonialism in the form of education dependency has taken a variety of forms. Foreign assistance and aid programs have been targeted at what the West considers problems, priorities, or appropriate solutions. From kindergarten to universities, Western influence is obvious. Despite the fact that neocolonialism operates with the consent and participation of the Third World nations, this dependency is a vicious cycle as seen by the fact that many of these efforts have thwarted, if not undermined, national development of new models and textbook production (Altbach 1977; Carnoy 1974).

The notion that this dependency relationship is not only an international phenomenon but one that has its internal counterpart in many Third World nations is the essence of a key work by Carnoy (1974) in which he analyzes the role that schooling has played in India, Nigeria, Brazil, and Peru. He concludes that in both India and Nigeria, upon which direct colonialism had been imposed, schooling was developed as an instrument of social control devised to maintain and expand colonial policies. The colonizer's role was only passed on to national elites who had been prepared for their role of oppressor by the British. After emerging from mercantile relationships with Spain, Brazil and Peru were extensively subjected to conditions of dependency or 'indirect colonialism' as defined by England and the United States, which were their dominant exporters and investors. Primary and secondary schooling in Brazil and Peru were developed by the elites of both societies who were attempting to maintain social hierarchies where the interests of both internal and external dominating groups are in control. Carnoy (1974:346) concludes, 'Schooling for hierarchical structures is a colonizing device.' This was no less the case in Africa (Ampene n.d.).

In summary, Third World nations, particularly new states, have faced complex political, social, and economic challenges in improving the quality of life of their citizenry. It is in the context of these complex and often conflicting if not competing interests that educational planning takes place. Much attention has been given the effort but then much is expected of it in the form of societal returns. Schools are expected to engender feelings of nationalism, to enforce national language policies, to solve problems of social inequity, to solve problems of development and much more. But educational systems have fallen far short of these goals. As is the case in the West, schools have been particularly unsuccessful for vernacular language speakers who are most often members of demographically and/or socially and economically isolated groups. Attempts at solving national problems based on Western models have largely been unsuccessful as has the quest for uniformity through mass compulsory education, a common language(s) of instruction, and an imposed national curriculum. These attempts have frequently resulted in new problems. A more focused look at curricula in the Third World suggests some reasons for past failures and raises concern for the future as well.

CURRICULUM ISSUES

What constitutes a curriculum? Any analysis of Third World vernacular language curricula is hampered by the fact that there are no widely accepted answers to this question. One broad definition by Doll (1976:6) has been suggested: 'The curriculum of a school is the formal and informal content and process by which learners gain knowledge and understanding, develop skills, and alter attitudes, appreciations, and values under the auspices of the school.' This definition offers the ingredients of curricula which most theorists today would agree are also found in other social institutions albeit unstated (Cremin 1975). More simply stated, the curriculum is the who, what, how, when, and what for of education (Kliebard 1977).

But, of course, though the definition is simple, the ability to document every aspect of curriculum is impossible since there exists in every situation what Illich calls the hidden curriculum. Not only is this a phenomenon of curriculum in countries around the world, but he (1972:106) warns that: 'Everywhere the hidden curriculum of schooling initiates the citizen to the myth that bureaucracies guided by scientific knowledge are efficient and benevolent. Everywhere this same curriculum instills in the pupil the myth that increased production will provide a better life. And everywhere it develops the habit of self-defeating consumption of services and alienating production, the tolerance for institutional dependence, and the recognition of institutional rankings. The hidden curriculum of schools does all this in spite of contrary efforts undertaken by teachers and no matter what ideology prevails.'

What is known about curriculum models of vernacular, bilingual, and multilingual education in the Third World? Very little. As has been stated, a number of nations have established language planning agencies, often part of government, to handle questions of broad-based language planning issues; however, this has not happened in all countries. International efforts to bring about even discussion on these topics have not been sufficient in number or scope. Note there was a span of 26 years between the two major conferences held by UNESCO (1951-1977). Some of the more recent efforts that have been carried out have increased international understanding of the nature and scope of problems while restating the need for more discussion. For instance, at a meeting of the Assembly of Heads of African States and Governments in 1966, the Organization of African Unity Inter-African Bureau of Languages (OAU-BIL) was authorized, although it was not established until 1973. The reports on the First Inter American Conference on Bilingual Education, 1974 (Troike and Modiano 1975), Educational Planning in Multilingual Countries, 1978 (Solá and Weber 1978), Georgetown University Roundtable on Languages and Linguistics, 1978 (Alatis 1978), also restated the need.

The literature that is available on experiences in Third World countries supports the perspective that it is within the context of complex and often conflicting linguistic, social, and economic interests that national language policy, language of instruction policies, and curriculum decisions are made. Furthermore, generalizations about curricula are impossible in the absence of the needed data base on curriculum models, content, methods, and materials, and on formative and summative evaluations. Even with such data, generalizations would be difficult, if not inappropriate, particularly from a comparative perspective, given the little that is known about the historical and sociolinguistic context in which these programs are being developed and implemented in each country/region/community.

The literature available at this point is only suggestive with respect to the practice of vernacular, bilingual, and multilingual educational systems of the Third World from the broader perspective of curriculum. One indication that there has been significant consensus on future directions of educational change in the Third World is the widespread acceptance of the report of the International Commission on the Development of Education, *Learning to Be.* Adopted as the master plan for educational reform by almost all the member states of UNESCO, it advocates a pervasive restructuring of educational systems to promote life-long learning (Faure et al. 1972:v-vi).

An essential element of the report is its philosophical underpinnings. Its premises on the role of school in society synthesize educational ideologies as diverse as those of Carl Rogers, Ivan Illich, and Mao Tse-Tung. To a large extent, there is a very substantial amount of agreement among the Commission's recommendations, particularly those related to educational goals, but to a much lesser extent regarding the means by which to achieve these goals.

A number of recurring issues of national experiences in the Third World emerge from the literature. These are most often perceived and described as needs and deserve attention. However, after reviewing them, a number of questions arise related to the assumptions on which these curriculum efforts are based and the consequent quality and potential impact the curricula will have on the individuals and groups they purportedly seek to more effectively educate.

The needs and issues most often raised in the literature available include:

1. The need to improve language planning efforts, to increase vernacular language instruction, to resolve the inadequacies of the vernacular as a medium of instruction, and to develop/obtain effective models for first and second or multilingual language learning;
2. The need to translate curricula and curriculum models;
3. The need for more textbooks, materials, technology, and methodologies in vernacular/bilingual language;
4. The need to include culture in the curriculum, most often seen as subject (history) or content (social studies) rather than form;
5. The need for teachers who speak vernacular languages and the need to improve their skills.

The fact that much of the literature on the subject of curriculum can be grouped or cross grouped into such a limited number of clusters is of concern. Certainly, design, implementation, and evaluation of curriculum in Third World countries should probably not be less complex an undertaking than similar efforts elsewhere in the world. The substance of the clusters is also of concern. Taken independently, the needs represented by the clusters are certainly legitimate; on the other hand from a broader perspective one is impelled to ask why they focus on only one aspect of the who, what, when, how, and what for of education—that is, the linguistic aspect.

Other necessary questions that must be raised relate to the assumptions with which curriculum developers are working. Are they assuming that curriculum can be translated? Are they assuming that changing the language of instruction has no bearing on any or most other aspects of the curriculum? Are concepts of learning and schooling being confused? Are educational systems approaching vernacular/bilingual curriculum design comprehensively from local and societal levels and including in the design process input from and coordination with other local and national planning efforts? Regrettably, I suggest that in most cases the answer to the first three questions is yes and the answer to the last question is no.

Other questions related to the substance and process of vernacular/bilingual curriculum development in the Third World should be raised. Some will be posed in a review of the five clusters of needs, but it should be noted that an exhaustive treatment of all the national/local contexts from which these needs emerge is not possible even in the broader sense. The intention is to identify recurring themes from the limited literature available, to raise questions, and to identify avenues for future research.

In the first cluster of needs (to improve language planning efforts, to increase vernacular language instruction, to resolve the inadequacies of the vernacular as a medium of instruction, and to develop/obtain more effective models for first and second or multilingual language learning), some trends seem clear and others are either still emerging or given no attention in the literature that is available.

The literature indicates that there is a substantial amount of support for the use of the vernacular as a medium of instruction as well as a subject. Though the reasons for this support vary from context to context, there is also strong resistance to its use. Many argue that the absence of an orthography, the lack of technical terminology, and the lack of vernacular language materials (literature, history) make vernacular inadequate as a medium of the instruction. One of the roles of the language planning agencies often is to develop orthographies where they do not exist and to sponsor the writing of materials and tests.

Most linguists today feel that these efforts are well directed. Many agree that there is no reason why vernacular cannot be used as the medium of instruction by developing where necessary the orthographies or technical terminologies (Fishman 1976; UNESCO 1977). Many accomplishments have been reported in India (Goel and Saini 1972; Khubchandani 1978a,b), Tanzania (Mhina 1974), Southeast Asia (Lester 1974), China (Barnes 1978;

Fincher 1978; Schwarz 1962), Haiti (Dejean 1975; Foster 1980), Micronesia (Topping 1975), and Africa (Bamgbose 1976).

It is the planning process that is costly and time consuming, but it can be accomplished, depending on the commitment made to the effort, in the span of a few years (Fishman 1972). Another consideration is the function of the vernacular in the curriculum; that is, whether the vernacular language is used transitionally as a bridge to the regional/national language (as is the case in the United States, the Soviet Union, and Europe as per Lewis 1980) or, whether the vernacular is to be used as the basis for minimal literacy (Ferguson 1978).

There are, of course, other sources of opposition to vernacular language instruction. The concern has been expressed that it could be used as a vehicle to enforce or reinforce existing systems maintaining the poor as speakers of less prestigious languages. This was a subject of concern at the 1977 UNESCO meeting of experts and is also discussed by Afolayan (1978).

Other resistance has come from less expected sources. While there has been a substantial increase in the demand for access to education, there are still members of rural societies who fear that increased schooling will lead to their young leaving the villages for urban areas, thereby losing their earnings and disintegrating their familial systems and lifestyles. Such resistance in India was described by Goel and Saini (1972).

In addition to arguments based on self-concept, respect, and identity, arguments in favor of vernacular language education usually involve the more efficient learning of reading (Engle 1975) and of the second language (Modiano 1973). While findings are still not definitive, some very strong statements have been made including UNESCO's (1953:11): 'It is axiomatic that the best medium for teaching a child is his mother tongue.' Tucker (1977:40), based on the positive outcome of the Canadian immersion programs, has argued that: 'No uniform recommendation (such as the UNESCO axiom) can be made that will suffice for all pupils. The available empirical data do not permit universal generalizations. Rather, they highlighted the fact that constellations of social and attitudinal variables interact in unique ways in diverse sociolinguistic settings to affect the child's ultimate level of linguistic development.'

He suggests that vernacular language instruction may be most appropriate in settings where the average number of years of schooling completed is low and where social and economic pressures 'mark' the language. However, where home language is highly valued and parents actively encourage literacy, where social factors are such that a child's success can be predicted, and where bilingualism is valued, beginning school in a second language may well be appropriate, as in Canada's immersion experience. This, however, is not a common educational context in the Third World.

Other broadly held beliefs have also been challenged. Paulston (1969) suggests that second language learning and foreign language learning are more dissimilar than originally thought and that more research is needed in this area. However, she (1977) has also supported the position that the major problem in implementing bilingual education is not the absence of models and methods of language teaching. There are many available to meet the needs (Fishman 1976). More critical questions relate to the description and understanding of social, political, and economic factors that interact and come to bear on an educational program to produce bilingualism/multilingualism.

It is rarely argued that the vernacular should be the only language of instruction throughout the school system. (This is not to be confused with the fact that there have been nations that have made a vernacular language an official national language.) Rather, vernacular language instruction is most often transitional and, hence, compensatory. Illich argues against this trend. He suggests there is no basis for the imposition and overt concern about the teaching of any language. He (1979:60) depicts the difference between taught colloquial speech and vernacular speech as costly language and that which comes at no cost. He (1979:68) warns that language has become so much a commodity that education's primary task is the provision of institutions or factories in which language producers can equip citizens with ever-increasing shares in language stock.

The amount of effort and time given to learning first, second, and foreign languages in countries around the world is enormous. Hartshorne (1967) reports that 45 percent of the school day was spent on such learning in South Africa. This may be supportive of Illich's concerns. Yet there is every reason to believe, as Illich suggests, that divorcing language learning from learning and living is neither logical nor productive in terms of the broader goals of education—and certainly the curriculum.

With respect to language planning within the context of education and planning for national and social development, *Educational Planning in Multilingual Countries* (Solá and Weber 1978) outlines a meaningful and comprehensive planning process that takes into consideration the range of institutional and technical development needs.

In summary, there are few indications that educational language planning and planning for development are being approached in a coordinated and purposeful way. On the other hand, there has been substantial, though again not enough, activity to meet the needs, with respect to the expansion of the nomenclature (and in some cases orthographies) of vernacular languages. The trend is consistently to use vernaculars in education as a transitional bridge to the regional/national language(s) from a compensatory framework. There are increasing trends to continue to include it as a

subject in upper grades after the transition has taken place. But most agree
that Third World nations are met with complex problems in deciding what
language to teach in, for what length of time, and how, whether, and when
to introduce the other language(s). (Khubchandani 1978a; Yabar-Dextre
1978; Erickson 1960).

The second cluster of needs (to translate curriculum and curricular
models) is based, it would seem, on the assumption that curriculum can be
translated from a national unmarked language to vernacular (or many
vernacular languages) with no changes or with only minor changes, which
are usually called making the curriculum 'culturally relevant'. But, is this
assumption valid? Can curriculum be translated and transferred? Though
some may feel that much can be learned from the experience of other
educational systems both within nations and among nations, there is a great
deal of concern about such undertakings in the Third World, particularly in
light of the problems and outcomes of the drive for mass education in many
post-colonial societies. Many have realized that transference of Western
educational models is inappropriate, yet many Third World nations have
centralized educational systems that in many cases have made adjustments
in the Western curricular models and content they have carried over from
precolonial times, but educational outcomes continue to fall far short of
those desired.

The reality is that no nation has developed a bilingual model curriculum
that is transferable to every possible educational context (Fishman 1976;
Paulston 1977; Trueba 1979). Furthermore, there never will be.

Kimball (1974:24), in his anthropological study of culture in the
educational process from an international perspective, warns that
educational systems can not be modernized 'by reshuffling the bits and
pieces of a curriculum, adding a little of this or subtracting a little of that.
The transformation required is much more fundamental... It means
modifying the curriculum so as to emphasize the basic disciplines of
thought.' After discussing the failure of 'transplanted programs in Latin
America', he concludes (1974:251): 'We should have learned at least that
the educational practices from one culture cannot be transferred to another
with the expectation of gaining the same results.' The extent of the problem
becomes clear in Filho's (1957) intensive analysis of the curricula of many
of the nations of Latin America, among which he found marked
correspondences. Curriculum then cannot be translated and transferred
from one national context to the next. But what is international translation
and transference? Can a national curriculum be developed that in its
entirety will be both appropriate and productive in every ethnolinguistic
context within a nation? The literature suggests that much attention is being
given to the development of nationally relevant curricula; however, there is

very little to indicate that there is a need to develop curriculum that is specific to the cultures and needs of vernacular language groups. This is evident in the efforts of many planning agencies that have given attention to the need for national relevancy but have taken the simple translation approach for vernacular language groups. Once again, old mistakes are being repeated.

Goel and Saini (1972:64) relate that India suffered from this misconception in approaching the use of vernacular languages as media of instruction and concluded that this misconception was a major factor in impeding the progress of this effort. 'The third factor which was equally important in retarding the process of change regarding the teaching of mother tongue lay in the mind of educationists themselves. For instance, it was thought that the teaching of mother tongue was more or less the same as teaching of certain textbooks in the mother tongue. This was a patently erroneous impression that continued to prevail for long.'

Curricula that are an outgrowth of national language policies that are transitional in nature (the temporary use of the vernacular during a limited period—one to five years—until the national or official school language(s) are introduced) have only limited potential for solving the many problems of rural poor populations. The average number of years of schooling completed by these vernacular language speakers is usually minimal. Educational resources and expenditures are disproportionate to those in urban areas.

If meaningful societal participation and preparation for personal growth, 'learning how to learn', are to any extent the answers to the 'what for' question that should be raised by curriculum developers, then the curriculum goals of many Third World countries are not being achieved. This is evident in the growing numbers of youths leaving rural villages. Urban flight is perceived by many as a result of the inability of the curriculum to relate schooling to the need for rural manpower and the often misdirected push for universal education and development. Instead, the curriculum gives more value to urban languages and lifestyles and encourages the flight from rural areas (Illich 1972; Sheffield 1976; Ward 1974). However, this has caused a crisis in the cities where the number of unemployed youths continues to increase. If national development is to be achieved, rural development must take place. The growing demands for agricultural products from the cities make one dependent on the other (Eisemon 1977). There may be hope, however. This is apparent in the substance of the UNESCO report *Learning to Be* (Faure et al. 1972) and in many endeavors in the Third World to integrate education with rural planning and development efforts (UNESCO 1968). Some notable examples include planning and reform efforts in Tanzania (Nyerere 1967) and Cuba.

Cuba obliterated illiteracy by providing instruction in the homes of the rural poor farmers, which was administered by the 'children of revolution' (Kozol 1978). Of course, these reform efforts were accompanied by substantial social change. Hawes on the other hand, is not optimistic. He (1972:17) concludes that despite the new syllabuses, the new books, the curriculum conferences, the curriculum centers, the international programs, relatively little impact is actually being made on the primary school curriculum. Nor, he suggests, is there any reason to believe that rapid changes are likely to occur unless there is a totally new approach to curriculum planning.

The need for new states to totally restructure their philosophy and social structures for schooling has been strongly supported by Illich (1972) and Freire (1978). However, though some gains have been made, many problems persist that may be rooted in allegiances to old practices. Many Western structural, sequencing, and organizational patterns have remained prevalent in the curriculum—the bureaucracies, the overemphasis on tests and testing, the tracking, the push to standardization (Hawes 1972). These trends can only stymie the development and experimentation needed in Third World contexts and increase social polarization.

Curriculum development from a local rather than national level was supported by Sweeney (1975) who sees education as a two-way process that can most effectively be developed by local microlevel analysis of needs rather than by national strategies.

The *Letters to Guinea-Bissau* written by Paulo Freire constitute a blueprint of how a new nation state went about analyzing the who, what, when, how, and what for of education. Essentially, it reflects a deeply rooted concern with the welfare and quality of life of the poorest segments of society—those who have been bypassed by so-called development efforts in the past. The reader emerges with a more humanistic view of development—one that would no longer be measured simply in terms of G.N.P. Freire (1978:104-5) offers hope: 'Needs of learners can be defined in close relation to new pedagogical methods. In the final analysis, the reorientation of the educational system can overcome totally the colonial inheritance. It demands different content, different conception of education. The definition of what should be learned even at the level of literacy education for adults and the creation of programmatic content cannot be thought of apart from the reorientation of the educational system so that it is consistent with the plan for a new society.'

Evidence that nations are asking the right questions in developing and analyzing the applicability of curriculum to specific contexts will emerge when there is evidence that there is less transference and more activity in the areas of specific language and culture curricula development. The literature from Third World countries describing the need for vernacular language texts and materials, the third cluster of needs, is abundant. This is a natural outgrowth already discussed. Consequently, the inadequacy of developing vernacular language materials, texts and methodologies using transference, translation, or other adaptive approaches will not be repeated.

However, it is appropriate to note that some very positive steps have been taken in a number of countries. Once again, these advancements must be viewed from the total international context of education in the Third World. The control of publishing, distribution, and pricing of books by European and Western powers has often had a deleterious effect on national textbook development and production efforts (Carnoy 1974).

In India, despite early misdirection of efforts and problems of the nature just described, changes in policies regarding the language of instruction have recently prompted an examination of the process and products of vernacular language textbook development with the result that some very good materials have been produced in some areas of the country (Goel and Saini 1972).

The fact that only one reading primer was developed in Cuba for its very effective literacy campaign (Kozol 1978) might be viewed as an argument against the need for massive production of textbooks. Yet, here again, application of this experience to other settings is almost impossible—the linguistic and political experience of Cuba is unique.

The need for vernacular language materials and textbooks has been described in Peru (Lagoria and Ballon 1976), South Africa (De Beer 1967), Southeast Asia (Lester 1974), the Philippines (Sibayan 1978), Africa (Afolayan 1978; Bamgbose 1976), and other international discussions focusing on vernacular/bilingual education. The proceedings of the First Inter American Conference on Bilingual Education also reflects the needs identified in Latin America (Troike and Modiano 1975). The new Inter-African Bureau of Languages has also set comprehensive goals for the development of textbooks, materials, and methodologies for vernacular and bi- or multilingual education efforts in many vernaculars (Kalema 1980). UNESCO (1977) recapitulated needs in this area from a broader perspective.

Experiments with new methodologies in Kenya, Nigeria, and Tanzania (Sheffield 1973), Peru (Paulston 1969, 1972; Solá 1979), Cuba (Kozol 1978), and other nations have in some instances been overwhelmingly successful, in others less so, but they may serve to support the experimentation and development efforts of other Third World nations.

A substantial amount of concern about the need and use of technology and media appears in the literature. Sweeney's (1975) criticism of the use of modern communications systems as viable mechanisms to reach the urban poor concurs with Illich's (1972) warnings and preoccupations. Both suggest that the massive expenditures have not had impressive impact on the rural poor: inappropriate technology and models, such as television, were imported. A second problem is the narrowness of the medium. Illich suggests that investment in audio cassette systems would be more appropriate than TV to achieve educational ends since people would be encouraged to record, listen, and use language rather than just be passive observers. In fact, much interest has surfaced in increasing the use of vernacular languages in all communication systems, newspapers, TV, and radio (Albo 1974; Engelbrecht 1980).

The fourth cluster of needs (to include culture in the curriculum) is perceived by many as a necessary component of the curriculum for two reasons, political and pedagogical—though the first is more apparent. Some may question whether vernacular language groups have distinct cultural patterns and heritages. While no axiomatic statement is possible because of the broad definition of vernacular language used here, the case may well be made that cultural heterogeneity almost invariably accompanies linguistic heterogeneity. Cultural diversity within and among nations of the Third World is considerable. However, increasing immigration concomitant with urbanization and technological advancement are increasing the incidence of multiculturalism, a fact that is the norm in human interaction around the world.

The question of the extent or nature of cultural variance must be raised for each group within each national/local context for which vernacular/ bilingual programs are being designed. In addition to purely cultural differences, there are other aspects of diversity, as has been discussed, that to some extent accompany or interact with linguistic and cultural differences. These include economic, social, and political differences. Variables that receive most attention in the literature (to the extent that they are confounded with one another at times) are those related to class, race, and urban vs. rural lifestyles. Increasingly, questions are being raised about the affective aspects of culture, class, and lifestyle and what bearing these have on linguistic and cognitive processes and outcomes of schooling.

The political impetus to include culture in the curriculum is most often an outgrowth of the perception of schools as socializing institutions. Just as many new states view language as a source of unity and identity, they also view a common culture as a source of national unity. While there is evidence that aspects of culture have been included in the massive curriculum development efforts that have taken place throughout the Third World (the Cultural Revolution in China being one of the most obvious examples), the endeavor in most countries limited itself first to curriculum content. The inclusion of subjects (history, religion, values, vernacular language) in the revision of curriculum from the perspective of culture as subject is, of course, relatively easily accomplished as it constitutes a rather minor accommodation of the curriculum. In addition, this type of reform is subject to less negative reaction from the dominant language and culture groups, particularly if these changes are limited to the curriculum offered vernacular language speakers. Minority group members, on the other hand, might feel that culture must be included in the curriculum because they fear the possibility of losing their culture as individuals or, from a collective perspective, the possible extinction of their culture.

In any event, culture as subject is most often a transitional accommodation to human diversity. In addition to tacking on subjects, other accommodations of the curriculum usually include the preparation of what are generally termed 'culturally relevant' texts and materials. That is, they are designed to reflect the culture by inserting names, places, and topics that are perceived to be germane to a group's cultural experience.

Since the quest for cultural transmission through the curriculum is so often political and based on conflicting motives and goals (the majority seeking uniformity and a national culture; minorities seeking to maintain cultural modes and perhaps 'unity in diversity'), understandably the literature contains little consensus and, in fact, contradictory evidence about the role of culture in the educational process. At the root of this controversy is the question: Are unity and diversity conceptually contradictory? Many suggest they are. Broudy (1972:143), a well known Western educator, states: 'Extreme cultural relativism, the principle involved to justify cultural pluralism and ultimately anarchic individualism is an interesting philosophy, but a misleading description of social reality. It makes social life impossible because each man—not man as distinguished from God—becomes the measure of all things and if schooling has any relevance to social reality, cultural pluralism cannot rule the curriculum and alternative programs cannot be multiplied indefinitely. For the schools to be accountable, responsibilities must be limited and to some extent directed to common goals.'

Others argue that culture is a necessary component of the curriculum since the culture of a society represents the ways in which a group of people have organized their experiences to give them a world view which provides them a basis for (1) explaining their environments in cause-effect terms; (2) framing purposes; (3) distinguishing the desirable from the undesirable; and (4) formulating the means by which recurring problems are solved (Goodenough 1963). The preferred outlook, values, modes of interaction, and cognitive skills children bring with them to the classroom must be taken into consideration in designing all educational experiences if they are to have positive cognitive and affective outcomes. (Irvine and Sanders 1972; Ramirez and Castañeda 1974).

On the other hand, the more substantive questions raised today relate to language and thought as well as culture and thought, and these are perceived to have implications for curriculum in the broader context of pedagogy. Ben Zeev (1977) and Cummins (1974, 1977) argue that there is an influence of bilingualism on cognitive growth and functioning and that a great deal more attention must be given the matter. With respect to culture, that is, questions are being raised, and research conducted on the relationships between culture and language learning, culture and perception, culture and conceptual processes, culture and problem solving, culture and learning, culture and memory, and many other relationships (Cole and Scribner 1974). Much has been done to eliminate the notion of the inferior 'primitive mentality' due to 'cultural deprivation'. As an outgrowth of research conducted in Liberia, Cole et al. (1971) argue that what differs between cultures is not the quality of thought processes, but the content premises of thought and the situations and conditions that elicit thinking. The nature and extent to which a group brings skills to a task differ as a function of the culture's emphasis on the task involved. Current neurological research on language processing and organization in multilinguals (Benderly 1981) are also contributing to our understanding. For cross-cultural discussions and studies that address some of these relationships from the following inter- and intranational populations, see: Mexican children in the United States (Holtzman et al. 1975), Meztizos and Indians in Mexico (Hunt and Hunt 1970), Navajo and Anglos in the United States (John 1972), Ugandan and British (Musgrove 1973), and many cases in other African contexts (Irvine and Sanders 1972) including Basutoland (Wallman 1972).

For the fifth and last cluster of needs (for teachers who speak the vernacular language and the need to improve their skills) much has been written throughout the Third World about the necessary linguistic skills, attitudes, and ability to apply culturally relevant teaching methodologies. The problems stem from a variety of realities. In many instances teachers called upon to implement new vernacular language policies were not trained to do so. Furthermore, they were often members of the upper class who had access to higher education, which might suggest a social distance between themselves and the vernacular speakers. They are often bilingual but not fluent in the vernacular of the groups they are supposed to teach. The push for mass compulsory education in the 1960's increased access to education but resulted in a similar demand for teachers. Disparities in the allocation of educational resources resulted in differences of quality between the teachers in urban and rural areas. For a discussion of this situation in South Africa, see Malherbe (1978); for discussions of these problems in other countries consult the following: India (Goel and Saini 1972); West Africa (Abiri

1976); Nigeria (Taiwo 1976); South Africa (Hartshorne 1967); and Black Africa (Afolayan 1978); international (Hawes 1972).

There are many questions about teachers' language skills. These include: What are the requisite affective, linguistic, and cognitive competencies of a vernacular/bilingual teacher in a Third World setting? How can these be developed? How can teachers with the needed skills be identified?

The fact that Western influences in schools of education in the Third World have been so prevalent, the fact that vernacular languages are not often used as the medium of instruction (though there is an increasing trend to introduce vernacular languages and cultures as subjects of instruction), and the fact that testing systems and other mechanisms have continued to a large extent to discriminate against the very vernacular language speakers who are needed, are all issues that need to be assessed within each national/local educational context. Though such treatment is not possible here, the reader is encouraged to read the paper by Saville-Troike and Troike in this publication, which treats the issues of vernacular/bilingual teacher training from an international perspective.

CONCLUSION

This review of vernacular language education in the Third World suggests that there is a need to document and describe vernacular/bilingual curricula content, models, and outcomes as well as the interaction between organizations and systems (from the school to the societal level) responsible for the curricula within the socio-political and economic national/local environments in which they are implemented. (Hawes 1972 states that Third World nations are currently spending about .2% of their budgets on research.) In the absence of such research, the literature suggests the following:

Curriculum development to meet the needs of linguistically complicated nations of the Third World is a complex undertaking. There are no simple answers that can be transposed from one nation to another. The reality is that linguistic heterogeneity will persist. If complex social, political, and economic problems of any nation are to be resolved in a manner productive for all segments of society, major changes must be made in education and schooling—language is only one of many considerations, though a key one.

New states would do well to reassess their concept of 'nation', and 'education', and the role language plays in each. This concept of nationhood should be an outgrowth of a philosophy of man. If it is a philosophy of free man, the education must be liberating. Curriculum must be guided by this new philosophy. However, the design and implementation of curriculum must be based on local micro-level needs rather than on imposed national edicts.

Countries that truly seek to develop by opening participation to broader bases of their citizenry must redefine other social structures and organizations. The new challenge for curriculum development in the Third World, then, is not only reaching decisions about what language minorities are educated in but who, what, how, when they are taught, and for what?

* * *

The prospects for educational reform then are mixed. Countries that seek to be responsive to the needs of linguistic minorities may change from a traditionalist view of education as the provision of knowledge and skills to a view that endeavors to liberate the human spirit and give opportunities for oppressed groups to contribute and participate and to have greater control over their own futures. However, if the elites, monied, and empowered by perpetuating social and linguistic controls allow their own parochial interests to assume priority in a world in crisis, then we can expect to see inadequate and temporary accommodations to the needs and potential contributions of vernacular language groups, limited in scope, potential, and impact.

EDUCATION REFORM AND THE
INSTRUMENTALIZATION OF THE VERNACULAR
IN HAITI

ALBERT VALDMAN

INTRODUCTION

Haiti is the leading creolophone country in the world: its entire population, estimated at more than five million, speaks the vernacular language, Haitian Creole (HC), and only ten per cent possess a fair command of the official language, French. Since the late 1940s, the vernacular has evidenced steady progress toward attaining the status of national language.[1] Although HC has not been granted official status, the constitution of the state stipulates the possible use of the vernacular in administrative or judicial matters in order to guarantee equal rights to monolingual Creole speakers. Increasingly, HC is displacing French in radio broadcasts; the readership of three monthly newsletters written exclusively in Creole (*Bon Nouvèl, Boukan, Bwa Chandèl*) has now reached more than 50,000; some of the more creative writers have adopted the vernacular, notably the playwright and novelist Frankétienne (*Pèlin Tèt, Dézafi*). The most significant event in this continuous extension of the domains of use of the vernacular has been a clearly enunciated shift in official educational policy. The Ministry of Education has proclaimed a new program whose keystone is the use of HC as the main classroom language at the first primary cycle, comprising the first four years of schooling (Bernard 1980).

But if Creole becomes in effect an auxiliary official language through which the children of the monolingual rural masses are to gain access to the written word, concerted efforts for its standardization and instrumentalization need to be undertaken. As has been the case in the development of other vernaculars, the introduction of HC in public and formal functions forces language planners to confront the problem of variation. Inevitably also, standardization and instrumentalization take place against a backdrop of economic, political, and social issues.

THE LANGUAGE SITUATION OF HAITI

Language planning in Haiti must start with an accurate characterization of the linguistic situation of the country. When Charles Ferguson (1959), in his seminal article, redefined the notion of diglossia, one of the four illustrative cases he chose was that of Haiti. However a closer look at the structural and functional differences between HC and French renders somewhat inappropriate the use of the term diglossia to describe the present linguistic situation of the Haitian nation as a whole. As will be shown below, that type of linguistic situation does apply to one of the country's two subcommunities, the bilingual elite.[2]

First, from a structural point of view HC and French differ significantly not only at the morphosyntactic level but at the phonological and lexical levels as well. A comparison of the two languages, if it is extended beyond the mere matching of phonemic inventories, reveals striking differences in phonotactic and sandhi phenomena. For example, the vernacular lacks the two most salient morphophonemic features in French, elision and liaison. These phenomena, it will be recalled, involve alternations in the forms of morphemes determined by the first segment of the following morpheme. Elision describes the obligatory deletion of the morphophoneme before any vowel; liaison subsumes the deletion, obligatory under certain syntactic environments, of latent consonants. In HC the vowels of certain morphemes are elided but the phenomenon affects a small set of lexical items (mostly pronouns and verb markers). Most importantly, in HC elision may be optional as well as obligatory and the triggering phonological environment may both follow or precede the truncatable vowel, e.g. *li ale/l ale* 'he/she went', *li kouri* 'he/she ran', *poukisa l kouri* 'why did he/she run', *kote pitit li* 'where is his/her child', *kote papa li/ kote papa l* 'where is his/her father.'

Although the lexicons of French and Creole contain many cognate terms, semantic shifts, and profound differences in culture, ecology, and external influences have introduced great lexical distance between the two languages. The large proportion of cognates is misleading, for their meanings often diverge markedly, e.g., *frekan* (Fr. *fréquent*) does not mean 'frequent' but 'insolent' (Fr. *effronté*); *demanbre* (Fr. *démembré*) means 'exhausted' and not 'quartered'. Finally, as a language that has evolved from French through the structural upheavals inherent in the processes of pidginization and creolization, Creole can in no way be considered genetically related to its base-language. Thus, French and Creole are two distinct languages rather than two closely related varieties of a single tongue.

True functional complementation does not obtain between HC and French (Dejean 1978). For the bilingual elite, on the one hand, French covers all vernacular functions, including intimate conversations and, on the other hand, no domain of use and no communicative situation are exempt from the encroachment of HC. Among this social group both languages are learned at home. In the countryside, HC has gained entry in most vehicular and referential spheres of rural life and culture; the religious domain (both sermons and proselytizing), local administrative matters, use in the classroom mainly as transitional and support language, and radio broadcasts. So far as rural masses are concerned (Dejean 1978):

Creole is the sole linguistic instrument serving all their mental, intellectual, psychological, social and individual activities. One can hardly state that Creole is excluded from various sophisticated domains of use to which an illiterate population has in fact no access.

Even though the respective domains of use of HC and French are not as rigorously demarcated as the classical definition of diglossia suggests, finely graded sociolinguistic observations would undoubtedly reveal a certain degree of functional complementarity between the two languages.

More accurately Haiti is a nation composed of two distinct linguistic communities: the urban elite and the rural masses. The former, constituting a politically and economically dominant minority, is both bilingual *and* diglossic. Its members have varying degrees of control of the country's two languages and use them in partial complementation. They acquire French and HC in the home environment and, as is the case for children in all francophone countries, perfect their control of the official language at school. The rural masses are unilingual for all intents and purposes. In view of the lack of interaction between the two communities, rare are the occasions for country folks to use French; the vernacular adequately meets all the communicative needs of their cultural, economical and political universe. More importantly, the mass media and the schools are the sole vectors that bring French to them (see Figure 1).

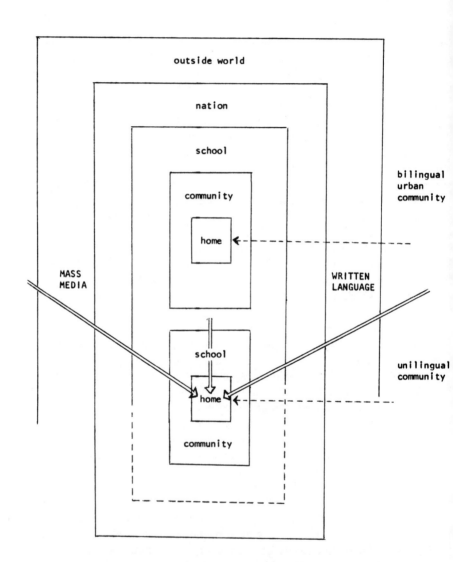

Figure 1. *Communication networks in Haiti*

In addition to HC unilingualism profound cultural, economic, and social differences set off the Haitian countryside from the cities. The rural masses comprising more than 80 per cent of the country's population, show little cultural, economic, and social differentiation. They are predominantly dark skinned, they engage in vaudoun practices and other African-based cultural activities, among them common law unions and some polygamy is the rule, and, except for a small group of fairly prosperous owners of large and medium-sized land'holdings, they eke out a living by subsistence farming and agricultural labor (Wingfield 1966). The urban dwellers are more differentiated. At the top are found the traditional bourgeoisie, comprising about two per cent of the nation's population. Its members, descendants of the free mulattoes of the colonial era, tend to be lighter skinned or to have some Caucasian physical features. They enter into legal marriage and are practicing Catholics. The next lowest urban social strata, the middle class and artisan group, form about five per cent of the population. Though usually dark skinned, their cultural, religious, and social characteristics differ little from the traditional bourgeoisie, except that among them the proportion of formal concubinage (*ménage* or *placée*) increases, as does participation in vaudoun ceremonies. The urban proletariat and unemployed or semi-employed members of the lower strata differ little from the rural masses from which they derive. The slums of Port-au-Prince, the capital and only large city of Haiti, are filled from displaced peasants trading one type of misery and marginal existence for another.

EDUCATIONAL UNDERDEVELOPMENT IN HAITI

Perhaps the most striking difference in economic development between the rural and urban communities of Haiti resides in the level of educational development. It was estimated that in 1971 78 per cent of the nation's population was functionally illiterate. The estimates range from 44 per cent in the urban centers to 87 in the countryside (Wiesler 1978). It is noteworthy that, whereas in the urban community male and female illiteracy rates differed by a factor of 3:2, the number of rural male functional literates was twice that of females' functional literacy. For that year 82 per cent of rural males and 94 per cent of rural females above the age of 20 had never attended school.

The 1971 estimates reported seven years later by Wiesler (1978), based on a ten per cent sampling, indicate that the wide gap between the level of education of urban and rural dwellers does not show signs of lessening. For the 6-11 year old group four times as many city children attend school as do offsprings of peasants:

Age Group	Haiti overall	Urban	Rural
6-11	24%	62%	14%
12-18	29	57	20
19-24	8	15	5

Not only do a minority of rural children enroll in school, but an infinitessimal proportion of those who enter the first grade complete the seven-year primary sequence. During the school year 1976-77 only three per cent of a total number of 136,381 pupils began the seventh year of the primary cycle. That year, nearly half the rural primary school population was concentrated in the Enfantine class, the first year of rural primary school (The percentage figures refer to the proportion of the total rural primary school population enrolled in 1971, e.g. 48% of enrollments were in the first-year classes.):

Grade (1-7)	Total Enrollment	Percentage	
Enfantine	64,996	48%	
Préparatoire I	24,883	18	
Préparatoire II	17,158	12.5	
Elementaire I	12,549	8.5	
			87
Elémentaire II	8,257	6	
Moyen I	5,228	4	
Moyen II	3,360	3	
			13
			100

The low level of school attendance and the catastrophic attrition rate reflected by the statistics in Figure 2 above stem from economic factors. The Haitian government, which controls schools in which are enrolled two-thirds of rural pupils, allocates the greater part of educational funds to the urban sector. There remain insufficient resources to build the necessary number of classrooms and to train and remunerate adequately teaching and supervisory personnel. In addition, many rural peasants cannot afford to release children from activities that assure family subsistence. Others cannot pay even the minimal school fees (less than $5.00 per year) and the cost of books and uniforms.

The minority of rural children who attend school and complete the first four years of the primary cycle seldom attains functional literacy. Typically, class size ranges from 75 to 100. It is not unusual for several classes to be held in the same room. The instructional model adopted may best be characterized as transitional monoliterate bilingual education (Fishman and Lovas 1970). French is the object of instruction and children are taught to read and write that language only. However, most teachers, cognizant of the fact that their charges seldom have an opportunity to use the official language and possess no effective competence in it, employ HC as medium of instruction. Under these conditions of instruction pupils may be able to recognize French words (particularly if they are cognates) and even pronounce them with fair accuracy, but, in view of the profound grammatical differences between the two languages, they are unlikely to understand written and spoken discourse. Since theirs is an exclusively unilingual HC environment, whatever linguistic skills they may have acquired at school will rapidly deteriorate. Finally, it is clear that the traditional system of rural primary education yields a relatively low level of formal learning and of control of instructional content.

Any endeavor aiming at fostering development in Haiti must aid in the bridging of the cultural, economic, and social gaps between the urban and the rural communities. One option would be to extend competence in French to all segments of the population through the intermediary of the schools and adult literacy programs. The prohibitive costs of this alternative force one to opt for the other choice: through language planning activities, to accelerate the extension of HC so that it may accede to those vehicular and referential functions relevant in the rural universe.

To achieve more cost-effective primary school programs and a significant increase in school attendance and retention in rural areas, the Ministry of Education has launched a reform program. The innovative program, supported by a loan from the World Bank, involves construction of new schools and a thoroughgoing change in pedagogical approach, and is predicated on the use of HC as the exclusive medium of instruction and as the object of instruction during a new four-year primary school cycle.

The new reform curriculum, now in its second year of trial in 600 classes, starts from the widely accepted premise that learning is more effectively imparted in a child's native tongue. Children are taught to read first in HC, and all instructional content is imparted by means of the vernacular. French is introduced from the first year of schooling, but as a foreign language in which pupils must receive explicit instruction and which they must practice orally. When children demonstrate the ability to read and write their native language and when they have acquired sufficient proficiency in spoken French, they are taught to read and write the official language. It is intended that, gradually, French will assume the function of classroom vehicle, so that it will serve as the chief means for the transmission of instructional content in the second half of the primary system (years 5-8) and, presumably, the exclusive one at the secondary and university levels.

The use of HC as principal educational tool in rural Haiti is eminently realistic and, if adequate resources are available for its implementation and generalization, the innovative educational model should lead to cost-effective instruction in the first four-year primary cycle. However, it does raise several problems not confronted heretofore in Haiti since the use of the vernacular educational medium was limited generally to adult literacy programs. Its introduction within the scope of a concerted national program requires the preparation of an extensive set of teaching materials and it directly involves the government in a variety of language planning activities. In this paper, I will deal with two of these: (1) the elaboration and adoption of a fairly uniform orthography, and (2) lexical enrichment necessitated by the accession of the vernacular to new domains of use.

THE ELABORATION OF A SPELLING FOR HC

From the acrimonious debate over a few minor alphabetical choices currently taking place in Haiti one would not guess that the elaboration of an autonomous phonologically-based spelling is more advanced in that nation than any other creole-speaking territory. The production of materials in HC is currently proceeding at a brisk pace. To the sizable amount of texts purporting to evangelize, edify, or educate are being added productions with literary and ludic intent and reference works. The debate over alphabetical conventions began nearly forty years ago when Ormonde McConnell, a Methodist pastor of Scotch-Irish origin, and Frank Laubach, the American specialist in mass literacy, introduced the first phonologically-based orthography.

That discussions over the choice of alphabet for the representation of HC have generated more heat than light stems in large part from the absence of global theoretical perspectives on the part of the proponents of various notations. Jean Bernabé is not altogether unfair when he qualifies these various attempts as 'empirical' (Bernabé 1976). In his admirable discussion of the elaboration of orthographies Jack Berry (1958) identifies four sets of factors that need to be considered: (1) linguistic, (2) psycho-pedagogical, (3) technical, (4) socio-political. It is the last set of factors that developers of orthographies for HC have failed to consider carefully or to address explicitly. In Haiti, the choice of alphabet and the degree of standardization imposed on an orthography cannot be dissociated from a fundamental socio-political issue: For whom is the orthography intended and toward what end? The central problems posed in the elaboration of an orthography reside in the diglossic relationship between HC and French in the Haitian linguistic community viewed broadly as constituted by the entire nation rather than one or the other of its two component sub-communities. In view of the bilingual elite's socio-political dominance and, accordingly, that of French, it is nearly impossible to conceive of an education program addressed to the unilingual masses that would be conducted through the intermediary of Creole alone. Even though numerous proposals have been put forward for adult literacy programs or basic elementary education programs using HC as instructional medium, their proponents have been careful to manage some sort of bridge to French; witness the recurrent deference to 'le passage au français'.[3]

The first attempts to represent HC featured a highly variable etymological spelling. The most systematic spelling of that type was employed by a Haitian diplomat and amateur man of letters, Georges Sylvain, in his adaptation in HC of La Fontaine's fables (1901). Although he adhered closely to the French model, Sylvain did attempt to note distinctive features of HC pronunciation, for example, the nasalization of vowels, in the environment of nasal consonants: *monmainm* ([mõmẽn], Fr. *moi-même*), *janmain* ([žãmẽ], Fr. *jamais*), *trinnin* ([trẽnẽ], Fr. *traîner*). He devised an efficient manner of noting final pronounced consonants, particularly in cognates of French lexical items whose final written consonant is silent: *lanuitt* ([lanɥit], Fr. *la nuit*), *laitt* ([lɛt], Fr. *lait*), *souritt* ([surit], Fr. *souris*). But the materials in HC produced by Sylvain and other Haitian intellectuals and writers were literary productions aimed at members of the bilingual educated elite; they were not designed to teach literacy to members of the unilingual rural masses.

Such was precisely the objective McConnell set for himself (McConnell and Swan 1945). His immediate goal was to impart reading and writing skills to adult illiterates in rural districts. Consequently he sought spelling conventions of as low a level of abstraction as possible that would provide a bi-unique representation of the phonemes of the language. Thus, he opted for the use of *w* and *y* in the notation of semivowels and for the use of the circumflex to represent the nasal vowels (see Table 3). But unfortunately, in the late forties Haiti was emerging from two decades of 'pacification' by the U.S. Marine Corps. Haitian intellectuals, favorably disposed toward an autonomous, as versus an etymological and frenchifying representation for HC, reacted intemperately against what they viewed as 'Anglo-Saxon' letters (Pressoir 1947).[4] In 1946 Pressoir and the then minister of education, L. Faublas, introduced a variant of the McConnell-Laubach spelling featuring French-inspired representations for the nasal vowel and the semivowels that departed slightly from bi-uniqueness (see Table 1). The Faublas-Pressoir counterproposal involved the use of the hyphen to distinguish the nasal vowel /ẽ/ from the corresponding sequence /in/ (*in* vs. *i-n*) and required several rules for the representation of the semivowel /j/ by means of *y* (initial, finally and intervocally) and *i* (pre-vocalically): *yo* 'they', *bagay* 'thing', *piyay* 'abundance'; *pié* 'foot', *misié* 'Mister'.[5]

Table 1. *Letter correspondences between three spelling systems for Haitian Creole*

IPA	McConnell-Laubach	Faublas-Pressoir (ONAAC)	IPN
Nasal vowels			
ẽ	ê	in	en
ã	â	an	an
õ	ô	on	on
ẽn	ên	inn	enn
ãn	ân	ann	ann
õn	ôn	onn	onn
ũn	ûn	oun	oun
ĩn	în	i-n	in
Oral vowel & N			
in	in	i-n	in
òn	òn	òn	òn
an	an	a-n	àn
un	un	oun	oun
Mid vowels			
e	è	è	è
ɛ	é	é	e
o	o	o	o
ɔ	ò	ò	ò
Semivowels			
j	y/i	y (initial, final, intervocalic) i (pre-vocalic)	y
w	w	w (initial and intervocalic) ou (pre-vocalic)	w
Initial and post-consonantal r			
w	r	r	w

The Faublas-Pressoir notation, rechristened 'alphabet ONAAC' when it was adopted by the government agency responsible for community development and literacy, is today the most widely used spelling for Creole. In 1974 the CRESH (Centre de Recherche en Sciences Humaines et Sociales) of Port-au-Prince organized a seminar during which the Québecois linguist, Gilles Lefebvre, and the noted Haitian scholar, Pradel Pompilus, presented an orthography sponsored by that organization. The CRESH spelling contained additional frenchifying features. Pointing out the systematic nature of the use of *c* and *qu* and *g* and *gu* to represent /k/ in French, the CRESH group advocated the use of this more abstract convention for HC; in addition, they proposed the replacement of the sequence /wa/ by the digraph *oi* and the use of *x* for the sequence /ks/.[6] These modifications of the Faublas-Pressoir spelling were incorporated in the 'Pan-Creole' orthography employed in bilingual readers distributed by the ACCT (Agence de Coopération Culturelle et Technique), a francophone agency, and they were advocated by members of a mission sent by the French Ministry of Foreign Affairs to assist Haitian educators in a pedagogical renovation of primary instruction.[7] Several years later, another French group, consisting of linguists from the University of Paris-V (René Descartes) was dispatched by the Ministry of Foreign Affairs to provide technical support to the ONAAC. They devised a spelling notation (labelled IPN in Table 1) that returned to the 'Anglo-Saxon' letters employed by the McConnell-Laubach system for the representation of the semivowels. In addition the René Descartes group streamlined the representations of the mid vowels by eliminating the use of the acute accent in the notation of /e/ and adhered to the use of *w* to note /w/ before rounded vowels. In Creole the distinction between the velar resonant /χ/ and the rounded semivowel and /w/ is neutralized in the latter environment; only a labialized velar glide occurs. But since words containing combinations of the labialized velar following a rounded vowel or labial consonant have French cognates showing *r*, both the McConnell-Laubach and ONAAC Faublas-Pressoir spellings represent them with the letter *r*: /wõ/ *rond* (ONAAC *ron*, IPN *won*), /wuj/ *rouge* (ONAAC *rouj*, IPN *wouj*). Undoubtedly the IPN orthography provides a more consistent representation for HC than the Faublas-Pressoir notation. But it should be underscored that the two schemes differ only by the choice of a half dozen phoneme-to-letter conversions; both are autonomous, systematic representations of the language. These two spellings depart from several of the bi-unique (one phoneme—one symbol) conventions of the McConnell-Laubach notations in the interest of an illusory facilitation of the 'passage to French' (Lofficial 1979). For example, the use of the circumflex accent to represent nasalization of vowels (see Table 3) instead of the diagraphs vowel *n* avoids potentially ambiguous sequences:[8]

McConnell-Laubach			IPN	
sêyê	'to bleed'		senyen	[sẽjẽ] or [sinjẽ]
vâyâ	'hard working'		vanyan	[vãjã] or [vanjã]

It also eliminated the use of the grave accent to disambiguate sequences oral vowel + *n*:

McConnell-Laubach				IPN	
pê	pin	'bread'	'penis'	pen	pin
pâ	pan	'edge'	'breakdown'	pan	pàn

In September 1979, by the same presidential edict that permitted the use of HC as medium of instruction in the new four-year primary cycle, the IPN spelling was declared official. All public and private organizations involved in education and the preparation of materials in the vernacular were enjoined to adopt the new orthography. Furthermore, a period of four years was allowed for 'experimentation'. This latter clause of the decree tended to cast some doubts about the permanency of the officialized orthography.

Since the elaboration of the McConnell-Laubach spelling in the 1940's most of the preparation of materials in HC has been undertaken by private, non-governmental groups. A consortium of Protestant groups (Comité Protestant d'alphabétisation) and a Catholic team (Bon Nouvèl) have been particularly active in disseminating periodicals (*Bon Nouvèl, Boukan*) and a variety of evangelical and educational materials. In the mid fifties these groups adopted the Faublas-Pressoir (ONAAC) spelling. Many adult literacy programs associated with them have imparted literacy to thousands of adults, and they have initiated the use of the vernacular at the primary school level (Valdman 1980). Understandably, these groups were disconcerted by the officialization of the IPN orthography, which left them in a quandary. Should they switch to the new orthography at the risk of alienating their readership? Or should they risk incurring the displeasure of government officials by adhering to their own spelling conventions until the end of the period of experimentation?

In a sense the new proposal served as a catalyst for modifications whose need was perceived by users of the Faublas-Pressoir system. For several years there had been discussions about the representation of the nasal vowel /ẽ/ (*in* or *en*), about a more systematic use of the hyphen (eliminating its use to resolve some of the infelicities of phoneme-letter conventions, e.g., the choice of *i-n* to represent the sequence /in/ because the use of *in* instead of *en* for /ẽ/), and about the representation of front rounded vowels (see

the section below). In recent issues of *Bon Nouvèl* the use of *i* for /y/ before
a vowel (e.g., *pié*), one of the key features of the Faublas-Pressoir notation,
has been abandoned in favor of the exclusive use of *y*, as has the choice of
ou for /w/. Even if the private sector groups do not accept all the features
of IPN, they are gradually adopting those of its features that represent a
simpler, less abstract representation of the phonemes of HC.

It is unfortunate that the proposals for the modification of the Faublas-
Pressoir were put forward by a group with foreign ties. It will be recalled
that the Faublas-Pressoir orthography developed as a reaction to a notation
viewed as an attempt by Anglo-Saxons to sever the cultural link between
Haiti and its French cultural tradition. That spelling had come to be viewed
by Haitian professionals in language planning and language development as
the national orthography.

NORMALIZATION AND THE DEMARCATION
OF SENTENCE CONSTITUENTS

The forty-year debate over slight alphabetical differences has diverted
attention from other important aspects of the elaboration of an
orthography for HC. In this section, I will focus on two of these:
normalization and the demarcation of sentence constituents.

Morphophonemic Alternations

Normalization refers to the codification of alternations in form (morphophonemic alternations), occurring within the speech of individual speakers
from the same geographical area and social group; the discussion of
standardization, the codification of dialectal variants will be taken up in the
final section of this contribution.

In HC morphophonemic alternations are found primarily in a small
number of function words: personal pronouns, tense-aspect markers, and
determiners. All five personal pronouns of the language occur in a full and
in a truncated form:[9]

(1) *mwen/m* '1st sg.'   *nou/n* '1st pl. inclusive'
    ou/w   '2nd sg.'   *yo/y* '3rd pl.'
    li/l   '3rd sg.'

The full form is obligatory when the pronoun follows a consonant, as is the
case when it functions as object (of a preposition or verb) and as possessive
determiner:

(2) *Jan bat li.* (**Jan bat l*)   'John beats him/her.'
   Koute matant ou? (**Matant w*) 'Where is your aunt?'

The obligatory use of the truncated alternant is quite rare; it is found for example before the continuative particle *ap*:

(3) *L ap chante* (**Li ap chante*)   'He/she is singing.'

In all other environments either of the two alternants may occur freely:

(4) *Mwen wè li.* /*Mwen wè l.*   'I see him/her.'
   /*M wè li.* /*M wè l.*

   Se pou n travay   'You/we must work.'
   /*Se pou nou travay.*

The 2nd person sg. pronoun *ou/w* and the 3rd person plural pronoun *yo/y*, both of which begin with a semivowel, differ from the other three personal pronouns in that the truncated form cannot appear before a consonant-initial word:

(5) *Yo bat ou.* (**Y bat ou*)   'They beat us/you.'
   Ou koute l. (**W koute l*)   'You listened to him/her.'

Another type of optional vowel truncation affects a small set of verbs, many of which function also as modals: *gen* 'to have', *se* 'to be', *vini* 'to come', *soti* 'to leave':[10]

(6) *Sa li gen?*   'What does he/she have?'
   Li g on bèl kabrit.   'He/she has a nice goat.'

A more complex type of final vowel change, involving rounding, occurs before the 2nd person sg. pronoun:

(7) *Ou blese pyòw* (*pye ou*)?   'Did you hurt your foot?'
   L ale avòw (*avè ou*)?   'Did he go with you?'
   M pral bòw (*ba ou*) *on bagay.* 'I'll give you something.'

The most variable behavior is that exhibited by the post-posed definite determiner. It is realized by five different phonemic shapes, depending on the phonological nature of the final or penultimate segment of the preceding word. Following a vowel, the basic form *la* undergoes truncation of the consonant:

(8) *lakou a*   'the yard'
    manje a   'the food'

The vowel is nasalized when the determiner follows a nasal segment:[11]

(9) *chen an*   'the dog'
    moun nan/moun lan   'the person'

and the *l* may be nasalized, as is shown by (9).

Scriptural Practice

Scriptural practice in the orthographic representation of these various morphophonemic alternations varies widely. The most consistent notation of this sort of variation is the version of the Faublas-Pressoir spelling adopted by foreign and Haitian missionaries, translators, and educators, most of whom have some sort of affiliation with religious groups. These constitute the most productive and experienced group among language planners and educators, and their strong commitment to the development of Creole manifests itself not only by their output (which includes the bulk of educational materials in HC and the two most widely disseminated periodicals, *Bon Nouvèl* and *Boukan,* totaling more than 50,000 copies) but also by the systematicity and consistency of their scriptural practice. Since many of these persons are grouped around an association called SEKA (Sant pour Etid Kréyòl Ayisyin 'Center for the Study of Haitian Creole'), I will refer to their scriptural practice by the acronym of their association.

Two models are readily available to Haitians for the representation of optimal morphophonemic alternations. The conventional French spelling notes the two forms of sandhi alternations of that language, elision and liaison, in a rather elegant and economic though abstract fashion. In the case of liaison, the full form always appears (*nous_allons, nous disons, ils parlent_avec moi*); in the case of elision of mute e, the elided form is indicated where it is obligatory: *l'ami* vs. *le garçon.* The other model that might serve as a basis for the normalization of spelling in Haiti is furnished by the representation of contraction of the negative, the copula and modal verbs in English. Texts show wide fluctuation between the full and contracted forms (*I'll leave* vs. *I will leave; I'm sorry* vs. *I am sorry; I can't do it* vs. *I cannot do it.*).

Current scriptural practice, to the extent that one can be identified, entails the choice of the full, lento form in the representation of optionally variable forms of personal pronouns and of all morphemes subject to final vowel rounding. All exceptions to this general principle are accountable in terms of one additional guideline:

Any optionally variable form preceded or followed by a vowel, is represented by the truncated form, consisting of a consonant, and is linked to the preceding or following word with a hyphen.

In the case of the definite determiner and the truncatable modal verbs, the graphic representation is less abstract, and the actually occurring forms are noted. Examples of the SEKA scriptural practice are provided in (10).

(10) SEKA Scriptural practice[12]

i. Bon Nouvèl

Lè yo poté méni-a ba msié, li touché ak douèt li.
'When they brought the menu to the man, he pointed with his finger.'

Malè pou li, sa-l touché, sété mayi moulin.
'Unfortunately it was corn meal that he pointed to.'

Msié vi-n ront.
'The man became embarrassed.'

Pou-l pasé ront la, li di li pral mandé yon lòt bagay.
'In order not be be embarrassed any more, he said that he wanted to order another thing.'

ii. Korijé tè nou

Lè n-ap mété pirin nan jadin nou, nou doué mélanjé-l ak dlo anvan nou mété-l nan tè-a.
'Before we spread liquid manure on our land, we must mix it with water before we put it on the earth.'

M-konnin anpil moun ap di yo pap fè sa.
'I know a lot of people who say they don't do that.'

iii. M'-komansé li kounie-á!

Bonjou méda-m yo, kouman nou yé?
'Good day, ladies. How are your?'

Jak ba-l manjé épi li vi-n fè yon gro zouazo.
'Jack gave it food and it became a big bird.'

Manman, ti chanté-a bèl. Chanté-l ankò, tanpri.
'Mother, this little song is beautiful. Sing it again, please.'

iv. Pélin Tèt

> *Sa ki di-ou sa? Mwin djès fin palé, trin-an èstòp rayt dévan*
> *(douvan) pyé-mwin. Ou wè, mwin té di-ou...*
> 'Who told you that? I've just told you, the train stopped right
> in front of my feet. You see, I've told you...'

> *M-ap kité-li désann anvan mwin alé.*
> 'I let her go before I left.'

Note that in the version of the SEKA scriptural conventions adopted by the authors of the school primer *M'-komansé li kounié-a!* ('I'm beginning to read now!') and the agricultural guide *Korijé tè nou* ('Let us improve our land'), the truncated form *m* is used in sentences initial position instead of the full form *mouin*. No doubt this usage attempts to mirror the greater frequency of the truncated variant in all styles. In fact, the full form *mwen* is quite rare and appears to be stylistically marked.

Thus, neither of the two available models have been selected in their pure form by these Haitian scriptors. While they lean toward the use of the form providing the fullest phonological information, they attempt to reflect usage by noting the short form in environments where it is optional. In the case of the more categorical alternation characterizing the definite determiner the actually occurring form is selected, e.g. *méni-a, trin-an.*

The text of the presidential decree (1979) recommending the experimental use of the IPN alphabet recommends the use of the apostrophe for the representation of truncated forms:

(11) *M' vini*   'I came.'
     L' al lekòl.[13]   'He went to school.'

However, no guidelines are provided for the use of the full or the short form in cases where the alternation is optional. Pierre Vernet (1980), a member of the committee that devised the IPN alphabet, attempts to fill the lacuna by recommending the categorical use of the full forms. Vernet does allow the use of contracted forms as an intermediary step within the context of the classroom (1980:79). But, by a rather curious reasoning, he argues that the use of variable representations poses less of a problem in written texts than in the learners' own production:

> C'est donc au niveau de l'écriture que les fautes existent. C'est donc à ce niveau que l'efficacité, la cohérence, la simplicité sont nécessaires et par lui qu'on doit les réaliser. C'est par ce biais qu'on doit empêcher l'installation d'une écriture compliquée, inefficace et anarchique. C'est

par lui qu'on doit éviter d'avoir une écriture qui change selon les individus (1980:132).

On the contrary, with the imminence of the widespread introduction of HC at the primary level, it would seem that the normalization of morphophonemic alternations is more urgent in published texts than in the production of individual speakers. Also, normalization is more easily implemented in carefully prepared and edited texts than in the production of individual speakers. It is, in addition, more easily implemented in carefully prepared and edited texts than in spontaneous written expression. Normalization entails the learning, on the part of new literates, of abstract and highly specific encoding rules which constitute violations of the bi-unique phoneme-to-grapheme correspondences which they have acquired as a first step. It might be preferable to allow new literates considerable leeway in written expression. In early stages, one might tolerate nonnormalized production; it should suffice that they adhere to the phoneme-to-grapheme correspondences. Thus, one should not penalize learners for such errors as

(12) *L ale avòw. (Li alé avè ou)*   'He went with you.'

assuming a normalized orthography of the type Vernet recommends.

In the SEKA scriptural practice some attempt is made to normalize morphophonemic alternations. In (10) note that lento forms are given for *fè yon* (allegro *fon*), item *iii*; the automatic nasalization of *ba* 'to give' before a nasalized segment (*ban msye*), item *i*. On the other hand, alternant forms are represented for personal pronouns (*pou l* vs. *li di li,* item *i*) and verbs with truncatable final vowels (*fin pale* vs. *fini pale,* item *iv*). The reluctance of these Haitian scripters to be constrained by a thoroughgoing system of normalization reflects cautious empiricism laudable in a situation where the vernacular has not yet undergone extensive instrumentalization. At the present stage in the elaboration of a written standard for HC there is no intrinsic merit in the generalized use of abstract full forms.

Once a decision is made on the degree of normalization to be imposed on the written form of HC, devices must be selected for the representation of truncated segments. McConnell, who opted for partial normalization, elected to use hyphens for truncated vowels:

(13) *m-vlé vs. mwê vlé*   'I want'
      Li té kité-l fè-l.   'He allowed him to do it.'

C.-F. Pressoir did not provide a wealth of texts illustrating his orthography. In the coda of his polemic booklet (1947:74) we find one attestation of the use of the apostrophe for the truncated form of the 1st person sg. pronoun:

(14) *Bon, sa fini! M'alé.*　　　　　'All right, this is the end!
　　　　　　　　　　　　　　　　　　　I'm leaving.'

The presidential decree of 1979 recommends the use of the apostrophe:

(15) *M'vini.*　　　　　　　　　　　'I'm coming.'
　　　L'al lekòl.　　　　　　　　　'He is going to school.'

As we have seen, so does Vernet (1980) for a transitional period during the initial learning stage. On the other hand, Yves Dejean, who switched from an impassioned defense of the ONAAC spelling (1973) to pragmatic acceptance of the officialized system (1980) prefers to retain the hyphen:

(16) *Y-aprann.*　　　　　　　　　　'They are learning.'
　　　K-ap peze-l.　　　　　　　　'Which is oppressing him.'

The Demarcation of Sentence Constituents

HC, like other varieties of Creole French, contains many homophonous function words: for example, the sequence *la* represents locative 'there' and one of the alternants of the post-posed definite determiner:

(17) *Poul-la kakaye.*　　　　　　　'The hen cackled.'

and *nan* may express the locative preposition 'in, at' or another alternant of the definite determiner:

(18) *Moun nan mache.*　　　　　　'That person walked.'
　　　　　　　　　　　　　　　　　　'The people at the market.'

In addition in complex noun phrases, including those composed of embedded clauses, all but the right-most definite determiner may be deleted, with the result that the domain of the determiner can not always be identified:

(19) *pitit sòt la*　　　　　　　　　'the stupid child'
　　　　　　　　　　　　　　　　　　'the child of the idiot'

Bernabé (1976) has proposed the use of the hyphen to disambiguate corresponding homophonous constructions in Martinican Creole. Adopting his suggestion to HC would yield the following linearly differentiated sequences:

(17a) *Poul-la kakaye.*   'The hen cackled.'
       Poul la kakaye.   'The hen that is there cackled.'

(18a) *Moun-nan mache.*   'The person walked.'
       Moun nan mache.   'The people at the market.'

(19a) *Pitit sòt-la.*   'The child of the idiot.'
       Pitit sòt la.   'The stupid child.'

The last example is to be interpreted as synonymous with *pitit-la sot* 'the child is stupid'. Indeed, the presidential decree (1979) recommends the use of hyphens to indicate the close syntactic bond between nouns and post-posed definite determiners or personal pronouns (equivalent to possessive determiners):

(20) *fi-a*   'the girl'
     pitit-mwen   'my child'

The authors of the first two systematic orthographies for HC shied away from the use of diacritics to signal syntactic organization. As was pointed out above, in McConnell's notations hyphens are preempted for the representation of the truncated alternants of personal pronouns. In the Pressoir alphabet and its modified ONAAC version the hyphen already serves as an ad hoc device to distinguish potentially polyvalent graphic sequences. The use of *in* for /ẽ/ in these notations requires the use of the hyphen to represent the sequence /in/:

(21) *vin* (*ven*) 'wine' vs. *vi-n* (*vin*) 'to come'

in the IPN alphabet the use of *en* for the nasal vowel leaves *in* available for the representation of the sequence /in/.[14]

The SEKA scriptural tradition, which makes use of the ONAAC alphabet, exhibits highly variable use of the hyphen as syntactic demarcator. In general, that use of the diacritic is relatively infrequent and usually occurs to mark the link between noun and singular forms of the definite determiner (see 10).

In HC derivational affixes have low productivity, so that compounding constitutes the chief internal means of lexical creativity (Valdman 1978:129-59). Compounds are derived from:

1. lexicalized idioms and metaphors: *gwo nèg* 'big shot' (big guy),
   je fò 'bold' (big eyes), *kouto famasi* 'treacherous' (pharmacy knife),
   fòk se li 'a type of gruel' (it must do);

2. lexicalized French loans: *kòm ki dire* (comme qui dirait) 'as one
   would say', *a lè ki lè* (à l'heure qu'il est) 'at this time';

3. lexicalized French loans analyzable, partially, in terms of HC
   lexemes; these compounds generally contain as morphological
   residue fused elements corresponding to French function words or
   sandhi variants: *ventnèf* 'twenty-nine' (containing the autonomous
   lexemes *ven* 'twenty' and *nèf* 'nine'; *nevè* 'nine o'clock' (containing
   the bound alternant *nèv* corresponding to the free form *nèf* 'nine'
   and *è*, the bound alternant of *lè*, 'time, hour'); *janmdebwa* 'wooden
   leg' (containing *janm* 'leg' and *bwa* 'wood' and the residual element
   de); *pabokit* 'by the bucket' (containing *bokit* 'bucket' and the
   incipiently productive quantifier *pa*).

In devising an orthography for HC, one needs to consider whether these
compounds should be represented as uninterrupted linear chains or whether
lexeme boundaries should be marked with some sort of diacritic, the
hyphen, for example. This would make it possible to differentiate, in
written HC constructions from lexicalized combinations:

(22) *je fò* vs. *je-fò* (there is a third homophone, *jefò* 'effort')
     kouto famasi vs. *kouto-famasi*

In the case of lexicalized French loans, there is no need to demarcate the
constituents since these are not available to naïve monolingual speakers of
HC:

(23) *kòmkidire, alèkile*

In the case of lexicalized French loans containing frozen residual elements,
such as *de,* only those residual elements that have become productive,
hence, separable, in HC need to be marked off: *janmdebwa* but *pa bokit,*
since we also find *pa mamit* 'by the pot', *pa lit* 'by the liter', etc. Pierre
Vernet (1980), who is the only Haitian language planner to have given
serious thought to the representation of these various types of compounds,
elects to write them as unanalyzed chunks; he also uses the hyphen to
distinguish constructions from lexicalized idioms and metaphors.

STANDARDIZATION AND LEXICAL ENRICHMENT:
THE PROBLEM OF GALLICIZATION

The major tasks in the instrumentalization of HC are lexical expansion and enrichment of the language. For both these tasks the major hurdle is potential gallicization which might trigger the formation of a creole continuum.[15]

Language planners in Haiti rapidly came to an agreement on the variety of HC to be reduced to writing. In fact, the vernacular shows little geographical variation and, in view of the high degree of political and economic centralization, concensus rapidly formed around the Port-au-Prince variety. HC shows little geographical variation at the phonological and morphosyntactic level. The three dialect zones—South, North, and Center (in fact West, including the capital city Port-au-Prince)—are set off primarily by lexical variants which, furthermore, are marked by two traits.

First, lexical variants that mark the North and South dialects are localized relic forms pushed out by competing forms emanating from the Port-au-Prince (Central) area. Second, the forms that impose themselves as less localized or socially deviant, that is, as standard, are in most cases closer to the French cognate:[16]

	French	Central	North-South-Gonvave island
'thirst'	soif	souaf	souèf/souaf
'pepper'	poivre	pouav	pouèv/pouav
'already'	déjà	deja	dija/deja
'to forget'	oublier	bliye	bilye, blilye/blie
'well behaved'	sage	saj	say, chay, chaz/saj
'garlic'	aïl	lay	laj/lay
'clothing'	habits	rad	had/rad
'eight'	huit	uit	wit/uit

In view of the functional distribution of the two languages in Haiti, namely the fact that to French are allocated the higher administrative and educational functions, and the fact that French serves as vernacular, vehicular, and referential language for the politically and socio-economically dominant bilingual minority, it comes as no surprise that variants viewed as frenchifying enjoy greater prestige. This is reflected by the urban versus rural distribution of variants containing front rounded vowels, final /r/, and final, unassimilated voiced stops:[17]

	French	Urban	Rural
'rice'	riz	duri	diri
'two'	deux	do	de
'sister'	soeur	seù	sè
'brother'	frère	frèr	frè
'story'	histoire	istwar	istwa
'leg'	jambe	janb	janm
'meat'	viande	vyand	vyann
'tongue'	langue	lang	lanng

It should also be underscored that any urban variant ranks higher socially than a corresponding rural feature in areas where these coexist. The French-oriented nature of linguistic variation in Haiti also manifests itself by hypercorrection, illustrated at the lexical level by the following creations (Orjala 1970):[18]

	Simple Creole form	Derived form	Corresponding French form
'to thank'	remesie	remesisman	remerciement
'end'	fini	finisman	fin
'subsistance'	viv	vivasyon	subsistance
'decision'	deside	desidasyon	décision
'completely'	fini	finman	complètement
'often'	souvan	souvaman	souvent
'always'	toujou	toujouman	toujours
'in general'	an jeneral	an jeneralman	en général

The tendency toward gallicization in what we might term informal standardization poses serious problems to Haitian language planners and language developers. These problems are aggravated by the base-language versus creole relationship existing between French and HC and the differences in political and socio-economic power between the country's two communities.

The acquisition of new domains of use by HC requires lexical enrichment and stylistic differentiation. When, for example, French evolved from a vernacular to a vehicular language in the course of the 16th century, a wide variety of sources for new lexical and rhetorical devices were available to the illustrators of the language: Greek and Latin, regional dialects, professional jargons and sociolects, rival vernacular and vehicular languages. The options for the development of HC are much more limited. The de facto quarantine imposed for more than a century by the European powers and the United States together with the metropolitan-oriented links between other Caribbean communities, especially the Creole French-speaking regions, and their European guardians have effectively insulated Haiti from cultural contacts with its immediate neighbors.

The writers and scholars who participated in the instrumentalization of French boldly used all the internal resources of the language. Although the derivational processes of French were not at that time as productive as those of, say, Italian and Spanish, they had not yet become congealed by puristic attitudes to prevent the illustrators of the language from heeding Du Bellay's exhortation: 'Tu composeras hardiment des mots à l'imitation des Grecs et des Latins.' Thus they created numerous abstract adjectives by: freely using available suffixes (*arbreux, boivard*); nominalizing adjectives and verbs (*le vert* for *la verdure, le frais* for *la fraîcheur; le vivre, le chant*); resorting to augmentatives or diminutives (*fleurette, tendrette*); coining compounds (*humbler-fier, aigredoux*).

The creolist Keith Whinnom has suggested (1971) that, because of their origin in reduced varieties of speech, creole languages suffer from congenital lexical deficiency and that the relative absence of productive word-building processes renders difficult linguistic repair and enrichment. Indeed, HC possesses only two truly productive derivational affixes, the denominal verb-forming suffix -*e* (*bourik* 'donkey' / *bourike* 'work like a mule'; *plog* 'plug' / *ploge* 'to plug') and the privative deverbal prefix *de/dez*: *bloke* 'to block' / *debloke* 'to unblock', *apiye* 'to lean / *dezapiye* 'to stop leaning' (Valdman 1978:129-49). However compounding constitutes a readily available process for lexical creation, although, compounds tend to be highly idiomatic and semantically opaque:

(22) *souse* 'to suck' +
    tire 'to pull, to milk'   *souse tire* 'to be a parasite'

   rete 'to remain' +
    pran 'to take'   *rete pran* 'to tolerate'

   non 'name' +
    jouèt 'toy, game'   *non jouèt* 'nickname'

   vye 'old' +
    moun 'person'   *vye moun* 'adult'

Explanations for the preponderance of French loans over neologisms in the newly coined terms found in materials being prepared in Haiti are to be sought not in structural factors but in the attitudes of speakers towards the country's two languages. Formality in spoken language is often achieved by nonce borrowing from French, usually in the forms of phrasal units. In (23) note the incorporation of the noun phrase *un petit peu orgeuilleux* triggering the switch to the frenchified vowel system:

(23) gèp li-menm ki rive ki *un pti peu orgeuyeu*
       (un petit peu orgeuilleux)
       'The wasp, herself, who was a little bit arrogant'

       kèk *seu*men yo vini *tre regulyèr* e depi yo komanse kapab li
       'a few weeks, they come very regularly and as soon as they begin
       to be able to read'

       pre*u*mye paj, d*eu*zyèm paj, yo pa tounen
       'the first page, the second page, they don't return'

One of the consequences of massive borrowing from French, particularly in the form of transfer of phrasal units, is the increased use of phonological features, such as the front rounded vowels and post-vocalic *r,* that mark the variety of HC employed by members of the bilingual elite.

In Haiti, despite the growing mass of written material in HC designed to educate, edify, entertain, or elevate the soul and the spirit, there has been little reflection on strategies for the lexical enrichment of the vernacular. The paucity of theoretical discussions on the subject of lexical expansion is in striking contrast to the wealth of concrete efforts deployed in the adaptation of the language to a growing number of domains and types of discourse. The situation is diametrically opposed to that which obtains in the French West Indies where, despite the paucity of materials written in the vernacular, there has developed a lively debate on the sociolinguistic and glottopolitical implications of various strategies of lexical expansion. The most creative and eloquent writer on that topic is Jean Bernabé, who serves as the theorist for a group of politically engaged younger linguists, writers, and teachers in Guadeloupe and Martinique associated with the Groupe d'Etudes et de Recherches en Espace Créolophone (GEREC). Bernabé points out that, paradoxically, those very language planners and developers who are rushing to mold the vernacular for the expression of new concepts and for the coverage of new functions, threaten the structural integrity of the language:

> ...certains créolophones (des intellectuels surtout), plutôt que de s'adonner à une quête exigeante des ressources actuelles de la langue et de ses potentialités néologiques, impatients qu'ils sont de faire dire à la langue autre chose qu'elle n'a jamais dit, préfèrent couler les mots français les plus sophistiqués dans le moule galvaudé des structures

linguistiques du créole: voulant témoigner du créole à travers une énonciation "phatique" du créole et pour le créole, ils se font, paradoxalement, les artisans d'un véritable "linguicide", situation pathétique, voire tragique car ne pas du tout parler le créole revient également à l'abolir (1976:55).

For Bernabé and his group the lexical enrichment and the forging of a written form of the vernacular must necessarily traverse a 'philological' phase during which writers of talent—poets—must assiduously inventory and develop the neological capabilities of the vernacular. This search cannot be limited to the everyday spoken idiom of the folk, in the case of Haiti, that of the monolingual rural masses. For the Martinican linguist the writers of talent who will evolve the written styles of Creole—the *écriture* of the language—must navigate with skill between the Scylla of gallicization and the Charybdis of transcription of the spoken idiom. The straight course lies in maintaining maximum deviance (*la déviance*) between the vernacular and the superordinate official language.

Attaining maximum deviance between Creole and French involves two approaches. First, the creole writer must search the treasure room of the folk lexicon. One obvious source for the words and the rhetorical devices that will be woven into the new written form of the vernacular is the folktale ('preserved from the ravages of frenchification at the level of syntax as well as that of vocabulary... [it constitutes] the socio-historical and linguistic root of the phenomenon of creolization' GEREC 1976). Second, the Creole writer must go beyond the resources of his own variety of Créole and appropriate those of Creole as a whole. That is, he must forge not a literary form of Martinican, say, but a literary form of *transcréole*. To illustrate the GEREC's theory of lexical enrichment D. Colat-Jolivière (1976) provides a literary transformation of a Guadeloupean folktale. To the core Guadeloupean syntax and vocabulary he adds features from HC, Dominican and Martinican. Unfortunately, the text of the transformed folktale is not accompanied by a transcription of the original recorded document, thus making it impossible to determine the proportion of native and imported material in the rewritten tale. It is claimed that the talented Haitian writer Frankétienne achieved the literary quality of his novel *Dézafi* ('The challenge'), unquestionably the most distinguished belletristic production in HC, precisely by a sort of transcreolization, except that the extraneous elements in *Dézafi* do not originate in other synchronic varieties of Creole but in older diachronic strata. The author, reportedly, dipped into Jule Faine's French-HC dictionary (1974) for archaisms no longer in current usage in Haiti (Bernabé 1978).

But the poetic quality of *Dézafi* derives not only from the marked nature of its lexicon (archaisms, specialized vaudoun and cockfighting vocabularies) and the resulting maximum deviance from French thus achieved, but also from Franketienne's skillful interlacing of rhetorical devices and evocative vocabulary. Consider the following passage in which the author described the cruel treatment inflicted on the zombies by the malevolent *houngan* (vaudoun priest) (Franketienne 1975:208):

(24) *Yo toufé-nou, toufounin-nou.*   'They choke us and hit us with their fists.'

Yo chiré-nou, chifonnin-nou.   'They tear us apart and quarter us.'

Yo raché-nou, rachonnin-nou.   'They cut us and cut us up in small pieces.'

Yo piyé-nou, déchèpiyé-nou.   'They rob us and leave us stark naked.'

Yo prijé-nou, déchalboré-nou.   'They press us and squeeze us out.'

Note that in all but the last line the second term, derived from the first by partial reduplication, contains in intensive form the nuclear meaning of the morphologically simpler form. Although they may be analyzed, semantically, as a simplex form plus an augmentative or intensive element, *toufounen, rachonnen,* and *déchèpiyé* cannot be considered, from a morphological point of view, as derivatives of *toufé, raché,* and *piyé,* respectively. Although the two items in each pair share a semantic feature and despite the morphological similarities between them, no intensive affix can be extracted. However, to deny any sort of morphological relationship between *toufe* and *toufounin,* for example, would lead one to overlook some of HC's productive lexical processes.

One would also underestimate HC's internal resources for lexical expansion by adhering too closely to French models. For example, one finds in Martinican Creole derivatives containing reflexes of the French denominal suffix -té (-ité, -eté): *kouyonste* 'stupidity' (from *kouyon* 'idiot'), *perozite* 'fear' (from *pè* 'fear'), *lapepazite* 'incapacity' (from *lapepa* 'not be able to'). As may be seen from the last two examples in particular, this pattern does not generally yield morphologically transparent forms and has limited productivity. But Martinican has another suffix *-te* which does not correspond to the French denominal *te.* It is in fact a moderately productive deadjectival suffix signifying 'having one or several', e.g. *fanm* 'woman' / *fanmte* 'having one or more women', *nòm* 'man' / *nòmte* 'having one or more men', *boug* 'guy' / *boute* 'having one or more guys' (Bernabé 1981).

It remains, however, that the diglossic relationship between French and HC results in the fact that any French word is, potentially, part of the lexicon of the vernacular tongue. Even those Haitian writers who exploit the internal resources of the vernacular for its lexical enrichment are led to borrow from French to achieve rhetorical effects. For example, in an article dealing with the literary potential of HC, E. Célestin-Mégie (1980) is obliged to resort to French loans in addition to native compounds in assembling a broad set of terms referring to the continuum language-jargon. It is interesting to compare his set to that identified for French by Jardel (1975):[19]

	French	HC
highly valued	langue	lanng
	langue de prestige (etc.)	lang banda, lang prestij
	idiome	langaj literè
	langage	dyalek
neutral	parler	
	dialecte	
	langue courante, populaire	pidjin bosal
	dialecte populaire, etc.	matchaka plizyè langajpale
	patois	dyalèk makanda
	jargon	patway (lanng moun sòt)
	petit-nègre	charabya beza
	langue enfantine	
highly devalued	idiome informe	
	baragouin	
	charabia	

Recourse to French loans cannot be completely eliminated in the elaboration of a written form of HC sufficiently differentiated stylistically to serve in the preparation of a broad spectrum of educational, literary, and technical works. Nor can writers restrict themselves to speech forms used in everyday conversation by the rural and urban masses. But gallicization, in the form of massive borrowing from French and standardization toward frenchifying features, would result in the creation of a standardized vehicular form of HC, employed for written discourse, that would diverge widely from folk speech. That form of the vernacular would be the one that would find its way in the materials of Creole used at the primary level and in adult literacy programs. This gallicized written variety of the vernacular would cause the unilingual creolophone masses to be doubly disadvantaged. At present, and for the foreseeable future, these masses have no access to

French models and, consequently, they have little opportunity to acquire functional mastery of it. If the written form of *their* language diverges markedly from their everyday usage, then they are effectively denied access to knowledge and to techniques transmitted by means of the written word.

If language planning and language development in Haiti are to contribute to the economic development of the masses, to give them more control over their political destiny, and to enhance social justice, then those involved in the enterprise must strive for the elaboration of a vehicular variety of HC that reflects inner creative processes of the vernacular form of the language and the communicative strategies of the rural monolingual speakers. They also must transcend spoken usage in forging a written vehicular form of the language. Fortunately there are signs that the most talented illustrators of HC have chosen this direction, witness the playwright and novelist Frankétienne's resort to specialized vocabularies and to archaisms in his novel *Dézafi*. Because of the relative inaccessibility of rural speakers and the difficulty for both foreign and local linguists to observe language functioning in rural communities, there are no doubt many lexical and stylistic resources characteristic of folk usage that remain to be tapped for utilization in the grand project of instrumentalization.

NOTES

[1] In this paper, I am using a model of language functioning in which three types of languages are recognized: *vernacular* (the language of daily communication within a social group), *vehicular* (the means of communication with outside groups, either within a polity or outside of it), *referential* (the vehicle of a valued cultural tradition). Many communities also have special religious languages. This functional classification is exemplified below for Haiti.

Language Function

Vernacular	Creole (rural masses; urban proletariat)
Vehicular	Internal: Creole, French
	External: English, Spanish, French
Referential	French
Religious	Latin, vestigial African languages

[2] Ferguson's definition of diglossia, and subsequent extensions of that notion suggested by John Gumperz and Joshua Fishman to encompass the complementary use of dialects and styles, accurately describe the alternative use of French and Creole in colonial Saint-Domingue (Valdman 1978). In that rigidly stratified plantocratic society:

1. vehicular and referential functions were attributed exclusively to French;
2. Creole was acquired spontaneously at home, even for the ruling group;
3. the vernacular was viewed as a debased and corrupted form of French.

[3] Even McConnell conceived his notation within a literacy campaign in which the ability to read HC served as a transitional goal: 'Its [the literacy campaign] aim is to teach adults to read and write Creole, with a view to their passing on to French afterwards' (McConnell and Swan 1945:7).

[4] Nationalism has strongly flavored discussions about choice of alphabet in Haiti. Pressoir attributed McConnell's 'erroneous' choice of the circumflex accent to denote nasality of vowels to the pastor's lack of knowledge of French. He claimed (1947:66) that, if he failed to adopt the French-oriented digraphs *in, an, on* for /ẽ/, /ã/, and /õ/, respectively, it was because for an English reader these graphs were associated with a vowel followed by a *n*. It is difficult to see, however, why the choice of the circumflex reflects the bias of anglophones. Why would that diacritic evoke nasalization for an English reader? More simply, McConnell's model was the IPA representation of nasal vowels with tilde in S. Comhaire-Sylvain's description of HC (1936). It may be that Pressoir's allegations stem from an earlier proposal by McConnell in which /š/ was noted with *sh* and /u/ with *u*. In the final analysis, Pressoir and other intellectuals saw in McConnell's radical departure from the French convention of representing nasal vowels a threat to the French cultural tradition to which even intellectuals favorable to a certain promotion of HC were strongly attached. Undoubtedly, the American economic and political control of Haiti, very much in evidence during the post-occupation period, could only reinforce this strong francophile sentiment. In the polemic over the representation of the nasal vowels the circumflex accent became a symbol of an alleged attempt by English and American residents in Haiti to seize control of the national vernacular: 'Les anglais et les américains d'Haïti purent facilement lire les textes du pasteur, qui les mettaient à l'aise et éliminaient les difficultés de l'orthographe à base française en créole' (Pressoir 1947:66). Jean Bernabé errs, then, in attributing the rejection of the circumflex accent to a popular reaction against a bizarre foreign graphic device: 'on peut y [the rejection of the use of the circumflex] voir une réaction d'essence populaire contre la sophistication et la technicité, ou encore une attitude écologique tendant à protéger la langue contre l'invasion de l'inesthétique confondu, alors, avec l'insolite' (1976:25).

In the more recent debate between proponents of the ONAAC and IPN notations (see below) Yves Voltaire (1980:19) attributes the latter to meddling on the part of the French: 'Ou wè vre se blan franse k'pa menm konn pale kreyòl ki fè travay sa-a (You see that it is really the French, who can't even speak Creole who are doing that work.'

[5] The McConnell and Pressoir notations underwent modification during the period 1943-47. McConnell and Swan (1945) used *i* to note /y/ before vowels, e.g., *pié* 'foot'; Pressoir first chose *w* to represent the back semivowel, e.g., *mwin* 'I, me' but later adopted the digraph *ou* before vowels, e.g., *mouin*. The Haitian journalist pays a debt of gratitude to A. de Saint-Quentin whose treatise on Guyane Creole (1872) contained the first autonomous and systematic notation ever devised for a Creole French. As Pressoir notes, that system is nearly identical with the one that he put forward as an alternative to the McConnell-Laubach alphabet. Had Saint-Quentin's description been more readily available and had it come to the attention of earlier scriptors, Haiti would have been spared forty years of generally sterile debate. Finally, despite the acrimony of the first debate on the orthographic representation of HC, Pressoir does not fail to recognize McConnell's signal contribution: 'Malgré ses erreurs, bien excusables d'ailleurs, le Pasteur McConnell demeure un pionnier qui à droit à la reconnaissance des Haïtiens' (1947:68).

[6] In the discussion that followed the presentation of the orthography in response to the charge from a participant that the spokesmen for the Académie orthography were not 'representative' (of the persons involved in the preparation of materials in HC?), G. Lefebvre retorted that the members of the Académie Française who have proposed rules for the standardization of French grammar were also not representative (CRESH 1974:24). He continued with an assertion put forward by all those who wish to close debate on matters orthographic: 'Une fois que vous aurez adopté cette orthographe, les gens ne la discutent plus, c'est une convention qui lie les écrivains et les lecteurs.' Indeed, any orthographic system is arbitrary, but the issue begged by the response is that orthographic proposals can be evaluated if criteria guiding the choice are stated explicitly. It is not clear what advantages, except closer alignment on the standard French spelling, accrue from the frenchifying features proposed by the Académie.

[7] The only exhaustive set of materials making use of that notation is a bilingual collection of folktales from a variety of Creole French-speaking territories (ACCT 1976).

[8] The use of *é* instead of *e* to represent /e/ avoids potentially ambiguous sequences *en*: *benyen* /bẽjẽ/ or /benye/.

[9] Henceforth all HC forms will be cited in IPN notation since it provides a nearly perfect biunique representation of the phonemes of the language. Note that the term Creole will be used to refer to Creole French varieties as a whole; otherwise, individual varieties will be mentioned: HC, Martinican, etc. No position is taken here on the issue of the demarcation of French Creole varieties, that is to say, whether they constitute a single language or different ones.

[10] This list of truncatable verbs is illustrative only; for a more complete discussion of sandhi variation (morphophonemic alternations occurring at word boundaries) in HC, see Tinelli (1974), Valdman (1978:81-8), and Vernet (1980).

[11] This is a somewhat simplified presentation of sandhi variation in HC. For example, among certain speakers, the definite determiner shows nasalization of the vowel in all environments (*pitit-lan* instead of *pitit-la, bank-lan, pitimi-an*).

[12] *Bon Nouvèl* ('Good News') is a monthly, established about ten years ago, with a circulation of upward of 30,000, published by a Catholic group; *Korijé tè nou* ('Let us improve our land'), a booklet on better agricultural practices, is published by the *Bon Nouvèl* press; *M' komanse li kounyé-a* ('I'm beginning to read now') is a primer used by a Catholic order in Northern Haiti; *Pèlin Tèt* ('The mouse trap') is a recent Frankétienne play evoking the moral plight of the Haitian immigrants to the United States while at the same time confronting cultural and social differences between the Haitian elite and working class.

[13] Note the use of the truncated form of *ale* 'to go' rendered without any graphic device.

[14] C.-F. Pressoir advocated the use of the apostrophe instead of a second *n* to demarcate more clearly nasal vowels: *ban'nann* for *bannann* 'plantain', *répon'* for *reponn* 'to answer'. If indeed readers find it difficult to differentiate between nasal vowels, sequences of nasal vowels plus *n,* and sequences of oral vowels plus *n* (*chen* 'dog', *chenn* 'chain', *menaj* 'girl friend or concubine'), this would constitute a strong argument for McConnell's use of a diacritic for the representation of nasal vowels: *chê, chên, ménaj,* respectively. It would also support the use of *é* instead of *e* to represent /e/.

[15] Creolists specializing in English-based creoles claimed that decreolization has not affected Creole French varieties. As a rule, these varieties seem to lack, at the grammatical level, the extensive alternation between basilectal forms and variants reflecting movement toward French. However, such variation, correlating with social factors, occurs widely in Reunion Creole, and is not altogether absent from HC. For example, in that variety of Creole frenchification (found more frequently among members of the urban middle classes) involves the use of the conjunction *ke* (often pronounced with a front rounded vowel, *keu*) in subordinate clauses: *li di m ke li te vin we m* 'he said that he had come to see me.'

[16] Except for Orjala (1970), there is no thorough study of regional variation in HC.

[17] Choice of sociolect was one of the major issues involved in the modification of the McConnell-Laubach spelling. Pressoir alleged that the British-born pastor standardized HC on the basis of rural rather than urban speech (1947:66): '...l'adaptateur [McConnell] ne connaissant pas assez notre idiome pour en saisir les nuances, ne s'appliqua à rendre que les voyelles du 'gros créole' sans tenir compte des doublets en usage non seulement dans le parler des haïtiens cultivés mais encore dans la langue d'un nombre considérable de prolétaires mêlés à la masse de ceux qui parlent le 'gros créole'. Ainsi, *i* élimina *u* (*diri,* jamais *duri*), *è* élimina *eu'* (*kwafè* et jamais *kwafeu'*), *é* élimina *e* (*ké* et jamais *ke*).'

[18] The data is from Orjala (1970) and has not been confirmed by other sources.

[19] Note that the author uses the more frenchified (sociolinguistically prestigious) variant of the word. In HC there is a variation *-aj/-ay:langay/langaj;* the first alternant marks more rural, 'gros creole' usage. Célestin-Mégie's use of items from the basilectal and frenchifying poles is characteristic of the styles of HC produced by bilinguals. This approach is particularly evident in radio broadcasts in which the speaker will often match French loans and HC equivalents or paraphrases, e.g. *pètwol brut,* c'est à dire *gwo soulye* 'unrefined oil, that is to say, raw'; the term *gwo soulye* is a pejorative expression denoting lack of polish and refinement.

THE RICHFORD EXPERIENCE: FRENCH BILINGUAL EDUCATION AS A 'BÀSIC' APPROACH TO LANGUAGE COMPETENCE

PHYLLIS L. HAGEL

OUR COMMUNITIES AND THE NEED FOR FRENCH BILINGUAL EDUCATION

The Franklin Northeast Supervisory Union is composed of five small towns located in the rural, northernmost section of Vermont astride the Quebec border. The principal occupation of the area is dairy farming, and approximately 43% of the population can claim French-Canadian descent.

The French were the first settlers in what is now the state of Vermont, when Fort Ste. Anne was established on Isle La Motte in 1666. The majority of the French-speaking immigrants did not come to Vermont, however, until the period 1840-1939, when Canadian workers were enticed by recruiters to labor in the big cotton and woolen mills of Winooski and Burlington. After 1930, many French Canadians left their farms, which were by then exhausted and arid, to seek better lives in the fertile counties of northern Vermont, including Franklin County, home of the Franklin Northeast Supervisory Union (FNESU).

Until 1950, the French Canadians were thought to be unassimilable, and thus little attention was paid to their social or educational needs. But during the 1960s, as parochial schools that had educated French-descent students in both English and French were forced to close for economic reasons, and as churches that had provided for French-language masses denationalized, the French Canadians began to be assimilated into the mainstream of Anglo-American cultural values and practices. In the northern border

171

communities, such as those within the FNESU, the assimilation was less rapid than in the cities and towns of New England, for farms led to isolation both from neighbors and from communications media. Because of language differences, close-knit family patterns, proximity to their native Quebec, and the absence of a supportive and accommodating educational and career experience, the Franco-Americans of our district have tended to remain outside the mainstream of social and economic prosperity. They have also remained unrecognized as a people who have enriched and contributed to our past and present-day society.

The rural Vermont setting is a particularly difficult one for persons who have little economic, educational, or linguistic security. Sometimes referred to as the most rural state, Vermont has many communities like ours that are small and geographically scattered. There are large areas of mountainous and undeveloped land reached only by secondary roads, many of which are impassable during the long harsh winter. Few social or health services are readily available, and none of these are bilingual. Incomes are low, and families are large.

What, then, is the relationship between the above factors and bilingual education within the FNESU? A study conducted by school administrators prior to the submission of an ESEA Title VII Bilingual Education program proposal to the federal government in 1977 established the percentage of Franco-Americans in local schools as ranging from 35-75%. It should be noted that the definition of 'Franco-American' used for the purposes of this study included both those who are dominant-language French speakers and children who are from second-generation Franco families, where French may or may not be spoken regularly in the home. The cultural heritage of such second-generation children, however, is clearly French-Canadian, and a critical educational factor is that these children have learned their English-language reading and speaking skills from persons in the home whose native language is French. Prior to the establishment of the FNESU bilingual education program, these were the characteristics of children of Franco-American background in our schools:

1. Franco-American children began the primary grades with no significant differences with respect to social skills and psychomotor development. There were, however, noticeable differences in self-concept and behavioral patterns in children who are native speakers of French: they were less verbal and more retiring.
2. Franco-American children experienced a significant cumulative negative effect on their rate of learning. The older they got, the more they were behind in basic skill areas.

3. Less concrete, but perhaps more significant, was the phenomenon of tracking by ethnic background. Teachers and administrators observed that Franco-Americans, as they fell behind in school achievement, became less academically oriented as they progressed through the educational system. Very few of the Franco-Americans appeared in the college preparatory curriculum groups; fewer still attended college. This was often caused by a combination of low family expectations and a lack of sensitive educational and career guidance in the schools.

4. Franco-American families have repressed and hidden their cultural heritage in the face of traditional hostility towards 'Canucks' and denigration of their language from traditional French foreign language teachers; they have attempted to assimilate with the dominant Anglo culture.

On all standardized measures, Franco-American children were typically behind grade level by the third grade. The cumulative effect of this regression became most significant by the eighth grade. The FNESU district's own school-referenced reading inventories bear out this effect of regression.

Since the bottom line by which many programs are measured today is 'educational progress', our French bilingual education program has to demonstrate clearly that it is bringing increased capacity in the basic skill areas to our children. In our geographic area, a second bottom line of effectiveness is the ability of students to secure and hold a job once out of school. Our area has a high rate of unemployment (over 13%), and family farms are failing. Our area will remain, of course, adjacent to French-speaking Québec regardless of the political developments in that province. Many families in the district have relatives on both sides of the border, and several even find the international border running through their property. These citizens and their children, most of whom remain in the area and inherit the farms and local businesses, have an urgent economic need to be able to use the French language fluently and as part of their daily lives. Many business people in Franklin county have openly stated that they could substantially increase and facilitate their business were they able to speak French fluently. In an area as economically depressed as northern Vermont, this is an important educational stimulus.

WHAT IS A 'BASIC' PROGRAM?

Once the need for bilingual education beginning at the elementary-school level was clearly established in the FNESU district, administrators looked to a proven model of French bilingual education. The public schools of the St. John Valley in Maine had developed such a program between 1970 and 1975. Their test and other results were convincing enough to the Joint Dissemination Review Panel in Washington that the Panel approved this program for nationwide adoption. The materials already packaged and available for purchase included such items as performance objectives, teacher's manual, and curriculum guide.

After examining these materials, the FNESU determined that the program would have to be modified to incorporate the basic competencies mandated by the state of Vermont for each grade level. These goals, known as *'Les Aptitudes de Base'* in their French-language version as prepared by the Vermont State Department of Education, include grade-by-grade goals in the skill areas of *'Lecture, Ecriture, Discours, Action d'écouter, Mathématiques et Raisonnement'*. The bilingual curriculum had to incorporate materials to teach these 'basics'. Here are some examples from the brochure:

(Ayant reçu:)
une liste de mots qui sont employés fréquemment, l'étudiant les reconnaîtra avec une exactitude de 80%;

des matériaux à copier, l'étudiant le fera sans erreurs ou omissions;

un choix de locations géographiques familières, l'étudiant donnera des directions claires et précises pour arriver à location choisie;

les directions de compter à cent, l'étudiant récitera les numéraux de 1 à 100 dans l'ordre habituel, sans erreurs;

les symboles +, −, X, et ÷, l'étudiant peut identifier le sens en donnant un example.

Thus, one element of the FNESU definition of a 'basic' bilingual program approach is the incorporation of the minimal competencies as defined by Vermont law. A second element of the definition is a French-language curriculum that reflects the methods and materials used by the English-language classroom teachers to achieve these goals.

Since the French-background child has a special need to be able to function effectively in the American, English-language school system, FNESU administrators determined to parallel as closely as possible both the classroom methods and the classroom materials commonly used by the English-language teacher in whose classroom we work. At the present time, we encompass all classes in grades K-4 in three public elementary schools within the FNESU, and we include all children in each class regardless of language background. Approximately 60-64% of the students come from a French cultural/linguistic background; the remainder are monolingual Anglophones. All children receive the same bilingual language experiences regardless of their background.

In order to integrate our bilingual curriculum with the teachers' local educational program, we sat down together and examined their curriculum alongside that provided by the St. John Valley model. Through this cooperative process, we developed French-language performance objectives that reflected both our combined perceptions of what the children needed and the state-mandated competencies. This process required a lot of curriculum development work by our staff, but it has resulted in a smooth transition from French- to English-language work in the classroom. Our curriculum includes a fully-developed French language elementary reading program (la 'Méthode Dynamique' from Québec), a French-language version of a mathematics series used in English, and our own locally-developed social studies units based on similar units produced by other French elementary bilingual programs in Canaan, Vt., and Berlin, N.H. Since our bilingual program includes both French and previously monolingual English-speaking children, this approach has helped the English-language classroom teacher and the Anglo-background student feel comfortable with our presence in the classroom. A weekly planning conference with all staff involved in the program keeps this cooperative effort running smoothly.

It cannot be overemphasized that one of the reasons our program has been so well accepted by the community as well as by the English-language teachers is precisely because we can demonstrate how our program complements and reinforces the basic skills areas every child must master (in whatever language) in order to progress through the system. It is our close integration within the regular school patterns that allows each child to learn in the language in which he or she feels most comfortable. This in turn fosters a more positive self-image and an accepting attitude on the part of all children in the bilingual classroom.

Subject-oriented instruction in French takes place for a minimum of a half hour daily and is provided by Project French bilingual teachers who work in the students' regular classroom. Additional French instructional and conversational time is provided daily by a bilingual teacher aide and by the classroom teachers (many of whom have had prior French study).

Another important factor in our acceptance by the local community is the manner in which we dealt with the question of language variety and dialect. We needed to consider the following issues:

a) The form of French spoken in northern New England is clearly French-Canadian in origin;
b) Franco-Americans have often in the past unjustly suffered ridicule for their language variety at the hands of traditionally-trained 'standard' French teachers;
c) There is a severe lack of trained Franco-American bilingual teachers;
d) The local community feared that due to the lack of trained Franco-American bilingual teachers that this pattern of rejection would repeat itself, and 'standard' (i.e. France) French would be imposed on their children;
e) Local residents were hostile to the use of 'standard' French, and were convinced that use of the 'standard' language would further alienate their children from themselves and from their Franco-American cultural and linguistic heritage;
f) Local residents had already had negative experiences with traditional French teachers with whom they could not communicate in their native French mother tongue during parent-teacher conferences at school.

We thus made a conscious and deliberate choice to use the local Franco-American speech as our instructional model. We hired 'standard' French teachers who were knowledgeable about elementary education, sympathetic to the Franco-American situation, and willing to learn and use the local French vocabulary (along with correct grammatical structure).

This mix of staff ethnic background and accents has been a model for inculcating attitudes of tolerance, mutual acceptance, and respect so necessary to the development of positive self-images. The children show no confusion at being exposed daily to widely varying French accents. The parents respect our efforts and are pleased to have outsiders take the trouble to learn and to value their own French speech.

A third element of our definition of basic bilingual education is our early-intervention homebased preschool program for four-year-olds. This program is a critical success factor in an isolated area such as ours. We bring education to the homes and provide a head start to our French- (and English-) background students. Our purpose is to reduce the differences in self-concept and verbal patterns that have in the past been characteristic of our French population. The preschool curriculum is based on the bilingual kindergarten objectives, but the areas of cognitive concentration are reinforced by the use of manipulative materials to develop muscle coordination, the selection of curriculum themes that reflect the reality of rural farm life, and by peer group play sessions to develop social skills that are difficult to acquire because of the rural nature of the area. The bilingual thematic curriculum includes the following units: *'Les fruits et les légumes'*; *'Les animaux de la forêt et des champs'*; *'Les vêtements et les sports d'hiver'*; *'le corps humain'*; *'La vie familiale'*; *'Les moyens de transport locaux'*; *'La vie sur la ferme'*; *'le sirop d'érable'*; *'Les plantes et la culture'*.

The Preschool bilingual specialist and the bilingual aides make three home visits weekly and work with the parents to provide further home activities to expand upon the skills learned each week. The program readies the child to enter the regular district kindergarten (or first grade) class at a functional ability level in both French and English. This preschool program has been such an unprecedented success in the FNESU district that a waiting list has had to be established.

These three factors, then, of incorporating bilingual minimal competencies, paralleling the English curriculum methods and materials, and providing bilingual early intervention for four-year-olds at home, constitute the FNESU definition of a 'basic' approach to developing language competence in our students. It is an approach that goes far beyond the traditional FLES program, since it deals with the whole range of student learning at the elementary school level.

Any successful educational program, however, also involves the abilities of teachers and the support of parents to carry on the 'basic' program in future years and after federal funds are no longer available.

INSERVICE EDUCATION

An important key to our success with our 'basic' approach is our extensive inservice training program. Our federal grant mandates the provision of teacher training, and the FNESU administrators felt that this money would be put to best use by training not only our bilingual staff, but also those English-language classroom teachers who deal on a daily basis with our Franco-background pupils. By providing them also with the sensitivity, methods, and language training to work more effectively with Franco students, we felt that everyone would benefit from the bilingual approach to elementary school. The extensive inservice education program is designed to insure ultimately the capability of local staff to continue the bilingual program at the close of federal funding.

At the beginning of the program we arranged a two-week preservice workshop, during which our bilingual staff was thoroughly trained in our performance objectives, in the customs and language variety of the local community, in local education methods, and in team teaching techniques. Through discussion and demonstration (and with an assist from the Bilingual Training Resource Center of the University of Southwestern Louisiana) we familiarized the district teachers with our staff, our objectives, and our methods. We also discussed individual classroom scheduling and arranged weekly curriculum meetings for the remainder of the year.

Next the Bilingual Education Program subcontracted with the Center for Bilingual Education at the University of Vermont to provide credits for inservice courses to be given within the district. During our first two years of operation, these courses included: French-Canadian history and civilization; French for teachers; Bilingual teacher aide training; Issues in bilingual education; Techniques for identifying local French culture; Classroom management and discipline; Developing community-based elementary curriculum; and Bilingual early childhood education.

The French-Canadian studies course was taught by several University of Vermont professors, each giving a seminar in his or her specialty. A similar seminar-type format was used for the courses on 'Developing community-based curriculum' and 'Bilingual early childhood education'.

'French for teachers' has been perhaps the biggest hit of the two years within the FNESU district. Over forty teachers enrolled, thus necessitating the services of two professors. (In this case, the Project Director was appointed an adjunct faculty member at UVM to assist in teaching within the district). The class was split into groups according to previous French background or ability. The objectives of the course were twofold: to give teachers a foundation course in French-Canadian language skills in the traditional sense, and to give teachers the means and confidence to use the French language in their daily classroom activities. A typical lesson plan for this course would include one hour of language skills practice, one half hour of weekly Bilingual Project-related student vocabulary, and three ten-minute demonstration mini-lessons suitable for use in the teacher's own classroom.

The Bilingual teacher aides' course has focused on the basics of teaching and learning skills and a review of formal French grammar. All of the bilingual aides are local women of French background but with no formal education beyond grade or high school.

'Issues in bilingual education' and 'Techniques for identifying local French culture' were given by staff from the Boston University Bilingual Training and Resource Center (also Title VII-funded). Those enrolled in this series of four all-day weekend seminars included both Project staff and cooperating FNESU district classroom teachers.

All courses are open to any interested teacher, parent, and school board or community member.

PARENT ADVISORY COUNCIL AND PARENT ACTIVITIES

A Parent Advisory Council (PAC) sponsors many activities for both our French and English parents. They support the bilingual project newsletter, which features interviews with the staff and examples of children's classwork, and the donation to preschool parents of helpful bilingual parent manuals with suggested at-home activities. They have arranged for community performances of the Celebration Pantomime Theater (a bilingual theater group from Maine), 'Les Sortilèges' (a traditional French-Canadian folkdance troupe), and the 'Festival des Deux Mondes' (a Franco-American traveling cultural festival). Another outstanding event sponsored by the PAC was a parent-child educational field trip to Montreal that included a tour de ville, a show at the Dow Planetarium, and a visit to the Aquarium. At present, the PAC is sponsoring a monthly series of parent workshops focusing on traditional French-Canadian crafts.

Parents have also been offered the opportunity to participate in a seminar on 'Coping with your child's behavior/ Se débrouiller avec la conduite des enfants' that was taught by a local guidance counselor. French parents also have the opportunity of becoming teacher aides with the bilingual program and thus of gaining both employment and further educational training.

EVALUATION

The bilingual education program has gathered independently verified data to confirm the effectiveness of our 'basic' approach to education. Students now pass the Vermont Basic Competencies in either French or English. The previous gap between French and English students on standardized tests and reading inventories has virtually disappeared in those grades that are part of the bilingual program; it has remained constant in other grades. No ethnic tension is visible in the early elementary grades, and learning in French is seen as a badge of honor for students with envious older siblings.

Annual parent survey results have been extremely positive: 80-97% of the parents who responded from the three towns agreed that their children were getting a good education in both French and English, while 90-97% of the parents who responded from the three towns agreed that their children had benefited as a direct result of the bilingual program; 75-96% of the parents also reported that their children discussed their bilingual classroom activities at home. From 90-95% of the parents indicated that they wanted the bilingual education program to continue to be made available to their children in future years.

An unexpected benefit of the Richford experience with French bilingual education has been the administrative view of bilingual education as a legitimate 'alternative education' experience for all children, regardless of ethnic or linguistic background. It also presents a means to parents of providing preschool education that would otherwise be impossible or very costly to obtain. As an optional program with an active parents' council, it offers parents a choice of how they wish their children to be educated. It also offers the cooperating district classroom teachers the opportunity of expanding the horizons of their traditional teaching situation.

SUMMARY

A bilingual education program such as ours squarely addresses the issue of using a second language in defining and teaching the 'basics' as they are currently being mandated by state areas covered by the Vermont competencies; it maintains a close working relationship with the English-language curriculum; it involves the classroom teachers in both planning and instructional time; and most important, it teaches subject matter through the use of a second language rather than by teaching language as an end or subject matter in itself.

The FNESU bilingual program also fosters 'competencies' for both learner and teacher. For the learner, 'language competence' is defined as the ability to communicate in both French and English during the course of everyday school activities. This competency is developed through the careful choice of structured language learning situations throughout the school day, whether in the classroom, the hall, the lunchroom, or the playground. For the teacher, 'language competency' is defined as the ability to instruct using both English and French. This competency is developed through formal inservice training activities and through observation and participation in the daily demonstration lessons conducted by the bilingual project staff. In the FNESU district, the bilingual 'return to basics' has thus become the means to a stimulating and relevant educational program in which there is a built-in potential for home, school, and community involvement.

*This paper originally appeared in *French Review* 54.3:393-400.

THE ROLE OF THE VERNACULAR IN TRANSITIONAL BILINGUAL EDUCATION

RODOLFO JACOBSON

INTRODUCTION

The professional literature abounds in studies stressing the philosophical as well as socio-political difference that holds between a maintenance-oriented and a transition-oriented bilingual program. However, there need not be any conflict between these two approaches, if, one, the maintenance of the vernacular code is stressed by means of a stable and balanced distribution of the two languages, rather than a gradual decrease of the use of the vernacular as some degree of proficiency in the nonvernacular tongue is being achieved; two, if the use of the vernacular as a medium of instruction is limited to the child's primary years (grades K to 3); and finally, if provisions are made for the child to understand that, even though the school language is the nonvernacular code from grade 4 on, the use of the vernacular outside the classroom is appropriate in a variety of home-, church-, and community-related situations. The value of the use of the vernacular code for the child during his early years of instruction is to provide time for him to make the needed emotional adjustment to the presence, in the country as a whole, of a language other than the one he speaks at home. The emphasis on an affective component in bilingual education seeks to accomplish for the child three goals, i.e. to reach the threshold level in his native language, to develop simultaneously the language skills in the second language that enable him to function well in a nonvernacular class environment after grade 3, and to allow sufficient time for the child to make the adjustment to the fact that his two codes are distributed in very specific ways. It is the objective of this paper to describe

181

the implementation of a non-conflicting approach that enables the child to make the transition to English as a medium of instruction and yet to recognize the functions of his own native dialect.

This country has been concerned, for a number of decades, about how to resolve two apparently conflicting realities. Numerous immigrations and territorial expansions led to the presence on American soil of speakers of scores of different languages, providing a richness of linguistic resources in this country. However, English rather than any of the indigenous, colonial, or immigrant languages, became the American medium of communication. Several ideologies were advanced that ranged from an extreme Anglo-Conformity position to a contrary, equally extreme, Cultural Pluralism position (Gordon 1961; Jacobson 1971; Kjolseth 1971). Although these ideologies were intended to be more culturally than linguistically relevant, it is easy to interpret them in a language oriented context, that is, to envision them as ends of a continuum stretching, at one extreme, from the only-English position to a multilingual position at the other extreme. Neither of the extremes represents current views but it is still an open question as to what extent one should allow, in addition to a standardized version of American English, the free use of languages like Spanish, French, Chinese, Vietnamese, and scores of others.

There are still over nine million persons in the U.S. for whom English is not a native language (Rogg 1978). Of these, more than five million are speakers of varieties of Spanish with Mexican-American, Puerto Rican, Cuban, or other Hispanic-American characteristics. In the homes, the neighborhoods, and the churches many non-English languages are heard and children must adjust to a situation where bilingualism becomes a necessity and diglossia a way of life. A non-English speaking child learns early in life that he will have to learn English in order to succeed in the broader society. The parent of that child knows it and so does the teacher of the school to which that child goes. What is not well understood is how to bring about a change in his language behavior so that the child may use the nonvernacular language effectively and also appropriately. Bilingual education was proposed to accomplish this. It also posed, however, the serious questions as to the fate of the child's vernacular. In the transitional approach, the home language might be consciously eradicated or allowed to vanish by attrition; in the maintenance approach, the home language was retained.

The argument for the retention of the home language becomes viable when one examines language in areas where two languages are in contact. South Texas is a case in point. A Spanish-speaking Mexican-American who has overcome the social and economic pressures and succeeded in educating himself, has usually acquired English to a degree that allows him to use either code as the situation may require. Although his literacy skills in Spanish, a language that was learned through oral transmission, do not always equal his English language skills, the *educated* Mexican-American has the choice of either language. The rationale for his choice is the appropriateness of the situation—a domain-oriented decision. On the other hand, and despite his ability to keep the two languages separate, he may engage in intersentential or intrasentential codeswitching, alternating languages at predictable grammatical boundaries (Jacobson 1977; Reyes 1976). Common as codeswitching actually is, it is only practised under very specific circumstances: (1) the interlocutors are bilingual, (2) the role relationship is one of peers, kin, or otherwise closely related persons, (3) the setting is informal, and (4) the topic reflects personal rather than transactional interaction.

As we examine this mode of interaction more closely and try to relate the community behavior to the language behavior appropriate for a classroom where a bilingual education program is implemented, it appears that a strategy of this nature—if it could be properly adapted—would be most appealing to children who every day witness the codeswitching of parents and peers, and for bilingual teachers who, for their communication with students, would want to utilize a communicative process that is natural and rapport-promoting at the same time. The switching back and forth from English to Spanish, as is observed in the Chicano community, must however be adapted to conform to sound pedagogical principles. The exposure to and the use of intrasentential codeswitching can hardly be recommended for a bilingual child who is trying to learn to keep his two languages apart. The switching at sentence boundaries, known as intersentential codeswitching, on the other hand, carries no risk as each sentence is a complete grammatical unit in its own right, regardless of the language used. Therefore, only intersentential switching is recommended for use in the method here described.

Three goals or foci tend to prevail in any educational setting regardless of the language or languages involved. The child's language has to be developed; the child is expected to achieve academically; and he must undergo socialization. The priorities according to which these three foci are arranged, however, tend to vary depending upon the professional bias of the designer of the school program. A psycholinguistically oriented curriculum specialist would give language development the highest priority. The curriculum specialist, especially if he also performs school administrative functions, would assign the highest priority to statistically verifiable academic achievement. The sociolinguistically trained program designer, on the other hand, would stress the children's social interactional norms. None of course underestimates the importance of any one of these foci within the whole instructional framework.

It is the sociolinguistically-oriented approach that has influenced the development of an approach of bilingual instruction known as the *Concurrent Approach.* The version of the approach described here, however, differs substantially from others bearing the same name, e.g., translation techniques are here usually avoided and comprehension difficulties are solved in a variety of different ways (see below). The 'Concurrent Translation Approach', as implemented mainly in California (Christina Bratt Paulston, personal conversation), engaged in random flipflopping between languages rather than premeditated and justifiable code alternations. Therefore, the instructional approach described here is called, more appropriately, the *New Concurrent Approach,* henceforth, the NCA method. Crucial to the NCA method is its language attitude aspect: the two languages used in the instruction of content during the primary years share mutual prestige. The bilingual teacher avoids any reference to what may lead to the assessment by the child that, say, English is the language of prestige and Spanish only a secondary or tolerated language. This is accomplished by a balanced *dual language use* and by the teacher's modeling of bilingual behavior. Dual language use means that the two languages are used concurrently and for the same amount of time, using L_1 during some portions of the class and L_2 during others. The teacher alternates between the two languages but stays within each for more time than in an intersentential codeswitching event as discussed above. Careful self-monitoring by the teacher ensures that equal time is spent in both languages. The cue-response technique developed for this purpose (see below) permits the teacher to rationalize the switching, that is, to specify what is accomplished by shifting to another language. Note that the teacher does not translate parts of the lesson nor does she provide a free interpretation of the material. She merely uses two different codes instead of one for the presentation of her carefully planned self-contained lesson and thus provides a model for her students to imitate. This modeling of bilingual behavior serves the purpose of showing that dual language use is not just an instructional gimmick but a strategy in which one engages if he knows two languages. As mentioned above, this strategy differs from the community-based codeswitching in that no language alternation within the sentence is encouraged. It is the intersentential, not the intrasentential, switching that allows the child to derive from each sentence the grammatical structure pertinent to English or Spanish. In other words, whereas the convergence of English and Spanish structures is commonplace in community switching, the sepration of the two codes is pursued in classroom switching. Taking advantage of the unique influence that she has on her students, a teacher can show that her language alternation practices are worth imitating, not only in the classroom, but also during recess, on the street, in the park, and at home. Thus, the language alternation perceived in the classroom and in informal settings conveys a very clear message to the child, that of equal status of home and school language.

The pressure in our communities to assign greater prestige to the nonvernacular code is strong. English is the language chosen for the domains of school (outside a bilingual program), employment, and government. As a result, those who seek to advance on the socioeconomic ladder must know English. The value attached to Spanish, on the other hand, seems to be limited in range and mostly confined to the domains of home, neighborhood, and church. And yet, time spent in the home, in the neighborhood, and at church covers a larger period of a person's life than time spent at school and is culturally, psychologically, and socially of greatest importance. Therefore, the teacher must demonstrate, during the adaptation years of the young child, the intrinsic value of the bilingual's two languages. By modeling bilingual behavior, the teacher shows the children what it means to be bilingual and encourages them to follow her example.

By the end of grade 3, the child in the NCA method has understood the value of his home language and its functional apportionment within the community. For the bilingual child, the fate of his vernacular is most important. His home language represents his home, the immediate neighborhood, and the persons with whom he associates. Therefore, he will find it rewarding that in the bilingual program his vernacular is respected and even used for instruction. He has been given time to adjust to the fact that English will be the medium of instruction and this gradual emotional adjustment to English has allowed him to develop proficiency in nonvernacular language skills over four years: a proficiency now instrumental to his academic achievement during the post-primary years. There is no reason to suspect that the child's school performance suffers because he knows both languages. Because of his English language skills he will do well in school. Because of his Spanish skills he can function with the people he cherishes and in settings that are familiar to him. This coexistence of the two languages gives him the self-identity that he needs during his primary grades. The NCA method therefore capitalizes on the equal prestige of the two languages, so that the self-awareness gained in this way can help the child learn the new language.

With this language attitudinal framework as a background, the bilingual teacher learns to view her class from a sociolinguistic perspective. The class takes on the characteristics of a social situation and the teacher, that of an analyst who seeks to uncover the cues that tell her how to conduct the class most effectively. Classroom strategies, curriculum matters, needed language development, and interpersonal relationships are all identifiable in this socio-educational network. Through training the teacher develops sensitivity to the system of cues (see below) and helps the child in an almost parallel development of the two languages as the latter acquires the knowledge of the school subjects. The decisions as to language selection in response to these cues constitute the core of the NCA method.

The linguistic repertoire of the teacher using the NCA approach includes, in addition to her proficiency in the majority language, familiarity with several codes that Hispanics in South Texas use. Regional variations, switching techniques, and knowledge of the standard variety of Spanish are all part of the teacher's repertoire. The linguistic demands on the bilingual teacher sound impressive but in reality are comparable to those made on the monolingual. Just as the latter has developed sensitivity toward stylistic variation, the former has developed an analogous sensitivity in language variation. Some additional training is necessary however in order for the bilingual teacher to develop the linguistic awareness that is here emphasized.[1]

The bilingual teacher is responsible for the language development of the children in either language. It may be overt as it is in the actual ESL or SSL class. The NCA method, however, is not implemented during the English as a Second Language or Spanish as a Second Language components of the bilingual program. Obviously, language alternation is impractical as a technique when English or Spanish is taught as a subject: ESL requires the use of English only and SSL, that of Spanish only. The covert language development that is part of the NCA method involves those language development efforts that the teacher pursues as she teaches math, science, social studies, or any other school subject. Regardless of the subject being taught, the teacher must provide additional practice to students in their weaker language or enrich their vocabulary or increase their ability to translate or interpret. These and similar activities are incidental but must be attended to in order to ensure the students' progress toward literacy in the two languages. They are all part of a design known as the System of Cues. Here, the teacher reacts to a series of cues by switching back and forth between languages as the content of a class may suggest.

The United Independent School District in Laredo, Texas has used and developed the new Concurrent Approach as the instructional method in one of its schools for the last six years. The following description, the component cues and the pedagogical areas to which these belong, is drawn from transcriptions of teacher-student dialogs in actual NCA classes.

Cues, in NCA, are signals that the teacher identifies in her class and that she wishes to respond to. As an ethnographer seeks to gather all the elements of a social situation and then arrange them in a meaningful order, so the teacher identifies the various aspects, pedagogical and social, that she feels she must address. These elements, or cues, are categorized depending on their relevance to classroom management, language development, curriculum, or teacher-student interactional norms. Classroom management, here called classroom strategies, and teacher-student interactional norms (interpersonal relationships) are pedagogical areas only in the broadest sense, but do follow set criteria established for the teacher during formal class performances.[2] Table 1 lists these pedagogical areas and the corresponding cues.

Table One

System of Cues

Classroom Strategies	Curriculum
Conceptual reinforcement	Language appropriateness
Review	Content
Capturing of attention	Text
Approval/Disapproval	

Language Development	Interpersonal Relationships
Variable language dominance	Intimacy/Formality
Lexical enrichment	Courtesy
Translatability	Free Choice
	Fatigue
	Self-awareness
	Rapport

Tables 2, 3, 4, and 5 are transcriptions that represent class segments in which language alternations occur as responses to cues. At times more than one cue may have triggered a given response; it is not always possible to infer from mini-lessons like these to which cue a teacher wished to respond. Each transcription is preceded by a general comment with reference to the cue or cues triggering the response. The grade level of the class is indicated and several comments provide further clarifications.

The four examples in Tables 2 through 5 show the significance of language alternation in response to certain cues that the teacher observes in her classroom. The teacher must develop an awareness of code selection. Normally, one does not pay attention to form but only to meaning; one focuses on what is said and not how it is said. In a bilingual situation, one grasps the content of the message, regardless of the language or languages in which it was conveyed. The teacher implementing the NCA method, on the other hand, is asked to be aware of any language switch that occurs in the classroom and also to alternate languages as necessary. In addition she must monitor her own code alternations for frequency, duration, and motive.

The teacher only switches languages when the alternation is pedagogically sound. As she plans the switching in advance, she must know exactly what she wants to accomplish by shifting from L_1 to L_2 or viceversa. This kind of language distribution is decided in principle when the lesson is planned. There she will focus on the following issues:

1. Based on the content to be taught, what will the expected teacher-student interaction be?
2. Which portions of the interactions should take place in English and which in Spanish?
3. What is accomplished, in each particular instance, by switching from one language to the other; in other words, why switch at all and in what way would the lesson be less effective if no language alternation occurred?

Although it may be difficult to predict the children's language choice decisions, the initial planning stage is important. Table 6 represents a part of a hypothetical lesson that teachers write in advance in order to identify the lesson segments where language alternation might be justifiable. This anticipated teacher-student dialog is comparable to a conventional lesson plan except that it goes beyond it by suggesting what the actual verbal interaction might be. The plan is laid out in three columns, the one at the left for Spanish, the one at the right for English and the central column for the cue that triggered the switch. A plan of this kind has been helpful to teacher trainees in order to decide where switches would be appropriate. Depending on the students' actual responses, the teacher makes whatever changes or adjustments are called for.[3]

The time frame of code distribution should be as balanced as possible. In order to obtain a near 50-50 distribution of the two languages, the teacher learns to detach herself from her teaching task and to monitor her own language distributional patterns. As she acquires greater confidence in her ability to carry out both objectives simultaneously, the teaching of content and the self-monitoring, she gradually feels more comfortable with the approach. The self-monitoring is designed to help the teacher maintain an accurate record of the time spent in either language, overall as well as in each switching event, and also to provide a rationalization for the switch. In other words, 'the teacher shall know each time a switch occurs *why* a language alternation is here appropriate and *what specific objective* is achieved by conducting the class in English and in Spanish or viceversa' (Jacobson 1981:15). This distributional pattern is intended to achieve, as pointed out before, these positive effects: first, the child will have developed his native language more fully by the time the bilingual education program ends; secondly, the student will be emotionally ready to shift to an only-English classroom in the upper grades, since he will be, by this time, proficient enough in English to achieve well academically.[4] Finally, he will have learned the functional distribution of two languages and their appropriate use in the community where he lives.

Because of its direct relationship to the community, the NCA method seeks to draw directly on the parent's cooperation. The parent must know the rationale of this approach. The patterns of language use at home must be correlated with the patterns of language use at school. If teachers using the NCA method view both languages as equally prestigious, and parents express the view that one language surpasses the other in prestige, a situation of conflict may be created. Therefore, if both languages are to be developed concurrently in the primary grades, strategies must be found at home to duplicate the language behavior observed at school. A teacher-parent workshop on language distributional patterns would determine the most appropriate criteria to follow in this respect.

Such direct interaction is a major departure from the traditional parent role in bilingual education. Most parent involvement programs either train parents or help them find work. As a result, one finds parents as aides, helpers, participants in extracurricular events, and so forth. One also finds them as members of parent advisory groups where they largely function, not as a decision-making body, but rather an information-receiving entity through which the school can comply with governmental regulations on parent participation.

To train parents in areas that may help them become more efficient in their child-rearing roles is an important aspect of any parent involvement program. This often enables them to assist their children better in their school-related tasks at home and cooperate more effectively with the school program. Equally meaningful is the type of training that some schools provide whereby parents are professionalized in many aspects of program administration, so that they may come to use more fully the advisory capacity for which the parent group was created in the first place. However, the parent is seldom seen as a resource person that brings to the teaching staff and the school administration a greater awareness of the values of the group or groups from which the school population comes. Teachers and administrators, including minority members, often fail to understand the realities and the aspirations of a group that has not participated in a uniformation process like that of secondary and college education. It is particularly in regard to language behavioral patterns that the school needs a greater input from the parents, so that the conflict situation that is often created by divergent goals of school and community is avoided.

The shift to English-only after the primary grades no longer holds the message for the child that English is more prestigious than Spanish but rather that out of two potential languages, English, for being the majority language, has been selected as the medium of instruction. By implication, Spanish can still continue being an important medium of communication, outside the classroom. Therefore, different strategies may be developed at home, in the neighborhood, in community centers, and at church, where the post-primary child finds challenging activities that not only keep his first language alive but develop it further. Such a goal could hardly be accomplished without a close school-home relationship whereby language patterns are devised that allow parents to match the school objectives in an effective manner.

The child educated through the NCA method is expected to have achieved a degree of English language proficiency that matches or approximates that of the monolingual English-speaking child. Linguistic precautions have been taken, since the Spanish-speaking child will have learned English through appropriate English as a Second Language (ESL) methods and will have increased his English by learning his school subjects in a program where approximately 50% of the instruction is given in English. Affective precautions have also been taken, since the child has found that his home language is also used in the instruction of content. In addition to proficiency in English and the recognition of the equal prestige of his two languages, the balanced language distribution helps the child to attain the threshold level in Spanish.

The threshold hypothesis as proposed by Cummins (1979, 1980) suggests that a second language is learned more successfully when the home language is developed fully and *all* its structure is internalized. This hypothesis has served as a rationale for Canadian immersion programs in which English-speaking children receive their instruction, except for English language arts, in French (Barik and Swain 1975, 1978; Chaudron 1977; Genesee 1979; Lambert and Tucker 1972). In the U.S. immersion programs are virtually nonexistent. Swain (1981) argues in this respect that the Canadian immersion

is in contrast to the situation—which in the United States is often referred to as 'immersion'—where children who are to learn the target language are mixed together with other children who are native speakers of the target language—a situation for the learner which we have referred to as 'submersion', not immersion.

And she continues saying that

...the submerged children find themselves in a necessarily handicapped position which can do little to enhance any sense of self-esteem or permit equality of learning opportunities.

This is also the concern of De Avila and Duncan (1978) who find it paradoxical that complete immersion in English has had the greatest success of the attempts to promote bilingualism (see Cohen 1975; Lambert and Peal 1972). The bitter irony, however, is that it doesn't seem to work in the absence of equal status for both languages. Chicano children, say De Avila and Duncan (1978:141):

are simply not going to want to learn standard English as long as their own language (substandard though it may be) is held as an object of scorn and ridicule.

It is proposed here that the threshold level can be reached when the first language is maintained while the second language is acquired and used concurrently for instruction, as in the balanced language distribution in the NCA method. By the time the child completes grade 3, the age when he presumably reaches the threshold level, he has had instruction of and in Spanish for the equivalent of two years.

K: one-half year (i.e. half of the instruction in Spanish)
1: one-half year (i.e. half of the instruction in Spanish)
2: one-half year (i.e. half of the instruction in Spanish)
3: one-half year (i.e. half of the instruction in Spanish)[5]

Simultaneous instruction of and in English in grades K to 3 is not detrimental in any way. Quite the opposite, it is the means by which the child learns the differential apportionment of his languages and their functions.

Other instructional models for second language acquisition often lead to first language attrition or even to its eradication. In the monolingual English-only model, the home language is totally ignored, and in the usual bilingual Spanish-English model, the gradual decrease in the use of Spanish constantly stresses the higher status of English. In both cases, the prestige of the vernacular is undermined, thus encouraging the child to limit or to avoid altogether the use of his first language. Since current bilingual programs are all transitional *from the start on,* the use of the home language is merely a tool for the acquisition of English and no vernacular language maintenance is ever contemplated. Monolingual education, by definition, leaves the vernacular to its own fate by showing no interest in the preservation of the ethnic language. The other-than-English language resources in the country are too valuable to waste. If their maintenance can be combined with the acquisition of English proficiency and an understanding of the functional distribution of the two languages, we would be spared the contradictory situation whereby a school contributes, in the elementary grades, to the loss of the first language and encourages, in the secondary grades, the relearning of that same language as a foreign language.

The dual language use in early schooling holds two important promises for the first language. The form used need not be restricted to the vernacular alone, but may also incorporate any nonvernacular counterpart. Secondly, the child learns to recognize and keep separate the grammatical structures of English and Spanish. In regard to the former, the child acquires bidialectal sensitivity that allows him to switch from the regional dialect to the nonvernacular as the situation demands it. The notion of language appropriateness is thus developed and assists the child in making his decision as to which variety is called for at a given moment. In regard to the latter, the separation of the two languages—an ability that he has acquired through the process of encoding his concepts with flexibility and speed in Spanish and in English—allows the child to speak either language without interference from the other, an ability that he must possess to interact with monolinguals. However, the child or later, the adolescent, may still favor the codeswitching dialect of the bilingual community when such a variety, because of the speakers, the topic, or the setting involved, is appropriate. In that case, it is the person's free will and not his language deficiency that makes him intermingle the two languages.

CONCLUSION

The author has attempted here to show the place of one method of bilingual instruction, the *New Concurrent Approach,* in the broad setting of school-community relations and consider the whole, with special emphasis on desirable language attitudes, within the context of American education. It has been predicted that the balanced development of the two languages, the child's vernacular and the majority language, from grades K to 3 will accomplish one of the main objectives of American schools, that is, the achievement of English language proficiency by children whose first language is not English. The successful achievement of this goal, it has been suggested, is the result of proper linguistic and affective strategies that allow the child to grow in an environment of sociocultural equality. This cultural and linguistic equal opportunity is intended to provide for the non-English speaking minority child the tools for academic achievement in English without severing his sociolinguistic ties with the community to which he belongs.

Table Two

To ensure that the concept of 'Thanksgiving' is fully understood (*Conceptual reinforcement*) or to review the significance of Thanksgiving (*Review*) or to explain it more thoroughly to the Spanish dominant (*Courtesy*), the teacher alternates in her discussion between English and Spanish, e.g.

> T: How do we celebrate Thanksgiving?[1] *Cómo celebramos el Día de las Gracias?*
>
> S₁: *Agarrando el guajolote y ...*
>
> T: *¿Comiendo qué?*
>
> S₂: We cook and eat it.
>
> T: That's right.[2] We cook and eat it. *Compramos un guajolote, lo cocemos y nos lo comemos.[3] Pero antes de la comida, qué es lo que hacemos?*
>
> S₂: *Damos las gracias por el guajolote.[4]*

(Grade K)

Comments

1. To provide a smooth transition, the teacher first asks a question in English and then follows it up by an identical question in Spanish.
2. To assure the child that his/her response was correct, the teacher not only accepts the answer in English but rewards the students by starting out in English also.
3. After a short additional comment in English, the teacher switches back to Spanish.
4. The child's shift to Spanish is now complete.

Table Three

Within the home domain, Spanish is more appropriate; hence, a switch to Spanish is warranted (*Language appropriateness*). At the same time, a language switch helps capture the attention of the group (*Capturing of attention*).

T: You can say, 'Mommy, I made some butter at school.' And you can tell your Mother how to make the butter.[1] *Tú le vas a decir a Mamá como hiciste la mantequilla en la clase*[2] *pero nada más si están calladitos van a ayudar a hacer la mantequilla.*[3] All right, who can tell me what this is right here?[4]

S: A recipe.

T: What is a recipe?

(Grade K)

1. The content here is taught in English. The first reference to the children's mother is in English.
2. The switch to Spanish illustrates language appropriateness as most children associate Spanish with their homes.
3. The continuation in Spanish alerts the children to the forthcoming activity.
4. The return to English suggests that the lesson now goes on.

Table Four

The teacher develops a concept simultaneously in the two languages (*Conceptual reinforcement* like above). By moving smoothly from one to the other code, he/she makes sure that children know the right terms in both languages (*Lexical enrichment*) or children are acquiring greater competence in the language in which they are not dominant (*Variable language dominance*).

T: *Mañana vamos a ver si la semilla ha crecido.*[1] Now when we add water to a seed, what happens to a seed?[2]

S: It cracks.

T: It cracks. *¿Y qué es lo que sale de la semilla?*

S: *El tallo.*

(Grade K)

1. A science concept is developed in Spanish.
2. By means of a smooth transition to English, the concept is reinforced as the other language is now used as a means of instruction.
3. The appropriate vocabulary is developed in both languages.
4. On continuing the unit, the teacher switches back to Spanish and elicits another science term, *tallo.*

Table Five

To ensure that children know the appropriate vocabulary (*Lexical enrichment* like above) and that they can render in L_2 what they have just heard in L_1 (*Translatability*), the teacher has her explanation restated in L_2.

T: (provides explanation in Spanish how to make breakfast with emphasis on preparing French toast from scratch). *Les expliqué todo detalladamente en español. Quiero saber quien me lo puede decir ahora pero en inglés.*[1] *Detalladamente, exactamente como yo lo dije.*

S : You get a pan, you put milk and the ... *allí entran*[2]

T: You mix it?

S : You take it, you throw it then into a pan, you wait for two minutes; you turn it *después* another four minutes, you turn it and then you get it; you put the cinnamon, the honey, ...

S : ... the bacon.

S : ... and then you get a glass of juice.

(Grade 3)

1. The ability to translate or interpret is here explored. To mention the language label, 'inglés', is here appropriate as the children have become more explicitly aware of the difference between the two codes.

2. As the child begins to interpret, there is no further significant switch. Two minor switches to Spanish do however occur, a *false start* switch and a *substratum* switch, as labeled by Jacobson (1977:240-242)[6] elsewhere.

Table Six

	T: Do you remember what we have been learning about air? Robert, what have we learned about air and weight?
	S₁: ... that air has weight.
	T: Very good. Isela, what have we learned about air and space?
	S₂: ... that air takes up space.
T: *¿Se acuerdan del experimento que hicimos el* ← Review	T: Very good.

T: *otro día con el vaso y la toallita de papel?*
Lorenzo, me puedes decir lo que hicimos?

S₃: *Pusimos una toallita en un vaso y no se mojó el papel.*

T: *Muy bien, Lorenzo.*

Conceptual
Reinforcement →

T: Who can tell me now why the paper didn't get wet?

S₄: ... because the air in the cup didn't let the water in.

T: *Muy bien, Laura. Tú sí pusiste atención. El papel no se mojó porque el aire ocupa espacio o lugar en el vaso y no permite que entre el agua.*

← Approval

Text →

T: Now, I want you to turn to page 18—a one and an eight. Here you will see another example.

NOTES

[1] This training is not described here because of the limitation in space, but see Rodolfo Jacobson (1981).

[2] For further discussion of the System of Cues, see Rodolfo Jacobson (1979a).

[3] For more details on the NCA dialogue plan, see Rodolfo Jacobson (1979b).

[4] A more appropriate time for the transition to English-only instruction would be grade 6 when the child would already have developed both languages completely but current legislation does not as yet provide for bilingual education through the upper elementary grades.

[5] A variant of this design would provide for two and one-half years of instruction in Spanish, e.g.,

    K: one year   (only Spanish)
    1: one-half year (i.e., half of the instruction in Spanish)
    2: one-half year (i.e., half of the instruction in Spanish)
    3: one-half year (i.e., half of the instruction in Spanish)

The Spanish-only instruction in grade K (in conjunction with some ESL instruction) would further strengthen the child's first language development. A Title VII Demonstration proposal to this effect has been recommended for funding by the Office of Bilingual Education and Minority Languages in Washington, D.C. and will be implemented in two schools of the Southwest Independent School District, San Antonio, Texas, in fall 1981.

6 Jacobson describes a *false start* as a switch that allows the bilingual to recast his thought in the other language because he could not get the message across in the first one. *Substratum* is a subconscious switch whereby a single word from L_1 surfaces into an L_2 discourse, usually because of the speaker's language dominance pattern.

TEACHER TRAINING FOR BILINGUAL EDUCATION: AN INTERNATIONAL PERSPECTIVE

RUDOLPH C. TROIKE and MURIEL SAVILLE-TROIKE

ISSUES AND NEEDS

Being a teacher has never been simple. Being a bilingual teacher is at least twice as complex. Preparing a bilingual teacher must certainly take account of this complexity if it is to adequately fulfill its purpose.

If the teacher is the principal figure in the educational process, mediating between the learner and the curriculum, his/her role becomes even more central in a bilingual education program. For here the teacher must serve not only to represent and interpret the adult world to neophyte learners from the same or closely similar linguistic and cultural background, but must represent and interpret a different cultural world through the means of the learner's language, at the same time attempting to teach the language which is the medium of that other cultural world. Training should minimally serve to prepare the teacher to handle these complexities.

What a bilingual teacher is and does is determined to a large extent by national and local educational practices, policies, and goals. In developing countries elementary or middle school graduates are often used as instructors in the primary grades. This fact defines the potential pool of teachers in bilingual programs and the parameters within which a teacher training program must operate. On the other hand, in some developed countries, bilingual teachers are required to have college degrees and special certification in bilingual education. This obviously allows for much more extensive technical preparation.

The educational structure in the country will also have a determining effect on the content and context of teacher training. In a country with a highly centralized system, training/certification requirements may be determined by the Ministry of Education, either on its own or in consultation with outside specialists. Where the tradition of local control is strong, however, requirements may be set by individual teacher training institutions or voluntary accrediting organizations, or even by local school boards.

National educational policies and goals, where any have been formulated, are often reflections of larger policies and goals, particularly in the economic, social, and political spheres. A UNESCO meeting of experts in 1977 proposed a typology of aims for bilingual education which in part illustrates this point. Ten possible aims were identified, as follows:

1. National development
2. National integration
3. Incorporation of marginal or minority groups into the national life
4. Provision of improved access to goods and services, employment, etc.
5. Assurance of civil rights, equal educational opportunity, and protection from discrimination
6. Maintenance of segregated educational systems ('apartheid')
7. Development of languages in themselves
8. Preservation or revival of languages
9. Increase of interethnic, interregional, or international communication
10. Assimilation of linguistically and culturally different groups

It was further noted in the report that 'These aims might be at variance with each other. It should therefore be recognized that potential conflicts exist, and that bilingual education can be a two-edged sword' (Unesco 1977).

It is important to realize that all education is political, and no matter how much researchers, philosophers, and technicians may focus on other aspects, the political 'bottom line' (to use popular accounting parlance) is inescapable. This fact needs to be remembered when on occasion bilingual education is attacked as political, since it is usual to view the status quo (the 'unmarked' condition) as nonpolitical, and any 'marked' deviation from it as political. If a society has traditionally suppressed minorities, for example, or denied equal employment opportunity to women, the domination of the society by men or by a particular group (often both) is not seen as a political issue, but merely as the natural 'unmarked' condition. Conversely, efforts to increase opportunities for minorities or women, when these do not emanate from the established authority structure as an unmarked and logically-justified part of a coherent national policy, are pejoratively labeled as 'political'. The provision of bilingual education for the upper classes is rarely seen as political, unless control of the society by the upper classes itself comes to be challenged and the opportunity for education in a second language is viewed as elitism.

We shall not pursue these political issues further here except to recognize that political factors of one sort or another may impinge on various aspects of teacher training, and we will touch on them as they arise. In what follows, we shall for the most part not be addressing elite bilingual education, but will be directing our comments primarily to situations where previously excluded linguistic minorities are involved.

Any program of teacher training must allocate resources, whether at the national, provincial (state), or local level. Decisions about how much training is needed, by whom, and how many people are to be trained will have implications for the use of people, time, funds, and other resources. If such decision-making is to be soundly based, it should be preceded by a needs assessment to determine the discrepancy between existing resources and those required to implement the policy. Policy decisions are sometimes made without adequate information on which to judge their cost implications, and may be tempered or abandoned when the costs are known.

To take an example, when the 1968 Bilingual Education Act was passed in the United States the need for some training of teachers in programs was recognized, but the lack of institutional resources among colleges and universities to conduct the training was not, nor were those institutions generally responsive to the need. Direct funding for such purposes was not authorized until 1974, at which time a number of programs sprang into being. It was also not until 1974 that Congress requested estimates of the number of children in need ('need' being defined as lacking skills in English). The estimates have finally (1980) been published, but they are valid only at the national level and for some of the more populous states. Furthermore, they are valid only for some of the major language groups, so that among American Indian groups, for example, separate figures are available only for the Navajo.

If the dimensions of need are so poorly known in a country where millions of dollars have been spent on determining the number of children with limited proficiency in the national language, how much more difficult it may be to estimate the need for numbers of teachers in a developing country with few resources to spend on planning. Nevertheless, language surveys such as the sociolinguistic surveys of East African countries, the Quechua dialect survey in Peru, or the Linguistic Archive of Oaxaca (Mexico) are essential instruments in the planning process and can provide important information for determining the need for teaching training (Troike and Modiano 1975).

One particularly critical educational policy issue which will have a major impact on teacher training is whether bilingual programs are to develop initial literacy skills in the native language or whether they will make use of the native language only orally while introducing literacy in the second language. This major dichotomy in bilingual education models used around the world directly affects training programs, since to implement the first model, teacher candidates must learn to read in their own language if they cannot do so already. For various historical reasons, in most instances they will be literate only in the national language, if they are literate at all. This need implicates teacher trainers as well, who should if possible be able to read in the language they are teaching teachers to read.

TEACHER SKILLS AND COMPETENCIES

While the skills and competencies which are needed by bilingual teachers will vary with different settings and types of programs, it may be best to begin with a more or less 'maximal' or 'ideal' set, which would be recommended for a four to five year college-level program in the U.S. or comparable environment. This set could be condensed or adapted in various ways for application in in-service training programs, for training paraprofessionals, or for training bilingual teachers in places where they are expected to have less than a college degree.

The requirements given here are based on a set of guidelines for bilingual teacher preparation developed by a group of leaders in bilingual education who were brought together in 1974 by the Center for Applied Linguistics (CAL 1974). They are given under four subject headings: (a) language proficiency, (b) linguistic, (c) cultural, and (d) pedagogical. The requirements are stated in terms of 'competencies' or skills/knowledge to be demonstrated by the teacher candidate. This mode of formulation has three purposes: (1) the characteristics identified might be taught within different courses in different institutions, so that a statement in terms of competencies is more flexible than one given in terms of specific courses; (2) the competencies can be satisfied through tests or other means of demonstration rather than only through taking particular courses; (3) the needed competencies can be identified quite specifically, whereas the content associated with a particular course title could be quite variable.

The following competencies, then, are adapted from the CAL *Guidelines*:[1]

A. Language Proficiency
1. Demonstrate the ability to understand, speak, read, and write the national/second language and the students' language at an acceptable level by passing an examination (standardized if possible).
2. Demonstrate the ability to provide content instruction (in mathematics, health, social studies, etc.) through the medium of both the national/second language and the students' language.

B. Linguistic Knowledge
1. Demonstrate an understanding of the basic nature of language, language change, and relation of language to society and culture, including bilingualism.
2. Demonstrate a knowledge of the phonological, grammatical, and semantic characteristics of the national/second language and the students' language and the ability to identify areas of possible interference and positive transfer.
3. Demonstrate understanding of basic stages/processes of first and second language acquisition and their implication for classroom instruction.
4. Be able to identify and explain regional, social, and developmental varieties of the students' language(s).
5. Demonstrate awareness and understanding of cultural differences in patterns of communication.

C. Cultural Knowledge
1. Demonstrate an understanding of the concepts of culture, ethnocentrism, and cultural relativity, and basic principles of social and cultural analysis (including acculturation and assimilation).
2. Demonstrate an awareness of the cultural diversity of the country or region.
3. Identify significant aspects of the mainstream culture to aid in recognizing similarities and differences.
4. Demonstrate an awareness of the history of the country or region.
5. Demonstrate a knowledge of the history of the target cultural group.
6. Demonstrate a knowledge of the culture of the target group.
7. Develop an awareness of the cultural group's folklore, and its function in the culture.

D. Pedagogical Competencies
   1. Demonstrate the ability to explain and apply one or more theories of learning.
   2. Show an understanding of and demonstrate the ability to apply appropriate methods for developing first and second (national) language skills, including listening, speaking, reading, and writing.
   3. Demonstrate the ability to plan and present content lessons in both languages in various curriculum areas.
   4. Demonstrate a knowledge of how to effectively incorporate students' culture in the curriculum.
   5. Utilize appropriate classroom management techniques, especially those which relate to individualizing instruction.
   6. Demonstrate ability to work with auxiliary persons in a classroom.
   7. Demonstrate ability to work with parents and community.
   8. Demonstrate ability to assess language proficiency in subject matter areas, and to utilize the results.
   9. Demonstrate ability to formulate objectives and develop evaluation strategies.
   10. Demonstrate ability to utilize various teaching techniques in content areas in the national/second language and the students' language.
   11. Demonstrate ability to evaluate instructional material in terms of the students' linguistic, cultural, and intellectual characteristics.
   12. Demonstrate ability to modify instructional materials to meet students' needs.
   13. Demonstrate ability to plan and implement team teaching.
   14. Demonstrate a knowledge of how to utilize in the classroom appropriate literature from the students' group.
   15. Demonstrate any other skills, information, competencies expected of a bilingual professional.

The language proficiency requirement is essential and in many ways the most important requirement of all. For a bilingual program to be meaningful, the teacher must be able to speak the language of the students fluently. For programs which utilize initial literacy in the students' language, the teacher must also be able to read and write the language. But beyond that, it is not enough merely to be proficient in the language. *The teacher must be able to use the language to teach content matter.*

Just as someone proficient in the national language cannot automatically be expected to be able to teach mathematics or history or science without special training, the same applies *a forteriori* to speakers of minority languages. Even if they are fluent speakers and can read and write their language, in most instances they will not have had the experience of using or hearing the language used in the academic domain, since their education will probably have been entirely through the medium of the national language. One of the biggest hurdles minority-language teacher trainees have to face is learning to use their language in a new sociolinguistic domain. This fact becomes painfully evident in studies of bilingual programs, which show over and over again that teachers continually regress into the use of the national language because of their limitations or insecurity in using the other language in the school or subject-matter domain.

The competencies dealing with linguistic knowledge are designed to prepare teachers for recognizing and dealing appropriately with processes and problems in second language acquisition and with development and variation in the first language, as well as with cross-cultural differences in patterns of communication. The purposes for requiring this knowledge on the part of teachers are several. First, teachers need to know something about the structure of the national language to give them a metalinguistic perspective on what they are teaching. Second, some formal knowledge of the students' language (which in most cases will be their own as well) can help teachers to diagnose and understand students' learning problems with the second language, and at the same time enable them to embue students with greater respect for their own language—an attitude which can have a positive effect on learning the second language.

Knowing something about variation in the students' language can help overcome undue prescriptivism or negative attitudinal reactions toward students' linguistic behavior. Many teachers in Spanish bilingual programs in the U.S., for example, reinforce students' low self-esteem by denouncing regional and social variants in their speech as *barbarismos*. Understanding the nature of code-switching as a normal process and a positive social skill among bilinguals can likewise help to remove this phenomenon from the shade of obloquy into which ignorance or prejudice has so long cast it.

Where teachers may have to develop curriculum materials in the first language, or where such materials exist, sensitization to variation in the language and understanding of the reasons for it can act as a brake on premature or inappropriate normativism. As an illustration of the type of problem which can arise because of lack of linguistic knowledge or awareness, one group which received funding for materials development used the pronunciation and usage of their own rather atypical community as the sole basis for their materials and made no provision for other varieties of the language. The result was that other communities speaking the language were unwilling to utilize the materials in their bilingual education programs, and the programs suffered because they had no materials.

By knowing about cross-cultural differences in communication patterns, teachers can be aware of the need to teach the patterns as such, and can help students adjust to them. Examples are not far to seek. Asian students often find it embarrassing to thank someone for a personal compliment, since such a reaction seems to imply lack of modesty. In some areas of the world compliments directed at children or growing plants may place them in peril, and so be inappropriate or require an off-setting remark (depreciation, in fact, may be required among some groups). Asking a person's name may be tabu, and there may be constraints on who may talk to whom about what (including between related students in the classroom), and when one should be silent or when one may talk. Where differences exist between such patterns in the students' language and the patterns in the national/second language, teachers can help to minimize learning problems that will arise, or can adapt or supplement curriculum materials which do not take those differences into account.

Training in cultural knowledge about both the mainstream national culture and the minority culture is essential in helping the trainee develop an informed perspective on cultural differences. If trainees are from the minority group, they may very well have acquired a negative self-evaluation of their cultural characteristics from stereotypes held by the dominant group. In addition, even fully participating members of the minority culture do not have an objective understanding of their culture which they can analytically compare and contrast with the majority/national culture. Further, to the extent that they are acculturated, they will probably lack familiarity with their own traditional culture. An understanding of cultural differences can therefore have significant affective consequences in teachers' pedagogical practices, and in the attitudes they in turn communicate to their students about their culture. At the same time, it can aid them in materials and curriculum design, and in choosing appropriate cultural material to include in their teaching. This is of crucial significance, since an important part of their function will be helping prepare minority students to survive in a sometimes hostile and often indifferent cultural world.

The pedagogical competencies given here are basically those of appropriate classroom management and instructional techniques, with additions and modifications essential to the bilingual and cross-cultural nature of the interactional setting in the bilingual program. Many programs in the U.S. include classroom aides (paraprofessionals) in their staffing;

these are persons without full teacher training and certification (sometimes with none) who assist the teacher in the classroom and who require supervision by the teacher. Also, programs in the U.S. have increasingly emphasized working closely with parents and the community to involve them in supporting and reinforcing the educational efforts of the school, as well as to make the school more responsive to their goals and interests. In short, these pedagogical competencies underscore the need for bilingual teachers to possess basic teaching skills *plus* first and second language teaching abilities and sensitivity to the unique needs found in the bilingual program.

CURRICULUM AND PROCEDURES [2]

The specific curriculum organized to prepare bilingual teachers according to the competencies given above will vary from one institution to another, and from one country to another, particularly where circumstances dictate that only a subset of the competencies are appropriate to include in the training. Circumstances will also dictate the amount of time available for preparation and the conditions under which training must take place.

In general, two kinds of training are usually recommended for both preservice and inservice programs: (1) formal training, including classes, workshops, and seminars, and (2) field-based training, including supervised observation and practice teaching.

In one institution, for example, second-language teaching methods might be taught in the modern languages department, while in another place the course might be given in the education department, college, or faculty. The mainstream/national culture might be dealt with in a course in sociology, history, or social psychology; the minority language and culture might be covered in the same department or they might be found in different departments. Competencies included in a single course in one institution might be distributed through two or more courses in another institution, perhaps in configuration with still other competencies. All of this must be worked out in terms of the history and existing faculty strengths of each institution.

Naturally, it is to be expected that the curriculum for teacher or paraprofessional training will reflect the content of the school program, which in turn as we have noted is determined to a large extent by the aims or goals adopted at the national, state, or local level.

It is in any event important that training include a practicum and supervised field experience under as realistic a situation as possible to prepare trainees for the conditions they will ultimately face. Bilingual education entails experiences in dual language instruction, second language development, and attention to cross cultural differences which are likely to be unique in the experience of the trainees, and a radical departure from the way in which they were undoubtedly taught themselves. The significance of this last point is to be found in the conventional wisdom that teachers tend to teach as they were taught—frequently to the despair of teacher trainers attempting to bring about changes in teaching methods. Supervised practice teaching is thus essential in order to inculcate in trainees the new methods and concepts involved in bilingual instruction.

Furthermore, observation and practice should take place in surroundings as similar as possible to those in which the trainees will eventually teach. Teacher attrition is usually highest after the first year of teaching because of the difficulties in adjusting to the stresses of the teaching situation. These stresses are accentuated if trainees have been 'protected' from exposure to the conditions they will face in actual teaching settings (we do not specify 'classrooms' here, since in some places, teachers will not even have the luxury of classrooms in which to teach). It is thus a disservice to trainees and their future students alike if a realistic experience is not provided.

For reasons of relevance and affect, as well as economic practicability, it is therefore often unwise to export prospective teachers to institutions in other countries for their training. Resources will generally be more efficiently and effectively spent on developing in-country capabilities in bilingual teacher training, although this may well include importing foreign expertise. Exceptions to this caveat occur where teachers who speak a minority language may benefit from having part of their training in a country where that language is dominant and used for a full range of sociolinguistic functions (such as Spanish speaking teachers from the U.S. studying in Mexico), or where the native language, even though dominant, has not traditionally been used for education (such as Arabic speaking teachers in Algeria studying in Egypt or Syria).

Training considerations in each of the four competency areas given above may now be taken up in turn:

A. Language Proficiency

The teacher candidate probably must already have considerable proficiency in the languages of instruction as a *prerequisite* to training in bilingual education, given the level of linguistic proficiency which is (or should be) required to teach in a language, and given the time it takes to reach such a level. Knowledge of the students' language need only be oral, however, with reading and writing skills taught as part of the curriculum if the program is to include literacy in the native language. The ability to provide content instruction through the medium of both the national/second language and the students' language is developed in large measure by having both languages used as media of instruction in the training program. Particular attention must be paid to teaching vocabulary in the students' language for concepts to be presented in the academic domains.

It cannot be emphasized enough that just because a person is a native speaker of a language, he or she is not automatically competent to teach in the language. If the language is one which has not traditionally been used as a medium of classroom instruction (as will often be true for indigenous languages), new terminology may have to be developed and taught to teacher trainees. For example, one American Indian language lacked a specific term for 'triangle', so one had to be agreed upon for teachers to use in talking about this shape (this example illustrates how culture-specific even such supposedly 'universal' concepts are).

Teacher trainees should be given sufficient guided opportunities to use their native language in unfamiliar academic contexts. Where the society has a traditional diglossic 'working relation' between languages whereby the national language is used for 'public' purposes and the native language for 'home' purposes, special attention must be given to helping trainees develop proficiency and security in using their first language in 'public' domains.

In addition, if trainees use a nonstandard variety of either the national language or the home language (or both), practice and training will have to be included in the program to help them develop comfortable fluency in standard varieties of one or both of the languages. Except in programs which utilize differentiated staffing and allow for team-teaching arrangements based on the relative language proficiency of teachers, teacher candidates who do not control a standard variety of the national language may find that they face restricted employment opportunities.

B. Linguistic Knowledge

Knowledge of the structures, varieties, and acquisition processes for first and second language is usually learned via formal training, in courses in linguistics, bilingualism, contrastive analysis, etc. Depending on training resources and the prior educational level of trainees, greater or lesser sophistication in this area may be considered adequate. Minimal competence includes understanding of the concept that all languages are systematic, as are the processes of language acquisition, and the knowledge that all varieties of a language are viable forms of communication (although not equally appropriate on all occasions). If literacy is to be developed in students' native language, knowledge of the relationship between language forms and symbols is also critical, and of how these differ in the two languages of education.

Whether training is to be completed in a few weeks or several years, it should address such questions as:

What are the elements of language?

How is language put together?

How does it work?

How is it used?

How is language learned?

How does it change?

Why does it vary?

How can language development be planned?

These questions should be asked of each language of instruction, both to emphasize their common nature, and to contrast the nature and context of first and second language acquisition.

The teacher with even minimal linguistic sophistication can do a great deal to guide students to an adequate command of the national language while at the same time preserving intact their respect for their native language. In language contact situations where people frequently engage in 'code-switching'—shifting between languages according to situation or topic, including shifts within sentences—teachers need to learn that this is a special linguistic skill to be valued. For academic learning purposes it may be desirable to keep presentations (or at least segments of presentations) in one language or the other, to encourage development of proficiency in each language, though there is no research evidence to demonstrate that this is necessary.

Above all, teachers must see language both as a powerful affective symbol (of identity, affiliation, attitude, rejection, control, etc.) and as an instrument for learning, and must feel free to use both languages to promote maximum learning by assuring that before everything else, students *understand* what is being taught.

The most fundamental principle in education is to *accept students where they are* and lead them where they need to go. This means accepting and respecting the linguistic skills a student brings to school and *building* on these. The teacher's goal should be to *add* to students' existing linguistic skills, not to reject or attempt to replace them. The teacher who understands the nature of language and language variation will have greater respect for the native linguistic abilities of students, and greater respect for his or her own personal native language ability.

C. Cultural Knowledge

Clearly knowledge about culture in general, or about any two or more cultures in specific, can be taught by various means; just as clearly, knowledge about a culture does not insure acceptance of people, or students, who are members of the group possessing that culture. On the other hand, the requirement cited in many job descriptions in the U.S. that bilingual teachers *be* bicultural does not insure that such teachers will be accepting of students from the same cultural background as they are (indeed, without appropriate training, such teachers may be more intolerant than someone from a different cultural background). Knowing a culture natively does not automatically enable one to teach it, or to be sensitive to it in teaching.

While recognizing and accepting the culture which students bring to school is important, however, the fact remains that the same reasons exist for learning the dominant culture in a country as for learning the national language: it is necessary for full participation in the larger society. The comparison with adding a second language is a useful analogy to continue, for adding a second culture has many of the same implications for both theory and training.

First, to understand and facilitate learning, teachers should know what it is that is being acquired, and how it compares with their students' native cultural system. Unfortunately, cultural rules have often been recognized only in their breach, and when the consequences have been dramatic or traumatic enough to the second learner to be of note—a kind of error analysis. More humane, if it can escape the lists of cultural stereotypes which are in circulation (i.e. present vs. future orientation, passive vs. active coping styles), would be a contrastive analysis to facilitate the identification of potential cultural conflicts for students and the development of instructional means and materials to teach to these points.

Having awareness, sensitivity, and knowledge about culture also entails being able to recognize cultural influences on oneself and others. All of us know that we have culture, too, but seldom do we recognize that this culture explains much of our own thinking and behavior. It is precisely because our culture is so much a part of us that it controls us at a subconscious level, unless we are trained to be conscious of its influence.

Formal training which may be offered in this area could include Cultural Anthropology, which contributes to notions of cultural relativity, and the Ethnography of Communication, which teaches methods for observing and describing communication events in different cultures, and is very relevant to describing classroom interaction. In addition to supervised observation, field-based training might include community visitation and collection and interpretation of data. Such a training component would be relevant not only in the development of awareness and sensitivity, but would also be applicable to relevant curriculum development and appropriate classroom practices.

Cultural sensitivity training does not mean just T-grouping and 'I'm OK, you're OK', but learning to observe cultural patterns and how to respond appropriately; it does not deal just with attitudes, but involves observational training and changes in unconscious microbehaviors.

While cultural awareness and sensitivity are very important in teachers, they are not enough. Teachers require knowledge about culture—about that of the larger society and that of their students—to select relevant instructional material when choices may be made, to utilize appropriate classroom procedures, and to maximize students' opportunities to develop to their full potentials. Teachers should have skills in cross-cultural interaction, in observation, in collecting cultural information from students and parents, and in creating and adapting culturally-relevant materials. All of this can and should be taught. Training can also heighten and guide the underlying cultural awareness and sensitivity that a teacher or teacher candidate brings to the program. But it is probable that the underlying *personal characteristic* of awareness and sensitivity must be a necessary *prerequisite* for training, just as basic language proficiency must be.

If a person is crassly ethnocentric, and basically intolerant of cultural diversity in students, then the function of the teacher training program can be a screening one, to withhold its approval and credentials, and to prevent that person from teaching in a bilingual program.

D. Pedagogical Competencies

Basic teaching skills in most countries begin with knowing how to teach reading and writing, and such content areas as mathematics, science, and social studies. In some, religious and moral content would be considered primary, or perhaps hygiene and agricultural methods. The scope and sequence of what is to be taught is in large part dependent on national priorities, and in large part on the social and economic conditions which determine how many years students are likely to attend school, and at what age.

Teacher candidates must first know the content themselves, usually through formal training or as a result of prior education; field-based training both reinforces this and effectively presents appropriate methodology in supervised observation and participation with master teachers who are teaching the target age group, and using the students' language for instruction.

In cases where reading is to be taught in a language which is not standardized, where students come to school speaking a divergent variety of the language, or where books printed in the students' language are not widely available, knowledge of how to teach reading from a language experience approach or how to teach reading through students' writing is particularly fruitful.

Knowledge of informal assessment techniques is also important for all teachers, even when formal assessment instruments and procedures are entirely prescribed by a central agency, if they are really to know what their students do not understand. So, too, is how to plan a daily lesson, even when objectives and course scope and sequence are determined at a higher level. Especially if the teachers' resource books or guides are printed in the national language, but class presentation is in the students' native language, it is crucial to be able to identify important concepts, and to understand the explanations well enough to interpret (not just translate) them for students. Practice in such interpretation should be part of the training program.

The need for such skills as developing instructional materials, working with paraprofessionals, and team teaching are not universal, but very important in many contexts.

TEACHER RECRUITMENT AND SUPPORT

In many places it is not traditional for members of the minority group(s) who are the target of bilingual education to be attracted to (or sometimes even allowed access to) the teaching profession. Additionally, negative attitudes by the majority group or linguistic purists toward the language variety spoken by the minority group may be a further inhibiting factor. In the U.S., in the state of Louisiana, for example, teachers for bilingual programs were initially imported from France because it was felt that the provincial/colonial variety spoken in Louisiana was not acceptable for educational purposes. It was not until a folklore-folklife festival stimulated sufficient ethnic self-acceptance that efforts began to utilize Louisiana French (Acadian) speakers as teachers in the schools.

The recruitment of appropriate teacher candidates is unquestionably one of the most crucial steps in mounting a bilingual education program. In most countries, the minority group involved will generally be greatly under-represented among those having the educational background required for admission to the program, so that there is at best only a small pool of potential candidates from which to draw (and since salary levels in education are often below those of other fields, the few qualified candidates may opt for higher-paying and/or more prestigious occupations). This will be true whether in the U.S. where Hispanic Americans have a much lower representation in college than Anglo Americans, or in Ecuador where Quichua speakers average less than one year of elementary school.

The scarcity of educated minority group members leads to several responses in attempting to meet the need for bilingual teachers. One response, exacerbated by negative evaluations of the language variety used by members of the group, is to recruit candidates from the dominant majority group who happen to know the language (usually from having studied it in school as a foreign language). Another is to establish short-term language training programs for majority-group teachers already in service, a response motivated to a large extent by the economic threat to jobs and job opportunities created by the language demands of bilingual education. In New York City and Texas, for example, English speaking teachers were certified as bilingual after taking 120 hours of instruction in Spanish (equivalent to less than one-tenth the amount normally required by trainees in the Defense Language Institute to reach a minimum level of proficiency in the language).

At the other extreme is a unique response employed on a few occasions in the state of California when speakers of relatively rare American Indian languages were needed to teach. Native speakers of these languages were found, and though they lacked any formal training they were given 'eminence' credentials, designed to enable schools to hire people with unique qualifications and avoid the problem of their securing regular certification.

A more common response has been to hire native speakers of the minority language as aides in a bilingual program, so that they would have immediate employment, and to provide training for them on-the-job and during vacation periods in the school schedule. Typically, a 'career ladder' program is established in cooperation with a college or university or a state or national authority so that aides can take courses and receive credits which will contribute toward their degree and/or formal teacher certification.

In many countries, it is necessary to go into the countryside to recruit trainees, who may at best have only two or three years of education and be minimally competent in the national language. In such situations, it may be desirable or necessary to locate the training site near the area from which the trainees are drawn, in order to minimize travel and the cultural and psychological dislocation involved in their training—since for many the training will involve their first extended period away from home and their first encounter with schooling since childhood.

In both developed and developing countries, preparing members of previously excluded minority groups for teaching will potentially involve dealing with problems of culture shock and other difficulties of personal adjustment common to many adult education programs. Because of their frequently precarious financial circumstances, trainees will often require subvention to enable them to participate in a training program. (This carries with it a danger that some trainees may take part only because of the subvention, but such persons can usually be screened out.) Adults have family and economic responsibilities which may take precedence over their education, and they need support and assistance with this, whether it be in dealing with a landlord regarding house repairs or finding a doctor for a baby. Further, trainees may have had previous negative experiences with schooling, and may have to be helped to recover the confidence that they *can* learn, as well as teach.

FACULTY SELECTION AND DEVELOPMENT

Because of the need for teachers themselves to have training through the medium of the language in which they will teach, there should be a high priority given to recruiting faculty in teacher education programs capable of teaching bilingually. In addition, opportunities should be provided for existing faculty members to develop such ability. Where feasible, team teaching or collaboration with a bilingual teaching assistant might be utilized as strategies to expand the number of offerings in indigenous languages for which formally qualified instructors may not be available.

When the students' native language (as Spanish or Chinese in the U.S.) is a dominant language elsewhere in the world, another readily available short-term means of securing faculty with ability to lecture in the language is through visiting appointments and faculty exchanges.

Faculty development should include provision for on-going intellectual stimulation and interaction, which may be abetted by establishing a regular faculty seminar to meet weekly or biweekly. Content for such meetings could include reports on research, reviews of research or reports on conferences, guest lectures, presentation and discussion of new course content, or observation of particular programs or master teachers in bilingual education. Graduate students could occasionally be asked to report on significant research.

The program can only be as good as the faculty, and one of the most rewarding motivations for continued professional growth and development is to be identified with a quality program.

If faculty are themselves to receive higher level training in other countries, priority consideration should be given to institutions where there are professors who can and will lecture in the teacher trainer's language, and where topics related to that language and its use in education will be accepted for course papers and theses.

COMMUNITY AND SCHOOLS

One of the major problems confronting bilingual education in many parts of the world, and unquestionably limiting its effect, is the need to build a grassroots constituency for it within the minority language communities concerned. Like other innovations launched in education, this has generally been imposed by the schools from above, with little or no consultation with parents or other community members, and little effort to educate them regarding the rationale involved. Since parents are understandably anxious to have their children learn the national language, they are not unnaturally uncertain about or even opposed to an approach which seems to focus rather on the native language. In another direction, because of the importance of culture in a bilingual program, schools frequently view the community as a resource to be exploited for cultural information, rather than as a partner in the educational process. For the partnership to be effective, parents and other members of the community must understand the purposes and methods of bilingual education, so that they can become active coparticipants in educating the whole child.

As evidenced in the UNESCO (1977) document cited early in this paper, the use of the native language can have a number of different purposes and roles, depending on the wishes of the community. The language can be simply tolerated, used for affective and cognitive support, employed to varying degrees as a medium of instruction, or developed as a social and communicative skill and cognitive instrument in its own right. Each of these alternatives requires different degrees of teacher training and curriculum development, as well as degrees of financial and emotional commitment on the part of the schools and instructional staff and of the community. No amount of use of the native language in the school can preserve it if the community does not in its own attitudes daily reinforce its use outside school.

EVALUATION

The evaluation of language proficiency is being addressed elsewhere in this volume, but consideration must also be given to evaluation of various aspects of teacher training. Ideally, evaluation procedures should be developed as an integral part of the design for the training program.

Intervening and background variables which should be taken into account include the age and sex of teacher candidates, the amount and nature of their previous education, previous teaching and other vocational experiences, and their language proficiency (in both the national/second language and students' language). Pre- and post-test measures of attitude should be administered (as unobtrusively as possible), including information on interest and commitment. The ultimate outcome variables are teacher performance in bilingual education contexts, and the levels of learning which their students achieve.

Evaluation should also determine the length of time required for various proficiency levels in reading the native language to be reached. A cost/benefit analysis of the native language literacy model is needed, including cost implications for teacher training.

Special training in evaluation should be provided for supervisors/inspectors, if that structure is appropriate; alternatives in other situations include evaluator training as part of teacher training or faculty development.

CONCLUSION

Throughout this paper we have tried to emphasize the political, social, and economic factors which to a great extent determine the goals, scope, and priorities of bilingual education. Either overtly or covertly, these factors affect every dimension of teacher training. This is not to imply negative 'politicization' of an academic domain, but to recognize that education is by nature a cultural institution which has as a primary and legitimate goal preparing students to participate in and contribute to their own society.

In spite of the many differences in the objectives, content, and duration of training programs which will be feasible or desirable in different parts of the world, however, the basic nature of bilingual education makes three universal requirements of teachers:

1. They must be able to communicate with students in a language they will understand.
2. They must themselves know the content of instruction.
3. They must be able to transmit their knowledge to students.

When there are inadequate numbers of teachers who possess these three characteristics to meet the need, efficiency would suggest that at least oral language proficiency is the most important prerequisite for additional training, since the required content competence can generally be added much more expeditiously than the required linguistic competence. In turn, the first two characteristics are prerequisites for the third.

Other factors may override efficiency in any given situation, so these cannot be considered an absolute hierarchy of criteria for selection of teacher candidates. The level of student achievement in bilingual programs in every country, however, will be dependent on the degree to which all three of these general competencies are developed in their teachers.

We have also tried to emphasize throughout this paper the importance of field-based training in relevant and realistic bilingual education contexts. While this should be provided along with formal training in the preservice phase, some of the most effective development of teaching competencies may occur in programs of inservice education. Especially where preservice training opportunities and facilities are limited, continuing training and assistance can be delivered to teachers who have the most immediate needs and applications. Depending on the location of programs and the resources which are available, technical assistance centers might be established, or a team of resource teachers/consultants might travel from site to site, perhaps with a mobile unit. A rotating substitute teacher might also be used to enable teachers to observe one another as a way to share ideas and experiences, or to allow one successful teacher to teach a demonstration lesson in several different places. Inservice training activities further provide means for faculty conducting preservice training to maintain contact with the actual situations for which teachers are being trained.

Finally, we have stressed the importance of understanding and support for bilingual education within the minority language communities concerned, and the potential impact of community wishes on the nature and goals of teacher training. Programs of parental and community education regarding bilingual education might be conducted, and mechanisms created and activated to assure more community participation in program planning and implementation.

One of the major barriers to the education of subordinated minority groups is attitudinal rather than purely linguistic. This is a common obstacle facing bilingual programs and teacher training, whether for aborigines in Australia, Quechua speakers in Bolivia, Spanish speakers in the U.S., or Turkish speakers in Germany. American Indian groups in the U.S. who have lost their ancestral languages without gaining educationally provide ample evidence for this. Using the native language as an instructional medium, training native-speaking teachers, and involving the community all have as an important part of their purpose enhancing the perceived status of the minority group. Only when this is achieved will the attitudinal barrier to educational opportunity and attainment be overcome.

NOTES

[1] The formulation of the competencies given here is basically a condensation of the original CAL ones, made by the authors in 1979 in the process of designing a basic program for an American university. They have been edited slightly to change references to 'English' and 'U.S. culture' to 'national/second language' and 'national culture'.

[2] See Saville and Troike (1971) for further detail on the design of bilingual programs in the schools, and background knowledge necessary for teachers. The work has also been translated into Spanish and adapted for application in Ecuador by Louisa Stark.

THE CAJUN FRENCH DEBATE IN LOUISIANA

GERALD L. GOLD

Ethnic nationalism is often accompanied by movements to restore all or some of the former importance of what has become a secondary language. When a minority language has evolved into a number of regional vernaculars, all of which are stigmatized and shorn of their public and literary importance in the wider society (and this was the outcome for the French language in post-Bellum Louisiana), attempts to reinstate standardized speech can by themselves become the symbolic objectives of ethnic revival. This discussion is centered on the revival of the French language in Louisiana and the resulting debate between those who would place their priorities in teaching an international or standard French, and those who prefer to perpetuate the vernacular that is still used in many regions of South Louisiana. The Cajun French debate, as it is referred to on occasion, is here presented not as a consideration of viable alternatives for minority language maintenance, but as a debate between social groups in South Louisiana for whom the French language and a 'Cajun' ethnic identity do not necessarily have the same meaning.[1]

To most participants in Louisiana's 'French movement', from the Governor to the rural Cajun French radio announcers, the debate over which French is the most appropriate instrument of linguistic and cultural revival has been charged with significance. Moreover, interest in language programs in Louisiana extends to Canadian and European observers who have participated in the steps taken to include standard French within the schools and in other public contexts. They are also aware that Cajun and Creole speaking speech communities have become virtually bilingual or, in many instances, almost entirely English-speaking. To the foreign francophones, demands for 'Cajunization' of the teaching program are

221

puzzling if not threatening. Nevertheless, they could not arrive at a comprehension of the dynamics of linguistic revival in Louisiana without a thorough understanding of the social organization of Louisiana French communities. It is at that regional level that explanation becomes possible, rather than at the level of a child enrolled in a second language program.

In this respect, minority language revival in French Louisiana is missing many of the elements of language revival that can be found in contrasting cases such as those of Quebec, New Brunswick, or Wales. Notably absent in Louisiana are persistent problems of structural accommodation within the dominant economy, that is, an ethnic division of labor.[2] This was not so initially, since South Louisiana francophones were discriminated against during the rapid development of the petroleum industry before and after the Second World War. This period was also a time when the structures for the dissemination of an English-language universal education were firmly consolidated in what had been isolated French-speaking regions. In virtually every corner of the triangle of French-speaking communities in South Louisiana, this period was characterized by a stigmatization of vernacular French and of regional Cajun and Creole identities.

Modernization, brought about through the schools and the general extension of state services, new technology such as air conditioning and the automobile, and the availability of mass media, has had far more extensive an influence on spoken French than the expansion of the oil industry or even development of large scale sugar and rice production at the expense of small farming. In practice, economic changes rapidly created opportunities for the many Cajuns who were already adept masters of the primary resource environment of South Louisiana. As a consequence, in many regions, French remains the dominant working language of primary resource work, though much of the work is in high technology blue collar fields.

The success of South Louisiana francophones in primary industries is cited by some respondents as the reason why the educational domain, within which many Cajuns are now teachers and administrators, is best left exclusively to the English language. This segment of the population, disinterested in a French written tradition, regards the school curriculum as the wrong place to fight for ethnic equality. Others, especially the urban professionals and the small 'Acadian' elite of South-central Louisiana, supporters of the parapublic CODOFIL (Le conseil pour le développement du français en Louisiane), have opted for the internationalization of Louisiana French, partially through the 'temporary' importation of 'international brigades' of second language teachers from France, Quebec, and Belgium (Gold 1980a:9-14; Smith-Thibodeaux 1977:85-87).

The conflict between these regional interest groups and urban-based elites is an essential feature of the Cajun French debate. The elite supporters of CODOFIL have sought to establish a symbolic importance for French within the context of a bilingual Louisiana that participates in an international francophone community. In particular, this has been the ideology most strongly supported by James Domengeaux, the Lafayette-based lawyer who is the persistent and authoritarian chairman of CODOFIL. In contrast, a grass roots regionally-based ethnic revival has been encouraged by merchants and primary producers whose emphasis on the cultural idioms of revival is centered on the revival of Cajun French music. An apparent resolution of this debate involves a merging of the two objectives through the penetration of the urban-based revival by advocates of the survival of popular culture (music and Cajun vernacular) who seek the institutionalization of elements of regional culture into the school curricula. An important consideration behind the action of regional leaders in this conflict resolution is a constant inability to find an audience in those communities where French is spoken on a daily basis.

To comprehend the issues underlying the vernacular-standard language debate, it is best to begin with a discussion of living speech communities and the ways in which regional speakers assess the status of their language and contrast their speech with more standard forms. Only then can the institutional response to the decline of French be provided with a context. Likewise, those who have opposed the maintenance of the linguistic status quo must be placed within the context of the regional, national, and international considerations that influence their stance on the course to be taken in language revival.

THE REGIONAL CONTEXT: CAJUN FRENCH
AS A LIVING LANGUAGE

Not only do both Cajun and Creole French vary in grammar and syntax from one region to the next, but there are also significant sociolinguistic differences between subethnic populations, age cohorts, occupational groups, and between males and females. Thus, although some interregional generalizations have been made about Cajun and Creole French, these nonlinguistic variables are as essential to an understanding of the regional basis of spoken French as they are inseparable from issues in the Cajun French debate.

Generalizations on patterns of French language use are limited here to three regions from which extensive household data is available for the years 1976 and 1977: Mamou Prairie in the Southwest, a cotton-producing region that has shifted to rice production with important consequences for the regional labor force; the Têche region around Breaux Bridge, where a similar phasing-out of manual cotton production has been accompanied by mechanization of the sugar plantations and by the expansion of a crawfish industry; and third, the fishing zone of South Lafourche where the persistence and capitalization of family-based fishing boats is accompanied by an oilfield service industry that is largely locally-operated.

Patterns of French use in these regions are closely related to occupational changes and corresponding shifts in the class structure. For present purposes, several generalizations that emerge from this research capsulize the patterns of Cajun and Creole French use in all three regions. A detailed analysis of change in each region has been published elsewhere (Gold 1979, 1980b; Larouche 1980; Maguire 1979).

i. In each region, there is a population of primary farmers or fishermen who are either continuing a family-based production unit, or who are retired producers, most of whom never changed occupations or modified their kin-based personal networks. These producers, whether they are men or women, tend to use only French in their everyday lives. In Mamou Prairie, 52.4% of the population use mainly French at home, and 24.2% are functionally unilingual French-speakers over the age of sixty.

The presence of these unilinguals and of others who are French dominant has a strong effect on the situational use of French both within families and within the community. For instance, it is this French-speaking subgroup that assured the transmission of French to children after parents began to force their children to speak English in the early 1950's.

The linguistic ideology of the unilinguals appears to be of no direct significance in the Cajun French debate. French use is a given for these individuals and many have a stigmatized image of their French as a barrier to full societal participation. However, virtually all of the unilinguals interviewed specify that speaking (Cajun) French is a sine qua non of being Cajun. This ethnolinguistic association has a strong influence on the bilingual advocates of Cajun French, most of whom, at least in the Southwestern Prairie, interact extensively with older Cajun musicians.

In both agricultural regions, the town centers include a small mercantile elite who were agricultural middlemen before the collapse of 'traditional' agriculture. In Mamou Prairie, this group was already very bilingual when the major migrations to town occurred after 1945, and in Breaux Bridge, the local elite has defined itself as 'Acadian' (though many are descended from French planter families) and it has long distinguished itself from the country-dwelling 'Cajuns'. The old town elite of Mamou became relatively insignificant during the 1960's and had little involvement in the 'popular revival' that was centered in the Prairies. During the same period, the old

'Acadian' elite of Breaux Bridge clung to its status and, with the support of newer local merchants and tradesmen, the Acadian leaders were instrumental in the launching of CODOFIL.

ii. A second subgroup that is found in all three regions are the bilingual merchants and tradesmen. These are people who attended primary school between 1932 and 1952 and were subject to forced linguistic acculturation in the classroom. Virtually all of this age group speak French most of the time at work, that is with peers, but English is the language in which they have socialized their children.

The range of public contexts where this bilingual group uses French varies from region to region. In South Lafourche, it is fishing and family contexts that predominate, but in Mamou Prairie and in the Têche region, French is used extensively in small business and, in Mamou Prairie, small businessmen energetically support local Cajun radio. In all three regions there are very spirited French-language election campaigns, private affairs, where the issues and the language used are entirely regional and politicians, in their speeches, make maximal use of 'the symbols of their "Cajun-ness" and of the metaphors that express, however indirectly, their unity against outsiders' (Gold 1981:161).

The bilingual Cajuns are a White group, in the sense that Black Creoles in Breaux Bridge (about 35% of the population) and in Mamou Prairie (about 15% of the population) do not actively support the aims of a Cajun popular revival, although Black musicians, such as Bois Sec Ardoin of Mamou Prairie, and Clifton Chenier, from the Têche region, are used in the symbolism of Cajun ethnic revival! Similarly, though the Indians of South Lafourche (about 10% of the population) still socialize their children in French, they are not active participants in Cajun cultural revival.

iii. The third group that is essential to language retention at the regional level are oilfield workers and students in their twenties and early thirties. It is in this age cohort that major male-female differences in French use appear in all three regions. Men who are recruited into the primary resource economy quickly move from being passive bilinguals to become active French-speakers. Few of their wives use French with the same frequency unless they were raised by a grandparent. In this way, women act as the mirrors to American society. They have more access to printed media and they prepare children for school. More women than men support the bilingual objectives of CODOFIL.

Within this group, the offshore oil workers lead dual lives. As they have up to three free weeks between shifts, they are able to establish a well-capitalized self-employed niche within their communities. Their children are usually taught some French, and the experience of being 'Cajun' somewhere else works to substitute any lingering traces of ethnic stigma with fierce ethnic pride. The oilworkers become full-fledged supporters of regional popular revival.

Of the same age, but with a different career pattern, are those who left their region for college and return with an interest in the revival of Cajun culture. This is a state-wide network that includes film-makers, musicians, and artists. From this group come some of the major protaganists in the Cajun French debate.

CODOFIL AND THE DEVELOPMENT
OF FRENCH IN LOUISIANA

As the French Creole planters lost their political control of Louisiana after the Civil War, provisions for French instruction were set aside (Kloss 1971:35). Many subsequent attempts were made to reinstate French language curricula. These were always made on a regional basis, and always as second language programs. There was some transnational encouragement. In the late 1930's, missions from Quebec and France discussed possible plans of assistance but their timing was probably inappropriate and neither country was prepared to act.

The years without collective action left the Louisiana French leaderless at the moment that national leaders might have had more input into the direction of a major expansion of public education after 1928. In New Orleans, the elitist Athénée louisianaise, oriented toward continental French 'civilization', represented a dwindling number of New Orleans (White) Creoles. The 'Acadians' of the Têche and of Lafayette faced similar difficulties in obtaining the support of rural Cajuns. One of their visible leaders, 'Cousin' Dudley Leblanc, wrote two volumes on the Acadian identity of the Louisiana French, and extended his network to Quebec and to New Brunswick, but his personal style of organization did not incorporate a response to the problem of language loss in Louisiana. Another potential source of leadership were the Louisiana French linguists,[3] James Broussard (L.S.U.), and Hosea Phillips (Southwestern) who had carried out and supervised studies of regional French in Louisiana. Their applied work, however, was directed to the founding of elaborate French houses with a European orientation.

By the time of the founding of CODOFIL in 1968, the situation of Louisiana French had continued to deteriorate. For voters and government alike, the rise of White ethnic movements throughout the country and the public response to Black Power and to civil rights agitation created a favorable climate for the creation of a State organization with the objective of preserving the French language in Louisiana. There was also the hidden agenda of consolidating more politically aware French-speaking voters.

In 1968-1969, two independent French language programs began in Louisiana schools: Federal Title VII Bilingual programs, which were initially confined to three parishes (St. Martin, Lafayette, and Evangeline), and the CODOFIL program which was administered by the Foreign Languages Section of the Louisiana State Department of Education in Baton Rouge. Initially, it was the CODOFIL program that went through very rapid expansion with the assistance of French and Quebecois associate teachers (and later, Belgians). This reliance on foreign teachers was to have profound effects on the ability of the new program to communicate with French speakers whose interests, as was already indicated, are very regionalized and have never been linked to the objectives of a national francophone organization. Moreover, the fact that the Louisiana identity of this organization was synonymous with a single individual, James Domengeaux, limited the breadth of popular support.

In the tradition of Louisiana personalistic politics, all major decisions taken with the CODOFIL program are said to have required the direct approval of Domengeaux. He negotiated the contracts with the foreign states, hired the teachers, kept constant communication with the Louisiana State Department of Education and the pedagogical representatives of Quebec and France (the Quebec Office was never more than a few doors away), dealt politically with school boards and principals, and appeared personally in the State House to assure CODOFIL its annual appropriation. To complete this aura of frenetic activity, CODOFIL activities have been monitored by the national and international press which were fed a steady diet of press releases, many of them prepared by foreign associate teachers working in the CODOFIL office.

CODOFIL AND THE CAJUN FRENCH DEBATE

The ideology behind CODOFIL deserves special attention and it is this set of directives that can be related to the situation of the French language at a regional level and with the exchange of opinions that is the Cajun French debate. The ideologies of participating governments are also important and are discussed in some detail elsewhere (Gold 1980a:9-23), but they do not relate directly to the issues of the debate. Moreover, foreign francophones in Louisiana have deliberately avoided entanglement in these discussions, often because they could not understand the regional basis of French.

The following aspects of the CODOFIL position must be kept in mind:
i. Bilingualism is a key concept in CODOFIL's official policy. Mastery of two languages, at least to an urban elite, means that French will be Louisiana's second language. As such, CODOFIL leaders see bilingualism

as an act of destigmatization. Louisianans, of any ethnic background, could assist their state in becoming a 'window on the French-speaking world' (Hébert 1974:6). The constant stream of foreign visitors to the state, and to the CODOFIL offices, is indirectly offered as evidence of this assertion. Within Louisiana, French is to be seen as a living language that would be a 'bond between peoples...' (Domengeaux nd:2). What the reader should note is that CODOFIL's bilingualism reifies language as a transportable element, whereas its Louisiana context is a highly embedded one.

ii. CODOFIL interpreted its mandate in a way that led to the justification of importing up to 400 foreign French teachers a year on short term contracts. Domengeaux repeatedly stressed that competent teachers could not be found in Louisiana given the urgency of preserving the French language (CODOFIL personnel carefully avoided discussions of the Federal Title VII curriculum). Therefore, a transition period was needed before properly trained second language specialists (SLS) could be deployed.

However, foreign teachers were given little training for work in Louisiana and many had no SLS accreditation. Initially, given its scarce resources, CODOFIL's assumption was that native speakers of French would not necessarily need training. But it repeatedly proved to be difficult to parachute foreign teachers into a conservative southern school system, often without the goodwill of the school personnel or of the members of the community. This was the operating norm in CODOFIL's first six years (1972-1978). When a teacher did adapt to Louisiana schools and communities (cf. Gold 1980a:33-34), he had to leave Louisiana to fulfill visa requirements, although marriages to Louisianans permitted some to stay and operate CODOFIL or work within the Louisiana State Department of Education.

A result of this imposition of fraternal outsiders is a widespread malaise over the appropriateness of the CODOFIL actions. More importantly, some began to doubt whether the CODOFIL program was what the Louisiana French needed to assure their cultural survival. Several respondents, each having had extensive contacts with CODOFIL, remark that after considerable initial enthusiasm, and a renewed popular confidence in the French language, CODOFIL's continued impact may have been negative. But in the context of Cajun regional politics language issues are virtually never raised. This makes popular disatisfaction with CODOFIL difficult to identify. To foreign teachers, an apparent absence of political opposition indicates either satisfaction or apathy in this reclaimed corner of francophonie.

iii. The emphasis on foreign teachers further reinforces the CODOFIL commitment to standard or international French. Domengeaux and CODOFIL supporters repeatedly emphasize that the regional variations in

Cajun French do not permit its widespread adoption as an instructional resource. Grammatical inconsistencies, errors in usage, and the loss over time of the quality of a written language are all cited as reasons why Cajun French must be avoided. The possible inconsistency between such a policy and the everyday reality of the large francophone speech community is resolved by the discourse of the educators having little practical relationship with that of members of the community. Only on very rare occasions do even the most ethnically-aware respondents not remind our interviewers that her or his French (although 'good and old', as Domengeaux puts it) is not the 'real' French.

This status given international French is related to the elite support that the CODOFIL program has received. CODOFIL is an appropriate 'solution' for a recently mobile segment of the population that has garnered considerable economic and political power in Louisiana. To CODOFIL planners, North Louisianians who receive the same standard French instruction are not to be confronted with a nationalistic, Cajun presence. These are the implicit terms by which Domengeaux was able to steer the enabling legislation for CODOFIL unanimously through the State House. Moreover, Domengeaux is emphatic that ethnic nationalism, such as the move toward Cajun French represents, cannot be permitted to surface within or even outside CODOFIL. In short, Cajun French represents a retrograde position to the architects of the CODOFIL program. It is a backward look at 'everything that the CODOFIL movement wished to resist' (Gold 1980a:7). It is noteworthy that those regions that have not readily accepted CODOFIL teachers, such as prosperous fishing communities of South Lafourche, the strongly French-speaking parishes of Acadia and Evangeline (the latter has had a modest Title VII program), are also regions where the majority of the local Cajun elites are not involved in interethnic contacts with Anglo-Louisianans and where most local leaders have not been participants in the political activities of ethnic renaissance at the State level.

In neither the CODOFIL program nor the Title VII program is Creole French given any serious attention. This has been the case despite the fact that a majority of the Black adults in St. Martin Parish, as well as many others in St. Landry, Point Coupée, and St. James Parishes (all former plantation areas), are Creole-speaking. Furthermore, many of the Whites in St. Martin Parish speak Creole, including all of the adult residents of villages such as Henderson and Catahoula. One reason for this situation is that CODOFIL has not been able to attract Black Creole support except through public school enrollments. Many Blacks perceive CODOFIL as a White organization and, to most, even the word 'Cajun' conjures up an image of White southerners. It is tempting to find some correlation between the rise of Acadian ethnicity and the insistence on Acadian and French origins, particularly in St. Martin Parish. Is this, at least partially, a response to a perceived encroachment by Blacks after the breakdown of the sugar plantation communities and of cotton sharecropping? Whatever the reason for this historical cleavage, a substantial constituency of potential supporters of the French Movement have been set aside.

The Creole-Cajun conundrum is yet another reason why the new French programs are not adapted to their cultural milieu. An exception is the Title VII program in St. Martin Parish which initially chose to use few foreign teachers and where a serious effort was made to develop a culturally-relevant curriculum. But even in this model program, initial plans to accommodate Creole-speaking children in grade one were set aside, and the cultural content of the program tends to idealize old customs and to stress their origins as transplanted traditions without bringing out enough of the indigenous and unique features of French Louisiana culture.

iv. In implementing the program, CODOFIL teachers and supervisors are asked to account for Louisiana French equivalents. On a very basic level, this involves admitting that there is 'another way to say it', even when the teacher is incapable of effectively communicating in that 'other way'. The 'other way', the 'Cajun way', is then implicitly presented as the 'wrong way'. With such an approach to bilingual education, CODOFIL and Title VII curricula are situated well within the guidelines of international French. The CODOFIL curriculum, which offers one ¼ hour a day as opposed to as much as an hour in some Title VII programs, is built around the Frère Jacques method designed for teaching French in Northern and Western Africa, rather than to North Americans. Little room is left for spontaneity and adjustment to local cultural form, and some teachers who were interviewed demonstrated how Frère Jacques can provide an illusion that the student is making progress.

To many Louisianans, a shift to Title VII Federal Bilingual Programs would resolve the inadequacies of the CODOFIL offerings (CODOFIL operated in as many as 40 Louisiana Parishes). As a new and potentially improved source of funding, the number of Title VII programs expanded from three to five and then to fifteen at the very time when CODOFIL was receiving its greatest criticism. But, as was already mentioned, the Title VII curriculum may also not reflect a living speech community. Moreover, because program proposals must prove that a substantial portion of the clientele is below the poverty line and of Limited English Proficiency (LEP), the politics of these proposals lead to an exaggeration of the number of French-speaking children. Some of the proposals, prepared by professionals, bear a remarkable similarity to each other.

Ironically, one result of this expansion is that the new programs have turned to CODOFIL for their supply of resource teachers, although every program must have the (rather illusory) objective of having home-room teachers self-sustain the program within the model schools. Such an administrative structure is not free of bureaucratic entanglement, since every program has its own personnel, sometimes politically appointed, and all of the programs share a regional resource center in Lafayette. Title VII programs are thus expensive and do not resolve the issues that create dissatisfaction with CODOFIL classes. Moreover, the foreign French teachers may even have a greater prominence than in a CODOFIL-linked school. In several cities, such as Lafayette and New Iberia, there has been sporadic resistance from parents who either find the curriculum to be unsuitable or whose ethnic consciousness moves them to oppose the incorporation of foreign francophones. Ancelet aptly refers to the issues that emerge as those peculiar to 'teaching the problem language in Louisiana' (Ancelet 1978:9).

THE CAJUN FRENCH DEBATE: THE MUSICIAN-ANNOUNCERS

Those who are working for the retention of Louisiana French have neither worked together, nor been in agreement as to what should be preserved and how this could be achieved. Within the living speech communities, there is no particular need for a precise strategy about what is to be done to maintain Cajun French, but in the universities and in the educational bureaucracy, the rationale is more explicit and often different from that provided by the community of speakers.

The issue of how much of the 'problem language' should be taught was latent from the first days of CODOFIL's existence. Initially, the question was raised publicly as part of an ongoing conflict of interests between agents of popular revival and those of elite or state-level revival. It was the Cajun radio announcers, most of whom are also small merchants and musicians, who assumed the brokerage role at a regional level by assisting in the creation of more regionally-uniform Cajun speech communities (there are no Creole broadcasts) and facilitating the construction of social networks between Cajun merchants and their clients.

CODOFIL attempted to organize the broadcasters in 1975 and began to request public service time in the same stations so that the foreign associate teachers could staff a series of CODOFIL broadcasts. Although asked to standardize some of their French (e.g. *avion,* instead of *aéroplane, émission,* instead of *program*), the announcers steadfastly refused to standardize their discourse or to diversify their menu of Louisiana Cajun music. Some CODOFIL announcements are read, and each announcer has a large stock of Quebecois, French, and Belgian music that is virtually never played; the announcers do not feel that the foreign French music is what their listeners want to hear. Moreover, they express uneasiness over apparent CODOFIL opposition to Cajun French. CODOFIL (through the Louisiana Mass Media Foundation, and French and Quebec Government support), has since gained access to what promises to be a full-time French language radio station, and may possibly be able to attract its own radio clientele. However, listeners still follow those stations and programs that are closest to their community and regional concerns, even when alternative French language broadcasts are available. In the short run, it appears that the announcers will continue to use Cajun music to communicate regional vernacular to a large audience, and CODOFIL may have to do the same thing in its own broadcasts.

CAJUN FRENCH I AND THE POPULIST RESPONSE TO INTERNATIONAL FRENCH

James Faulk, a high school French teacher from Vermilion Parish, published his *Cajun French I* in 1977, incorporating the material that he had used with high school students in Crowley, Louisiana. The reaction to Faulk's book was immediate and far-reaching. In Baton Rouge, Cajun French I provided a political petard against CODOFIL for a newly-created Cajun Club at Louisiana State University (LSU). In Lafayette, the vitriolic reaction by Domengeaux and other CODOFIL leaders permitted a group of recent university graduates to define a brokerage role for their fledgling association (founded with the assistance of the Quebec Government), l'Association des Francophones de la Louisiane, in an attempt to mollify the CODOFIL position. From Domengeaux's Lafayette office came a Telexed press release that set the tone of the debate. *Cajun French I* was referred to as unsuitable as a school text and unrepresentative of anything more than 'red neck French'. The battle had emerged into the open and CODOFIL felt obligated to defend the legitimacy of its own program in the columns of the regional media.

Faulk's textbook, based on the French spoken in Vermilion Parish, is particularly controversial because it is written in his own phonetic spelling, without any accompanying standard French text. Faulk claims that his phonetic system will sound like good Cajun French when it is read by a Louisiana English-speaker of his region. He makes not attempt to relate his examples to regional variations within South Louisiana, and he will not add accompanying standard French explanations so that a compromise could be worked out with the Lafayette-based l'Association des Francophones de la Louisiane or with COFODIL. Figure One provides a sampling of Faulk's method.

---

p. 69 'Conversation: subject nouns and pronouns, verb forms in 3rd column, and adjectives'

1. She's *absent*.	1. Ahl ā *ahb sont̄*.
10. They are alike.	10. Ee soñ *pah re-ee*.
25. He's deaf.	25. Eel ah toñ pay.
(Lit. He doesn't hear)	

---

p. 127 'Foods...'

16. There's a bargain on eggs today. They're only forty-nine cents a dozen.	16. Yaw añ bahrgin su lāz uhf ojoordwee. Ee soñ jus kahroñt nuhf soo lah doozan.

---

p. 240 'The 1st past tense...'

English Infinitive	Cajun Infinitive	
bend	*kobir*	changes to *ko bee* ...
learn	*ah prahn*	changes to *ah pree*

Figure 1. *A Sample of James Faulk's method for teaching Cajun French*

(James D. Faulk. 1977. *Cajun French I*. Abbeville: Cajun Press.)

To the USL academics and, in particular, to the French language advisers to the CODOFIL Program, Faulk's book is an anathema. The private fear of CODOFIL leaders and of bureaucrats in the Louisiana State Department of Education, Foreign Languages Section, is that the book might be accepted by those school boards who have been the most lukewarm to initiatives from CODOFIL, and used as a substitute for the Frère Jacques method. What Domengeaux probably did not expect is that his unfavorable public reaction to *Cajun French I* would bring public sympathy to James Faulk and create a possible rift within what CODOFIL supporters themselves refer to as the statewide 'French Movement'.

In Baton Rouge, the leaders of the LSU Cajun Club, most of whom are from rural families in French-speaking parishes, met with initial opposition from university authorities over their plans for recognition and funding for a Cajun French course. They then petitioned successfully for intervention from the State Governor, Cajun French-speaking Edwin Edwards, and meetings were held with James Faulk and other potential instructors to arrange for an accredited Cajun French course within the LSU curriculum. At the same time, more than thirty members of the LSU Cajun Club began to interact regularly with young Cajuns from other regions. One specific objective was to forge linkages with the musician-announcers of the Southwest Louisiana Cajun radio programs.

Significantly, the LSU Cajun Club included at least three Black Creoles in their group. Their members also were intent on making contacts with the Franco-American student movement at the University of Maine, Orono, and several car trips were made to Orono, Montreal, and Quebec City. The club became the nucleus of a short-lived social movement that had the objective of confronting those who claimed to represent the French language in Louisiana universities. At LSU, this meant a Cajun presence at French Department wine and cheese parties and, at a state level, the LSU Cajun Club strategy was to confront l'Association des Francophones de la Louisiane which they saw as a CODOFIL front of little or no use to Louisiana French-speakers. More importantly for Domengeaux, press releases to the nationally-syndicated media, issued by spokesmen of the LSU group, challenged the assumptions of CODOFIL that Cajun French was a dying language, that it could not be used to communicate with francophones outside of Louisiana, and that it was not a written language. The message was worded in a very confrontational manner: 'Faulk's book could save a fading culture', and 'young Acadians prefer to hear Cajun rather than classical French, to be able to communicate with their grandparents, and sometimes (sic) even their parents'.

ASSOCIATION DES FRANCOPHONES DE LA LOUISIANE

The response from Lafayette came in the autumn of 1977 when the Association des Francophones de la Louisiane was organized with the quiet assistance of the Quebec Government delegate in Lafayette, and the even less acknowledged blessing of Domengeaux and CODOFIL. The first president of the new organization was Richard Guidry, a French teacher in the St. Martin Parish Bilingual Program, who speaks both Cajun and Creole French. Guidry's constituency was not a university group, but a larger network of about fifty people in their late twenties who spoke Cajun French and had, for the most part, completed courses in French as a foreign language, at USL.

The linguistic ideology of the Association des Francophones de la Louisiane is reflected in Guidry's 'Hallo, Gramman's fine, an'y'all?', a Cajun French radio dialogue about a unilingual French grandmother who could not communicate with her English-speaking grandchildren. Determined to take a more active position in favor of Cajun French, Guidry and his network found themselves sympathetic toward James Faulk in his dispute with CODOFIL.

When Guidry and friends began defending Faulk's book, Domengeaux (n.d.) responded in a letter that singled out USL folklorist Barry Ancelet for 'inciting a controversy where none in reality exists'. Domengeaux then repeated his stance that it was not in the realm of 'practicality' to teach Cajun French in the public schools. Ancelet answered his missive with the assertion that Cajun French 'when well-spoken', does not differ from standard French or 'any other regional variation of the French language among speakers of comparable competence and social standing'. Ancelet rounded his reply with a written excerpt of Iry Lejeune's music (a Cajun folk hero⁴) to illustrate how Cajun French could be a literate language and how the Cajun oral tradition could be recorded.

The first round of the Cajun French debate ended in an apologetic tone. Guidry assured Domengeaux that the two sides had common goals, and CODOFIL was informed in an evaluation by its transnational partners that its program must begin to reflect Louisiana culture and speech (Debyser et al. 1978). Although CODOFIL made few immediate changes, it was clear that the French Movement now had a nascent intellectual elite and that these leaders would no longer be satisfied with anything less than a Louisiana French identity and a linguistic revival that was not wrenched from its sociocultural context.

A CAJUN FRENCH TEXTBOOK?
THE SECOND ROUND OF THE CAJUN FRENCH DEBATE

The next phase of the debate, a more serious challenge to CODOFIL, followed Faulk's attempt to have his textbook approved for the Louisiana State public school curriculum. Although he somehow missed his own hearing, Faulk drove to Baton Rouge with a convoy of rural neighbors toting English language placards calling on the State to 'Save our Cajun French', and exorting CODOFIL to stop tampering with their venerable language and to take their Belgians and Frenchmen back to where they came from. In a sequence of power politics which is not of importance to this discussion, Domengeaux is said to have personally assured that the Faulk book would not appear on the curriculum. However, the Faulk protest had implications far beyond the adoption of *Cajun French I*. The renewed debate had expanded the original conflict and CODOFIL had come under popular pressure to do something toward 'saving' and teaching the vernacular.

The refusal of Faulk's book was reported on the front pages of most weekly and daily newspapers in the Lafayette region. Only in Lafayette, Domengeaux and CODOFIL's base, was the story relegated to page 48 of the *Advertiser*. In the areas where French is spoken daily, Faulk's case was discussed in bars, on the street, and at the dinner table. The question that was the major topic of conversation could be summarized as: 'Was it not time to save the Cajun language?'. The latent class conflict that was not as apparent in the previous decade now seemed to be more visible.

In the regional press the renewed exchange was reported in this manner (a condensation of several articles):

Domengeaux: This is not an issue of Cajun or standard French... (but one) of using a method that is suitable to teach. Do we teach red neck English in the schools?

Faulk: I represent the people who work in the rice fields, the people who fish the bayous...we simply want Cajun French to be added to the curriculum and give the children a chance to choose...Most CODOFIL teachers are young and some of them are not certified to teach in their own countries.

Domengeaux: But they can speak French better than any damn Louisianan!

The debate raged on through the spring state elections of 1979. Faulk was approached by at least one delegate of a candidate for Superintendent of Education, who offered to bring the textbook issue into statewide politics (his opponent, the incumbent superintendent, was strongly supported by Domengeaux). Faulk declined, but the *Abbeville Meridional* and other regional papers continued to represent his case as 'CODOFIL versus local man', and they gave prominent display to Faulk's assertion that 'hard-earned tax dollars are being used to destroy our language'.

The Faulk issue must be put into a context of Louisiana politics which tend to be consociational rather than confrontational when an election is not in progress. The Faulk textbook probably damaged the public image of CODOFIL, and it had led to a loss of support. But, since language conflict is not perceived in the regions as a legitimate election issue, and since CODOFIL has more resources at its disposal than James Faulk, Domengeaux chose to settle the dispute in a move that would make CODOFIL appear to be a saviour of Cajun French. The turn of events was therefore somewhat similar to the outcome of similar debates in Quebec or New Brunswick in the late 1960's. Like its francophone counterparts to the north, Louisiana has an indigenous ethnic elite and intelligentsia. The ethnic intellectuals, some of whom had been highly critical of the transnational aid to schools, were now valuable to the leaders of the movement in the task of standardizing a Cajun vernacular. In Louisiana, that task implies making Cajun French palatable to the educational establishment.

STANDARDIZING THE VERNACULAR:
THE LEGITIMIZATION OF CAJUN FRENCH

The third and last phase of the debate removes the issue from the community and regional level and returns it to the universities where Louisiana French had not been systematically studied since the 1930's. Accompanying this new role for the universities is a long-standing rivalry between LSU, in Baton Rouge and USL, in Lafayette. Both universities were under simultaneous pressure to improve the training programs for second language teachers. USL, located closer to the French-speaking population and to CODOFIL, is taking a more culturally-oriented route than LSU, where greater structuring of French teaching is perceived to be the answer to the demand for higher standards in second language training.

Much of the direction of a USL position on Cajun French teaching came initially from folklorist Barry Ancelet who worked from the vantage point of his Center for Acadian and Creole Folklore, then located within the Department of Foreign Languages, to defend the interests of regional French within a department that looked to France for intellectual inspiration. Ancelet attempted to criticize the construction of the Faulk text, without depreciating the desirability of a 'regionally appropriate' method to teach the French language in Louisiana'.

Specific projects for the development of a Cajun text were supported initially by the USL-based National Bilingual Resource Center. Shirley Abshire-Fontenot, and a Californian, David Barry, began the task of preparing a course and an accompanying textbook for USL students who had completed two years of instruction in standard French. The USL team wisely sidestepped the issue of orthographic representation by adhering to the conventions of International French spelling. However, they have retained local syntactic constructions, lexical items, and pronunciation features. For example in Lesson I (Abshire-Fontenot and Barry 1980) they introduce the local form of the *passé composé* of verbs of motion in which the auxiliary 'to have' is used instead of 'to be': *Tu as été au fais-dodo hier soir?* (St. Fr. *tu es allé*). No attempt is made to represent local phonological features and departures from the conventional spelling are made only for local lexical items without Standard French counterparts, e.g. *asteur* 'now' (St. Fr. *maintenant*). Morphological variants appear in the conventional spelling even when they diverge considerably from the metropolitan norm, e.g., *ils répondont* (*ils répondent*) 'they answer', *vous-autres* / vuzot / (*vous*) 'you all'.

Despite the importance of the textbook project, at this time it appears as though its distribution will be somewhat limited because CODOFIL and the Louisiana State Department of Education have not officially approved its use in either elementary or secondary school programs. However, some teachers have begun testing the Cajun French materials with high school students and many respondents expect that the Abshire-Fontenot and Barry publication may well prove to be a turning ponit in Louisiana bilingual education. It is the first step in moving from the teaching of a 'neutralized'[5] standard French, which accounts for 'the other way to say it', to a text that posits the 'other way' as the familiar one, and the standard form as the necessary variant. Since none of these materials are designed to replace existing teaching methods at the critical elementary level, their impact may not be felt until the new approach filters through the school system, or until the fourth round of the Cajun French debate.

The Cajun French debate coincided with the appearance of the first literary productions to be published in the vernacular.[6] These tales, plays, and poetry have become part of the debate in that they form an essential legitimization of Cajun French. Together with the large musical repertoire, it constitutes Louisiana's first French literature since the decline of the French Creole publications in New Orleans. As is the case in other comparable settings, the authors of the new literature are also major participants in the language debate. Although they have published largely in Quebec, some materials are published in the *Mamou Prairie* and in the *Revue de la Louisiane*. The university presses in Louisiana publish books on Cajuns but they have not released works written in Cajun or Creole dialect.

A close parallel to the Louisiana linguistic conflicts is that of New Brunswick where French language publishing, despite the many glossaries of Pascal Poirier, did not take Acadian French seriously until the publication of Antonine Maillet's *La sagouine,* by a Montreal publisher. The vernacular of Maillet's novels takes on an ideological significance for francophone readers in Quebec and in France who associate the colloquial French of Acadia and of Louisiana with a traditional rural life that has disappeared in both nations, but is still an essential component of cultural identities. This is not at all the association that Louisiana writers would attach to their intellectual production. The same can be said for the films and paintings that are currently being produced in South Louisiana. Will this romanticism not be the filter through which future generations of high school and university students will regard the new literature? The others, the majority who cannot read or write French, are not likely to be exposed to any of this work. They are likely, however, to continue a conservative defense of Cajun and Creole French.

CONCLUSION

This discussion has used the example of a contemporary linguistic conflict to illustrate the relationship between the regional basis of Louisiana French culture and the possibilities for the emergence of a unified 'French Movement'. The Louisiana materials are also shown to present a special case in that most school children are only second language speakers of French, although many of their parents participate in an active living French speech community. When the schools attempt to further isolate children from their parents' cultural enclave, conflict emerges over the rationale and logic behind such training. It has been suggested in this discussion that the origins of the ideology behind the CODOFIL program are not grass roots but can be found in the socio-structural position of certain groups within Louisiana.

The living speech community in Louisiana has already, in many instances, rejected the schools as the means of effectively retaining French as an everyday language. It does not at all follow that inserting Cajun French into the programs would improve the acceptability of using French in the schools. The educators themselves lack a resource base of literary materials in Cajun French. Moreover, there is always a danger that an attempt by the schools to standardize vernacular Cajun dialects could rigidify and formalize dialects that were already going through rapid structural changes.

Efforts to standardize the Cajun vernacular and incorporate a 'neutralized' version within school texts are likely to have other unforeseen consequences. A 'cleaned-up' version of the vernacular is likely to meet with less resistance from parents and to facilitate intergenerational communication. In the long run, extensive teaching of Cajun French in Louisiana schools could broaden the base of interregional communication within the francophone population of the southern part of the state. Cajun youth from one region are already seeking contacts in other regions, particularly in the Lafayette area. Given the strength of regional networks, as opposed to the weakness and lack of continuity in the elementary French programs, it is still likely that regional French speech communities could outlast the new courses that were designed to preserve their French.

NOTES

[1] Research in South Louisiana began in 1975 with the aid of Université Laval and the Wenner-Gren Foundation for Anthropological Research. Most subsequent fieldwork was supported by the Social Science and Humanities Research Council of Canada, and by the Ford Foundation. My sincere thanks to Eric Waddell, Louis-Jacques Dorais, Dean Louder, Barry Ancelet and Regna Darnell for listening to some of the ideas that are incorporated into this paper.

[2] By ethnic division of labor I am referring to the unequal representation of ethnolinguistic groups in the labor force. The term was probably first used by Michael Hechter (1975), though its application can be found in earlier studies by Everett C. Hughes (1943) and his students.

[3] Broussard did his work on Creole dialect in St. Martin Parish and Phillips, a native of Ville Platte, did his research on the dialect of his home parish of Evangeline. Many of the theses on variants of Louisiana French were prepared for William A. Read of LSU who wrote numerous articles and a book on the subject. There are, of course, many non-Louisianans who have written on the subject of Louisiana French, but these works would not be germane to this discussion.

[4] Iry Lejeune was an accordionist and musical poet from the Church Point area of Southwestern Louisiana. Though he has been dead almost thirty years, his records are still regularly purchased and played on the Cajun radio shows. Much of the repertoire of other groups is based on Iry Lejeune's renditions of traditional music. He is probably the best-known individual in the French-speaking regions of the Southwest.

[5] For example, Ancelet (1980), Marcantel (1979), Reed (1976).

[6] This notion of 'neutralization' of the vernacular was suggested to me by Albert Verdoodt.

THE STATUS OF LANGUAGES IN EUROPE

GUY HÉRAUD

INTRODUCTION

Can a language be applied like a label to a place? Can areas be 'linguistified'? To put it yet another way, does territory have a linguistic dimension? This is the question that the present article intends to answer. Given a positive response, it then becomes possible to establish a typology of the linguistic situations or, more precisely, of the linguistic characteristics of a territory. Figuratively speaking, it could be said that every territory has a linguistic description, its 'linguistic identification card'.

This 'linguistic identification card' does not necessarily correspond to political boundaries; the majority of states do not have territorial linguistic homogeneity. Therefore, in order to label them linguistically, their territories must be divided into several distinct parts, each according to a particular linguistic regimen. The sum of these different territorial 'identification cards' becomes the 'linguistic identification card' of the state.

A question arises immediately: Is the language with which an area is to be labeled the effective language (sociolinguistic perspective) or the legal language (jurolinguistic perspective)? The topic is open to these two different, but legitimate approaches. The term 'status' in the title indicates that this topic is viewed here largely from a juridical perspective. However, it is not possible to omit totally the sociolinguistic (or ethnopolitical) perspective. Contemporary epistemology has firmly established that an object cannot be treated, and above all defined, without using outside points of reference; an object can be considered only in relation to other objects or to reality as a whole. Thus it is essential to consider, in addition to the status of language, the sociological and factual aspect of the linguistic dimension of territory.

This incursion into the sociolinguistic domain within a juridical approach is justified to the extent that social factors influence the question of status. We present factual situations, therefore, not simply as a gratuitous addition, but in a comparison of jurolinguistic status and sociolinguistic reality, which reveals a new aspect of status, 'adequacy' and 'inadequacy'. (See Sections 5.1 and 5.2).

A discussion of linguistic status leads us to distinguish three issue areas.

I. The issue of qualification. By what juridical means is linguistic status defined? By custom or by specific legislation? If the latter, by constitution, law, or administrative act?

II. The issue of juridical quality. How is the language used? Is it an official language and/or a national language? An auxiliary language or a language of the state? A regional language or a territorial language without administrative significance?

III. The issue of linguistic characterization of the geographic area. Is it unilingual or bilingual? If the latter, is it bilingual by linguistic superimposition, juxtaposition of unilingual populations, or both? Is there territorial bilingualism within a state or within a region?

This study is limited to the level of general jurolinguistic typology. It offers no in-depth examinations of individual language functions and situations. General jurolinguistic typology constitutes an introduction to linguistic law.[1]

As André Martinet states, 'Language cannot be considered to be simply a means of communication', but has 'a thought-organization function, an expressive function, and an aesthetic function as well' (1961:13).[2] The interest of states and minorities in the linguistic questions attests to the reality of the expressive function on the collective scale. Language is one of the most salient and prestigious symbols of collective identity; like a flag waving in the breeze, the language of public signs, of government, of the educational system, of radio, of television expresses the pride of collective identity. This is true to such an extent that groups which have lost the daily use of their language, and could therefore function without it in public life, insist that it be continued on street and highway signs, for example. In Aosta, the Italianized capital of a French-speaking region, all public roads bear signs in both languages, even though French is rarely used. In Ireland as well, place names are indicated first in Gaelic and then in English, although more than three-quarters of the population no longer speak the national language. The impassioned opposition to German signs in Alsace reflects the same phenomenon in its opposite extreme—a part of Teutonia repudiating its own essence in order to blend into the French nation.

It is interesting then, both psychologically and politically, to look at how states settle their linguistic problems. Are governments faithful to ethnic character, or do they repudiate it? Is the diversity of the country taken into consideration, or ignored? Is problem-solving approached pragmatically, or sentimentally? Is action inspired by a desire for internal harmony, or for international favor?

The intention here is to emphasize typological, descriptive, and geographical substance more than method. Moreover, the focus is not on a detailed examination of the use of languages in various public and private domains of juridical life, but on the formulation of a classification of territories according to the language or languages recognized officially. The discussion will deal with Europe specifically, and a synthetic inventory of recognized langauges will be proposed, using some examples from other parts of the world. A summary typology, presented below, can be drawn for the various situations. This typology will structure the discussion.

Section 1.0   Problems of Qualification
Section 2.1   Official Language
Section 2.2   National Language
Section 3.1   Language Status Equality
Section 3.2   Language Status Inequality
Section 4.1   Territorial Bi- or Multilingualism
Section 4.2   Individual Bi- or Multilingualism
Section 5.1   Adequate Linguistic Regimens
Section 5.2   Inadequate Linguistic Regimens
Section 5.3   Linguistic Regimens for Immigrants

1.0   PROBLEMS OF QUALIFICATION

In the past, constitutions generally did not indicate the language of the state, no more than they indicated state symbols (motto, anthem, flag). There were exceptions, of course, specifically in those bi- or multilingual states which respected their linguistic diversity. Switzerland, in its Federal Constitution of 1848, mentioned three languages, German, French, and Italian, and the Belgian Constitution of 1831 posed the question, but did not resolve it.[3]

In recent decades, states which are unilingual, or aspire to be so, specify the 'national' language as well as flag, motto, and anthem in their constitutions. The French Constitutions of 1946 and 1958 do not fit this pattern. It is surprising that language is not mentioned, considering that the text stipulates a national emblem, an anthem, and a motto (article 2 of the Constitution of 4 October 1958). This omission is significant, since France

is by no means unilingually French. This omission cannot be explained by
the desire to avoid politicial problems, because in both 1946 and 1958 ethnic
sentiment in France was hardly perceptible. The omission attests, rather, to
the fact that the French mentality was and remains, by and large, closed to
linguistic issues.

The French legal system establishes no more than a minimum of linguistic
standards. In the press, for example, the ordinance of 13 September 1945,
considered illegal by many, prescribes narrow limits for the use of German
in the newspapers of Alsace and Moselle. With regard to education, the
decree of 18 December 1952, later modified, pertains to the instruction of
German in the three departments (Bas-Rhin, Haut-Rhin, and Moselle). The
Deixonne Act of 11 January 1951[4] permits the optional instruction of four
'vernacular' languages, Basque, Breton, Catalan, and Occitan, later
including Corsican as well, on the primary and secondary levels.[5] The
Bas-Lauriol Law[6] prohibits, with penalties, the use of any language other
than French in both written and television programs. Even the use of
foreign words is prohibited whenever there is an equivalent in French.

Despite an awakening of linguistic consciousness in France, the fact
remains that there is no text which explicitly establishes French as the
official national language. France is one of those nations where the
qualification of the official language is effected primarily through custom.
It could be said that French is unofficially the official language of France.

The Grand Duchy of Luxembourg is characterized by an official
language, *de facto*. Though the Constitution of 17 October 1868 (article 29)
established French and German as official languages, a 6 May 1948
amendment deconstitutionalized the linguistic regimen and deferred power
to the legislative body: 'The law determines the use of languages in
administrative and judicial matters' (article 29). Seemingly, only the basis
of linguistic qualification was changed, from the Constitution to ordinary
law. However, since parliament has so far remained silent on linguistic
qualification, there exists a *de facto* situation which has lasted 32 years.

In Luxembourg there are three relatively well defined linguistic areas—
one for each of the two 'unofficial official' languages and one for
Letzenburgesch, the German dialect (Moselfrankisch). Being monethnic,
the Grand Duchy cannot be bilingual, but is rather, triglossic; Luxembourg
is not composed of two juxtaposed populations, but of a single people using
either French or German in both its literary and dialectal forms.
Letzenburgesch is the common spoken language, whereas German
predominates in the churches and the press. French is the 'calling card',
appearing alone on almost all public signs, official or private. There are a
few exceptions. German is used in public notices and Letzenburgesch is used
on street signs in the city of Luxembourg. In Esch-sur-l'Alzette, the second

largest city, street names are in French and German. Lately many areas have added names in Letzenburgesch to French signs, but in small letters.[7] Treaties and laws are in French, whereas minutes of parliamentary deliberations and town councils are written in the language of the proceedings, though never in German. German is not used by individuals, and since World War II it has lost its value as a national symbol, French having assumed this role. Postage stamps and currency are printed in French, often with a few words in Letzenburgesch.

In summary, French is, *de facto,* the official language of the Grand Duchy (as linguistic symbol of a state determined to differentiate itself from the other German-speaking peoples). Letzenburgesch, the household language, has some value as a national language, because, although used in Germany, Belgium, and France, it is omnipresent in the Grand Duchy.[8] Literary German retains its solid position only as an auxiliary language.[9]

The situation of Malta is analogous to that of Luxembourg, though different from the point of view of linguistic qualification. As in Luxembourg, three languages complement each other, reflecting triglossia rather than trilingualism.[10] Maltese is the ethnic language of the inhabitants, English is the former colonial language, and Italian is the traditional language of culture.[11] But, in contrast to Luxembourg, Malta officially and explicitly defines linguistic status in its Constitution: 'The national language of Malta is Maltese; Maltese and English, as well as any other language prescribed by Parliament (by a two-thirds vote), will be official languages, and the government may use them for all official acts' (article 5:1). Further, the Constitution states that 'the authorities must know them and use them indifferently in dealing with the public' (article 5:2). Italian is not mentioned at all, but it is the language (with literary Arabic) which, by popular usage, would have the best chance of being established as the third official language. On Malta then, the definition of national and official languages is explicit and official. However, since Italian plays a definite auxiliary role on the island and has not received legal ratification, Maltese language status remains incomplete.

2.1, 2.2 OFFICIAL LANGUAGE—NATIONAL LANGUAGE

The case of Malta introduces a distinction which states recognize between official language (OL) and national language (NL). Ireland, Switzerland, and Spain are other examples.

The Irish Constitution of 1937 (article 8) declares Irish 'as the national language, the first official language'. But, in fact, English functions as the first official language, Gaelic not having regained its former importance as had been hoped at that time. In 1938 Switzerland modified article 116 of its Constitution, by inserting a paragraph stating that 'German, French, Italian, and Romansch are national languages of Switzerland', whereas only German, French, and Italian are confirmed as official languages. The Spanish Constitution of 27 December 1978, more explicit on the import of this distinction but more evasive as to the specific languages, makes the same distinction. The Constitution decrees that 'Castilian is the language of the state. All Spaniards have the duty to know it and the right to use it' (article 3:1), while acknowledging 'the richness of the diverse linguistic varieties in Spain' as a 'cultural heritage which is to enjoy particular respect and protection' (article 3:3). Even if the term 'national language' is not used, the concept is implicit. Although the languages 'to be respected and protected' are not listed, they logically include the 'official languages of the autonomous communities' designated by the 'respective statutes' (article 3:2).[12]

Outside of Europe in former colonial territories this dual concept of 'official language' and 'national language' is most significant. English is an official language of India with Hindi, but only for 50 years. Unlike Hindi, it is not a national language; however, since Hindi is only one of 14 principal indigenous languages, resistance of non-Hindi states to the prospect of Hindi as the sole official language gives English an important advantage. Senegal, in a solution diametrically opposite that of the Republic of India, recognizes six African languages as national and makes French the only official language. The Central African Republic, to cite another example, recognizes Sango as national and French as official.

Similar to the OL/NL distinction is the distinction between official language (OL, with the double meaning of official and national) and auxiliary language (AL). Such is the case in the French-speaking Arabic countries of North Africa, where French is still used by the government in an auxiliary role. On Cyprus, English plays this secondary role.

As a general rule, if the OL/NL distinction is not made, the OL is also the NL. Luxembourg is an exception. French, the OL, cannot be considered the NL, since, located within Teutonia, the people use the Letzenburgesch dialect in daily life. However, given the distinction, two situations are possible: either the official language is foreign (English in India, black Africa, and originally Ireland), or it is one among other indigenous languages. In the latter situation, to accept all indigenous languages as OL, especially those in limited use, would greatly complicate governmental operations. Thus, Romansch is not an OL in Switzerland, and only Castilian is recognized as official in Spain. Historical and ideological reasons as well as practical considerations account for this. It would be politically difficult for the reformist administration of King Juan Carlos to move directly from a policy of ostracism (under Franco) to completely equal recognition (such as the status of French and Italian relative to German in Switzerland) of three languages now considered by most Spaniards as detrimental to the unity of the *patria* and the *Estado* (Basque, Catalan, and Galician).

When a state recognizes multiple national languages, it is accepting cultural diversity. Thus, even if it does not seem possible or desirable to use these languages officially, the state accepts the responsibility for their protection. The jurisprudence of the Swiss Federal Tribunal considers it the responsibility of the cantons to watch over the integrity of the four linguistic areas of the Confederation. The association 'Défense et promotion des langues de France' is trying to end governmental opposition to the seven minority languages used in metropolitan France by 'nationalizing' them.

3.1, 3.2 LANGUAGE STATUS EQUALITY — LANGUAGE STATUS INEQUALITY

The problem of status equality and inequality involves two distinct concerns: the relationship between the OL and the NL, and the relationship between the official state language (SL) and the official regional language (RL).

A. Official Language and National Language

A national language often enjoys more acceptance than an official, nonnational language; but in terms of positive prerogatives, the official language predominates. Thus, in Switzerland Romansch plays no part in domestic governmental operations, public and private relations, and foreign relations.

Sometimes languages recognized by the state as official are 'demoted' to serve only as RL. For example, in the U.S.S.R., the languages of the 14 union republics other than the Soviet Federated Socialist Republic of Russia, though official, are relegated to regional use. Slovene and Macedonian in Yugoslavia and Slovak in Czeckoslovakia have been similarly demoted.[13] Whereas in the U.S.S.R. this demotion reflects the actual situation, in Yugoslavia Serbo-Croatian has been legalized, since it is the only language recognized in the army.[14] In Belgium German, though theoretically cofficial, has been in fact completely demoted in favor of French and Dutch.

B. State Language and Regional Language

RL is not to be defined solely as a language that is used in only part of the state territory, since the SL also may have a limited territorial range. This is generally the case where there is bi- or multilingualism through juxtaposition of unilingual territories.[15] Theoretically, Belgium French is not used in Flanders nor Dutch in Wallonia. In Switzerland it is still necessary to speak the language of the region even with agents of the government. Fortunately, in practice this principle has been relaxed a great deal, through political concern for the French and Italian speakers and for the foreign tourists. Thus it was possible to allow the English and Japanese translations of destinations in certain train stations in the popular Bernese Oberland.

RL should be defined as that language which can be employed in contacts with regional government (and possibly as the language used within this government). The concept of 'region' carries wider meaning of 'territorial circumscription': the autonomous *region* of the Aosta Valley, the autonomous *province* of Bolzano/Bozen, the *district* of Bienne in the canton of Bern, the 19 communes of the *arrondissement* of the Capital District of Brussels, the German *linguistic region* of Belgium, and the Romansch *communes* of the Graubünden, to cite a few examples. 'Region' may also refer to federate states: the states of the Republic of India with languages other than Hindi, and the union republics of the U.S.S.R. other than the Soviet Federated Socialist Republic of Russia (which are *de facto* necessarily bilingual).

The existence of a RL implies bilingualism, with formal priority given to the SL. Thus, the Aosta Valley, South Tyrol, and the province of Trieste in Italy are bilingual, Italian-French, Italian-German (and Ladin), and Italian-Slovene, respectively. The only exception is the Faeroe Islands, where Faeroese is spoken so widely compared to Danish that the archipelago may be considered unilingually Faeroese.

Sometimes a SL is simply a RL in a certain part of the state. In the Flemish communes with French 'facilities' (the six communes around the Capital District of Brussels and various communes along the linguistic border) and in various Walloon communes with Dutch 'facilities' along the same border, this is the case.[16] The entire part of Belgium that is officially considered German-speaking is subject to French 'facilities', in such a way that this linguistic region is completely bilingual, though German has priority. Inversely, the communes of Malmédy and Waimes, now Walloon but a part of Prussia prior to the signing of the Treaty of Versailles, have German 'facilities'. Moreover, German does not appear on public signs.

Romansch, a national but not official language, is a RL in part of the Graubünden. Romansch has the quality of an official idiom, yet only on the cantonal level, and on the communal level in almost all the communes in the traditionally Romansch area.[17]

The status of a RL varies. It is sometimes officially proclaimed as a RL. Sometimes the juridical texts consider it an auxiliary language, such as German in South Tyrol before the promulgation of the reforms commonly known as 'The Packet' in 1971.[18] Sometimes its position is purely factual. In these cases there is 'acceptance' on the part of government agencies allowing public use of a language not mentioned in legal texts. The Alsatian dialect in eastern France suffers this indefinite and threatened situation.

The SL/RL distinction provides a formal, precise definition for the term 'linguistic minority'. A linguistic minority is an indigenous population whose language is not recognized by the state as an official language. From this point of view, Swedish-speaking Finns are not a minority (although they constitute only 6.6% of the population of Finland), nor are the Ticinese (between 5 and 6% of the Swiss), because Swedish and Italian are officially recognized, whereas the Catalans (29% of the population of Spain) and the Ukrainians (42 million, or 16%) are to be considered minorities, since their dialects are not officially recognized.

4.1, 4.2 TERRITORIAL BI- OR MULTILINGUALISM— INDIVIDUAL BI- OR MULTILINGUALISM

Territorial bi- or multilingualism (TBM) exists when two or more languages thrive in two or more territorially distinct parts of the same state. Switzerland, Belgium, and Finland are well-known cases of TBM in Europe, to which we may add Czechoslovakia and Yugoslavia. In reality, almost all nations are TBM, because very few are monoethnic: in Europe only Iceland, Luxembourg, and, to a lesser extent, Portugal. France, for example, is octolingual. These situations, however, are not taken into consideration, most particulary in France. TBM constitutes a situation similar to that of states with a juxtaposition of unilingual territories (JUT) (see footnote 20).

Individual bi- or multilingualism (IBM) occurs when two or more languages thrive in the same territory. Two distinct situations are possible. One is bi- or multilingualism of a territory resulting from the juxtaposition and mixing of two or more unilingual populations—Brussels, the bilingual communes of Finland, the district of Bienne, and Cyprus before it was divided into two zones, for example. In this case we have JP territories, bi- or multilingual by juxtaposition of unilingual populations.

A second possibility is bi- or multilingualism existing on the individual level while the territory remains homogeneously populated. In this case we have bi- or multilingual territories by linguistic superimposition (LS).

It is obvious that, as populations mix, JP tends to become LS; but populations never fuse completely. Every group, even after becoming bilingual, prefers its ethnic tongue, or at least preserves a sense of ethnic consciousness, as do the Anglicized Irish.

Linguistic superimposition raises many questions, because, as François Fontan (1975) states, unilingualism is the norm. What, then, are these origins of bi- and multilingualism and diglossia? Three situations can be distinguished.

First, a phenomenon widespread in German-speaking countries, Italy, and Spain, though unknown in France, is the superimposition of dialects on the language of culture. This often leads to diglossia, rather than bilingualism in the strict sense, since the dialects in question are only particular regional forms of the same language. German Switzerland and Luxembourg exemplify this phenomenon in that the population invariably speaks in dialect, reserving German or French for writing. In Ticino, the Swiss canton, Italian is already competing with Lombard in the oral tradition, as are dialects throughout Italy itself. In French Switzerland only a few valleys, Val d'Hérens and Val d'Anniviers, the heights above Sion, and, more generally, French Fribourg, still use Franco-Provençal dialects in verbal interactions.[19] In Greece we find a variant of this situation. There the opposition between Katharevousa and Dimotiki is between a learned language and the vernacular, not between a learned language and different dialects. Moreover, Dimotiki, a language written as well as spoken, is gaining ground.

A second linguistic phenomenon is the superimposition of an imported foreign language on the local language. Such is the case in Luxembourg and on Malta, where French and English, respectively, have never been ethnic languages. In Luxembourg this phenomenon results from the desire to distinguish itself from neighboring Germany (where other *Moselfränkisch* dialects are spoken). In most of the other cases, including Malta, Ireland, North Africa, the Levant, and India, the maintenance of a foreign language as official or auxiliary language is a vestige of colonialization.

Finally, a third situation is found in all JP territories when two unilingual populations mix over time and develop a generalized bilingualism. This phenomenon occurs when the languages in contact enjoy the same 'prestige'.[20] If the difference in 'prestige' is too great, as between French and Dutch in Brussels, the population which speaks the 'prestige' language will not make the effort to learn the other, and bilingualism does not result.

TBM and IBM can exist separately or jointly. Pure TBM exists when each territory in which two or more languages are spoken is officially considered bilingual. This occurs when the OL of the territory is also a state language (SL), as in Flanders and Wallonia (with the exception of the communes with 'facilities'), German Switzerland, French Switzerland, Italian Switzerland, unilingually Finnish Finland, and unilingually Swedish Finland. The state territory is a group of juxtaposed unilingual territories; Belgium, Switzerland, and Finland are not, because in these states bilingual regions are added to unilingual regions.

Another form of pure IBM exists when the entire state territory is subject to one and the same bi- or multilingual linguistic regimen. When two distinct linguistic groups live together, the state territory forms only a JP, as Cyprus before the partition or Singapore, quadrilingual by juxtaposition.

In another possibility the population is homogeneous, but uniformly bi- or multilingual, in which case there is LS in the state territory— Luxembourg, Malta, Ireland, and Lebanon (Arabic-French *de facto*).

The TBM-IBM combination is found when the indigenous language of one part of the state territory is not a SL but simply a RL. As the SL is necessarily superimposed (SL/RL bilingualism), the part of the state territory in question is IBM. But the state itself is TBM-IBM, since it is composed of two or more linguistic regions, that is, of two or more territorial elements with different statuses. Belgium, Switzerland, and Finland belong to this type, Belgium comprising seven different linguistic zones,[21] Switzerland five,[22] and Finland three.[23]

The TBM-IBM combination is also found in every state that is bi- or multilingual in a diffuse way. In all these states there are limited domains where the use of diverse OL is authorized concurrently in all areas of the territory. This authorization may result from express legal stipulation or from tacit popular acceptance. For example, Brussels National Airport in Zaventem, located in a commune in Flanders without French 'facilities', is bilingual Dutch-French by virtue of a legislative stipulation. In the U.S.S.R. *de facto* 'personalization' goes so far in favor of Russian, officially only a RL, that Russians can feel totally at home throughout the entire nation (cf. Section 3.1, 3.2 A above).

5.1, 5.2 ADEQUATE/INADEQUATE LINGUISTIC REGIMENS

'Adequate' and 'inadequate' regimens (ALR and ILR) are those which correspond or do not correspond to the indigenous languages of the territories under consideration. These terms do not constitute value judgments as to why a particular linguistic regimen was adopted, but are used merely to define language characteristics.

Linguistic adequacy is a rare phenomenon. To establish this, we have only to compare the limited number of states with diverse linguistic statuses and the high number of polyethnic states. Almost every state in the world is a linguistic composite, even if we do not consider foreign immigration and language importation.

The adequate linguistic regimens are found in those few states which are historically unilingual, such as Iceland and Portugal. No naturally multilingual state (TBM) has attained perfect adequacy. Belgium, for example, has bilingual regimens in territories that were originally Flemish (Brussels and communes with 'facilities'), and it treats the territory of Welkenraedt (Plattdeits dialect) and the arrondissement of Arlon (Letzenburgesch) as unilingually French. There is near perfect adequacy in Switzerland, but for a few exceptions. The city of Bienne replaced the Alemanic dialect with German-French bilingualism in the nineteenth century; the neighboring commune of Evilard, with which Bienne forms a district and which was originally French-speaking, is also officially bilingual. Gurin, the only Alemanic commune in Ticino, could not remain unilingually German, and therefore became Bosco/Gurin. Romansch has succeeded in gaining respect neither for the principle of linguistic territoriality, nor even less for Romansch unilingualism (except, from a purely toponymic viewpoint, in about half of the communes). In Finland, in addition to two unilingual zones, there is a mixed Finnish-Swedish zone which is encroaching on originally Swedish communes rather than on originally Finnish communes. Norway has, with less rigid localization, a zone where Nynorsk is spoken (the northwest) and another (the larger) where Bokmål is spoken.[24]

Besides these cases, to which may be added Denmark (the Faeroe Islands), Yugoslavia, and Czechoslovakia, other TBM states are taking steps toward quasi-adequacy by establishing bilingual regions, instead of the unilingualism necessary for strict adequacy. Among these states are: Italy, in the South Tyrol, the Aosta Valley, and the Provinces with Slovene minorities (Gorizia and Trieste); the Netherlands, in bilingual Friesland; Spain, in Euzkadi, Galicia, and Catalonia; Great Britain, in Wales; and East Germany, with the Sorbs.

A third group of states remains closed to ALR. In Europe these include France and Greece. Greece is obliged, however, to recognize certain facilities for the Turks of western Thrace, as a counterpart to the limited rights granted by Turkey to the Greeks of eastern Thrace.

Quite often states combine ALR and ILR, which establishes discrimination among minority groups. Though the Italian Constitution declares, 'The Republic protects linguistic minorities through appropriate measures' (article 6), this protection exists only in the Aosta Valley (French), South Tyrol (German and Ladin), and the provinces of Gorizia and Trieste (Slovene). Yet, Italy has no fewer than 11 indigenous linguistic minorities; in addition to those mentioned above, there are also the

Albanians, the Catalans, the Croats, the Greeks, the Mediolanese,[25] the Occitans, and the Sards. In fact, this protection applies only within regions with particular autonomy, and even then not for all such regions (none for the Sards and Catalans of Sardinia), nor for all minorities within these regions (none for the 'Walsers' of the Aosta Valley, for the Ladins and Germans of Trentine,[26] for the Friulans and Germans of Friuli-Venezia-Giulia, nor for the Slovenes of the province of Udine). The limited application of article 6 is not random, however; the only minorities protected are, with the exception of the Aosta Valley, those for which there is an international obligation[27] or which have benefited from international support.[28]

The discrimination resulting from this state of affairs exists not only among the ethnic groups, but also within these groups. Protection is available for the Slovenes in the province of Gorizia and Trieste but not for those in the province of Udine, for the Ladins and Germans of South Tyrol but not for those in Trento and Belluno (in this case, only Ladins) or the Walser Germans.[29]

Though the situation in Italy has been emphasized, because it is a nation rich in minorities, there are other less positive examples. Greece, Turkey, and even Sweden do not recognize their linguistic minorities.[30]

5.3 LINGUISTIC REGIMENS FOR IMMIGRANTS

The purpose here is to point out the cases where the phenomenon of immigration is translated on the level of the OL or the RL by at least a partial symbolic recognition of the languages and cultures of certain categories of immigrants.

In Europe indigenous communities have a long historical tradition. Most of these communities were formed through fissiparous evolution: the diverse Romanic, Germanic, and Slavic ethnic groups, for example. In America as well, the term 'native' refers only to the first inhabitants, Indians and Eskimos. But there, in addition to these groups, a second 'indigenous' group formed out of the first European immigrants, from England, France, Spain, and Portugal. These ethnic groups imposed their respective languages in their areas of colonization. Later immigrants, despite their large numbers—the Italians in Argentina, the Germans, Dutch and Scandinavians in Canada and the United States—had to accept these languages, at least publicly.

Dissatisfaction with linguistic assimilation has begun to emerge in the United States, together with the practical interest involved in the preservation of these various languages. Under the impetus of intellectuals such as the sociologist Joshua Fishman (Kloss 1977) and the reality of large-scale legal and illegal immigration, the United States is modifying the traditional 'melting pot' ideal and is now tolerating a policy of linguistic pluralism. This 'new direction' benefits particularly the Spanish-speaking populations in the Southwest and Florida.

Other countries are adopting this mode. German, for example, enjoys *de facto* status as a protected minority language in the federal states of Santa Catarina and Rio Grande do Sul in Brazil, as well as in southern Chile, in the region of Valdivia and Puerto Montt. In Canada, when Prime Minister Trudeau tried during his first term to establish unilingual or bilingual (English-French) districts in the Quebec-Ontario border, it was suggested that this system—reminiscent of the proposal made by Karl Renner in the final years of Austria-Hungary—be extended to the 'nonfounding' races— Germans, Ukrainians, Dutch, Polish, Italians. The idea had little chance of success, due to the nongeographic nature of the immigration, but it reflected the reality of increasing linguistic pluralism. In the Republic of Singapore, Chinese (80% of the population) and Tamil are officially recognized as OL, with Malay (the only indigenous language) and English.

In Europe and the other regions of the world which are not areas of modern settlement, the principle of indigenity prevails, *de facto* and *de jure*. It is indeed normal to prevent these territories, which are not 'res nullius', from becoming 'res communes'. The inhabitants have a right to preserve their identities; and Europe and the rest of the world gain just as much from protecting this diversity.

Linguistic problems can become acute with the growing presence of migrant workers. Various host states, including Belgium, France, the Netherlands, West Germany, Switzerland, have not offered these minorities linguistic recognition. Services offered in the foreign language have the objective of promoting the assimilation of those immigrants who remain and of providing those immigrants returning home with a certain amount of the culture of the host state. The presence in the host state of a constantly renewed foreign population might produce a new 'indigenous' ethnic minority, but today there are different political, economic, and social conditions which impede this process. The European settlers in America and Australia, the Water Croats in Burgenland (Austria), the various minorities of the Banat (Vojvodina in Yugoslavia and Banat in Rumania), the Albanians and Greeks of southern Italy, the Catalans of Alghero/Alguer in Sardinia: all are examples of such a historical process. Other cultural characteristics besides language, such as religion, must be considered, as in the growing openness to the Moslem minority in France.

An association for the defense of minorities, the Federal Union of European Nationalities (FUEN) recognizes the 'indigenization' of immigrant minorities by including in its ranks the Polish of the Ruhr (Rohrpolen). Even more significant is the admission of German as an auxiliary language in the French part (Malmédy-Waimes) of Eupen-Malmédy, annexed from Germany in 1918 and again in 1945. Likewise significant is the ratification of Czech as a minority language, taught in schools, in the province of Vienna (whereas Czechoslovakia ruthlessly expelled in 1945-46 its indigenous Teutonic 'Austrian'): the minority protection clause of the Treaty of Saint-Germain-en-Laye was renewed in the Treaty of Vienna, 5 May 1955, and ratified by law with the creation of a Czech *Beirat* (advisory council), similar to the councils formed for the indigenous minorities (Slovens, Croats, Hungarians).

Why limit such good efforts? Why not recognize, then, the Turks of Voralberg in Austria, the Portuguese in Alsace, the North Africans and Hausas in the Parisian region, the South Moluccans in the Netherlands, and the speakers of Hindi, Urdu, and Tamil in the United Kingdom?

A little known case of 'indigenization' is found in the Norwegian possession of Svalbard (of which the largest part forms Spitsbergen). Of the 3800 inhabitants of Longyearbyen and Barentsburg on the island of West Spitsbergen, 2500 are Russians (and others from the U.S.S.R.) and only 1300 are Norwegians. The Soviets, who work in the coal mines, live by themselves, with their own educational systems.

Finally, there is the situation of the military bases—the American bases at Guantánamo in Cuba and Thule in Greenland, the British bases on Cyprus: these bases constitute *de facto* real and political enclaves. The Allied troops stationed in various countries (Americans, British, and French in West Germany) represent a situation even more similar to that of migrant populations, since the soldiers and their families are living on territory that is under effective sovereignty of the host country. However, these people are clearly separated from the community, since there is no question of assimilation or absorption, and since their presence, like that of the bases themselves, is considered temporary. Nevertheless, this phenomenon brings foreign languages and cultures, with their own structures (schools, mass media, theaters, etc.), into the host state.

CONCLUSION

In this essay I have treated the topic of language and ethnicity on a political level as a social or group phenomenon. I have attempted a conceptual scheme for the role of language in European politics. Language has no simple mode of relationship to both the state and other groups. Nor is language static: it is a dynamic force in the mobilization of ethnic groups.

Finally, I have urged autonomous solutions—the protection of minorities by majority rulers. Language rights are an integral part of human rights. If Europe is to become united, it must be on the basis of linguistic and ethnic self-determination. The compatability of regionalism and European integration is possible, but it will depend on the good will of Europeans.

Translated by Robert Magnan, Charles Foster, and Karen Foster.

NOTES

[1] On linguistic law see Héraud (1971).

[2] See Héraud (1970) on thought-organization function, and Héraud (1973, 1977) on aesthetic function.

[3] Constitution of 7 February 1831, article 23: 'The use of the languages of Belgium is free. It can be regulated only by law and only for the acts of public authorities and legal matters.'

[4] Of which the real promoter is Occitan professor Jean Bonnafous.

[5] Of the six minority languages used in metropolitan France (not including German, which has its own regimen), only Dutch (Flemish) remains excluded under the Deixonne Act. But the Haby reform (1975), which practically annuls the Deixonne Act, should remove any obstacles preventing the teaching of Flemish at the primary level. The exclusion of Flemish is based on the argument that it is not a 'vernacular' language but a foreign dialect, since it is a form of Dutch. Corsican has escaped this ostracism because it is considered distinct from Italian ('lingua corsa').

[6] Law no. 75-1349, published in the *Journal Officiel* 4 January 1976. Implementation was deferred by one year: see AGULF 1978 and the Barre memorandum of 19 March 1977.

[7] Thus, Soleuvre/Zolver.

[8] Except in Lasauvage, located on the French border.

[9] Primary school instruction begins in Letzenburgesch, then German is used, to be replaced by French midway through the secondary level. Since the Grand Duchy has no university, students continue their studies either in French (in France and Belgium) or in German (in West Germany).

[10] On Malta, there are three distinct languages: the Arabic dialect Maltese, English, and Italian. In Luxembourg, the three languages derive from only two distinct languages, German and French.

[11] Formerly co-official with English, Italian was excluded in favor of Maltese with the threat of Italian fascism in 1934. See Vieter (1979:123-32).

[12] The Constitution of Finland (article 14), in a similar case, establishes Finnish and Swedish as 'national languages'. When no distinction is made between 'national' and 'official', 'national language' obviously carries the meaning of 'official language'. The French translation of the Constitution should also be checked against the Finnish and Swedish texts.

[13] Slovak officially has been a co-official language of Czechoslovakia, with Czech, since 1968; formerly it was simply the RL of Slovakia.

[14] It was excluded from international use when Macedonian succeeded in asserting itself in the drafting of international treaties; the same is true *mutatis mutandis* for Slovene. Yugoslavia respects the equality of the alphabets as well, though sometimes to an extreme. The names of train stations are indicated nationwide in both alphabets—understandable in the republics using Serbian/Croatian, but surprising in the republics of Slovenia (since Slovene uses only the Roman alphabet) and Macedonia (since Macedonian uses only the Cyrillic alphabet).

¹⁵We must be careful to distinguish between the juxtaposition of unilingual territories (JUT) and the juxtaposition of unilingual individuals in the same territory (JP). This typological term, used in passage 4.1, 4.2 of the text, deserves a more developed presentation. In addition to these two types of 'juxtaposition', there is the phenomenon of 'superimposition', in which a territory is bi- or multilingual by superimposition (LS) when it has a bi- or multilingual (or diglossic) population. Examples include:

JUT: German Switzerland, French Switzerland, Italian Switzerland, Dutch Belgium (Flanders), French Belgium (Wallonia), German Belgium (Eupen-Saint-Vith).

JP: Arrondissement of the Capital District of Brussels (French, Dutch), district of Bienne (German, French), cities of Helsinki, Turku, Vaasa, and others (Finnish, Swedish).

LS: Luxembourg (Letzenburgesch, German, French triglossia for all inhabitants), Malta (Maltese, English, and Italian triglossia), Ireland (Gaelic and English diglossia, with priority of one or the other according to the region).

JP situations tend to become situations of LS through contact between the populations; but in general ethnic consciousness is not replaced by 'bilingual' patriotism. This feeling is found less and less among the inhabitants of Brussels, and almost never in the other JP areas of Europe. Inhabitants of SL territories show the same tendency to rally around one language, sometimes when it is not the language usually spoken. For example, the English-speaking Irish often wish to be considered Celts, which is why they established Irish as their only national language.

¹⁶Bilingual signs have finally been raised in Comines/Komen in the Walloon province of Hainaut. There have always been such signs in Ronse/Renaix, in the province of East Flanders, because of the Gallicized Flemings there. Not only the name of the commune appears in both languages, but all public and private signs and notices as well.

¹⁷The others, for the most part Germanized, have switched to German (Sankt-Moritz, Bonaduz, etc.), and one to Italian (Bivio, Beiva in Romansch).

¹⁸Constitutional law, published 5 January 1972. Paradoxically, French in the Aosta Valley, which is used much less than German in the South Tyrol, was proclaimed 'official language of the Valley, equal to Italian' (article 38, Statute of 26 February 1948). At that time there was hope for a revival, which has not yet occurred.

¹⁹Or 'Bougondien', a term which I have proposed together with Guiu Sobiela-Caanitz.

²⁰The prestige of a language is due not to any intrinsic value or to the literature produced in that language, but to the historical and contemporary power relationships between the two ethnic groups involved. Thus, French is 'prestigious' in Brussels, though less so in Montreal, and even less in the Aosta Valley, where it must compete with English and Italian respectively.

²¹The seven zones: the Dutch linguistic region (LR) (Flanders, excluding communes with French 'facilities'), the French LR (Wallonia, excluding communes with Dutch and German 'facilities'), the German LR (Eupen-Saint-Vith) incorporated into Wallonia, the bilingual French-Dutch LR of the Capital District of Brussels (19 communes), the Flemish communes with French 'facilities' (divided into two categories: the six communes around the Capital District of Brussels and the communes strung out along the Flanders-Wallonia border, including the famous commune of Voeren/Fouron), the Walloon communes with Dutch 'facilities' (along the Wallonia-Flanders border), and the two Walloon communes with German 'facilities' (Malmédy and Waimes). There are provisions for an eighth zone, the 'region' of Welkenraedt, Walloon and unilingually French, where French-German-Dutch trilingualism could be established (cf. the law of 8 November 1970). Other zones include the arrondissement of Arlon, officially unilingually French, but where, apart from the commune of Arlon and a few villages, Letzenburgesch is spoken.

²²The five zones: unilingual German Switzerland, unilingual French Switzerland, unilingual Italian Switzerland, the German-French bilingual district of Bienne, the German-Romansch zone of the Graubünden, the Italian-Romansch zone on the Graubünden (Bivio), the purely

Romansch zone of the Graubünden, and the Italian-German commune of Bosco/Gurin in Ticino. These boundaries are less strictly defined than in Belgium.

Furthermore, there are three distinct levels—confederation, canton, and commune. Thus, there is no purely Romansch zone at the confederate level, since Romansch is not an official language of Switzerland; that zone must be considered Romansch-German. Moreover, there are communes where the territory is divided between two zones: the communes of Fribourg, La Neuveville, Cerniat, and Charmey, for example, have German sections, and Maloja is a Romansch-German section of the Italian-speaking commune of Stampa. The choice of a linguistic regimen in the communes of the Romansch Graubunden and the definition by canton in Fribourg, for example, is based on a custom and was ratified by the Federal Court in the Constitution (Héraud 1974:373-86, and especially Viletta 1978).

[23]If the Lapp zone (population about 3000) is omitted, Finland is divided into three linguistic zones: a unilingual Finnish zone, a unilingual Swedish zone, and a bilingual zone. But this is not a static situation. Whereas the province of the Åland Islands is permanently established as unilingually Swedish by virtue of a League of Nations statute (27 June 1921), the other linguistic areas are shifting. Several times revised to compensate for the effects of the decline of the Swedish minority, the law states that communes are bilingual when the minority constitutes 10% or more of the population and unilingual when less than 8%, except if the town council decides to maintain bilingualism. Moreover, each city with at least 5000 inhabitants using the minority language (Swedish) is necessarily bilingual, whatever the percentage, as in Helsinki, Turku, and Vaasa. In 1962 there were 438 Finnish, 47 Swedish, and 44 mixed communes. Cf. Merikoski 1957 and Modeen 1970:121-39.

[24]The Nynorsk zone (of which the center is Trondheim) uses pure Norwegian, a western Scandinavian language related to Icelandic-Faeroese (which itself has two distinct dialectal forms). The main part of Norway originally used an eastern Scandinavian language of the Swedish branch (Bandle 1973). On the other hand, in Jämtland, Sweden, Norwegian is spoken. Bokmål, or Dano-Norwegian, is an imported language in that it was the language used by the Danish government at the time of the Kalmar Union, which progressively changed in pronunciation.

[25]An expression coined by Guiu Sobeila-Caanitz for the tongue of northern Italy, which (with the exception of Venetian and Istrian) are not properly Italian.

[26]The Ladins of Trentino, however, are affected by the stipulation of Constitutional Law 5 of 26 February 1948, establishing the status of the autonomous region of Trentino-Alto Adige.

[27]Peace Treaty of Paris, 10 February 1947 (supplement IV) for South Tyrol; London Memorandum, 5 October 1954, and Treaty of Ósimo (Ancora), 10 November 1975, for the Slovenians in the province of Trieste.

[28]The Aosta Valley was believed to have the support of France, although such was not the case. The Slovenes in the province of Gorizia were supported by the Anglo-Saxon occupying forces.

[29]The regional government, under the impetus of Mario Andrione, has brought German courses into the communes of the upper Vallaise. Thus the Aosta Valley is the only region protecting an ethnic group by statute.

[30]In Sweden, the Skåne (*lato sensu:* the counties of Blekinge, Halland, and Skåne) belongs to the Danish ethnic area but has become very Swedish. There are now signs of a certain awakening of ethnic consciousness.

APPENDIX

Recognized Languages of the Different States of Europe

By 'recognized languages' are meant the languages used by the government and in the legal system, not only those which benefit from status in the educational system and the mass media. This 'recognition' may be either explicit or implicit.

Andorra is listed, although it is not a state but rather a cofief or, more generally, a condominium. Cyprus, Turkey, and the U.S.S.R. are not considered.

Abbreviations:

AL: Auxiliary language.

ML: Language of minorities having no territorial organization; territorial concentration will also be indicated, especially when the linguistic regimen is territorially limited, as for the Germans in Denmark and the Danes in Germany, for example.

NL: National language. When the NL is not indicated, the OL is considered the NL (more often implicitly than explicitly).

OL: Official language.

RL: Regional language in force in a specific area.

Albania

OL: Albanian.

Andorra

OL: Catalan.

ML: *de facto* Spanish, French.

Austria

OL: German.

ML: (Groups having Beirate, advisory councils): Hungarian, Serbo-Croatian (in its Croatian form), Slovene, Czech. The first two groups are in Burgenland, the third in southern Carinthia, and the fourth in Vienna. (See Veiter 1979).

Belgium

OL: *de jure* Dutch, French, German; limited *de facto* to Dutch and French (which makes the three OL *de facto* NL).

Territorial Zones:

— Brussels region (arrondissement of the Capital District of Brussels or greater Brussels, that is, the commune of Brussels and 18 others), OL: French and Dutch.
— Flemish region, OL: Dutch.
— Walloon region, excluding the linguistic region known as 'German Belgium' or Eupen-Saint-Vith, OL: French.

Within the Flemish region and the Walloon region:

— communes of the Walloon region having Dutch 'facilities', OL: French, AL: Dutch (application vague).
— communes of the Walloon region having French 'facilities', that is, Eupen-Saint-Vith, OL: German, AL: French.
— communes of the Walloon region having German 'facilities', that is, the communes of Malmedy and Waimes, OL: French, AL: German.
— unestablished: German and Dutch 'facilities' in Welkenraedt and surrounding communes (Walloon region using Germanic dialect).

Bulgaria

OL: Bulgarian.
ML: Rumanian, Turkish, and others; Macedonian is not recognized because the government considers it simply a Bulgarian dialect.

Czechoslovakia

OL: Czech (Bohemia-Moravia), Slovak (Slovakia): Czech and Slovak are two codified forms of the same language.
ML: German (readmitted, in theory, during the Dubček era), Hungarian, Polish.

Denmark

OL: Danish.
RL: Faeroese (a form of Icelandic-Faeroese) in the autonomous possession of the Faeroe Islands; Greenlandic or Inuit or Eskimo in Greenland.
ML: German (southern Jutland, south of the Konge River).

Finland

OL: Finnish, Swedish.

The unilingual French zone includes the second largest city, Tampere.
The unilingual Swedish zone includes the autonomous province of the Åland Islands.

The bilingual zone includes the major cities (Finnish name given first): Helsinki/Helsingfors, Turku/Åbo, Vaasa/Vasa.

Same/Lapp is protected but not recognized, neither as an OL nor as a NL, except implicitly, nor as a RL. At best it can be considered an AL in the zone inhabited by the Sames.

France
OL: French.

Germany (Democratic Republic)
OL: German.

Germany (Federal Republic)
OL: German.
ML: Danish, Frisian (both in Schleswig, Danish north of the Eider River, Frisian in the Kreis of Nordfriesland).

Great Britain and Northern Ireland
OL: English.
RL: Welsh (Wales).
— islands in British waters:
       Isle of Man, RL: Manx.
       French has been abolished as a RL on the Channel islands of Guernsey and Jersey.

Greece
OL: Greek (in its two forms, Dimotiki and Katharevousa).
ML: Turkish (in Thrace).

Hungary
OL: Hungarian.
ML: German, Serbo-Croatian, Slovak, Rumanian, Slovene.

Iceland
OL: Icelandic (a form of Icelandic-Faeroese).

Ireland
OL: Gaelic, English.
NL: Gaelic.

Italy
OL: Italian.
RL: German, Ladin (a form of Rhaeto-Romanic) in the autonomous
      province of Bolzano/Bozen or south Tyrol, French in the
      autonomous region of the Aosta Valley, Slovene in the provinces
      of Gorizia and Trieste. Ladin is a RL *de jure* in the autonomous
      province of Trent, but this constitutional arrangement stated in
      the Statute of the Region of Trentino-South Tyrol is not yet in
      effect.

Leichtenstein
OL: German.

Luxembourg
OL: *de facto* French.
NL: *de facto* Letzenburgesch (German dialect).
AL: *de facto* German.

Malta
OL: English, Maltese (Arabic dialect).
NL: Maltese.

Monaco
OL: French.

Netherlands
OL: Dutch.
RL: Frisian (province of Friesland).

Norway
OL: Norwegian   (Bokmål/Riksmål),   Neo-Norwegian   (Nynorsk/
      Landsmål).
For Same/Lapp the situation is the same as in Finland.

Poland
OL: Polish.

Portugal
OL: Portuguese.

Rumania
OL: Rumanian.
ML: Hungarian, German, and others.

San Marino
OL: Italian.

Spain
OL: Spanish.
NL: Spanish, Basque, Catalan, Galician.
RL: Basque in the autonomous region of Euzkadi, Catalan in the *Generalitat* of Catalonia, Valencian (a form of Catalan) in the autonomous region of Valencia, Galician (a form of Portuguese) in the autonomous region of Galicia.

Sweden
OL: Swedish.
For Same/Lapp the situation is the same as in Finland.

Switzerland
OL: German, French, Italian.
NL: German, French, Italian, Romansch (form of Rhaeto-Romanic).

Vatican City
OL: Italian (Latin is the language of the Church and not of the state).

Yugoslavia
OL: Serbo-Croatian, Slovene, Macedonian (a form of Bulgarian).
RL: Hungarian, Rumanian, Ruthenian (a form of Ukrainian), Slovak in the autonomous region of Vojvodina, Albanian in the autonomous region of Kosovo-Metohija.
ML: Hungarian (communes of Lendava and Murska-Sobota in Slovenia), Italian (communes of Buje/Buie, Izola/Isola, Koper/ Capodistria, Novigrad/Cittanova d'Istria, Piran/Pirano, Umag/ Umago in Slovenia; communes of Porec/Parenzo, Pula/Pola, Rijeka/Fiume, Rovinj/Rovigno in Croatia), other languages than the above mentioned (in Vojvodina, as well as in Macedonia and Kosovo, including Turkish).

*The original version of this paper appeared in *Language Problems and Language Planning* 4. 195-223.

EDUCATION FOR SEPARATISM: THE BELGIAN EXPERIENCE

ELIZABETH SHERMAN SWING

When Charles Baudelaire visited Belgium in 1865, he commented somewhat condescendingly on a peculiar schizophrenia in the heart of the young nation: 'Une partie peut s'en aller à la Prusse, la partie flamande à la Hollande, et les provinces wallonnes à la France. —Grand malheur pour nous! (1953:196). Were Baudelaire to return today, he might not find Belgians as ready to embrace another national identity, but he would find the same centrifugal forces in their society that he had observed a century ago, including a clearly articulated federation movement. The high-rise apartment buildings, the acres of concrete parking lots at the new shopping centers, the everyday traffic jams—all symbols of Belgium's frenetic embrace of postwar technocracy sometimes referred to as 'Americaniza-tion'—might momentarily suggest one hundred years of change. Yet if Baudelaire were to ask about political developments, he would learn that semiautonomous communities—Dutch-speaking Flanders, Francophone Wallonia, and a small German-speaking area in the eastern section of Liège Province—have begun to replace a unitary Belgian nation-state; that throughout the 1970's and into the 1980's cabinets fell over the implementation of this communal structure. The linguistic divisions still remain.

The trend is toward more linguistic separatism. In Belgium today there are separate French- and Dutch-language Ministries of Education, separate French and Dutch TV channels and radio stations, separate French and Dutch theaters and symphony orchestras, separate French and Dutch libraries and sports federations.[1] The Royal Conservatory of Brussels has two student orchestras—one for Francophones, one for Flemings. Dual signs in Brussels identify, as one and the same, places such as *Avenue du*

Commerce and *Handelstraat, Boulevard des Arts* and *Kunststraat, Mons* and *Bergen, Anvers* and *Antwerpen, Bruxelles* and *Brussel;* and it is not uncommon for partisans of one group or the other to paint over their rival's name. Nor is more overt friction unusual. In 1976 riots broke out in Schaerbeek, a predominantly Francophone commune in Brussels, over the refusal of its mayor to create dual service windows—one for Francophones, one for Flemings (Courrier Hebdomadaire du CRISP 1978.786:24-25); in 1979 marches and demonstrations took place in villages on the language line in Voeren and the Comines over schools for linguistic minorities (Courrier Hebdomadaire du CRISP 1979.859; Le Soir 1979:2). Although French is a language most Flemings know well, a visitor frequently encounters Flemish shopkeepers who refuse to speak French even to a foreigner—and Walloons who claim no recollection of Dutch, their second national language which they studied in school. In a country once considered a model for the study of bilingual education, bilingualism now seems more a product of the internecine quarrel than an educational ideal.

The paradox within this bilingual quarrel is, of course, not new. 'Tout le monde affecte de ne pas savoir la flamand,' observed Baudelaire of Brussels society in 1865 (1953:76). Another observer, T. R. Dawes, an Englishman who visited Belgium in 1901 hoping to find a bilingual model for education in Wales, recorded a similar enigma. He found much to praise in bilingual Brussels. There he observed schools with classes for both language groups, separate classes for Flemings and Walloons for the first four years, mixed classes thereafter. Although French was the language of instruction in all the upper grades in Brussels, Dawes noted that lessons in some schools were given first in one tongue then in the other, that children communicated with one another unselfconsciously in both languages on the playground; and he remarked that 'the prejudice formerly felt against Flemish dies away as its utility in a country which is becoming more and more bilingual asserts itself' (1902:11).

Visits to schools in Flanders, however, caused Dawes to modify these optimistic conclusions. Flemings had reason to learn French, an international language which was the medium of instruction in all secondary schools and universities in 1901. It was a one-sided bilingualism —for the Francophone students denigrated Flemish, a tongue they considered no more than a local patois. Even so, these Francophone students did better on the *concours général,* which was still given entirely in French, than did the bilingual Flemings. The director of a school in Flanders explained: 'The pupils are somewhat confused with the two languages, and there is a great mental effort in changing from one language to another' (Dawes 1902:49-50). Thus, imbedded in the Dawes Report, whose purpose was to find practices in Belgian bilingual education that could be emulated in Wales, was the assumption that learning advanced cognitive subjects in a second language put Flemings at an intellectual disadvantage. Bilingualism was a necessity for Flemings, and not always a beneficent necessity. Flemings learned French more thoroughly than Walloons learned Flemish, yet Walloons got ahead professionally and economically because theirs was the dominant language.

Although the era of unilingual Francophone economic, political, and cultural hegemony is past and the civil service has rewarded bilinguals throughout most of the twentieth century, the centrifugal forces in Belgium today still reflect the legacy of this French-language dominance. There exists a widespread assumption that bilingualism is at best a necessary evil: a necessity for national unity, at least in bilingual Brussels, but a danger to intellectual development if introduced too early and a one-way road to language loss.[2] Language planning in this bilingual country reflects this assumption, for it fosters the development of linguistic ethnicity through separatism: geographical separatism, division of the country into unilingual regions—Dutch-speaking Flanders, Francophone Wallonia—plus a Dutch-French bilingual capital zone; institutional separatism, the transformation of political, social, cultural, and educational institutions into unilingual French and Dutch-language regimes.[3] In the past Flemings were educated for integration into a Francophone world. Today they are educated for linguistic ethnicity.

LINGUISTIC IMPERIALISM

In Drogenbos, a Flemish commune peripheral to Brussels, stands a sixty-year-old *athenée* where today the language of instruction is Dutch. Over the front door, carved in stone, is the word *école,* souvenir of the era when French was the language of all schools that went beyond primary level. The fact that until 1932 all Flemings who went to secondary school had to use French as a language of instruction, for most if not all of the day, is part of a constellation of painful group memories that permeate the Flemish Movement, memories similar to those colonists share of outrages under an occupying imperialist power. A Flemish spokesman speaks of nineteenth century conditions in these terms:

The Flemish were governed in a foreign language, tried by judges who addressed them in an idiom which they did not understand, and, in the army, commanded by officers with whom they could not speak. Moreover, in secondary schools they were forbidden to use their own language. (Haegendoren 1965:27)

Another Fleming, Dirk Wilmars, recalls that in his grandfather's youth Flemings were not only forbidden to use their own language in school, they were punished for using it. Dutch was taught only as a second language, and even in Dutch class the language of instruction was French (1966:55).

French was the language of state long before Belgium became an independent nation in 1830. Its use became widespread under the Burgundians, but it was also used in governmental and cultural affairs by a series of subsequent rulers—the Spanish (1579-1713), the Austrians (1713-1792), the French (1792-1815)—even in Flanders where a majority continued to speak one or another dialect of Flemish (Dutch). However, it was not until Napoleon designated French the official language of instruction for a new model state school system that an instrumental use of language led to the 'francisation de la bourgeoisie', as Henri Pirenne, the Belgian historian has noted (1926-32.6:92), and to the emergence of language as a political issue. During the years that Belgium was united with the Netherlands (1815-1830), William of Holland adopted a similar pattern of linguistic imperialism, but in this case designating Dutch as official, demanding that it be taught in all schools and be prerequisite for official employment—policies which outraged the recently augmented Francophone bourgeoisie, temporarily uniting free-thinkers and Catholics. And it was this unlikely coalition which led to the Revolution of 1830 and the establishment of an independent Belgium in which language was a political issue from the very beginning.

Once the new nation was born, this Francophone bourgeoisie reinvented the wheel by treating the schools as the instrument of *their* power. As a contemporary observer has pointed out, William had suppressed 'la liberté de l'enseignement'; now the government suppressed 'le cours spécial de langue hollandaise' by doing away with Dutch instruction in Walloon schools (Juste 1844:332). Legislation did call for use of the language best suited to the needs of students and, therefore, appeared to safeguard both language groups. In actuality, however, government was conducted in the language of the social class from which the legislators came—French. All laws were written in French and all official discussions took place in French. As far as the leaders of the newly independent nation were concerned, Flemish was a dialect destined eventually to disappear.

From the Flemish standpoint, most subsequent history represents an attempt to redress this linguistic imbalance. The school law of 1842 reestablished the right of Flemish school districts to conduct primary schools in Flemish, but in secondary schools French continued to dominate. Legislation was introduced in 1850 to make Flemish the required *second* language in secondary schools in Flanders and for it to have parity of esteem in the French area; but instruction on an advanced level could not take place in Flemish, for there were neither books nor trained teachers. And the universities, where French replaced Latin in 1848 as the language of instruction, were empowered to give instruction in other languages only in exceptional cases:

> Les lecons sont données en langue française; néanmoins le Ministre pourra, par exception, authoriser l'emploi d'une autre langue dans certaines branches de l'enseignement universitaire. (Greyson 1892-93. 1:192)

Clearly only the most favored Fleming stood any chance to advance under this educational system.

It was not until the 1870's that the Flemish Nationalist Movement, originally a group concerned with Dutch-language orthographic reform, began to have an impact on the political structure by demanding that Flemish be used in judicial proceedings and in public administration in Flanders. Not until 1890 was it required that lawyers pass an examination in Flemish in order to demonstrate ability to converse with Flemish clients, not until 1883 that serious language reform began to take place in state schools. The point of reference was still French, however, as the following excerpt from a memo sent to school directors demonstrates:

> Une société flamande réclame pour que dans les Athénées flamands les instructions données aux élèves par voie d'affiches, et qui ordinaire-ment ne sont rédigées qu'en français, le soient en même temps en langue flamande.
>
> Je ne vois aucun inconvénient à faire droit à cette demande et je vous prie donc, Monsieur le Préfet, de faire désormais afficher ces instructions dans les deux langues. (Greyson 1892-93.2:94)

The condescension displayed in the suggestion that schoolmasters should meet the linguistic needs of Flemish students only if doing so brings no inconvenience (i.e., if the teacher happens to know Flemish) explains much about the reactive aggression of many Flemish Nationalists in the years ahead.

In 1898 Flemish was proclaimed the second national language. But it was not until after World War I, an era when tensions between the language groups were exacerbated because the German occupier openly courted Flemish activists, that schools in Flanders became vehicles for flamandization. The Nolf Plan provided for the gradual conversion of the University of Ghent into a Dutch-language university between 1923 and 1930. Between 1925 and 1927, Camille Huysmans, Minister of Science and

Art, reformed the curriculum of state secondary schools in Flanders so that henceforth two-thirds of all courses would be taught in Dutch, thus ensuring a pool of students able to take advantage of the new regime at Ghent. The Language Law of 1932 extended the Huysmans' reforms to all secondary school subjects by establishing the principle of territoriality in education (*landstaal*). As Louis Franck, Minister of State, noted: 'Les classes populaires veulent reconquérir leurs élites' (1932:42). It was not, however, until 1943 that the University of Ghent began to graduate Flemings who had gone all the way through school in Dutch; and these graduates had in turn been taught by teachers who were educated in French, a point which still rankled as recently as 1965 (Haegendoren 1965:33). Even today one meets middle-aged products of the earlier system, some of them fervent Flemings, all of whose education, or a large part thereof, was in French.

LANGUAGE AND IDENTITY

Two disparate language groups, one Germanic, one Latinate, have coexisted in the territory that is now Belgium since the fifth century A.D. when Franks invaded this northern outpost of the Roman Empire. Details of the Frankish invasion are still debated. Scholars hypothesize, however, that the division between Germanic north and Latinate south which still exists today marks the limit of a territory assimilated by Roman civilization, not necessarily the limit of a Roman defense line but the limit of a region so densely populated that the invading Franks adopted its Latin vernacular; whereas they established their own Germanic tongue in the sparsely settled northern region. Whatever its origin, this north-south language division has persisted for fifteen hundred years.[4]

In Flanders, however, although the masses continued to use a Flemish mother tongue, the ruling class adopted French. We have, of course, no accurate record of the degree to which French penetrated into Flanders, but we do know that it was the language of the nobility in Brussels, seat of the Burgundian Court but once a Flemish village, and of international entrepreneurs in such cities as Antwerp. There existed a lively tradition of bilingual education in the cities of Flanders in the sixteenth century. Nevertheless, except in Brussels, where a language shift has gone on for centuries, the bilingual Fleming appears to have been an exception until the advent of mass education in the late nineteenth century. In 1834 it was estimated that in the village of Eckloo 'from among 800 inhabitants... only 300 can understand French and not 100 speak it fluently' (Clough 1930:20). In 1836 attempts to impose French as the language of instruction in an industrial school in Ghent failed because workers could not function in that language (van Nérum 1838:143-44). Even in the twentieth century it was still the complaint of radical Flemings that the masses in Flanders were separated from their leaders by language.[5]

Those ambitious young Flemings who did adopt French in order to advance within the Establishment often paid a heavy price. For in accepting Francophone education, the Fleming also accepted a Walloon image of reality, a reality which equated French with the values of civilization and viewed Flemish as 'une langue barbarique'. Nevertheless, Francophones became increasingly defensive about their language as the power of Flemings increased and the movement for use of Dutch in their schools began to take hold. As a Walloon educator, M. Putanier, pointed out at a conference of teachers in Brussels in 1923:

Et voilà par quelles mesures on cherche en Belgique à réduire à expulser cette belle langue française qui y régnait avec éclat et qui eût été la langue des Dieux si elle avait fleuri aux temps sereins de l'Hellade antique.... La langue française! Mais son destin n'est-il pas associé à celui de la civilization. (Lepetit 1925:259).

Doubtless equating French with the gods was an exaggerated claim even at the time it was made, but the universality of such views can hardly have contributed to a heightened sense of self-esteem on the part of the Flemish community.

From the standpoint of this community, however, the greatest danger came from within, from the Frenchified Fleming whose passion for Francophone culture could lead to disparagement of the Flemish world. Such a process was already underway in the late eighteenth century—as witness the testimony of J. B. C. Verlooy in 1788:

The Flemish language is especially maltreated in Brussels. In this city it it not only neglected but also despised.... There are those who refuse to speak Flemish in society or in the streets, others who purposely speak Flemish badly in order to give the appearance of having been educated in France. (translation adapted from Kluff 1938:17)

Verlooy describes a familiar phenomenon, more characteristic of Brussels than of other cities north of the language line, where bilingualism was likely to be characterized by diglossia, a differentiation of linguistic function— Flemish for home, French for business. Nevertheless, the often commented upon 'low intellectual level of Frenchified Flemings' (Haegendoren 1965:13) was frequently the price of adopting a Francophone identity, although individuals who found themselves master of no language were likely to be first generation immigrants to Brussels. By the third generation a large shift had usually taken place. In either event, the Flemish community lost.

Even more important was the price frequently paid for a Francophone education by the Flemish child—the shock of being wrenched from a familiar milieu and transported to a world of strangers, foreigners. One meets Flemings who have successfully made the transition; one may also hear tales from them of what the transition costs. An urbane, intelligent teacher at the Interpreter's School of Brussels, for example, looks back upon the years his parents moved from Antwerp to the capital city and placed him, at the age of eight, in a French-language school as the most painful and lonely of his life. The memory of his linguistic incompetence during that year still rankles, as does the image he formed of his own unworthiness.[6] And his experience was not unique. Generations of Flemings were educated in French-language schools, particularly in Brussels. One may still find families who have chosen a similar road for their children.[7]

Given the high cost of assimilation with Francophone culture, it is not surprising that the Flemish Movement should have come to focus on communal solidarity. According to Max Lamberty, the foremost philosopher of the Flemish Movement, Flemings must protect their people against pressure to assimilate even if an 'enforcement of segregation' is needed in order to ensure survival. 'Is Belgium the only country where the political leaders recognize, alongside the rights of man, also the rights of the community?' asks Lamberty (1971:47). In order to define their community, however, Flemings must possess their own language, a language which has come to have mystical qualities:

Language is the mirror of the personality and, conversely, language has a marked influence on the personality. Through language our personality assimilates its environment.... From a means of communication the language grows into a creative spiritual force. Language lends the culture of a people its identity and its form. (Haegendoren 1965:34)

Metaphysics of the mother tongue notwithstanding, Flemish intellectuals have designated *Dutch,* not *Flemish,* as their language—even though Dutch is not always the dialect spoken at home by the child's mother. Indeed, there are members of an older generation who encountered standard Dutch for the first time in school, their mother tongue being a discreet Flemish dialect.[8] Nevertheless, Dutch is now the language of the schools, the language heard by young Belgians on radio and TV from early childhood.

Old customs die slowly, however. Despite the adoption of Dutch as the official language of the Flemish Nationalist Movement in the nineteenth century, linguists continued to specify *Flemish* rather than *Dutch* as the language of northern Belgium until well into the twentieth century.[9] The Flemish Cultural Council did not change the word *Flemish* (*Vlaams*) in its title to the word *Netherlandish* (*Nederlandse*) until 1972. It is a matter of pride for Flemings to avoid any evidence that French has influenced their language. Certain Flemish intellectuals even question whether imitation of Hollanders is the best way of stabilizing their mother tongue (Geerts 1972). There is, in other words, a lively interest in the vernacular in some Flemish circles.

Interest in the vernacular is not unique to Flemings. The strong influence of France has mitigated the dialect issue for Francophones, but a small group still use Walloon, engage in revivals of the Walloon theater, write books and articles on the preservation of 'belgicismes' (Hanse et al. 1974). *Le Soir* prints discussions of the syntactical differences between Belgo-French and the French of Paris. Foreign students studying French at the University of Brussels are instructed in the Belgian inflection, and are told that Belgo-French is the more ancient, presumably the more honorable, dialect. The trend in both Walloon and Flemish circles is toward in-group identification.

This trend is, of course, part of a world-wide phenomenon, as much a part of life in Wales, Scotland, Quebec, Zambia, for example, as it is in Belgium—a global concern with particularity, with ethnicity, with preservation rather than assimilation, a movement, therefore, which provides assumptions and corroborates the needs of both Walloons and Flemings. Perhaps one may gain some insight into this process, as it appears to be unfolding in Belgium, by looking at a similar situation in Tøndor, a bilingual village near the German border in Denmark, which has a population three-fourths Danish, one-fourth German. In Tøndor, each group takes elaborate precautions to preserve a separate identity. Danes from Tøndor go to much greater trouble to identify themselves as Danes than would Danes from the homogeneous world of Copenhagen:

Acceptance as a Dane in good standing seems as a minimum to require that one speaks Danish even in contact with members of the out-group, sends one's children to a Danish school, avoids identifying oneself with out-group associations and institutions, and does not sell land (especially not farmland) to members of the out-group (Svalastoga and Wolfe 1969:26-44).

Through their school structure, Flemings and Walloons seem to be signalling a similar message: that acceptance of themselves as human beings requires minimal contact with members of the out-group. Indeed, the Final Report of the Harmel Center, where major research on the relationship between Belgian linguistic groups took place during the decade after World War II, concludes that 'intellectual life, education, and administration must be unilingual':

The Walloon community and the Flemish community should be homogeneous. Flemings who settle in Wallonia and Walloons who settle in Flanders must be resorbed [sic] by the environment. In this way the personal element is sacrificed for the territorial element. Consequently all the cultural system must be French in Wallonia and Flemish in Flanders. (translated by Senelle 1972:12)

This separatism is extended even to bilingual Brussels, for the Report rejects 'bilingualism in education' (Centre de recherche.326:6)—a significant conclusion which became the basis for language legislation in the 1960's.

Some radicals have extended these separatist premises even further. The Flemish political party *Volksunie,* for example, has proposed the establishment of an official *subnationaliteit* whereby all Belgians would be issued an identity card designating each as Walloon, Fleming, or German-speaking. Minorities living in Flanders or Wallonia would automatically acquire the subnationality of their region after living there for ten years. In Brussels children would acquire the subnationality of parents, with the possibility that products of a mixed marriage between a Fleming and a Walloon could change subnationality after twenty years of residence in the bilingual capital—long enough to go through school in the initial language (Vandezande 1971). Granted that this proposal represents a radical extreme not yet realized: it is an extreme that expresses a psychic reality for at least some Belgians.

SCISSION

Linguistic and education laws in the 1960's laid the foundation for the separatism of present-day Belgium: the definition of geographical communities in which the administrative, cultural, and educational institutions are conducted in the language of the region—Dutch in Flanders, French in Wallonia (except for a small German-language area); and in the bilingual city of Brussels, use of French *and* Dutch, but in separate but equal institutions. This separatism was already imbedded in the provisions for educational and administrative linguistic regionalism in the Language Laws of 1932, but language legislation of the 1960's went much further. The 1930's legislated for flexible boundaries between linguistic regions, thus making it possible for Flemish villages contingent to Brussels to become a part of that bilingual agglomeration when a Francophone minority reached 30 percent—a sore issue when the census of 1947 showed significant Francophone gains. In 1962 the linguistic census was abolished. The Law of 8 November 1962 froze the language line, making it changeable only through act of Parliament. Later legislation did allow for protection of minorities in a few villages on the language line and on the Brussels border (the six *communes à facilités*), but the Brussels border was to remain immutable.

The Language Law of 1932 had allowed minorities in Flanders of Wallonia to begin school in their mother tongue. The Law of 30 July 1963, on the other hand, mandated total hegemony of the regional language. The Law of 14 July 1932 had allowed Flemings and Francophones to coexist within the same school in Brussels, sometimes even within the same class where a teacher taught first in one national language, then in the other.[10] The language Law of 1963 not only split such schools into two separate linguistic regimes separately administered, it also empowered a linguistic inspectorate to determine whether the mother tongue of the child coincided with the language of the school.[11] By 1969 there would be two ministries of education, one for Dutch, the other for French-language schools. By 1971 two semiautonomous Cultural Councils, one Dutch, one French, would be responsible for administering to the educational, social, and cultural needs of Flemings and Walloons.[12] This is a bilateral design, each community a mirror image of the other; but basic to it is the scission which makes the complementary images possible.

Except for a few international schools and a few private French-language schools still remaining in Flanders which may not grant a legal diploma or receive government subsidies, all education in Belgium now takes place in separate but equal linguistic communities.[13] The era when building a wall between Dutch-language and French sections of schools in such cities as Antwerp in order to retain subsidies has long passed.[14] And in Brussels dual-language schools such as T. R. Dawes observed in 1901 no longer exist. Instead, Flemish children learn French and Francophones Dutch as a mandatory *second* language which may not be used as a language of instruction, only as a *subject* in the modern language classroom. No school may even employ a teacher who did not receive his or her diploma in the language of the linguistic community to which the school belongs unless the teacher has passed a special examination before a state board and has shown 'profound' knowledge of the second language—or 'sufficient' knowledge in the case of some modern language teachers.[15]

The universities fall within this pattern, too, even though they were not specifically included in the 1963 legislation. The state universities of Liège (traditionally French) and Ghent (Dutch since 1930) are balanced by the newer universities of Mons-Hainaut (French) and Antwerp (Dutch). Each of the private universities, the University of Louvain (Catholic) and the University of Brussels (free-thinking) have split into autonomous linguistic segments. The University of Brussels became the *Vrije Universiteit te Brussel* and the *Université Libre de Bruxelles* in 1969,[16] just one year after language riots at the University of Louvain led to the downfall of the government of Premier Vanden Boeynants and to a decision to move the entire French-language faculty from Louvain (*Leuven*) on Flemish soil to new facilities, built at great government expense at Louvain-la-Neuve near Ottignes in Wallonia.

None of the transformations has taken place peacefully, however. In Flanders conflict has centered around the rights of Francophone minorities, a group of whom filed appeals with the Court of Human Rights in Strasbourg between 1962 and 1964 over the lack of alternatives to a Dutch-language for their children. From the standpoint of these Francophones the future looked ominous. French-language 'transmutation classes' provided by the Law of 1932 had been discontinued. Boarding schools in Brussels or Wallonia were expensive and disruptive to family life. What private French-language schools still existed could not grant a legal diploma, and anyway, enrollment in such schools would lead to the nonvalidation of the school certificate (homologation issue) and to the prospect that entrance to higher education or to a civil service career would be closed (European Court of Human Rights 1967-68.1:181-85, 193). The new laws, in other words, denied a French-language education to a child of Francophones living in Flanders.

That the European Court should have ruled in favor of these laws signifies the power shift that has taken place. However, even before this ruling the arguments of Francophones attempting to maintain their status quo had begun to sound like mirror images of Flemish arguments in the past for education in the mother tongue. For according to these Francophones, learning is impaired when children are obliged to cope with:

> abstract ideas—such as those of mathematics, religion, ethics, physics, and chemistry—in a language they understand only with difficulty, or even initially not at all, ... [and they] cannot fully exercise their intellectual function of reflection. (European Court of Human Rights 1967-68.1:29)

And the Flemish counterargument, which was also the official position of the Belgian government, recalls points made in the past by the Francophone hierarchy: that the aim of the 1963 legislation was to create an intelligentsia in Flanders with a sound knowledge of their mother tongue, Dutch; that a child who speaks one language (French) at home and another language (Dutch) at school has the advantage of knowing two languages well—despite testimony to the contrary. The balance of power had shifted in favor of the Flemings—a complement to the shift of industry from the depleted coal mines of Wallonia to Flanders.

Evidence for this shift in power abounds, but the case of the Royal Conservatory of Music in Brussels, a world-famous institution, presents special incongruities. In the fall of 1970, the conservatory completed division into two sectors, a French sector and a Dutch-language sector, with the two faculties housed in the same building, each with its own director, its own catalogue, its own enrollment of students, its own classes, its own performing groups, its own diplomas. When the linguistic split took place, Professor André Gertler, the celebrated Hungarian violinist, surprised many people by deciding to align himself with the Dutch-language sector—even though he spoke no Dutch. To gain a faculty member of Gertler's international eminence was no small coup for Heer Kamiel D'Hooghe, the Flemish Director, who accepted this ally amidst a storm of protest from the French-language press (Le Soir 1970). The impact of Gertler's alignment was especially interesting for the international students in his master violin class: Gertler teaches in French because he knows no Flemish, but his students must take all their courses in Flemish, even *solfège,* because they must enroll in the Flemish sector of the Conservatory.[17]

LIBERTÉ DU PÈRE DE FAMILLE

On one issue Flemings have not had total victory. In Brussels, the city where Flemings most often have experienced language loss, a city where a shift from Dutch (or a Flemish dialect thereof) to French has taken place for centuries, Francophones succeeded in gaining partial restoration in 1971 of *liberté du père de famille,* the right of a father to select the language of education for his children—a curious human right in that *fathers* might select a *mother* tongue that was rarely used at home. The feminist implication of this paradox was not the issue, however. At issue was the father's right to make the choice.

Language laws throughout the twentieth century have specified that in Brussels the language of education be the mother tongue or 'usual language' of the child. The Language Law of 1932 even provided for language inspectors to check enrollments in Brussels schools. It was not until 1966, however, that the provisions for direct surveillance of school enrollments by the language inspectorate and court review of contested language declarations envisaged in the Language Law of 1963 went into effect; however, between the fall of 1966 and the spring of 1971 when the freedom to select a language of education was restored, the schools of Brussels were the center of a major political storm. Small wonder this was an explosive issue. The protagonists in the conflict were innocent children, often very young children, whose parents, often very bewildered parents, were trying to interpret experience according to the norms of a society in the midst of change. Small wonder the language inspectorate seemed more like adversaries than the hard working civil servants that they really were, civil servants who moved in bilateral tandem, one from the French-language Ministry of Education, one from the Dutch-language Ministry, both reviewing language declarations for each school to which they were assigned.

The inspectors did their jobs with professional impartiality, but they had a complicated role. 'Le contrôle ne sera ni tracassier, ni arbitraire, mais efficace', stated a Ministerial directive (Internal memo 1967:5). However, for the inspector to be efficacious and at the same time to avoid harassment of the child and the child's family represented a particular challenge. The inspector had to be able to recognize a case of 'réel bilinguisme de l'enfant', because in that case the parents could indeed decide which language would be the medium of instruction. He could not directly interrogate the child, but he could query the head of the school and the child's teachers—and he could visit the child's classes along with his colleague from the other language regime and discuss with the child matters other than language:

> En outre, l'inspecteur linguistique, comme tout inspecteur pédagogique, a accès à la classe en cause et peut, dans le cadre de l'activité de la classe et avec le tact voulu, poser des questions et parler avec les enfants de cette activité. (Internal memo 1967:8)

He could, in other words, learn to walk on eggshells while gathering evidence for his report.

How effective was this inspectorate? That it was efficient in carrying out its functions we have no reason to doubt. Even so, the number of cases actually tried before the first court of appeal, the Commission, was not large: 26 in 1967-68, 21 in 1968-69, 39 in 1969-70, 47 in 1970-71. Of these 133 cases, however, only 41 terminated with a mandate to send a child to a Netherlandish school—and of these, 20 were appealed to the Jury (see Table

1). As for the second court, the Jury, it heard 116 cases, sent 33 children to Netherlandish schools, and of these four appealed to the *Conseil d'Etat* (see Table 2). The *Conseil d'Etat,* in turn, reversed one Jury decision and accepted the other three. In total, during this period only 53 children were placed in Netherlandish instead of in French-language schools because of the new linguistic controls.

These figures, of course, give us no idea of the degree to which the inspectorate functioned as a deterent, no idea of the extent that enrollment patterns reflected compliance with the law simply because the inspectorate was there—or even because school officials refused a provisional enrollment because of irregularities in the language declaration. We *do* have school enrollment figures for these years, however, and from them fairly conclusive evidence that very little had actually changed despite the political hue and cry. For between 1959 and 1971, the enrollment in Dutch-language schools continued its steady decline (see Table 3).

Table 1. *Commission Cases: 1967-1971*

Disposition	1967-68	1968-69	1969-70	1970-71	Total
Allowed to stay in French schools	19	11	10	15	55
Required to go to Netherlandish schools	7	10	18	6	41
Allowed to stay in Netherlandish schools	--	--	1	6	7
Classed as without merit	--	--	10	--	10
Still in progress*	--	--	--	19	19
Total	26	21	39	47	133
Appealed to Jury	4	7	9	--	20**

SOURCE: Ministerie van Nationale Opvoeding en Nederlandse Cultuur. Memo dated March 13, 1971.

*As of March 13, 1971.

**Other cases during these years went directly to the Jury, i.e., cases where *both* language inspectors challenged the placement of the child in a particular linguistic regime.

Table 2. *Jury Cases: 1967-1971*

Disposition	1967-68	1968-69	1969-70	1970-71	Total
Allowed to stay in French schools	8	15	23	4	50
Required to go to Netherlandish schools	4	10	15	4	33
Allowed to stay in Netherlandish schools	--	--	3	5	8
Classed as without merit	--	--	4	--	4
Jury incompetent to judge	1	2	--	--	3
Binding agreement	--	1	--	--	1
Still in progress*	--	--	1	16	17
Total	13	28	46	29	116

SOURCE: Ministerie van Nationale Opvoeding en Nederlandse Cultuur. Memo dated November 3, 1971.

*As of March 13, 1971.

The issues for those whose language declarations were challenged by the inspectorate were both more universal than *liberté du père de famille,* and more narrow: more universal because freedom was the issue, more narrow because the legal framework sometimes revolved around points of law that had little to do with language or freedom. Some families tried to evade the law by filling out two language declarations, one for one language, one for the other. In some cases, they even argued that a declaration signed by the mother could not be valid because only a male could be *chef de famille,* [18] an argument which presented a curious dilemma for families in which no father was present. The universal human right to family life, to freedom, to an education was all too frequently a peripheral issue for families intent on proving a legal point that would make *liberté du père de famille* once again possible. It was even peripheral to arguments based on the probable impact of a new school regime on the emotional and scholastic future of a child, particularly a child who has already had a difficult school adjustment (Dossier 80/70 Jury).

The fact that families had to fight before a Commission or Jury—and in four cases before the *Conseil d'Etat* [19] for a freedom previously viewed as a

Table 3. *Percentage of students enrolled in Dutch and in French nursery and elementary schools in Brussels between 1959 and 1971*

Year	Nursery Schools		Elementary Schools	
	French	Dutch	French	Dutch
1959-60	81.11	18.89	83.20	16.80
1960-61	81.88	18.12	82.89	17.11
1963-64*	82.79	17.21	83.00	17.00
1964-65	83.85	16.15	83.29	16.71
1965-66	84.11	15.89	83.70	16.30
1966-67	84.61	15.39	83.79	16.21
1967-68	84.69	15.31	84.51	15.49
1968-69	85.38	14.62	84.92	15.08
1969-70	85.61	14.39	85.26	14.74
1970-71	86.30	13.70	85.56	14.44

SOURCE: Ministerie van Nationale Opvoeding en Nederlandse Cultuur. Unpublished tables.

*No data was given for 1962-63.

fundamental right exacerbated the already explosive linguistic tensions within the city. There were families who lost their appeal. The father of Maria Kouvas, a Greek immigrant who tried to argue that because he had never signed a language declaration while living in Flanders he could now enroll his daughter in a French-language school in Brussels, lost his case (Conseil d'Etat Dossier 3/67). So did Dominique le Fevere de ten Hove, whose earlier education had taken place entirely in the Netherlandish regime, first in Flanders, then in Brussels, and who tried to claim that he was really a Francophone despite twelve years in Flemish schools. His father even sent a series of letters to the Jury outlining long-term plans to send the boy to a French-language university and giving 'permission' for his son to attend a French-language technical school, but to no avail. Dominique, who was eighteen at the time these proceedings took place, had already become—in the eyes of Belgian law—a Fleming (Dossier 50/69 Jury). The courts were frequently *very* strict in upholding the letter of the law when dealing with an individual who had gone to school in a territorial language, who had been assimilated into the territorial cultural community, and less strict with the children of Francophone Flemings in Brussels. This was, indeed, a legal maze.

Only a minority of cases actually went against the parents—a fact which in itself became a political issue. As Senator René Bourgeois, a Francophone, pointed out, the number of cases won by the parents 'prouve que, deux fois sur trois, la décision prise par les inspecteurs linguistiques est contestable ou même incorrecte' (Sénat de Belgique 1970:7). As often as not, the letter of the law did *not* win the day. The father of Irène Parmentier freely admitted that he filled out two language declarations, one stating that Netherlandish was the mother tongue or usual language, one stating that French was. But he argued that his intent was not to disobey the law, that his intent was to give the child opportunity to learn both national languages, that he had always planned to have his daughter attend secondary school in the French regime because he was a Francophone—and the Jury let him do so (Dossier 31/69 Jury). Judith Spikerman, a child born in the United States of Dutch parents, was allowed to stay in a French-language school despite the claim of the language inspectorate that she was subject to Belgian language law because she knew Dutch, one of Belgium's national languages (Dossier 80/70 Commission). Anne Marie Breckpot was allowed to stay in a French-language school even though she had previously attended a Dutch school in Flanders. The argument: the mother tongue of the child was really French, but only a Dutch-language school was available in the unilingual territory (Dossier 3/67 Commission). Anne Pourvoyeur, whose father was a member of the Francophone faculty at the University of Louvain, was eventually allowed to enroll in a French language school, a decision rendered in January 1968 when the Louvain riots were at their height (Dossier 5/67 Commission). The traditional language structure was far from dead.

For the citizens of Brussels, the harassment eased in September 1971 with partial restoration of *liberté du père de famille.*[20] Hereinafter, the family could choose *either* a French- or a Netherlandish-regime—or even switch a child from one regime to the other. Immigrants from Flanders would still have to prove that they were really Francophones if they wished to enroll their children in French-language schools, and residents of the six *communes à facilités,* including Americans, were still subject to stringent regulations.[21] But for the majority of *Bruxellois,* conflict over this particular school issue had been defused.

COMMUNITY TENSIONS IN THE 1970's

Community is an ambiguous concept in modern Belgium, connoting, at once and the same time, rival linguistic groups whose members share a world view defined by mother tongue *and*—except for the bilingual capital—rival unilingual regions where linguistic identity is prescribed by geography. That the revised Constitution of 1971 provides all Belgians, including citizens of the bilingual capital, with membership in one or the other of three semiautonomous communities—one French, one Dutch, one German, each administrated by its own Cultural Council—implies that language determines cultural identity (Article 3C). But that this Constitution also recognizes four geographical regions as language zones— Dutch, French, German, plus the Brussels bilingual zone—implies that, except in Brussels, language is a function of geography (Article 3B).

This distinction is particularly important for schools, the central institution in the power struggle. Although the two Ministries of Education supervise schools in both the linguistic regions and in Brussels,[22] a fundamental difference exists between schools and communities in Brussels and in the unilingual territories. In Brussels, membership in a cultural community is largely a matter of self-identification, as symbolized by the language of the identity card or by choice of a language regime in the schools, virtually a free choice since restoration of *liberté du père de famille* —provided that parents can prove their residence within the city.[23] In the unilingual territories, on the other hand, assimilation of linguistic minorities continues to be the policy and—except in certain villages on the language line—there exists no legal alternative to education in the regional language except for a child to commute to a school in a different linguistic region, a solution not always logistically feasible. Small wonder that Francophones living in Flemish villages on the Brussels perimeter, even those living in communes with limited 'facilities' for Francophones, eye the freedom enjoyed the French-language community in Brussels with envy. Small wonder these Francophones are themselves a source of tension within the capital. Boundaries between linguistic territories are determined by law, but an individual's perception of his or her linguistic identity is not easily subject to spatial or legal containment.

Another difference exists between schools and communities in Brussels and schools and communities in the rest of Belgium. In bilingual Brussels where two fully articulated French and Dutch school systems are in competition with one another, there is exaggerated necessity to articulate differences; whereas in the unilingual territories schools are assumed to reflect the values and priorities of the communities in which they are located. There is a paradox here: in Brussels study of French in Dutch-language schools and of Dutch in French-language schools may now begin as early as first grade.[24] In the unilingual territories, on the other hand, second language study may not begin before the fifth year when English or another modern language may be substituted for French in Flanders or Dutch in Wallonia. Only in Brussels are the centripetal patterns of the past still mandated.

There was a point shortly after restoration of *liberté du père de famille* in 1971 when officials in both Ministries of Education wondered whether a new educational pattern might emerge from attempts on the part of members of both language communities to educate their children for linguistic pluralism by sending them one year to a school in one language regime, the next year to a school in the other—a Brussels equivalent of immersion classes such as are found in Ottawa or Montreal. Such a pattern, however, has not become firmly established—although some Flemings continue to send their children to French-language secondary schools after completion of Dutch-language elementary school, a familiar traditional pattern approved by neither the French nor the Dutch Ministry.[25] However, it is not possible to speak of bilingualism in Brussels schools except in terms of these anomalies. The primary function of the separate but equal regimes is still to educate for membership in *either* a French or a Netherlandish community—not to educate for membership in both.

Nevertheless, members of both communities have—in one way or another—signaled their recognition of the *de jure* existence of linguistic parity. That the *Taal Aktie Komitie* called for curtailment of the study of French in Dutch-language schools in Brussels after the fifth year in order to allow more time for study of the mother tongue is the stance of a radical group still defensive about language maintenance (Le Soir 1979:2). But that the Francophone community, the group which has traditionally resisted study of a second language and has continued to do so, should begin to recognize the utility of Dutch, that a leading daily such as *Le Soir* should devote a front page editorial to a discussion of the necessity for 'passive bilingualism', i.e., the ability to understand, if not to speak or write the second language, is a measure of the times (Le Soir 1976:1). In 1979 *Le Soir* even published an editorial called for improvement in the quality of Dutch language classes in French-language schools because Francophone children must compete with bilingual Flemings for government jobs (Le Soir 1979:2).[26]

The rivalry continues in other ways. Now that no established contact takes place between the two Ministries of Education,[27] degrees granted by each school regime must be equivalent, but even the idea of equivalence is open to cultural variation. *L'enseignement rénové/vernieuwd onderwijs*, for example, the Belgian adaptation of reforms found in schools throughout Western Europe, seeks to achieve similar goals in both school regimes: selection of a new elite from a wide socio-economic base, postponement of a premature choice of a scholastic track, emphasis on small group work, use of the 'discovery' method as a teaching tool, recognition of the need for personality development (Corijin 1976; Verdière-de-Vits 1971; Ministries of National Education 1975). But the means to these ends, according to spokesmen from both Ministries, are not similar: there is much greater emphasis on the development of individualism in French-language schools, much greater emphasis on community values in Netherlandish schools. The visitor does not necessarily discern such cultural demarcations, but educators in each regime affirm that they exist.[28]

In Brussels, moreover, where Flemings constitute less than 20 percent of the population, efforts to maintain school enrollments have exacerbated tensions. Flemings entered the era which began in 1971 with certain legislative safeguards—a kind of affirmative action program: the promise of ten new Dutch-language schools a year,[29] the right to preferential scholastic norms on which to project further expansion. Where Francophones needed thirty students in order to form a second class, Flemings would need only fifteen (see Table 4). Where a French school would not be entitled to a director until three hundred students were enrolled, a Flemish school would need only one hundred students (Le Soir 1971:2). This was a controversial program: 'Demain, on prendra les enfants au berceau, et on les mettra de force dans les institutions flamandes', complained the French-language press (Le Soir 1971:2). But the program survived a legal challenge. In 1973 the *Conseil d'Etat* declared these scholastic norms to be justifiable inequality because Flemings could not have real freedom of choice until they had a complete network of Dutch-language schools in Brussels (Conseil d'Etat 1973).

Neither promises of new schools for the Dutch regime nor differential norms have fully compensated for the decline in school population, however. Expansion in the Dutch-language sector did take place, particularly between 1971 and 1977 when the *Nederlandse Cultuur Commissie* created no less than 76 Dutch-language schools (Monteyne 1977:4). By the end of the decade, however, even the *Nederlandse Commissie* had concluded that demographic considerations no longer justified further use of funds for the building of new Dutch-language schools, that hereinafter emphasis would have to shift to expansion of existing facilities (Monteyne 1977:4). In a city where one school child in four is the child of foreign laborers who are much more likely to select education in French than in Dutch for their families, some of the enrollment losses in the Dutch-language regime may be more apparent than real. But that losses have occurred, no one denies (see Table 5).

Table 4. *Projected class size for Dutch- and French-language elementary schools in Brussels, 1971*

Number of Classes	Flemish Sector	French Sector
1 class	no minimum	20 students
2 classes	15 students	30 students
3 classes	35 students	55 students
4 classes	55 students	80 students
5 classes	70 students	105 students
6 classes	85 students	130 students

SOURCE: *Le Soir,* May 31, 1971.

Given the new monetary and demographic reality, the announcement in December 1979 that the two Ministers of Education, Jacques Hoyaux and Jef Ramaeckers, had reached a compromise that would lead to release of funds for construction of schools was welcome news. The new school pact allocated funds to schools in both language communities, with favorable terms for schools experimenting with educational reform. In such schools enrollments as low as 120 students in the first two years (versus 185 for traditional schools) would qualify for subsidy. Dutch-language schools in Brussels and its periphery were even more favored, for they need only three-fourths the normal norms (Le Soir 1979:2). With such preferential treatment still available, the future of Dutch-language schools remains good even with declining enrollment.

The most inflamatory conflict over schools at the end of the 1970's did not directly involve the rivaly between the Dutch- and French-language regimes of Brussels. Instead the conflict centered over the immutability of geographical divisions and the disparity between language communities that are a function of geography and those that are a function of cultural identity—a sore point in villages on the language line where linguistic minorities are a significant part of the population. Amid the continuing tumult in the Voeren and Comines, areas of unrest since the freezing of the language line in 1962, there were increased tensions in the six *communes à facilités* on the Brussel's periphery, Flemish villages with French-language nursery and elementary schools (facilities) for Francophones resident in them, schools supervised by the Dutch-language Ministry of Education—a point which rankles; for Francophones argue that *their* cultural community should control *all* French-language education. Flemings, however, insist on controlling schools within the boundaries of *their* geographical territory and

Table 5. *Percentage of students enrolled in Dutch and in French nursery and elementary schools in Brussels between 1960-1961 and 1977-1978*

Year	Nursery Schools		Elementary Schools	
	French	Dutch	French	Dutch
1960-1961	81.88	18.12	82.89	17.11
1963-1964*	82.79	17.21	83.00	17.00
1964-1965	83.85	16.15	83.29	16.71
1965-1966	84.11	15.89	83.70	16.30
1966-1967	84.61	15.39	83.79	16.21
1967-1968	84.69	15.31	84.51	15.49
1968-1969	85.38	14.62	84.92	15.08
1969-1970	85.61	14.39	85.26	14.74
1970-1971	86.38	13.62	85.56	14.44
1971-1972	86.71	13.29	85.87	14.13
1972-1973	86.73	13.27	86.30	13.70
1973-1974	86.79	13.21	86.67	13.33
1974-1975	87.10	12.90	87.22	12.78
1975-1976	87.37	12.63	87.73	12.27
1976-1977	87.76	12.24	88.06	11.94
1977-1978	87.68	12.32	88.55	11.45

SOURCE: Years 1960-1961 through 1967-1968, Ministerie van Nationale Opvoeding en Nederlandse Cultuur. Unpublished tables.

Years 1968-1969 through 1977-1978, Ministerie van Nationale Opvoeding en Nederlandse Cultuur, *Onderwijs-Statistieken, Schooljaar 1978-1979*, pp. 59, 61.

*No data given for 1962-1963.

have backed their claims to such power with action—as in February 1979 when the Minister of Dutch-language Education terminated subsidy of the French-language school in Linkebeek because of its long-standing policy of enrolling children whose parents were not legal residents of the village (Le Soir 1979:1).

As Brian Weinstein has pointed out: 'Manipulation of language variation accompanies the expansion and contraction of political frontiers over the centuries' (1979:346). In Belgium the boundaries are now fixed, and—tensions, riots, marches, notwithstanding—the traditional language hierarchy based on French-language dominance is dead. Three generations of Flemings have gone all the way through school in their own language. Immigrants from Flanders no longer arrive in Brussels with an inbuilt sense of inferiority, for they know that a diploma from a Dutch-language school can guarantee entreé to jobs previously reserved for a Francophone elite. Flemings are the majority in Belgium if not in Brussels, the stronger political group with an emerging economic strength and a virtual renaissance in the arts. And they have achieved these goals in large measure by insisting on autonomous educational structures that will allow each group access to positions of power. It remains to be shown that these separate but equal linguistic communities will become creative sources of growth for the individual in Belgium rather than a symptom of fragmentation which will lead to further splintering of a broken mirror.

*An earlier version of this paper appeared in *Western European Education* 5.4 (Winter 1973-4):6-33. Expanded treatment of the subject may be found in Swing (1980).

NOTES

[1] See *Courrier Hebdomadaire du CRISP.* 1978. L'autonome culturelle et l'aide communautaire aux fédérations sportives. nos. 791-2 (24 mars); and *Courrier Hebdomadaire du CRISP.* 1979. La lecture publique dans la Belgique des communautés. nos. 843-4 (15 juin).

[2] See, for example, Verheyen (1929). A more recent statement is found in Bustamante, van Overbeke, and Verdoodt (1978).

[3] There is also a small German-language area in the eastern section of Liège Province, whose German and German-French schools (the only legal dual-medium schools in Belgium) are supervised by the French-language Ministry of Education. The revised Constitution of 1971 provided for a separate Cultural Council for these German-speaking Belgians (less than one percent of the total population).

[4] The seminal study of the language line is still the most important: Kurth (1896-98). See also Dhondt (1947); Draye (1942); Stengers (1959); and Volkhoff (1944).

[5] See Wilmars (1966) for a discussion of the historical dimensions of this phenomenon. See also Picard (1942-59).

[6] Conversation with Guy Toebosch, Brussels, September 11, 1970.

[7] The author encountered a Flemish family in Brussels in 1970-1971 who had elected to send all seven of their sons to French-language Catholic schools, even though neither parent felt as comfortable speaking French as speaking Flemish—an illegal decision at the time. They explained that the school in Flanders near Antwerp which the boys had previously attended had not taught proper French, a failing that would handicap the boys' advancement in careers. On subsequent trips to Brussels in 1976 and 1979, the author encountered similar families, although by then *liberté du père de famille* had been restored.

[8] A librarian at the Bibliothèque Royale recounted his linguistic adventures to the author during the summer of 1976. A native of East Flanders where he learned the local dialect as a mother tongue, he learned standard Dutch, then French, German, and English in school; but he still communicates with his mother, who is unilingual, in the East Flanders dialect.

[9] See Meillet and Tesnière (1928), and Rundle (1946).

[10] A few of these 'bilingual classes' existed as late as 1962. Archives de la ville de Bruxelles, *Bulletin communal: rapport annuel,* 1962:407.

[11] Law of 30 July 1963, Articles 17, 18. The executive order putting these provisions into effect was not issued until 30 November 1966.

[12] This design was provided in the revised Constitution (1971). The Netherlandish Council remained an organic unit, supervising institutions in Flanders and in the Dutch-language community of Brussels. The French-language Cultural Council subdivided into a Council for Wallonia, a Council for French-language institutions in Brussels, and a Council for the whole.

[13] A few French-language schools for handicapped children and for the children of armed services personnel exist in Flanders but are supervised by the French-language Ministry. Similar Dutch-language schools in Wallonia are supervised by the Dutch-language Ministry.

[14] A school in Antwerp had built a wall between its French-language section (Lycée d'Anvers) and its Dutch-language section (Institut St. Josef) in the early 1960's in a futile attempt to qualify for government subsidies. The author saw a similar wall in a school attended by children of French-language faculty not yet removed to Louvain-la-Neuve when she visited *Leuven* in 1970.

[15] Law of 30 July 1963, Articles 13, 14, 15.

[16] For details of the scission of the University of Brussels, see Dejean and Binnemans (1971). See also *Courrier Hebdomadaire du CRISP.* 1969. Le dédoublement linguistique de l'Université de Bruxelles no. 458 (14 novembre); no. 463 (14 décembre).

[17] Private conversation with members of André Gertler's Master Class, May 1971.

[18] Dossier 49/69 Jury. The father *did* have more rights than the mother until 1974 when 'le principe de l'égalité de droit absolu entre époux à l'égard des enfants' was affirmed by the Ministries. Note de 14 novembre 1974, ref. I/MCM/13.11.02821 in compliance with the *Loi du 1er juin 1974.*

[19] The *Conseil d'Etat'* rendered the final ruling in cases concerning Maria Kouras, Dossier 3/64, A.15.676/VI 3696, No. 13. 680; Marlys vande Weerdt, Dossier 13/68, A.16.217/VI 4155, No. 13. 920; Catherine Kerstiens, Dossier 20/69, A.16.348, No. 13.679; Peter Vermiere, Dossier 47/69, A.17.121/VI 4452.

[20] Law of 26 July 1971, Article 88.

[21] These six communes, officially in Flemish territory, offer limited facilities to Francophones. Americans, however, encountered particular difficulty enrolling their children in Francophone schools, for the inspectorate was especially vigilant during the years under discussion in matching enrollment to legal requirements: residence in the commune, French as a *usual* language in the household—a requirement frequently difficult for Americans to fulfill. No exact statistics were made available to the author, but she was told in a private conversation in June 1976 with J. Doppagne, language inspector for the French Ministry of Education, that the Commission or Jury had decided against Americans in these villages more than twenty times, thus forcing them to find alternatives for their children to French-language schools close to home.

[22] The French-language Ministry of Education also supervised schools in the German-language area in the eastern section of Liège Province, including German-French schools, the only dual-medium schools in Belgium.

[23] Law of 26 July 1971, Article 88. The new inscription form requires parents to give their official resident but not their mother tongue or usual language. Ministère de l'Education Nationale et de la Culture Française, 9 september 1974. 7/4261, III/3/44 (mimeographed memo).

[24] The Law of 27 July 1971 modified Article 10 of the Law of 30 July 1963 to allow instruction in the second language to begin as early as the first year of school provided that such instruction is in oral use of the second language.

[25] Interview with M. Knaepen, Brussels, June 1976; with A. Doppagne, Nivelles, July 1979; with M. Toté, Brussels, July 1979.

[26] This reassessment of the need for bilingualism correlates with public opinion samples reported by Verdoodt (1976).

[27] Interview with M. Totté, Brussels, July 1979.

[28] These observations are based on interviews with officials in both the French and the Netherlandish Ministries of Education in 1976 and in 1979, as well as visits to schools in both language regimes.

[29] These schools were first mentioned in the Law of 30 July 1963, Article 21.

AMERICAN BILINGUALISM: THE NEED FOR A NATIONAL LANGUAGE POLICY

CHARLES R. FOSTER

Bilingualism—in its truest sense—should be appreciated as the ability to function fluently and interchangeably in two languages; the choice of one language or the other depends on the situation. In the United States, where English is the 'official' language of government and business, most daily transactions are carried out in English. The use of other languages tends to be restricted to private family or social situations involving other speakers of these languages.[1] In fact, English monolingualism is the most obvious sign of assimilation into American culture. Hence, bilingualism is seen by many as evidence of insufficient assimilation.

Concomitantly, bilingual education, as it is commonly understood in the U.S. today, rarely focuses on the development of equal skills in both English and another language; instead, its objective is to impart English language skills to the nonnative speaker within as short a time as possible. However, true bilingual education, in its most effective form, must take place within a cultural context, since language is both a product and expression of the culture in which it develops (see Ramirez and Castañeda 1974; Saville-Troike 1978). Once associated primarily with the education of the privileged in prestigious schools, bilingual education increasingly refers to government mandated and funded programs established to accommodate the growing number of non-English speaking children in America. This link to court rulings and government financing, however, has transformed the concept into a social issue with political overtones. It is unfortunate, therefore, to hear the confusion between educational and political aspects of bilingual education reinforced by the President. In a speech to the nation's mayors on March 2, 1981, he charged bilingual programs with deliberately impeding the acquisition of English skills among minority groups and thereby limiting their vocational preparation.

This attitude is in line with the conservative view that many of our social innovations are at the root of the country's current problems, that these problems were handled better in the past without the intervention of the Federal government. In fact, however, this outlook reflects only one of several phases through which bilingual education has passed as the nation has grown.[2]

In the nineteenth century numerous immigrant groups resisted pressures to abandon their native language and culture. Many established bilingual education programs through their churches or synogogues to preserve their cultural heritage. After 1840, public schools began to offer instruction in German, Spanish, and French as well as English, often trying to draw students from these parochial schools. The predominately Spanish-speaking population of the newer southwestern states actively supported such programs.

The wave of isolationism that swept the U.S. after World War I left few of these programs intact. A national identity based on democracy and free enterprise was commonly felt to require the solid foundation of a common language. During this time of growing support for the melting pot concept, monolingualism became the certification of assimilation. Bilingualism, it was felt, could only perpetuate cultural diversity; it was a social and economic handicap to the individual and a burden or even a threat to society. These same attitudes are still prevalent in much of today's thinking on bilingualism (Casteñeda 1975).

After World War II, bilingual education was again relegated to the private school curriculum as foreign language instruction lost support in the public schools. The European model of education based on a study of the classics disappeared, and the study of living languages never acquired the fundamental role in the U.S. that it played in European education. Language study was required mainly for the college-bound, and, in most cases, primarily to satisfy entrance requirements. Then, in the late 1960's, when institutions of higher education began to reduce or abolish their language requirements for entrance or graduation, elementary and secondary schools reduced foreign language offerings even further. Poor teaching methods combined with minimal course offerings led to virtual ignorance of foreign languages by a majority of American students. Most colleges today require only a foreign language reading proficiency, thereby indirectly discouraging active verbal and comprehension skills. Few high schools make more than a desultory effort to teach their students the basics of a foreign language let alone use the language to teach the skills of listening, speaking, reading, and writing. Serious language instruction is begun too late and seldom pursued beyond basic grammar and vocabulary instruction.

At the heart of the melting pot position and its practical effects on the American educational system is the belief that immigrants—whether they actually did immigrate or were merely absorbed within its expanding borders—are obligated to master the English language and that once English is mastered, the native tongue is no longer needed to learn or communicate. On the practical side, a common language does make classroom instruction easier and more efficient; and for minorities it does assure a more rapid and complete assimilation. With language instruction downgraded, the decline in student enrollment and hence the need for fewer instructional personnel is seen not as a loss, but as a release of resources for other uses.

While the trend in the secondary school has been to deemphasize language skills, social changes during the last decade have made such language teaching a necessity in the elementary grades. The sheer increase in enrollment of 'limited English proficient' (LEP) children has had a great impact on schools, especially on elementary schools. Enrollment of LEP children is estimated at about five million today, with the largest increases found among Hispanic and, most recently, Southeast Asian children.[3] And it has become increasingly evident that standard educational methods used by the public schools fail to reach large numbers of these children. The dropout rate among Hispanic students, for example, is 50 percent and even higher in large urban centers (Hernandez-Alvarez 1976). These factors, in turn, have brought pressure from community groups and mandates from the legislative and legal systems for special efforts to accommodate these students. In 1970 the Department of Health, Education and Welfare directed school districts with enrollments of more than five percent non-English-speaking children to provide language programs to equalize their educational opportunities, according to an interpretation of the Civil Rights Act of 1964.[4] In 1974 the U.S. Supreme Court upheld HEW's interpretation in the landmark case of *Lau v. Nichols.*

The result has been a proliferation of bilingual education programs in two-thirds of the states.[5] The majority of the programs are based on the transitional model of bilingual education in which the mother tongue is used only as an interim medium of instruction until the child acquires fluency in English. Students are typically enrolled in these programs for three to four years. Derived from the assimilationist view of society, bilingual programs are rightfully identified as compensatory or remedial in their objective of 'curing' the English language deficiencies of ethnic children so that they can enter and function in regular classrooms.[6] In their planning and organization many transitional programs are marked by the absence of attention to sociocultural and linguistic concerns of the ethnic community. Their main purpose is to teach English language skills.

An alternative model aims at the maintenance of the child's native language by giving it equal emphasis with English as a medium of instruction.[7] The goal is to insure the continuation of the child's native language by the development of linguistic skills in both languages for academic and social purposes. This model enjoys greater support among educators and ethnic groups seeking to maintain their native tongue in the face of strong social pressure to abandon it. Both models focus mainly on ethnic students, although some programs, as, for example, those in California, are open to native speakers of English so that each group can serve as a linguistic model for the other.

In addition to the debate over the goals and relative merits of alternative models, the role of the Federal government in bilingual education programs and the cost of these programs has generated much controversy (Epstein 1977). Established a decade ago with a budget of $7.5 million, federal bilingual education programs have reached a current federal expenditure of about $160 million, the largest federal categorical program in the recent Reagan budget for the Department of Education. This expenditure is more than matched by state and local outlays. In some states, such as Illinois, New York, and California, state funds for bilingual education are more than double the federal funds (Cardenas 1977; Garcia 1977).

The United States, in contrast to many other countries providing bilingual education, is faced with a very complex situation. Here bilingual education serves a most diverse group of children with differing needs for which different educational strategies must be designed. Six major target groups with various degrees of linguistic competence can be identified.

The first group is comprised of children who arrive in the U.S. as immigrants speaking no English at all. The largest numbers have come from Cuba, Haiti, and most recently, from Southeast Asia. They also include migrant workers from Mexico.

The second group includes children who come from non-English speaking homes, but who were born or have resided in the U.S. Many Puerto Rican, Mexican-American, and Portuguese children fall into this category. These children may have some knowledge of English gained from exposure to television or English-speaking playmates, but the dominant language is not English and their cultural background is not Anglo-American. Their home language is frequently a vernacular.

Children who speak English and another language with equal fluency constitute the third group, which includes immigrants such as Italians and Germans who are easily assimilated. Bilingual imbalance will tend to develop rapidly as concept development and reading and writing are pursued in English. English soon becomes the dominant language and these children assimilate easily.

The fourth group contains children who become literate in English but who do not possess equal skills in the language of their ancestors. The children understand their home language but their speaking skill is so limited that even intra-family communication takes place in both languages; i.e., the children understand the home language but respond in English. Many Franco-American or Chinese-American children would belong to this group. These children identify themselves as Americans and not as members of their ethnic group. Frequently, the foreign roots of their parents may make them feel inferior and cause them embarrassment. However, as has happened to many of these children, they may later take pride in and try to recapture their ethnicity.

The fifth group is comprised of American English monolingual children with nonstandard language skills. These are the children or grandchildren of immigrant or native-born parents who are frequently poorly educated themselves. Many Black Americans are likely to be included in this group. Legally, bilingual programs may not be established for this group.

In the last group, which includes the vast majority of students, are the English monolingual native children who may some day be disadvantaged if the U.S. becomes a pluralistic society. They should be given the opportunity to develop skills in a second language. Persons who speak only English are in some way disadvantaged. Not only do they have fewer career options open to them in international business or the foreign service, for example, but more importantly they lack a sensitive tool for understanding other cultures, both at home and abroad. 7 Contrue an.

This taxonomy presents a picture of the diversity of language competencies both in English and in other languages in the United States. It also illustrates the pedagogical challenges faced by the schools: language programs should be tailored to the particular needs of each group and to individuals within each group.

The relevance and utility of these distinctions depends on the goals of bilingual education. The transitional model tends to focus on building the English language proficiency of the children in each group and, therefore, reduces instruction in the mother tongue as greater English proficiency is acquired. The maintenance model, on the other hand, seeks to prevent any loss of facility in the native language. (Another problem is to determine whether the standard form of the language or the vernacular ought to be maintained.) However, with emphasis on assimilation, it is often difficult for children to become bilingual. For children in the third category, those who speak two languages fluently from early childhood, English, because of its increased use, becomes dominant and fluency in the native tongue is lost. Moreover, this group represents at best a small portion of students enrolled in language programs. The assimilation process, depending on the type and quality of the bilingual program that is offered, may well put many students for varying periods into a seventh category—the most disadvantaged category—no mastery in either language.[8]

Given the importance of language facility for educational success and, more basically, for the complete development of cognitive capabilities, the dangers of leaving children in an educational limbo without mastery of any language must be carefully avoided. The transitional model should assure a steady and rapid acquisition of English without neglect of subject matter achievement, and the maintenance model should devote sufficient attention to instruction in both languages.

If the goal of bilingual education is seen as encouraging bilingualism (and hence biculturalism) then these categories of language competence illustrate the wide range of needs to be met. Where a diversity of languages and skills mastery within each school exists, it may well prove impossible to tailor instruction and curricula to meet the needs of the individual student. This may well require complementary instruction outside the public school system within the ethnic community itself. The disadvantage of this approach is the isolation of bilingual programs from the standard curriculum.

Where maintenance-model programs can be integrated into the regular classroom, the interaction between language minority students and the majority population is beneficial to both. This, in fact, is one of the recommendations of the 1979 report of the President's Commission on Foreign Languages and International Studies, *Strength through Wisdom*. Where the English-dominant majority receives part of its instruction in another language along with the minority students who are learning English, bilingual programs benefit the larger body of English speakers who otherwise might never be exposed to a foreign language. In addition, the minority group has provided a model for the majority and thus overcome any negative image associated with speaking the second language.

Unfortunately, the report too frequently views language merely as a medium of communication rather than as a sensitive and sophisticated means of enhancing understanding and empathy between peoples of diverse cultural background both at home and abroad. It emphasizes the declining numbers of persons with foreign language proficiency in trade, diplomacy, and security. Domestically, bilingual education offers a means of overcoming stereotypes and prejudices that have become increasingly dysfunctional in a society of linguistic and cultural pluralism. The universal benefits of bilingual education must be stressed in order to counter any narrow association with civil rights programs and create a broader basis of support within our society.

A second means of defusing the political controversy surrounding bilingual programs is with hard evidence of their success and educational *leads to two countries programs*

benefits. By focusing attention on measurable learning improvements and test scores, discussion may be shifted to a more realistic level, overcoming the emotionalism attached to particular philosophies. For example, evidence may well prove that certain groups of language minorities benefit most from immersion in English-language classrooms, while others respond better to transitional programs and still others to continued instruction in both languages. Unfortunately there is not enough empirical evidence to decide the matter objective; and, until evidence becomes available, theory and emotion will dominate debate.

Additional credibility can be lent to bilingual programs through a national plan which would provide a framework both for federal policies and activities at the state and local level (Fishman 1972, 1976; Foster 1980). *NEED for a NATIONAL PLAN* At present, even the statistical base for such a plan is lacking; data on minority language groups exist at the local but not at the national level. For constitutional and historical reasons, education has remained the domain of local and state governments, and this is true for the implementation of bilingual programs as well. Regional diversity indeed argues for maximum flexibility at the local level. Still, the growing importance of the federal government in formulating policy and providing funding for these programs indicates the need for a coherent plan which would require a thorough assessment of the country's language needs and make explicit the basis for policy directives (National Advisory Council for Bilingual Education 1981).

Bilingual education has a long history of helping minority language groups adjust to American society without eradicating the linguistic foundation of their social and cultural heritage (Gaarder 1977). At the same time, public educational policy has vacillated between active support and determined opposition. More recently, bilingual programs have been integrated into public education on the coattails of legal and political actions promoting civil rights and social programs for minorities (Santiago-Santiago 1978; Hufstedler 1980). Only when bilingual education is seen as a normal part of the instructional process which raises achievement levels will these programs cease to generate controversy. *closing*

Defusing the issue will require concrete analysis of the effectiveness of alternative teaching models to support or refute theoretical and emotional posturing. More important, the universal benefits of acquiring and possessing competence in another language to promote an awareness and understanding of other cultures and ensure successful foreign relations will need greater recognition. In this, our national opinion makers and statesmen, including the President, can play a crucial role by providing an accurate assessment of the country's language needs and by furthering thoughtful understanding of the role bilingual education might play in meeting them.

No country in the world has bilingual education problems as complex as the United States. This complexity, coupled with the lack of a national language policy, makes it even more difficult to plan, evaluate, or discuss effective bilingual education programs. Although many individual programs serve children well, only a rational and informed national debate will safeguard the language resources of the American people.

NOTES

[1] See Fishman (1966) for a discussion of language loyalty in America.

[2] For a comprehensive history of language policy and bilingual education in America see Kloss (1977).

[3] For an analysis of LEP population statistics see *National Advisory Council for Bilingual Education* 1981 and *National Center for Education Statistics* 1981.

[4] The so-called 'Pottinger Memorandum' of 1970.

[5] Irizarry (1978) offers a complete overview of existing state laws and the type of programs they authorize.

[6] Cárdenas and Cárdenas (1972) have argued that these result in a matrix of incompatabilities between the school and the language minority student that lead to underachievement.

[7] Blanco (1977) and Trueba (1979) offer a timely review of current models of bilingual education.

[8] A 1977 report by the Education Commission of the States highlights the underachievement of Hispanics in English language skills.

ISSUES IN BILINGUALISM:
A VIEW TO THE FUTURE

BEVERLY S. HARTFORD

Concerns with bilingualism and bilingual education are certainly not new: in fact throughout most of the world multilingual communities are the norm and unilingual communities are the exception. In spite of this, however, many educators have acted as though this were not true, and as if multilingualism were a deviant condition, an attitude which emerged as a correlative to universal education and spreading literacy.

In the Western world, from about the time of the Middle Ages, the need to know and use more than one language was generally accepted as necessary, especially for two major groups of people: the educated elite, and those whose mother tongue did not provide the means by which to accomplish daily work.

Among the elite, for example, educated persons learned Latin and often Greek, in order to pursue any other studies, since these languages were the media of education. Moreover, they might also learn other, non-Classical languages, since fluency in more than one prestigious language was regarded as a mark of education.

At the same time, others, such as peasants, slaves, indentured individuals, and freemen of some bourgeois standing might well be fluent in a language other than the one used at home. Within each stratum of a population, there were individuals who regularly interacted with members of other strata. At least one of the parties would have to speak some form of the language of the other, should the groups have different languages. These people were, however, not necessarily literate or formally educated.

Because of the confinement of literacy to an elite, educators were not faced with the same kinds of decisions demanded by multilingual communities today. Education in the native language might or might not be considered desirable, depending on its prestige and literary history. Therefore, decisions about what were to be the languages of education were not of any major concern.

With the advent of universal education multilingualism began to be viewed as problematical. The population which was to be educated grew in size and diversity, and attitudes changed towards the rights of people to education. Those responsible for providing education had to seriously consider how to determine the content of curricula. In many nations, such as the United States, monolingualism came to be desired and cherished. Problems of universal education seemed to be lessened by at least one factor if an entire population were to be educated in one unifying language, apparently putting less strain on educational resources and national unity. As a result, for some time, monolingualism was encouraged, and in many instances, prescribed by government authorities.

Attitudes towards multilingualism are changing once again, partially as an outcome of the very phenomenon which introduced the case for monolingualism: universal education. As education has provided people with the means for more extensive contacts with the world beyond their own immediate communities, they have realized that ethnic languages are being lost and fear the concomitant loss of ethnic identity. The resultant concern has been how to view multilingualism, especially in education.

This is no small concern. For example, in North America alone, with relatively few linguistic groups (compare, for example, with Héraud's typology of languages in Europe, this volume), the demand for preservation along with full rights and duties of citizenship resulted in complex, confusing, and confused policies of language use and language education. So too in many other parts of the world. This time, however, the groups who were most concerned about the status of language use were those who would have had little voice in any such decision (had there been any made) in the past. These were the newly enfranchised, who saw themselves in danger of becoming disenfranchised from their own heritage unless something were done to prevent it. These were speakers of vernaculars, languages which enjoyed less prestige in their particular settings than did the language(s) of education, government, and other institutions. As the demands for the respect and use of the vernaculars grew, issues arose which had to be addressed and which were the concern of educators, governments, and other policy makers.

This present volume came about as an attempt to address some of the issues which have arisen in education as a result of such concerns. The theme of the volume—the role of the vernacular in international bilingual education—is unique. Other volumes have addressed one or the other aspects of this theme, but have not integrated the two and focused on them as inseparable issues.

Three major areas of concern emerged from this focus: the problem of language variation; the implications of multilingualism for third world and minority ethnic communities; and the role of educational, social, economic, and political institutions in determining language policy.

The first area of concern, language variation, has been the focus of much recent research among linguists. Traditionally grammars have described idealized representations of speech communities, and those communities have been regarded as relatively linguistically stable, often having some degree of linguistic prestige. In a sense, then, such descriptions have been prescriptive, since they reflect an ideal rather than daily language usage. Moreover, where such communities have had written traditions, there has been very little overt concern with language norms and standardization (with the exception of the rare language academy): for the most part such norms have been taken for granted, and the written language has provided, at least partially, the basis of grammatical description. Even in less 'traditional' communities, where there may be only a fairly recent written language, or none, the trend has been to abstract away from *parole* to *langue,* with resultant static grammars.

The problem for bilinguals and bilingual communities, however, is that often their linguistic behavior appears quite different from that of their monolingual counterparts. Frequently at least one of the language systems involved is some nonprestige form. Furthermore, since they are also language contact situations, interlanguage influences are inherent. There arises the problem of whether (and how) to describe some ideal speaker of such a community and at the same time to describe as accurately as possible individual behaviors.

This is no small problem, because the decision about how and why to conduct such work bears directly on language planning policies and educational policies. Claims about what linguistic abilities are brought by the child to school, and about what linguistic abilities he should be expected to have upon finishing his formal education are directly dependent on perceptions of how the individuals of his speech community behave and how they *ought* to behave. Such perceptions are held both by members of his community and by influential nonmembers, and may or may not reflect the actual situation. Thus, we must understand the linguistic systems as fully as possible in order to understand how to proceed.

Recent work in linguistics points a way to such understanding. Variation theory, and systemizations of code-switching have begun to bear fruitful results, particularly for describing vernaculars. Here lies the foundation of methodological procedures for isolating and describing vernaculars.

Certainly much work remains, but it must be done in order to deal most fairly with vernacular speaking groups and individuals and to understand their linguistic powers, potentials, and needs. Accurate description of language variation, based on some notion of predictability, is absolutely essential—not only does it proffer insights into the nature of human language and its use in general, it can also provide information for the educator on how to design curricula, and how, for example, to develop means for providing literacy for the speakers. Thus any abstractions about ideal speakers must be based on reliably gathered speech data from real speakers, and reflect accurately their competencies.

Our second area of concern is the nature of the members of the ethnic and third world communities. Most speakers of the vernacular belong to a minority group (ethnic, political, or social), or come from third world areas, or both. It is important to know what universal education means to them, and particularly the implications for such groups of bilingual education which employs the vernacular. Even if we obtain accurate descriptions of language variation, they are not enough for the educator, but are only a beginning, although an immensely important one. We must understand how each group views its own uniqueness, especially in the context of spreading universal education. What do such groups have in common, what do they have in common with nonethnic, nonthird worlders, and how do they differ? For example, what is the difference between being a southwestern Hispanic in the United States and a northeastern Franco-american? What is the difference between being a member of one of these groups and being an Ewe in Togo? Are immigrant groups different from historically colonized groups; are speakers of some local variety of a prestige world language different from speakers of smaller, less prestigious community languages?

In particular, we need to understand the nature of cognition and development of cognitive abilities in multilinguals, especially as they encounter, more and more frequently, formal educational models. We need greater understanding of possible learning styles of children who will be the targets of such models. Claims made, for example, about relative field dependency of various groups and how such cognitive preferences influence the ways in which materials are best learned require a great deal more investigation before maximally effective curricula can be developed.

Such questions must be investigated because educational systems tend to import from other systems without understanding clearly what the necessary modifications must be. Just because a particular curriculum appears successful with one group, there is no reason to believe that it will work in unchanged form for others. Thus, standardized tests, procedures designed for particular cognitive-learning styles, and assumptions about motivations and attitudes not based on the target population, are bound to lead to frustration and upheaval if they are not carefully adapted to each new situation. This cannot take place until the nature of the new situation is well understood. Can we say, for example, that a transitional bilingual program is never desirable, or can we accurately determine contexts in which it is extremely desirable? Can we say that bilingual education is always desirable in bi- or multilingual communities? Is it ever the case that education in the vernacular *only* is the best approach? Or in the nonvernacular? In order to understand the possible answers to such questions, we have to understand the particular demand for education and the goals of the community, which means attempting to understand the members of the community and their relationship to the rest of the world.

This brings us to the last area of concern in the volume: the influence of institutions on bilingual education. In spite of accessibility of good linguistic descriptions, and of understanding the people most affected by bilingual education, policy determination depends on much more. There are, for example, economic factors which must be considered in looking at the feasibility of bilingual education and of the use of the vernacular in any such program.

Costs which are directly observable, such as the design of materials, the multiple printing, in each language, of various legal and quasi-legal documents, are only some of the economic concerns which influence policies. As educational levels grow, other economic problems arise, such as, in third world countries, the loss of a supply for certain workforce areas and an overabundance of supply in others. Such imbalance can easily upset the economic structure of a nation. At the same time, political structures may be affected. If bilingual education becomes the norm, then potential separatism occurs as ethnic groups obtain resources to seek political and economic power. In a country where political power has traditionally been in the hands of a dominant language group, change to bilingual education can lead to the vying for more control of political institutions by nondominant groups. The result may be profound change. Such change, of course, is not limited to third world countries: witness the growing political voice of minority groups in the United States.

All of these effects may be seen reflected in higher education. It has normally been the case that educational institutions maintain social and economic status quo, socializing their members towards acceptable citizenship. When change and upheaval occur in education, it is often a sign of concurrent change and upheaval in the society in general. With the establishment of bilingual education where it has been monolingual, with the inclusion of languages previously thought 'unfit' for educational purposes, great demands are made on the educators. Questions arise about who is qualified to teach, and who is qualified to train the teachers.

In this microcosm we see the unbalancing of social structures and economic structures. Teachers who had, until this point, been considered fully qualified are no longer necessarily so: monolingual, dominant-language speakers may find their careers in jeopardy. At the same time, those who had so long been barred from the educational systems may now find a disconcertingly wide range of choices open to them. And yet, who is to decide how to train teachers for these new systems? And who is to train them? In some places, the solution has been to import trainers and teachers from other countries: many ESL teachers are in demand in oil-producing countries throughout the world; Louisiana imports French-speaking teachers from Europe and Canada. This solution also contributes to the economic and social imbalance. For example, it may be distasteful to members of the minority/ethnic community, for two reasonss particularly: the imported teachers usually speak a 'standard' form of the vernacular, thus provoking further confusion about the worth of the indigenous language; and those jobs which go to the outsiders may be viewed as jobs lost to members of the community. Yet, until such time as the community can produce qualified teachers, they may indeed have to depend on these outsiders.

This leads to another question which is of major concern in this volume: what, exactly, ought to be the qualifications of teachers in vernacular bilingual education programs? Usually such qualifications are determined by legislative and educational institutions, often with one another's interests in mind. Local community input has been minimal, and unless these decision makers are attuned to community wants and needs, their decisions may not be satisfactory to the target populations. However, these institutions have the advantage of a broader viewpoint, an understanding of the needs of the political entity (e.g. region, state, nation) as a whole, which the individual community may not have, and reach decisions based on widespread considerations, such as the political and economic constraints mentioned above. Thus, the entire process of determining teacher qualifications involves numerous factors weighed differently by different participating institutions.

All of these concerns highlight the fact that the implementation of bilingual education is no easy task. It is not just a matter of making decisions about linguistic concerns, but rather about concerns of the whole spectrum of educational policy. The world is rapidly becoming literate: universal education is unlikely to wane. The field is and must be inter-disciplinary, and that is reflected in this volume. The issues raised here come from scholars in different fields, but proper examination and application of these concerns will better enable the cognitive, affective, and linguistic development of children and provide them the means to move between and across cultures in multicultural societies.

REFERENCES

Abiri, J. O. O. 1976. Preparation of the secondary school mother tongue teacher. *West African Journal of Education* 20.7-16.

Abrahams, D. and C. Troike, eds. 1970. *Language and cultural diversity in America.* Englewood Cliffs, N.J.: Prentice Hall.

Afolayan, A. 1976. The six year project in Nigeria. *Mother tongue education: the West African experience,* ed. by A. Bamgbose, 113-34. Paris: UNESCO.

_____. 1978. Towards an adequate theory of bilingual education for Africa. *GURT* 29, ed. by J. Alatis, 330-88. Washington, D.C.: Georgetown University Press.

Agence de Coopération Culturelle et Technique. 1976. *Lectures bilingues graduées (créole-français).* Paris: ACCT.

Alatis, E. 1978. International dimensions of bilingual education. *Georgetown University Round Table in Language and Linguistics.* Washington, D.C.: Georgetown University Press.

Alba, O. 1980. La /s/ final de palabra en el español de Santiago, República Dominicana. Paper presented at the Vth Symposium on Caribbean Dialectology. Universidad Central de Venezuela.

Albert, M. and L. Obler. 1978. *The bilingual brain.* New York: Doubleday.

Albo, J. 1974. Idiomas, escuelas y radios en Bolivia. *Cuadernos de investigación 3.* La Paz, Bolivia: Centro de Educación y Promoción del Campecino.

Allen, B. and G. N. Underwood. 1971. *Readings in American dialectology.* New York: Appleton-Century Crofts.

Altbach, P. G. 1977. Servitude of the mind? Education, dependency, and neocolonialism. *Teachers College Record* 79.187-204.

Ampene, E. K. n.d. Persistent issues in African education. *Occasional Papers in Continuing Education* 96.

Ancelet, B. J. 1978. Teaching the 'problem language' in Louisiana. *Le FAROG Forum,* dec. 9.

_____. 1980. *Cris sur le bayou.* Montreal: Editions Intermède.

Annamalai, E. 1971. Lexical insertions in a mixed language. *Papers from the Seventh Regional Meeting,* Chicago Linguistic Society, 20-27.

_____. 1978. The Anglicized Indian languages: a case of code-mixing. *International Journal of Dravidian Linguistics* 7.239-47.

Ansre, G. 1970. *Language policy for the promotion of national unity and understanding in West Africa.* Legon: Institute of African Studies, University of Ghana.

_____. 1971. The influence of English on West African languages. *The English language in Africa,* ed. by John Spencer, 145-64. London: Longmans.

Apte, M. L. 1974. Pidginization of lingua franca: a linguistic analysis of Hindi-Urdu spoken in Bombay. *International Journal of Dravidian Linguistics* 3.21-41.

Archives de la ville de Bruxelles. 1962. Bulletin Communal: Rapport Annuel: 407.

Arsenian, J. M. 1937. *Bilingualism and mental development.* New York: Columbia University Press.

Ashby, W. 1976. The loss of the negative morpheme *ne* in Parisian French. *Lingua* 39.119-37.

Asher, J. J. 1969. The total physical response to second language learning. *Modern Language Journal* 53.3-18.

Assemblée générale des usagers de la langue française (AGULF). 1978. *Review of 'La France en français'.*1. 47 rue de Lille, Paris 7e.

Attinasi, J. 1979. Language attitudes in a New York Puerto Rican community. *Ethnoperspectives in bilingual education research: bilingual education and public policy in the United States,* ed. by R. Padilla, 408-61. Ypsilanti, MI: Eastern Michigan University.

Bachman, L. F., and A. S. Palmer. 1980. *The construct validation of the FSI Oral Interview.* Presented at the Fourteenth Annual TESOL Convention, San Francisco, March; at the Fifteenth Regional Seminar of the Southeast Asian Ministers of Education Organization at the Regional English Language Center, Singapore, April; at the Language Testing Conference, Albuquerque, June. To appear in *Language Learning.*

Bailey, W., and M. Görlach, eds. In press. *English as a world language.* Ann Arbor: University of Michigan Press.

Bain, B. C., and A. Yu. 1978. Towards an integration of Piaget and Vygotsky: a cross-cultural replication concerning cognitive consequences of bilinguality. *Aspects of bilingualism,* ed. by M. Paradis, 113-26. Columbia, S.C.: Hornbeam Press.

Baker, O. R. 1980. Categories of code-switching in Hispanic communities: untangling the terminology. *Sociolinguistic Working Paper* No. 76. Austin, TX: Southwest Educational Development Laboratory.

Balkan, L. 1970. *Les effets du bilinguisme français-anglais sur les aptitudes intellectuelles.* Bruxelles: Aimav.

Bamgbose, A. 1976. *Mother tongue education: the West African experience.* Paris: UNESCO.

Bandle, O. 1973. *Die Gliederung des Nordgermanischen.* Stuttgart: Helbling Lichtenhahn.

Barik, H. C., and M. Swain. 1975. Three year evaluation of a large scale early grade French immersion program: the Ottawa study. *Language Learning* 25.1-30.

_____. 1976. A Canadian experiment in bilingual education: the Peel study. *Foreign Language Annals* 9. 465-79.

_____. 1976. A longitudinal study of bilingual and cognitive development. *International Journal of Psychology* 11.251-63.

_____. 1978. Evaluation of a French immersion program: the Ottawa study through grade five. *Canadian Journal of Behavioural Science* 10.192-201.

Barke, E. 1933. A study of the comparative intelligence of children in certain bilingual and monoglot schools in South Wales. *British Journal of Educational Psychology* 3.237-50.

Barkin, F. 1980. The role of loanword assimilation in gender assignment. To appear in the *Bilingual Review.*

Barnes, D. 1978. The language of instruction in Chinese communities. *International Review of Education* 24.371-74.

Basell, C. E., J. C. Catford, M. A. K. Halliday, and R. H. Robins, eds. 1966. *In memory of J. R. Firth.* London: Longmans.

Baudelaire, C. 1953. *Pauvre Belgique,* ed. by J. Crépit and C. Pichet. Paris: Jacques Lambert.

Baugh, J. 1979. *Linguistic style shifting in Black English.* Unpub. Ph.D. thesis. University of Pennsylvania.

Bautista, Ma. S. 1975. A model of bilingual competence based on an analysis of Tagalog-English code switching. *Phillippine Journal of Linguistics* 6.51-89.
_____. 1977. The noun-phrase in Tagalog-English code-mixing. *Studies in Phillippine Linguistics* 1.1-16.
Belgium Ministry of Education. 1967. *Le fonctionnement de l'inspection linguistique en matiere d'enseignement.* Internal Memo. 5 octobre.
Benderly, B. L. 1981. The multilingual mind. *Psychology Today* 15.3:9-12.
Berlin Bilingual Education Program. 1979. *Program description.* Burgess School, Berlin, N.H.
Bernabé, J. 1976. Propositions pour un code orthographique intégré. *Espace Créole* 1.25-57.
_____. 1978. A propos de lexicographie créole. *Espace Créole* 3.87-101.
_____. 1981. *Integration, créativité et aménagement linguistique en espace créolophone.* Paper presented at the Troisième Colloque International des Etudes Créoles, Saint-Lucia, May, 1981.
Bernard, J. C. 1980. Allocution. *Créole et enseignement primaire en Haiti,* ed. by A. Valdman, 6-8. Bloomington, Ind.: Creole Institute.
Bernstein, Basil. 1965. A sociolinguistic approach to social learning. *Penguin Survey of Social Sciences,* ed. by J. Gould, 144-168. Harmondsworth, Eng.: Penguin Books.
Berry, J. 1958. The making of alphabets. *Proceedings of the Eighth International Congress of Linguists,* 752-64. Oslo: Oslo University Press.
Ben-Zeev, S. 1972. *The influence of bilingualism on cognitive development and cognitive strategy.* Unpub. Ph.D. thesis. University of Chicago.
_____. 1977a. The effect of Spanish-English bilingualism in children from less privileged neighborhoods on cognitive development and cognitive strategy. *Working Papers on Bilingualism* 14.83-122.
_____. 1977b. Mechanisms by which childhood bilingualism affects understanding of language and cognitive structures. *Bilingualism, psychological, social and educational implications,* ed. by P. Hornby, 29-55. New York: Academic Press.
Bhatia, K. C. 1967. *A linguistic study of English loanwords in Hindi.* (in Hindi). Allahabad: Hindustani Academi.
Bialystock, E. 1980. *The role of linguistic knowledge in second language use.* Ms. Modern Language Centre, The Ontario Institute for Studies in Education.
_____. n.d. *Form/function relationships in second language learning.* In prep., Modern Language Centre, The Ontario Institute for Studies in Education.
Bills, G., ed. 1974. *Southwest areal linguistics.* San Diego: Institute for Cultural Pluralism.
Bills, G. D. 1975. Linguistic research on United States Hispanics: state of the art. *Spanish and English of United States Hispanics: a critical, annotated linguistic bibliography,* ed. by R. Teschner, G. Bills, and J. Craddock, v-xxii. Arlington, Va.: Center for Applied Linguistics.
Blake, L., W. E. Lambert, N. Sidoti, and D. Wolfe. n.d. *Students' views of inter-group tensions in Quebec: the effects of language immersion experience.* Ms., Psychology Department, McGill University.
Blanco, G. 1977. The education perspective. *Bilingual education: current perspectives, education,* 1-68. Arlington, Va.: Center for Applied Linguistics.
Bloomfield, L. 1933. *Language.* New York: Holt.
Botel, M., J. Dawkins, and A. Granowsky. 1973. A syntactic complexity formula. *Assessment problems in reading,* ed. by W. H. MacGinitie. Newark, Del.: International Reading Association.
Brault, G. J. 1961. New English French vocabulary. *French Review* 35.163-75.
_____. 1972. New English French culture. *French Review* 45.831-37.
Broudy, H. S. 1972. *The real world of the public schools.* New York: Harcourt, Brace, Jovanovich.

Brown, P., and S. Levinson. 1979. Social structure, groups and interaction. *Social Markers in speech,* ed. by J. Scherer and H. Giles, 291-341. New York and London: Cambridge University Press.

Brown, R., J. Fournier, and R. Moyer. 1977. A cross-cultural study of Piagetian concrete reasoning and science concepts among rural 5th grade Mexican- and Anglo-American students. *Journal of Research in Science Teaching* 14.329-34.

Bruck, M., W. Lambert, and G. R. Tucker. 1973. Cognitive and attitudinal consequences of bilingual schooling: the St. Lambert project through grade six. *International Journal of Psycholinguistics.*

Buck, H. M., and G. E. Yocum, eds. 1974. *Structural approaches to South Indian studies.* Chambersburg, Pa.: Wilson Books.

Bustamante, H., M. van Overbeke, and A. Verdoodt. 1978. Bilingual education in Belgium. *Case studies in bilingual education,* ed. by B. Spolsky and R. L. Cooper, 3-21. Rowley, Mass.: Newbury House.

Canaan-Norton Bilingual Education Program. 1979. *Program description.* Burgess School, Berlin, N.H.

Canale, M., and M. Swain. 1980. Theoretical bases of communicative approaches to second language teaching and testing. *Applied Linguistics* 1.1-47.

Candlin, C. N. 1980. Discoursal patterning and the equalizing of integrative opportunity. *English for cross cultural communication,* ed. by L. Smith. London: Macmillan.

Cárdenas, J. A. 1977. Budgeting for bilingual education. *Bilingual education: current perspectives, education,* 69-77. Arlington, Va.: Center for Applied Linguistics.

———, and B. Cárdenas. 1972. *The theory of incompatibilities: a conceptual framework for responding to the educational needs of Mexican American children.* San Antonio, Tex.: Intercultural Development Research Association.

Carnoy, M. 1974. *Education as cultural imperialism.* New York: David McKay.

Carroll, J. B. 1980a. Foreign language testing: persistent problems. *Readings on English as a second language,* ed. by Kenneth Croft, 518-30. Cambridge, Mass.: Winthrop.

———. 1980b. *Psychometric theory and language testing.* Presented at the Second International Language Testing Symposium, Darmstadt, Germany, May; at the Language Testing Conference, Albuquerque, June. To appear in Oller (in press).

Castañeda, A. 1975. Persisting ideologies of assimilation in America: implications for psychology and education. *ATISBOS, Journal of Chicano Research* 79-91.

Cazden, C. B., et al., eds. 1972. *Functions of language in the classroom.* New York: Teachers College Press.

Cedergren, H. 1973. *The interplay of social and linguistic factors in Panama.* Unpub. Ph.D. thesis. Cornell University.

Célestin-Mégie, E. 1980. Richès ak bélte lang ayisyin an. *Créole et enseignement primaire en Haiti,* ed. by A. Valdman, 190-200. Bloomington, Ind.: Creole Institute.

Center for Applied Linguistics. 1974. *Guidelines for the preparation and certification of teachers of bilingual/bicultural education.* Arlington, Va.

Centre sur Académie des Sciences Humaines et Sociales d'Haiti (CRESH). 1974. Séminaire sur l'orthographe du créole. *Revue de la Faculté d'Ethnologie* (Port-au-Prince) 24.

Chaudron, C. 1977. Teachers' priorities in correcting learners' errors in French immersion classes. *Working Papers on Bilingualism* 12.21-44.

Cheavens, S. F. 1957. *Vernacular languages in education.* Unpub. Ph.D. thesis, University of Texas.

Cicourel, A. V., et al. 1974. *Language use and school performance.* New York: Academic Press.

Clough, S. B. 1930. *A history of the Flemish movement in Belgium.* New York: Richard R. Smith.

Clyne, M. 1972. *Perspectives on language contact: based on a study of German in Australia.* Melbourne: Hawthorne Press.

Coballes-Vega, C. 1979. *A comparison of the form and function of code-switching of Chicano and Puerto Rican children*. Ph.D. thesis, University of Illinois at Urbana-Champaign.

Cohen, A. D. 1975. *A sociolinguistic approach to bilingual education*. Rowley, Mass.: Newbury House.

Colat-Jolivière, D. 1976. Essai de transformation d'un conte. *Espace Créole* 1.59-65.

Cole, M., J. Gay, J. A. Glick, and D. W. Sharp. 1971. *The cultural context of learning and thinking*. New York: Basic Books.

_____, and S. Scribner. 1974. *Culture and thought: a psychological introduction*. New York: Wiley.

Comhaire-Sylvain, S. 1936. *Le créole haïtien: morphologie et syntaxe*. Port-au-Prince and Wetteren (Belgium): De Meester.

Commissioner of Official Languages. 1980. *The language file*. Ottawa: Ronalds Printing.

Conseil d'Etat. 1973. *Contentieux de l'annulation (6)*. 1er février, no. 15693.

Coombs, P. H. 1968. *The world educational crisis*. New York: Oxford University Press.

_____. 1974. *Attacking rural poverty*. Baltimore, Md.: Johns Hopkins Press.

Corijn, H. 1976. *Het V.S.O. en de Universiteit*. Unpub. ms.

Courrier Hebdomadaire du CRISP. 1969. Le dédoublement linguistique de l'Université de Bruxelles. No. 458. 14 novembre; No. 463. 14 decembre.

_____. 1978. L'évolution du Rassemblement wallon d'avril 1974 à mars 1977. No. 786. 3. février.

_____. 1978. L'autonomie culturelle et l'aide communautaire aux fédérations sportives. Nos. 791-92. 24 mars.

_____. 1979. La lecture publique dans la Belgique des communautés. Nos. 843-44. 15 juin.

_____. 1979. Le problème des Fourons de 1962 à nos jours. No. 859. 23 novembre.

Cremin, L. A. 1975. Public education and the education of the public. *Teachers College Record* 77.1-12.

Criado de Val, M. 1966. *Gramática Española y comentario de textos*. Madrid: SEATA.

Cummins, J. 1976. The influence of bilingualism on cognitive growth. *Working Papers on Bilingualism* 9.1-43.

_____. 1977. Psycholinguistic evidence. *Bilingual education: current perspectives, vol. 4. Education*, 78-89. Arlington, Va.: Center for Applied Linguistics.

_____. 1978. Metalinguistic development of children in bilingual education programs: data from Irish and Canadian Ukranian-English programs. *Aspects of bilingualism*, ed. by M. Paradis, 127-38.

_____. 1979a. Cognitive/academic language proficiency, linguistic interdependence, the optimum age, and some other matters. *Working Papers on Bilingualism* 19.198-205.

_____. 1979b. Linguistic interdependence and the educational development of bilingual children. *Review of Educational Research* 49.222-51.

_____. 1980a. The construct of language proficiency in bilingual education. *Current issues in bilingual education*, ed. by James E. Alatis, 81-103. Washington, D.C.: Georgetown University.

_____. 1980b. The cross-lingual dimensions of language proficiency: implications for bilingual education and the optimal age issue. *TESOL Quarterly* 14.175-87.

_____. 1980c. The entry and exit fallacy in bilingual education. *NABE Journal* 4.25-59.

_____, and M. Gulutsan. 1974. Some effects of bilingualism on cognitive functioning. *Bilingualism, biculturalism, and education*, ed. by S. Carey. Edmonton: University of Alberta Press.

_____, and R. Mulcahy. 1978. Orientation to language in Ukranian-English bilingual children. *Child Development* 49.1239-42.

Damico, J. S., and J. W. Oller, Jr. 1980. Pragmatic versus morphological/syntactic criteria for language referrals. *Language, Speech, and Hearing Services in Schools* 11.85-94.

Damico, J. S., J. W. Oller, Jr., and M. E. Storey. 1980. *The diagnosis of language disorders in bilingual children: pragmatic and surface-oriented criteria.* Presented at the 2nd Annual Summer Meeting of TESOL, Albuquerque, July.

Darcy, N. T. 1946. The effects of bilingualism upon the measurement of the intelligence of children of preschool age. *The Journal of Educational Psychology* 37.21-43.

────. 1953. A review of the literature on the effects of bilingualism upon the measurement of intelligence. *Journal of Genetic Psychology* 82.21-57.

────. 1963. Bilingualism and the measurement of intelligence: review of a decade of research. *Journal of Genetic Psychology* 103.259-82.

Dave, R. S. 1973. *Lifelong education and the school curriculum.* Hamburg: UNESCO Institute for Education.

Dawes, T. R. 1902. *Bilingual teaching in Belgian schools.* Cambridge: Cambridge University Press.

Day, R. R. 1979. The acquisition and maintenance of language by minority children. *Language Learning* 29.295-303.

DeAvila, E., and S. Duncan. 1978. A few thoughts about language assessment and a sociolinguistic alternative to the Lau remedies. *Educación bilingüe,* ed. by H. Lafontaine, B. Persky, and L. Golubchick, 137-42. Wayne, N.J.: Avery Publishing Group.

────. 1979. Bilingualism and the metaset. *NABE Journal* 3.1-20.

De Beer, A. G. 1967. *The teaching of English as a second language in Africaans high schools.* Pretoria: The English Academy of Southern Africa.

Debyser, F., et al. 1978. *Evaluation of Louisiana state-wide CODOFIL French program.* Baton Rouge: Louisiana State Department of Education.

Dejean, C., and C-L. Binnemans. 1971. *Université belge: du pari au défi.* Brussels: Editions de l'Institut de Sociologie, Université Libre de Bruxelles.

Dejean, Y. 1973. *Comment écrire le créole d'Haíti.* Unpub. Ph.D. thesis, Indiana University.

────. 1975. *Dilemme en Haiti: français en peril ou peril francais?* Port-au-Prince: Edicions Connaissance d'Haiti.

────. 1978. *Nouveau voyage en diglossie.* Unpub. paper.

Denison, N. 1968. Souris: a trilingual community in diatypic perspective. *Man* 3.578-92.

Dhondt, J. 1947. Essai sur l'origine de la frontière linguistique. *L'Antiquité Classique* 16.261-81.

Dil, A. 1972. *The Hindu and Muslim dialects of Bengali.* Ph.D. thesis, Stanford University.

Doll, D. C. 1978. *Curriculum improvement: decision making in process.* Boston: Allyn and Bacon.

Domengeaux, J. n.d. Unpublished speech (mimeo).

Draye, H. 1942. *De studie van de Vlaamsch-Waalsche Taalgrensli in Belgie.* Brussels: Standaard Boekhandel.

Duncan, S., and E. De Avila. 1979. Bilingualism and cognition: some recent findings. *NABE Journal* 4.15-50.

Ebel, Robert L. 1972. Must all tests be valid? *Perspectives in educational and psychological measurement,* ed. by Glenn H. Bracht, Kenneth D. Hopkins, and Julian C. Stanley, 74-87. Englewood Cliffs, N.J.: Prentice-Hall.

Education Commission of the States. National Assessment of Educational Progress Project. 1977. *Hispanic student achievement in five learning areas: 1971-75.* Washington, D.C.: Government Printing Office.

Edwards, H. P., and F. Smyth. 1976. *Evaluation of second language programs and some alternatives for teaching French as a second language in grades five to eight.* Toronto: The Ontario Institute for Studies in Education.

Elias-Olivares, L. 1976. *Ways of speaking in a Chicano community: a sociolinguistic approach.* Ph.D. thesis, University of Texas at Austin.

Eisemon, T. 1977. Educational transfer: the social ecology of educational change. *Teachers College Record* 78.359-70.

Emeneau, M. N. 1956. India as a linguistic area. *Language* 32.3-16.
Engle, P. L. 1975. The use of vernacular languages in education: language medium in early school years for minority language groups. *Bilingual education series 3.* Arlington, Va.: Center for Applied Linguistics.
Engelbrecht, G. 1980. Literacy in rural Bolivia: implications for bilingual programs. *Reading Teacher* 33.933-35.
Epps, E. G. 1979. *Educating an ethnically diverse population.* ERIC/CUE Urban diversity series, 59W.
Epstein, N. 1977. *Language, ethnicity and the schools: policy alternatives for bilingual bicultural education.* Washington, D.C.: Institute for Educational Leadership, George Washington University.
Erickson, G. W. 1960. *Grade placement of the non-vernacular language and readiness for advanced study in schools of Central Africa.* Unpub. Ph.D. thesis, University of Minnesota.
Ervin-Tripp, S. 1972. On sociolinguistic rules: alternation and co-occurrence. *Directions in sociolinguistics: the ethnography of communication,* ed. by J. J. Gumperz and D. Hymes, 213-50. New York: Holt, Rinehart, and Winston.
European Court of Human Rights. 1967-68. *Cases relating to certain aspects of the laws on the uses of languages in education in Belgium,* 2 vols. Strasbourg: Council of Europe.
Faine, J. 1974. *Dictionnaire français-créole,* ed. by G. Lefebvre. Montreal: Lémeac.
Farhady, H. 1980. *On the plausibility of the unitary language proficiency factor.* Presented at the Language Testing Conference, Albuquerque, June. To appear in Oller (in press).
Faulk, J. D. 1977. *Cajun French I.* Abbeville, La.: The Cajun Press.
Faure, E., et al. 1972. *Learning to be: the world of education today and tomorrow.* Paris: UNESCO.
Feldman, C., and M. Shen. 1971. Some language-related cognitive advantages of bilingual 5-year-olds. *Journal of Genetic Psychology* 118.235-44.
Feldman, D. H. 1980. *Beyond universals in cognitive development.* Norwood, N.J.: Ablex Publishing Company.
Felix, S. W. 1980. *The effect of formal instruction on second language acquisition.* Presented at the Second Language Research Forum, Los Angeles.
Ferguson, C. A. 1959. Diglossia. *Word* 15.325-40.
Ferguson, C. A. 1978a. Multilingualism as object of linguistic description. *Linguistics in the seventies: directions and prospects,* ed. by B. B. Kachru, 97-105. *Special issue of Studies in the Linguistic Sciences.* Department of Linguistics, University of Illinois.
_____. 1978b. Patterns of literacy in multilingual situations. *GURT* 29, ed. by J. Alatis, 582-88. Washington, D.C.: Georgetown University Press.
_____, and S. B. Heath, eds. 1981. *Language in the U.S.A.* Cambridge: Cambridge University Press.
Fernando, C. 1977. English and Sinhala bilingualism in Sri Lanka. *Language and Society* 6.341-60.
Filho, M. B. L. 1957. *Primary school curricula in Latin America.* Paris: UNESCO.
Fincher, B. H. 1978. Bilingualism in contemporary China: the coexistence of oral diversity and written uniformity. *Case studies in bilingual education,* ed. by B. Spolsky and R. L. Cooper, 72-87. Rowley, Mass.: Newbury House.
Fishman, J. A. 1956. *Language loyalty in America.* The Hague: Mouton.
_____. 1968. *Readings in the sociology of language.* The Hague: Mouton.
_____. 1969. National languages and languages of wider communication in developing nations. *Anthropological Linguistics* 11.111-35.
_____. 1972. *The sociology of language: an interdisciplinary social science approach to language in society.* Rowley, Mass.: Newbury House.
_____. 1976. *Bilingual education: an international sociological perspective.* Rowley, Mass.: Newbury House.

Fishman, J. A., C. Ferguson, and J. Das Gupta, eds. 1968. *Language problems of developing nations.* New York: Wiley and Sons.

Fishman, J. A., and J. Lovas. 1971. Bilingual education in a sociolinguistic perspective. *The language education of minority children,* ed. by B. Spolsky, 83-93. Rowley, Mass.: Newbury House.

Floyd, M. B. 1978. Verb usage in southwest Spanish: a review. *The Bilingual Review* 5.76-90.

_____. 1979. *Language variation and mood usage in southwest Spanish.* Paper presented at 6th Annual Colloquium on Hispanic Linguistics, Adelphi University.

Fontan, F. 1976. *Ethnisme, vers un nationalisme humaniste.* Bagnols-sur-Crèze: Libraire Occitane.

Foster, C. R. 1980a. Creole in conflict. *Migration Today* 8.8-13.

_____. 1980b. Issues in American bilingual education. *Australian Teacher Education Journal* 38.12-17.

Franck, L. 1932. *La nationalité belge et le mouvement flamand.* Brussels: Lamertin.

Frankétienne. 1975. *Dézafi.* Port-au-Prince: Editions Fardin.

_____. 1978. *Pèlin tèt.* Port-au-Prince: Les Presses Port-au-Princiennes.

Franklin Northeast Supervisory Union Title VII Bilingual Education Program. 1979. *Program description.* Canaan, Vt.

Freed, B. F. 1978. *From the community to the classroom: gathering second language speech samples.* Arlington, Va.: Center for Applied Linguistics.

Freedle, R. O., and J. B. Carroll. 1972. *Language comprehension and the acquisition of knowledge.* New York: Winston.

Freire, P. 1972. *Pedagogy of the oppressed.* New York: Herder and Herder.

_____. 1978. *Pedagogy in process: the letters to Guinea-Bissau.* New York: Seabury.

Fried, V., ed. 1972. *The Prague school of linguistics and language teaching.* London: Oxford University Press.

GEREC (Groupe d'Etudes et de Recherches en Espace Créole). 1976. En guise d'explication sur le conte... *Espace Créole* 3.66-9.

Gaarder, A. B. 1977. *Bilingual schooling and the survival of Spanish in the United States.* Rowley, Mass.: Newbury House.

Garcia, J. D. 1977. Analyzing bilingual education costs. *Bilingual education: current perspectives, education,* 90-107. Arlington, Va.: Center for Applied Linguistics.

Geerts, G., ed. 1972. *Taal of Taaltje?* Leuven: Acco.

Genesee, F. 1979. Scholastic effects of French immersion: an overview after ten years. *Interchange* 9.20-9.

_____, and E. Hamayan. 1980. Individual differences in second language learning. *Applied Psycholinguistics* 1.95-110.

_____, and M. H. Stanley. 1976. The development of English writing skills in French immersion programs. *Canadian Journal of Education* 1.1-17.

_____, G. R. Tucker, and W. E. Lambert. 1975. Communication skills of bilingual children. *Child Development* 46.1010-14.

Giles, H. 1979. Ethnicity markers in speech. *Social markers in speech,* ed. by K. Scherer and H. Giles, 251-89. London: Cambridge University Press.

Gladwin, T., and W. Sturtevant, eds. 1962. *Anthropology and human behavior.* Washington D.C.: Anthropological Society of Washington.

Goel, B. S., and S. K. Saini. 1972. *Mother tongue and equality of opportunity in education.* New Delhi: Central Electric Press.

Gold, G. L. 1979. The French frontier of settlement in Louisiana: some observations on culture change in Mamou Prairie. *Cahiers de Géographie du Québec* 23.263-80.

_____. 1980a. The changing criteria of social networks in a Cajun community. *Ethnos* 1-2.60-81.

_____. 1980b. *The role of France, Quebec, and Belgium in the revival of French in Louisiana schools.* Quebec: Centre International de Recherche sur le Bilinguisme, Université Laval (Publication B-91).

Goodenough, W. H. 1963. *Cooperation in change: an anthropological approach to community development.* New York: Russell Sage Foundation.

Gordon, M. M. 1961. Assimilation in America. *Daedalus* 90.263-85.

Gould, J., ed. 1965. *Penguin survey of social sciences.* Harmondsworth, England: Penguin Books.

Graham, V. T. 1925. The intelligence of Italian and Jewish children in the Habit Clinic of the Massachusetts Division of Mental Hygiene. *Journal of Abnormal and Social Psychology* 20.371-76.

Granda, G. de. 1968. *Transculturación e interferencia lingüística en el Puerto Rico contemporáneo (1898-1968).* Bogotá: Instituto Caro y Cuervo.

Greyson, E. 1893-96. L'enseignement publique en Belgique. *Histoire et exposé de la législation a 1892,* 3 vols. Brussels: Charles Rosez.

Grierson, G. A. 1911. *A manual of the Kashmiri language.* (Two parts). Oxford: Clarendon Press.

Gringràs, R. 1970. Verbal strategies in multilingual communication. *Language and cultural diversity in America,* ed. by R. D. Abrahams and R. C. Troike, 184-97. Englewood Cliffs, N.J.: Prentice-Hall.

_____. 1974. Problems in the description of Spanish-English inter-sentential code-switching. *Southwest areal linguistics,* ed. by G. A. Bills, 167-74. San Diego: Institute for Cultural Pluralism.

Guilford, J. P. 1956. The structure of intellect. *Psychological Bulletin* 53.267-93.

Gumperz, J. 1964. Linguistic and social interaction in two communities. *The ethnography of communication,* ed. by J. Gumperz and D. Hymes. Special Publication, American Anthropologist 66. pt. 2.137-53. Washington, D.C.: American Anthropological Association.

_____. 1968. The speech community. *International Encyclopedia of Social Sciences* 9.381-86.

_____. 1970. Verbal strategies in multilingual communication. *Language and cultural diversity in American education,* ed. by R. D. Abrahams and R. C. Troike, 184-196. Englewood Cliffs, N.J.: Prentice-Hall.

_____. 1971. *Language in social groups.* Stanford, Ca.: Stanford University Press.

_____. 1972. Introduction. *Directions in sociolinguistics: the ethnography of communication,* ed. by J. Gumperz and D. Hymes, 1-25. New York: Holt, Rinehart, and Winston.

_____. 1976. The sociolinguistic significance of conversational code-switching. *Working Papers of the Language Behavior Research Laboratory No. 46.* Berkeley: University of California.

_____. 1980. Pragmatics of non-native varieties of English. *English for cross-cultural communication,* ed. by L. Smith, 15-39. London: Macmillan.

_____, and E. Hernandez-Ch. 1971. Bilingualism, bidialectalism, and classroom interaction. *Language in social groups,* ed. by A. S. Dil, 311-39. Stanford: Stanford University Press.

_____, and D. Hymes, eds. 1972. *Directions in sociolinguistics: the ethnography of communication.* New York: Holt, Rinehart and Winston.

_____, and R. Wilson. 1971. Convergence and creolization: a case from Indo-Aryan/ Dravidian border. *Pidginization and creolization of languages,* ed. by D. Hymes, 151-68. London: Cambridge University Press.

Gunnarsson, B. 1978. A look at the content similarities between intelligence, achievement, personality, and language tests. *Language in education: testing the tests,* ed. by John W. Oller, Jr., and Kyle Perkins, 17-35. Rowley, Mass.: Newbury House.

Guru, K. 1962. *Hindi grammar.* (In Hindi). Benares: Nagari Pracharani Sabha.

Guy, G., and M. L. Braga. 1976. *Number concordance in Brazilian Portuguese.* Paper presented at N-WAVE V. Georgetown University.

Hagel, P. L. 1978a. Resources for the teaching of Franco-American culture. *Modern Language Journal* 62.182-6.

————. 1978b. *A resource guide for New England libraries: bilingual-bicultural education/Franco-American studies.* Bedford, N.H.: National Material Development Center.

Halliday, M. A. K. 1970. Language structure and language function. *New horizons in linguistics,* ed. by J. Lyons, 140-65. Harmondsworth: Penguin.

————. 1973. *Explorations in the functions of language.* London: Edward Arnold.

————. 1978. *Language as a social semiotic.* Baltimore: University Park Press.

————, A. McIntosh, and P. Strevens, eds. 1964. *The linguistic science and language teaching.* London: Longmans.

Hanse, J., A. Doppagne, and H. Bourgeois-Gielen. 1974. *Nouvelle chasse aux Belgicismes.* Brussels: Charles Plisneir.

Harbison, F. H. 1975. Education: nationwide learning systems. *Teachers College Record* 76.539-62.

Harley, B., and M. Swain. 1977. An analysis of verb form and function in the speech of French immersion pupils. *Working Papers on Bilingualism* 14.31-46.

————. 1978. An analysis of the verb system by young learners of French. *Interlanguage Studies Bulletin* 3.35-79.

Hartshorne, K. B. 1967. *The teaching of English in Bantu schools in South Africa, some comments on the present situation.* Pretoria: English Academy of Southern Africa.

Hasselmo, N. 1972. Code-switching as ordered selection. *Studies for Einar Haugen,* ed. by E. Firchow et al. The Hague: Mouton.

————. 1979. Code-switching and modes of speaking. *Texas studies in bilingualism,* ed. by G. Gilbert, 179-210. Berlin: Walter de Gruyter and Co.

Hatch, Evelyn. 1979. Simplified input and second language acquisition. Presented at the annual meeting of the Linguistic Society of America, Los Angeles.

Haugen, E. 1956. *Bilingualism in the Americas.* Publication No. 26 of the American Dialect Society, University of Alabama Press.

Hawes, H. W. R. 1972. *Planning the primary school curriculum in developing countries.* Paris: UNESCO.

Heath, S. B. 1972. *Telling tongues: language policy in Mexico—colony to nation.* New York: Teachers College Press.

————. 1978a. Bilingual education and a national language policy, *GURT* 29, ed. by J. Alatis, 53-64. Washington, D.C.: Georgetown University Press.

————. 1978b. *Teacher talk: language in the classroom.* Arlington, Va.: Center for Applied Linguistics.

Hébert, F. E. 1974. The new Louisiana story. *Congressional Record. Proceedings and Debates of the 93rd Congress,* 2nd session, March 5.

Héraud, G. 1970. *La monda lingvoproblemo.* Amsterdam.

————. 1971. Pour un droit linguistique comparé. *Revue Internationale de Droit Compare* 303-330.

————. 1973. Introduction à l'ethnopolitique. *Contre les Estats, les régions d'Europe* 15-32. Nice: Presses d'Europe.

————. 1974. L'arrêt du TF suisse du 31 mars 1965 et la protection des aires linguistiques. *Melanges couzinet* 373-86. Université des Sciences Sociales, Toulouse.

————. 1977. Le clivage linguistique et le fait national. *Régions et régionalisme en France, du XVIIe siècle à nos jours,* 461-80. PUF.

Herbert, R. K., ed. 1979. Metatheory 111: applications of linguistic theory in the human sciences. *1979 Conference Proceedings.* East Lansing: Department of Linguistics, Michigan State University.

Hernandez-Alvarez, J. 1976. *Social factors in educational attainment among Puerto Ricans in six U.S. metropolitan areas, 1970.* New York: Aspira of America, Inc.

Holtzman, W. H. et al. 1975. *Personality development in two cultures.* Austin, Tex.: University of Texas Press.

Hornby, P. A. 1977. *Bilingualism: psychological, social and educational implications.* New York: Academic Press.

Houis, M. 1976. The problem of the choice of languages in Africa. *Prospects: Quarterly Review of Education* 6.393-405.

Hufstedler, S. M. 1980. Bilingual education, civil rights and language minority regulations. *NABE Journal* 5.63-70.

Hunt, R., and E. Hunt. 1970. Education as an interface institution in rural Mexico and an American inner city. *From child to adult,* ed. by J. Meddleton, 314-25. Garden City, N.Y.: Natural History Press.

Hymes, D. 1962. The ethnography of speaking. *Anthropology and human behavior,* ed. by T. Gladwin and W. Sturtevant, 15-53. Washington, D.C.: Anthropological Society of Washington.

_____. 1972. Introduction. *Functions of language in the classroom,* ed. by C. B. Cazden, et al., xi-lvii. New York: Teachers College Press.

_____. 1974. *Foundations in sociolinguistics: an ethnographic approach.* Philadelphia: University of Pennsylvania Press.

Ianco-Worrall, A. 1972. Bilingualism and cognitive development. *Child Development* 43.1390-1400.

Illich, I. 1972. *Deschooling society.* New York: Harper and Row.

_____. 1979. Vernacular values and education. *Teachers College Record* 81.31-75.

Ireland, D., K. Gunnell, and L. Santerre. 1980. *A study of the teaching and learning of aural/oral French in immersion classes.* Ms. Ottawa: Ontario Institute for Studies in Education.

Irizarry, R. A. 1978. *Bilingual education: state and federal legislative mandates.* Los Angeles, Cal.: National Dissemination and Assessment Center.

Irvine, S. H., and J. T. Sanders, eds. 1972. *Cultural adaptation within modern Africa.* New York: Teachers College Press.

Jacobson, R. 1971. Cultural-linguistic pluralism and the problem of motivation. *TESOL Quarterly* 5.265-84.

_____. 1976. *The social implications of intra-sentential code-switching.* Paper presented at the Annual Meeting of the South Central Modern Language Association, Dallas, Tex. ED 136 587.

_____. 1977. The social implications of intrasentential codeswitching. *New Scholar* 6.227-56.

_____. 1978. The social implications of intrasentential codeswitching. *New directions in Chicano scholarship,* ed. by R. Romo and R. Paredes, 227-56. San Diego, Ca.: University of California.

_____. 1979a. Beyond ESL: the teaching of content other than language arts in bilingual education. *Working papers in sociolinguistics,* ed. by R. Bauman and J. Sherzer. Austin, Tex.: Southwest Educational Development Laboratory.

_____. 1979b. Can bilingual teaching techniques reflect bilingual community behaviors? —A study in ethnoculture and its relationship to some amendments contained in the new Bilingual Education Act. *Ethnoperspectives in bilingual education research I,* ed. by R. V. Padilla. Ypsilanti, Mich.: Eastern Michigan University.

_____. 1981. The implementation of a bilingual instruction model: the NEW concurrent approach. *Ethnoperspectives in bilingual education research II,* ed. by R. V. Padilla. Ypsilanti, Mich.: Eastern Michigan University.

Jardel, J. -P. 1975. *Du conflit des langues au conflit interculturel: une approche de la société martiniquaise.* 3e cycle doctorate dissertation. University of Nice.

Jensen, J. V. 1962. The effects of childhood bilingualism. *Elementary English* 39.132-143, 358-66.

John, V. P. 1972. The silent Indian child: styles of teaching: reflections on the education of Navajo children. *Functions of language in the classroom*, ed. by C. Cazden, V. P. John, and D. Hymes, 331-43. New York: Teachers College Press.

Jones, W. R. 1952. The language handicaps of Welsh-speaking children. *British Journal of Education* 22.114-23.

————. 1966. *Bilingualism in Welsh education*. Cardiff: University of Wales Press.

Juste, T. 1844. *Essai sur l'histoire de l'instruction publique en Belgique depuis les temps les plus reculés jusqu'à nos jours*. Brussels: Librairie Nationale.

Kachru, B. B. 1966. Indian English: a study in contextualization. *In memory of J. R. Firth*, ed. by C. E. Basell, J. C. Catford, M. A. K. Halliday, and R. H. Robins, 225-87. London: Longmans.

————. 1973. *An introduction to spoken Kashmiri. A basic course and reference manual for learning and teaching Kashmiri as a second language*. Urbana, Ill.: Department of Linguistics, University of Illinois.

————. 1978a. Code-mixing as a verbal strategy in India. *International dimensions of bilingual education*, ed. by J. E. Alatis, 107-24. *GURT*. Washington, D.C.: Georgetown University Press.

————. 1978b. *Linguistics in the seventies: directions and prospects*. Special issue of *Studies in the Linguistic Sciences*. Urbana, Ill.: Department of Linguistics, University of Illinois.

————. 1978c. Toward structuring code-mixing: an Indian perspective. *Aspects of sociolinguistics in South Asia*, ed. by B. B. Kachru and S. N. Sridhar, 27-46. Special issue of *International Journal of the Sociology of Language* 16.

————. 1979. The Englishization of Hindi: language rivalry and language change. *Linguistic method: papers in honor of Herbert Penzl*, ed. by I. Rauch and G. F. Carr, 199-211. The Hague: Mouton.

————. 1980a. Models for new Englishes. *TESOL Studies* 1980, 117-50.

————. 1980b. *Pragmatics of non-native varieties of English for cross-cultural communication*. London: Macmillan.

————. 1980c. Socially-realistic linguistics: the Firthian tradition. *Studies in the Linguistic Sciences* 10.85-111.

————. 1981a. Bilingualism. *Annual review of applied linguistics*, ed. by R. B. Kaplan, 2-18. Rowley, Mass.: Newbury House.

————. 1981b. *Kashmiri literature*. Wiesbaden: Otto Harrossowitz.

————, ed. 1982. *The other tongue: English across cultures*. Urbana, Ill.: University of Illinois Press.

————. In press. *The Indianization of English: the English language in India*. New Delhi and New York: Oxford University Press.

————, and R. Quirk. 1980. Introduction. *English for cross cultural communication*, ed. by L. Smith. London: Macmillan.

————, and S. N. Sridhar, eds. 1978. *Aspects of sociolinguistics in South Asia*. Special issue of *International Journal of the Sociology of Language* 16.

Kachru, Y. 1979. The quotative in South Asian languages. *South Asian languages analysis* 1. Urbana, Ill.: Department of Linguistics, University of Illinois.

————, and T. K. Bhatia. 1978. The emerging 'dialect' conflict in Hindi: a case of glottopolitics. *Aspects of sociolinguistics in South Asia*, ed. by B. B. Kachru and S. N. Sridhar, 47-58. Special issue of *International Journal of the Sociology of Language* 16.

Kagen, J., H. Moss, and I. Sigel. 1973. Psychological significance of styles of conceptualization. *Basic cognitive processes in children*, ed. by J. C. Wright and J. Kagen. Chicago, University of Chicago Press.

Kalema, J. 1980. The Inter-African Bureau of Languages: a progress report. *Language and Development* 1.4.

Kaplan, R. B., ed. 1981. *Annual review of applied linguistics*. Rowley, Mass.: Newbury House.

Kessler, C. 1971. *The acquisition of syntax in bilingual children.* Washington, D.C.: Georgetown University Press.

————, and M. E. Quinn. 1977. *Child language development in two socio-economic environments.* Paper presented at the annual meeting of the American Educational Research Association, New York. ERIC Report ED 139 253.

————, and M. E. Quinn. 1979. Piaget and the bilingual child. *Piagetian theory and the helping professions,* ed. by M. Poulsen and C. Lubin. Los Angeles: University of Southern California.

————, and M. E. Quinn. 1980a. Bilingualism and science problem-solving ability. *Bilingual Education Paper Series 4.* No. 1. Los Angeles: National Dissemination and Assessment Center.

————, and M. E. Quinn. 1980b. Positive effects of bilingualism on science problem-solving abilities. *GURT* 31, ed. by J. Alatis. Washington, D.C.: Georgetown University Press.

Khubchandani, L. M. 1977. Language ideology and language development: an appraisal of Indian education policy. *Linguistics* 193.33-51.

————. 1978a. Languages of instruction in India. *International Review of Education* 24.275-80.

————. 1978b. Multilingual education in India. *Case studies in bilingual education,* ed. by B. Spolsky and R. L. Cooper, 88-125. Rowley, Mass.: Newbury House.

Kimball, S. T. 1974. *Culture and the educative process: an anthropological perspective.* New York: Teachers College Press.

Kjolseth, R. 1971. Bilingual education programs in the United States: for assimilation of pluralism. *The language education of minority children,* ed. by B. Spolsky, 94-121. Rowley, Mass.: Newbury House.

Klein, F. 1976. *A quantitative study of syntactic and pragmatic indicators of change in the Spanish of bilinguals in the United States.* Paper presented at N-WAVE V. Georgetown University.

Kliebard, H. M. 1977. Curriculum theory: give me a 'for instance'. *Curriculum Inquiry* 6.257-76.

Kloss, H. 1977. *Les droits linguistiques des franco-ámericains aux Etats-Unis.* Centre International de Recherches sur le Bilinguisme, Québec: Les Presses de l'Université Laval.

————. 1977. *The American bilingual tradition.* Rowley, Mass.: Newbury House.

Kozol, J. 1978. *Children of the revolution: a Yankee teacher in the Cuban schools.* New York: Dell.

Krashen, S. 1976. Formal and informal linguistic environments in language learning and language acquisition. *TESOL Quarterly* 10.157-8.

————. 1979. The monitor model for second language acquisition. *Second language acquisition and foreign language teaching,* ed. by R. Gringas. Arlington, Va.: Center for Applied Linguistics.

————. 1980. The theoretical and practical relevance of simple codes. *Second language acquisition,* ed. by R. Scarcella and S. Krashen. Linguistics Dept., University of Southern California. Ms.

Kurth, G. 1896-98. *La frontière linguistique en Belgique et dans le nord de la France,* 2 vols. Brussels: Société Belge de Librairie.

Labov, W. 1966. *The social stratification of English in New York City.* Washington, D.C.: Center for Applied Linguistics.

————. 1970. The study of language in its social context. *Studium Generale* 23.30-87.

————. 1972a. *Language in the inner city.* Philadelphia: University of Pennsylvania Press.

————. 1972b. *Sociolinguistic patterns.* Philadelphia: University of Pennsylvania Press.

————. 1976. Systematically misleading data from test questions. *Urban Review: Issues and Ideas in Public Education* 9.146-171.

Labov, W., P. Cohen, C. Robins, and J. Lewis. 1968. *A study of the non-standard English of Negro and Puerto Rican speakers in New York City.* Report on Co-Operative Research Project 3288. New York: Columbia University.

LaFontaine, H. 1975. *Bilingual education for Puerto Ricans: ¿sí o no?* Paper presented at the National Conference on the Educational Needs of the Puerto Rican in the United States. Cleveland, Ohio.

_____, B. Persky, and L. Golubchick, eds. 1978. *Educación bilingüe.* Wayne, N.J.: Avery Publishing Group.

Lagoria, C. A., and L. Z. Ballon. 1976. Peru: institutionalizing Quechua. *Prospects: Quarterly Review of Education* 6.424-9.

Lambert, W. E. 1977. The effects of bilingualism on the individual: cognitive and socio-cultural consequences. *Bilingualism: psychological, social and educational implications,* ed. by P. A. Hornby, 15-27. New York: Academic Press.

_____. 1978. Some cognitive and sociocultural consequences of being bilingual. *GURT,* ed. by J. Alatis, 214-27. Washington, D.C.: Georgetown University Press.

_____, J. Havelka, and R. C. Gardner. 1959. Linguistic manifestations of bilingualism. *Journal of Verbal Learning and Verbal Behavior* 8.77-82.

_____, and E. Peal. 1972. The relationship of bilingualism to intelligence. *Language, psychology, and culture,* ed. by A. S. Dil, 111-59. Stanford, Cal.: Stanford University Press.

_____, and G. R. Tucker. 1972. *Bilingual education of children: the St. Lambert experiment.* Rowley, Mass.: Newbury House.

Lamberty, M. 1971. The rights of minority groups, people, and the state. *Plural Societies.* Autumn:47.

Landry, R. G. 1974. A comparison of second language learners and monolinguals on divergent thinking tasks at the elementary school level. *Modern Language Journal* 58.10-15.

Langer, J. 1969. Disequilibrium as a source of development. *Trends and issues in developmental psychology,* ed. by P. Mussen, J. Langer, and M. Covington, 22-36. New York: Holt, Rinehart, and Winston.

Language Policy Task Force. 1980. *Social dimensions of language use in East Harlem.* Center for Puerto Rican Studies. Working Paper No. 8.

Lapesa, R. 1965. *Historia de la lengua española.* Madrid: Escelicer.

Larouche, A. H. 1980. *Ethnicité, pêche et pétrole: les cadjins du Bayou Lafourche en Louisiana française.* Unpub. M.A. thesis. Social Anthropology, York University, Downsview, Ont., Canada.

Lau vs Nichols. 1974. 414 U.S. 563.

Lawton, D. 1980. Language attitude, discreteness, and code-shifting in Jamaican Creole. *English World-Wide: A Journal of Varieties of English* 2.211-26.

Laygo, T. M., ed. 1977. *What is Filipino?* Berkeley, Cal.: Asian American Bilingual Center.

Leap, W. 1973. Language pluralism in a south-western Pueblo: some comments on Isletan English. *Bilingualism in the southwest,* ed. by P. R. Turner, 275-93. Tuscon, Az.: University of Arizona Press.

Legum, S., C. Pfaff, G. Tinnie, and M. Nicholas. 1971. *The speech of young Black children in Los Angeles.* Technical Report 33, Southwest Regional Laboratory.

Leidtke, W., and L. Nelson. 1968. Concept formation and bilingualism. *Alberta Journal of Educational Research* 14.225-32.

Leopold, W. 1949. *Speech development of a bilingual child.* Vol. 3. Evanston, Ill.: North-western University Press.

Lepetit, J. 1925. *Écoles libres et écoles officielles.* Brussels: Frameries.

Lepicq, D. 1980. *Aspects théoriques et empiriques de l'acceptabilité linguistique: le cas du français des élèves des classes d'immersion.* Unpublished Ph.D. thesis, University of Toronto.

Lester, M. 1974. Bilingual education in the United States, the Pacific, and Southeast Asia. *Topics in Cultural Learning* 2.137-46, ed. by R. W. Brislin. Honolulu: East-West Cultural Learning Institute.

Lewis, E. G. 1978a. Types of bilingual communities. *GURT* 29, ed. by J. Alatis, 19-33. Washington, D.C.: Georgetown University Press.

————. 1978b. What are the international dimensions of bilingualism in education? *GURT* 29, ed. by J. Alatis, xi-xix. Washington, D.C.: Georgetown University Press.

————. 1980. *Bilingualism and bilingual education: a comparative study.* New Mexico: University of New Mexico Press.

Lindholm, K. J., and A. M. Padilla. 1978. Language mixing in bilingual children. *Journal of Child Language* 5.327-78.

Linguistic Reporter. 1975. OCR sets guidelines for fulfilling Lau decisions. 18.1, 5-7.

Lipski, J. M. 1978. Code-switching and the problem of bilingual competence. *Aspects of bilingualism,* ed. by M. Paradis, 250-64. Columbia, S.C.: Hornbeam Press.

Lofficial, F. 1979. *Créole-français: une fausse querelle?* Quebec: Collectif Paroles.

López-Morales, H. 1980. Nasals in Puerto Rican Spanish. *Proceedings of the 8th Conference on New Ways of Analyzing Variation,* ed. by D. Sankoff and H. J. Cedergren. (to appear).

Lyons, J., ed. 1970. *New horizons in linguistics.* Harmondsworth: Penguin.

McClure, E. 1977. Aspects of code-switching in the discourse of bilingual Mexican-American children. *GURT* 28, ed. by J. Alatis. Washington, D.C.: Georgetown University Press.

————. n.d. *The acquisition of communicative competence in a bicultural setting.* NIE Grant NE-G-00-e-0147 final report.

————, and J. Wentz. 1976. Functions of code-switching among Mexican-American children. *Papers from the Parasession on Functionalism, Chicago Linguistic Society,* 421-32. Chicago: Department of Linguistics, University of Chicago.

McConnell, H. O., and E. Swan. 1945. *Let's speak Creole.* Petit-Goave (Haiti): Imprimerie du Sauveur.

McLaughlin, B. 1978. *Second language acquisition in childhood.* Hillsdale, N.J.: Lawrence Erlbaum Associates.

McMagh, P. 1967. *The teaching of English as a second language in primary schools in the Cape Province.* Pretoria: English Academy of Southern Africa.

Ma. R., and E. Herasimchuk. 1968. The linguistic dimensions of a bilingual neighborhood. *Bilingualism in the barrio,* ed. by J. Fishman, et al., 347-464. New York: Yeshiva University.

Mackey, W. F. 1970. A typology of bilingual education. *Bilingual schooling in the United States,* ed. by T. Anderson and M. Boyer, vol. 2.64-82. Washington, D.C.: U.S. Government Printing Office.

————. 1978. The importation of bilingual education models. *GURT* 29, ed. by J. Alatis, 1-18. Washington, D.C.: Georgetown University Press.

Macnamara, J. 1967. The bilingual's linguistic performance: a psychological overview. *Journal of Social Issues* 23.58-77.

————. 1970. Bilingualism and thought. *GURT* 21, ed. by J. Alatis, 25-46. Washington, D.C.: Georgetown University Press.

————. 1972. The cognitive basis of language learning in infants. *Psychological Review* 79.1-13.

Maguire, R. 1979. Creoles and Creole language use in St. Martin Parish, Louisiana. *Cahiers de Géographie du Québec* 23.281-302.

Malherbe, E. G. 1978. Bilingual education in the republic of South Africa. *Case studies in bilingual education,* ed. by B. Spolsky and R. L. Cooper, 167-202. Rowley, Mass.: Newbury House.

Marcantel, D. E. 1979. (pseudonym of Marc Untel de Gravelles). *Milles misères—laissant le bon temps rouler en Louisiane.* Document de travail no. 5, Projet Louisiane, Département de Géographie, Université Laval.

Martinet, A. 1961. *Elements de linguistique générale.* Paris: Armand Colin.

Maseman, V. L. 1980. Comparative perspectives on multicultural education. *Multicultural Education: Perspectives for the 1980's.* Buffalo, N.Y.: State University of New York at Buffalo.

Masica, C. 1976. *Defining a linguistic area: South Asia*. Chicago: University of Chicago Press.

Matluck, J. 1961. Fonemas finales en el consonantismo puertorriqueño. *Nueva Revista de Filolgía Hispánica* 332-42.

Mead, M. 1927. Group intelligence tests and linguistic disability among Italian children. *School and Society* 25.465-68.

Meillet, A., and L. Tesnière. 1928. *Les langues dans l'Europe nouvelle*. Paris: Pauot.

Merikoski, V. 1957. Le regime linguistique de la Finlande. *Revue Internationale de Science Politique.*

Mhina, G. 1974. *The role of Kiswahili in the development of Tanzania*. Pasadena: Munger African Library, California Institute of Technology.

Ministries of National Education. 1975. *Education in Belgium: the main trends*. Report presented at the XXXVth International Conference on Education. Brussels: Direction Generale de l'Organisation des Etudes/Ministrie van Nationale Opvoeding en Nederlandse Cultuur.

Miranda, R. V. 1978. Caste, religion, and dialect differentiation in the Konkani area. *Aspects of sociolinguistics in South Asia*, ed. by B. B. Kachru and S. N. Sridhar, Special issue of *International Journal of the Sociology of Language* 16.77-91.

Mishra, V. 1963. *The influence of English on Hindi language and literature 1870-1920*. (in Hindi). Dehradun: Sahitya Sadan.

Mitchell, T. F. 1978. Meaning is what you do—and how he and I interpret it: a Firthian view of pragamtics. *Die Neuren Sprachen*. Heft 3/4.224-53. Frankfurt am Main: Verlag Moritz Diesterweg.

Mitchell-Kernan, C. 1969. *Language behavior in a Black urban community*. Berkeley: Language Behavior Research Laboratory. Working Paper No. 23.

Modeen, T. 1970. The situation of the Finland-Swedish population in the light of international, constitutional law, administrative law. *McGill Journal* 16.121-39.

Modiano, N. 1973. *Indian education in the Chiapas highlands*. New York: Holt, Rinehart, and Winston.

————. 1979. The most effective language of instruction for beginning reading: a field study. *Bilingual multicultural education and the professional: from theory to practice*, ed. by H. T. Treuba and C. Barnett-Mizrahi, 282-88. Rowley, Mass.: Newbury House.

Monteyne, A. 1977. Le monde flamand de Bruxelles. *Courrier Hebdomadaire du CRISP*. no. 786.12 octobre:4.

Morrison, J. 1958. Bilingualism: some psychological aspects. *The Advancement of Science* 14.287-90.

Mougeon, R., C. Brant-Palmer, M. Bélanger, and W. Chichocki. 1980. *Le Français parlé en situation minoritaire: volume 1*. Toronto: Ontario Ministry of Education.

Munby, J. 1978. *Communicative syllabus design*. Cambridge: Cambridge University Press.

Musgrove, F. 1973. Education and culture concept. *Culture relevance and educational issues*, ed. by F. A. J. Iannai and E. Storey, 12-28. Boston: Little, Brown.

Nadkarni, M. V. 1975. Bilingualism and syntactic change in Konkani. *Language* 51.672-83.

Naiman, N., M. Froehlich, H. Stern, and A. Tadesco. 1978. *The good language learner*. Toronto: Ontario Institute for Studies in Education.

Nash, R. 1977. Aspects of Spanish-English bilingualism and language mixture in Puerto Rico. ed. by A. Makkai, V. B. Makkai, and L. Heilman, 205-25. Lake Bluff, Ill.: Jupiter Press.

National Advisory Council for Bilingual Education (NACBE). 1981. *The prospects for bilingual education in the nation: fifth annual report*. Rosslyn, Va.: National Clearinghouse on Bilingual Education.

National Center for Education Statistics (NCES). 1981. *The children's English and services study: a methodological review*. Washington, D.C.

National Materials Development Center. 1979a. *D'la Boucane*. Bedford, N.H.

National Materials Development Center. 1979b. *A Franco-American bibliography of New England.* Bedford, N.H.
_____. 1980. *A Franco-American overview,* vol. 1-4. Bedford, N.H.
Nyerere, J. K. 1967. *Education for self reliance.* Dar es Salaam, Tanzania: Government Printer. Reprinted in 1972 in *Ujamaa: Essays on socialism,* 44-75. London: Oxford University Press.
Obina, M. E. 1979. *The perception of Nigerian change agents in the use of vernacular or English in the implementation of educational goals.* Unpub. Ph.D. thesis, Catholic University of America.
Ogbu, J. 1974. *The next generation: an ethnography of education in an urban neighborhood.* New York: Academic Press.
Ogeltree, E. J. 1978. Where is bilingual education going? Historical and legal perspectives. *Educación bilingüe,* ed. by H. Lafontaine, B. Persky, and L. Golubchick, 52-7. Wayne, N.J.: Avery Publishing Group.
Oller, J. W., Jr. 1974. Bilingual education: promises and paradoxes. *On TESOL 74,* ed. by R. Crymes and W. Norris, 111-20. Washington, D.C.: TESOL. Also in *English as a second language in bilingual education,* ed. by J. E. Alatis and K. Twaddell, 65-75. Washington, D.C.: TESOL.
_____. 1976. Evidence for a general factor of language proficiency. *Die Neuren Sprachen* 76.165-74.
_____. 1979. *Language tests at school: a pragmatic approach.* London: Longman.
_____. In press. *Issues in language testing research.* Ms. Department of Linguistics, University of New Mexico, Albuquerque.
_____, and F. B. Hinofotis. 1980. Two mutually exclusive hypotheses about second language ability. *Research in language testing,* ed. by J. W. Oller, Jr. and K. Perkins, 13-23. Rowley, Mass.: Newbury House.
_____, and K. Perkins. 1980. *Research in language testing.* Rowley, Mass.: Newbury House.
_____, and V. Streiff. In press. *The language factor: more tests of tests.* Rowley, Mass.: Newbury House.
Orjala, P. R. 1970. *A dialect study of Haitian Creole.* Unpub. Ph.D. thesis, Hartford Seminary Foundation.
Pandharipande, R. 1979. *On the nativization of lexicon: the case of Marathi.* Unpub. ms. Department of Linguistics, University of Illinois.
_____. 1980. *Language contact and language variation: Nagpuri Marathi and Hindi.* Unpub. ms. Department of Linguistics, University of Illinois.
Pandit, P. B. 1972. *India as a socio-linguistic area.* Poona: Poona University Press.
_____. 1977. *Language in a plural society: the case of India.* New Delhi: Devraj Channa Memorial Committee.
_____. 1978. Language and identity: the Punjabi language in Delhi. *Aspects of socio-linguistics in South Asia,* ed. by B. B. Kachru and S. N. Sridhar, Special issue of *International Journal of the Sociology of Language* 16.93-108.
Paradis, M., ed. 1978. *Aspects of bilingualism.* Columbia, S.C.: Hornbeam Press.
_____. 1979. Contributions of neurolinguistics to the theory of bilingualism. *Metatheory III: applications of linguistic theory in the human sciences,* ed. by R. K. Herbert, 180-211. 1979 Conference Proceedings. East Lansing: Department of Linguistics, Michigan State University.
Passow, H. A., H. J. Noah, M. Eckstein, and J. R. Mallea. 1976. The national case study: an empirical comparative study of twenty-one educational systems. *International studies in evaluation VII.* New York: Halsted/John Wiley.
Paulston, C. B. 1969. *Las escuelas bilingues: the Peruvian experience.* Paper presented at the Third Annual TESOL Convention, Chicago, Illinois. March.

Paulston, C. B. 1972. Las escuelas bilingues en Peru: some comments on second language learning. *International Review of Applied Linguistics in Language Teaching* 10.351-56.
_____. 1974. Linguistic and communicative competence. *TESOL Quarterly* 8.347-62.
_____. 1975. Ethnic relations and bilingual education: accounting for contradictory data. *Working Papers on Bilingualism* 6.1-44.
_____. 1977. Viewpoint: research. *Bilingual education: current perspectives—linguistics V*, 87-125. Arlington, Va.: Center for Applied Linguistics.
Peaker, G. F. 1976. An empirical study of education in twenty-one countries. *A technical report: international studies in evaluation VIII*. New York: Halsted/John Wiley.
Peal, E., and W. Lambert. 1962. The relation of bilingualism to intelligence. *Psychological Monographs* 76. No. 27.
Pedraza, P. 1979. *Ethnographic observations of language use in El Barrio*. Ms. New York: Center for Puerto Rican Studies.
Pfaff, C. W. 1975. *Syntactic constraints on code-switching: a quantitative study of Spanish/English*. Paper presented at the LSA Annual Meeting.
_____. 1976. Functional and structural constraints on syntactic variation in code-switching. *Papers from the Parasession on Dyachronic Syntax*. Chicago: Chicago Linguistic Society.
_____. 1979. Constraints on language mixing: intersentential code-switching and borrowing in Spanish/English. *Language* 55.291-318.
Piaget, J. 1952. *The language and thought of the child*. London: Routledge and Kegan.
_____. 1970. *Genetic epistemology*. New York: Norton.
_____, and B. Inhelder. 1969. *The psychology of the child*. New York: Basic Books.
Picard, L. 1942-59. *Geschiedenis van de Vlaamsche en Groot-Nederlandsche Beweging*, 2 vols. Antwerp: De Sikkel.
Pillai, S. 1974. Code-switching in the Tamil novel. *Structural approaches to South Indian studies*, ed. by H. M. Buck and G. E. Yocum, 81-95. Chambersburg, Pa.: Wilson Books.
_____. 1978. *Syntactic structure and social function of code-switching*. Working Paper no. 22. New York: Center for Puerto Rican Studies.
Pireene, H. 1926-32. *Histoire de Belgique*. 7 vols. Brussels: Maurice Lamertin.
Platt, J. T. 1977. A model for polyglossia and multilingualism (with special reference to Singapore and Malaysia). *Language and society* 6.361-78.
Pohl, J. 1975. L'omission de *ne* dans le francais parlé contemporain. *Le Francais dans le Monde*. Fév.-Mars. 17-23.
Poplack, S. 1978a. Dialect acquisition among Puerto Rican bilinguals. *Language in society* 7.89-103.
_____. 1978b. Syntactic structure and social function of code-switching. To appear. *Latino discourse and communicative behavior*, ed. by R. Duran. New Jersey: Ablex Publishing Company.
_____. 1979. *Function and process in a variable phonology*. Unpub. Ph.D. thesis. University of Pennsylvania.
_____. 1980a. *Variable concord in sentential plural marking*. Working Paper No. 6. New York: Center for Puerto Rican Studies. To appear in *The Hispanic Review*.
_____. 1980b. The notion of the plural in Puerto Rican Spanish: competing constraints on /s#/ deletion. *Locating language in time and space*, ed. by W. Labov. New York: Academic Press.
_____. 1981. 'Sometimes I'll start a sentence in Spanish Y TERMINO EN ESPANOL': toward a typology of code-switching. *Linguistics* 18.708.
_____, and A. Pousada. 1980. *A comparative study of gender assignment to loanwords*. Paper presented at IX Conference on New Ways of Analyzing Variation, University of Michigan.
_____, D. Sankoff, and A. Pousada. 1980. *Borrowing: the synchrony of integration*. Paper presented at the LSA Annual Meeting, San Antonio.

REFERENCES 323

Pouler, C., and E. Wright. 1980. An analysis of the influence of reinforcement and knowledge of criteria on the ability of students to generate hypotheses. *Journal of Research in Science Teaching* 17.31-7.

Pousada, A., and S. Poplack. 1979. No case for convergence: the Puerto Rican Spanish verb system in a language contact situation. To appear. *Bilingual education for Hispanic students in the United States,* ed. by G. Keller and J. Fishman. Columbia University: Teachers College Press.

President's Commission of Foreign Language and International Studies. 1979. *Strength through wisdom: a critique of U.S. capability.* Washington, D.C.

Pressoir, C. -F. 1947. *Débat sur le créole et le folklore.* Port-au-Prince: Imprimerie de l'Etat.

Project Savoir. 1979. *Program description.* St. John Valley Bilingual Education Program, Madawaska, Me.

Project F.A.R.I.N.E. 1979. *A Franco-American resource inventory of New England.* Orono, Me.: FAROG, University of Maine.

Quinn, M. E. 1971. *Evaluation of a method for teaching hypothesis formation to sixth-grade children.* Unpub. Ph.D. thesis, University of Pennsylvania.

_____, and K. George. 1975. Teaching hypothesis formation. *Science Education* 59.289-96.

_____, and C. Kessler. 1976. *The relationship between science education and language development.* Paper presented at the annual meeting of the American Educational Research Association, San Francisco. ERIC Report ED 123 112.

Quirk, R. 1960. The survey of English usage. *Transactions of the Philological Society* 40-61.

Ramirez, M., et al. 1974a. *New Approaches to bilingual, bicultural education: developing cognitive flexibility.* No. 6. Austin, Tex.: The Dissemination Center for Bilingual Education.

_____. 1974b. The relationship of acculturation to cognitive style among Mexican Americans. *Journal of Cross-Cultural Psychology* 7.451-62.

Ramirez, M., and A. Castañeda. 1974. *Cultural democracy, bicognitive development, and education.* New York: Academic Press.

Rauch, I., and G. R. Carr, eds. 1979. *Linguistic method: papers in honor of Herbert Penzl.* The Hague: Mouton.

Reed, R. 1976. *Lâche pas la patate, portrait des Acadiens de la Louisiane.* Montreal: Éditions Parti Pris.

Reyes, R. 1976. Language mixing in Chicano bilingual speech. *Studies in Southwest Spanish,* ed. by J. D. Bowen and J. Ornstein, 183-88. Rowley, Mass.: Newbury House.

Robinson, P. 1978. *Language management in education: the Australian context.* London: Allen and Unwin.

Robinson, W. P. 1979. Speech markers and social class. *Social markers in speech,* ed. by K. Scherer and H. Giles, 211-49. London: Cambridge University Press.

Rogg, E. M. 1978. The special assimilation problems of Americans of Spanish speaking origin. *Educación bilingüe,* ed. by H. Lafontaine, B. Persky, and L. Golubchick, 74-9. Wayne, N.J.: Avery Publishing Group.

Romo, R., and R. Paredes, eds. 1978. *New directions in Chicano scholarship.* San Diego, Ca.: University of California.

Rosier, P., and W. Holm. 1980. The Rock Point experience: a longitudinal study of a Navajo school program. *Papers in Applied Linguistics: Bilingual Education Series 8.* Washington, D.C.: Center for Applied Linguistics.

Rubin, J. 1978. Toward bilingual education for Paraguay. *GURT,* ed. by J. Alatis, 189-200. Washington, D.C.: Georgetown University Press.

Rundle, S. 1946. *Language as a social and political factor in Europe.* London: Faber and Faber.

Saer, D. J. 1923. The effect of bilingualism on intelligence. *British Journal of Psychology* 14.25-38.

Saint-Quentin, A. de. 1872. Notice grammaticale et philologique sur le créole de Cayenne. *Introduction à l'histoire de Cayenne, suivie d'un recueil de contes, fables et chanson en créole avec traducion en regard,* A. de Saint Quentin. Antibes: J. Marchand.

Salomon, G. 1970. *Cue attendance and hypotheses generation as two procedures of training for producing uncertainty in teachers.* Technical Report USOE, ED 045 622. Stanford University.

Samarin, W. J. 1976. *Language in religious practice.* Rowley, Mass.: Newbury House.

Sankoff, G. 1980. *The social life of language.* Philadelphia: University of Pennsylvania Press.

Sankoff, D., and S. Poplack. 1980. *A formal grammar for code-switching.* Working Paper No. 8. New York: Center for Puerto Rican Studies.

Sankoff, G., and D. Vincent. 1977. L'emploi productif du *ne* dans le français parlé à Montréal. *Le Français Moderne* 45.243-56.

Santiago-Santiago, I. 1978. *A community's struggle for equal educational opportunity: Aspira vs Board of Education.* Princeton, N.J.: Educational Testing Service.

Saville, M., and R. C. Troike. 1971. *Handbook of bilingual education.* Revised ed. Washington, D.C.: Teachers of English to Speakers of Other Languages.

Saville-Troike, M. 1978. *A guide to culture in the classroom.* Rosslyn, Va.: National Clearinghouse on Bilingual Education.

Scherer, K. R., and H. Giles, eds. 1979. *Social markers in speech.* London: Cambridge University Press.

Scherre, M. 1978. *A regra de concordância de número no sintagma nomial em português.* Unpub. M.A. thesis. Rio de Janeiro: Pontifícia Universidade Católica.

Schumann, J. 1978. The acculturation model for second-language acquisition. *Second-language acquisition and foreign language teaching,* ed. by R. Gringras. Arlington, Va.: Center for Applied Linguistics.

Schwarz, H. G. 1962. Communist languages policies for China's ethnic minorities: the first decade. *China Quarterly* 12.170-83.

Scollon, R. forthcoming. Variable data and linguistic convergence. To appear in *Language in Society 6.*

Scott, S. 1973. *The relation of divergent thinking of bilingualism: cause or effect.* Unpub. research report, McGill University.

Scotton, C. 1976. Strategies of neutrality. *Language* 52.919-41.

Segalowitz, N., and E. Gatbonton. 1977. *Bilingualism: psychological, social, and educational implications,* ed. by P. A. Hornby. New York: Academic Press.

Sénat de Belgique. 1970. *Interpellation de M. Bourgeous.* Séance du 25 mars:7. Brussels: Moniteur Belge.

Senelle, R. 1972. *The revision of the constitution. Memo from Belgium 144-145-146.* Centre de recherche pour la solution nationale des problemes sociaux, politiques, et juridiques en régions wallonnes et flamandes (Harmel Center) ca. 1958. Brussels: Ministry of Foreign Affairs, External Trade, and Cooperation in Development.

Sheffield, J. R. 1973. *Education in Kenya: an historical study.* New York: Teachers College Press.

————. 1974. Educational policies for developing nations. *Teachers College Record* 76.89-100.

————. 1975. New perspectives on education and international development. *Teachers College Record* 76.534-38.

————. 1976. The rediscovery of poverty: a review of aid policies in education. *Teachers College Record* 77.527-37.

Sibayan, B. P. 1978. Bilingual education in the Philippines: strategy and structures. *GURT* 29, ed. by J. Alatis, 302-24. Washington, D.C.: Georgetown University Press.

Sibelman, L. 1978. Bilingual education: a mosaic of controversy. *Educación bilingüe,* ed. by H. Lafontaine, B. Persky, and L. Golubchick, 39-42. Wayne, N.J.: Avery Publishing Group.

Sinclair, J. M., and R. M. Coulthard. 1975. *Toward an analysis of discourse: the English used by teachers and pupils.* London: Oxford University Press.

Skutnabb-Kangas, T., and P. Toukamaa. 1976. *Teaching migrant children's mother tongue and learning of the language of the host country in the context of the socio-cultural situation of the migrant family.* Helsinki: The Finnish National Commission for UNESCO.

Smith, Frank. 1978. *Understanding reading: a psycholinguistic analysis of reading and learning to read.* Second edition. New York: Holt, Rinehart, and Winston.

Smith, L., ed. 1980. *English for cross cultural communication.* London: Macmillan.

Smith, P. M. 1979. Sex markers in speech. *Social markers in speech,* ed. by K. R. Scherer and H. Giles, 109-46. London: Cambridge University Press.

Smith-Thibodeaux, J. 1977. *Les francophones de Louisiane.* Paris: Éditions Entente.

Snow, C., and C. Ferguson, eds. 1977. *Talking to children: language input and acquisition.* Cambridge: Cambridge University Press.

Le Soir. 1970. 4 novembre.

Le Soir. 1971. 31 mai:2.

Le Soir. 1979a. 21 février.

Le Soir. 1979b. 26/27 août:2.

Le Soir. 1979c. 4 décembre.

Solá, D. 1979. Flexible technology model for bilingual education. *Ethnoperspectives in bilingual education research: bilingual education and public policy in the United States,* vol. 1.295-314, ed. by R. V. Padilla. Ypsilanti, Mich.: Eastern Michigan University.

_____, and R. M. Weber, eds. 1978. *Educational planning in multilingual countries: a report on a working conference.* NCLBE.

Spencer, J. 1971. *The English language in Africa.* London: Longmans.

Spilka, I. V. 1976. Assessment of second-language performance in immersion programs. *The Canadian Modern Language Review* 32.543-61.

Spolsky, B., and R. L. Cooper. 1978. *Case studies in bilingual education.* Rowley, Mass.: Newbury House.

Spolsky, B., and P. Irvine. 1980. Sociolinguistics of literacy: an historical and comparative study. *Proceedings of the Eighth Annual Southwest Areal Language and Linguistics Workshop. Anthropological Research Papers 20,* ed. by F. Barkin and E. Brandt, 246-51. Tempe, Az.: Arizona State University.

Sridhar, S. N. 1978. On the function of code-mixing in Kannada. *Aspects of sociolinguistics in South Asia,* ed. by B. B. Kachru and S. N. Sridhar. Special issue of *International Journal of the Sociology of Language* 16.109-17.

_____, and K. K. Sridhar. 1980. *The syntax and psycholinguistics of bilingual code-mixing.* Unpub. ms.

Srivastava, R. N., et al. 1978. *Evaluating communicability in village settings.* (Two parts). Delhi: Department of Linguistics, University of Delhi.

Stengers, J. 1959. *La formation de la frontière linguistique en Belgique ou de la légitimité de l'hypothèse historique.* Brussels-Berchem: Latomus.

Stern, H. H. 1978. French immersion in Canada: achievements and directions. *The Canadian Modern Language Review* 34.836-54.

_____. 1980. *Directions in FL curriculum development.* Presented at ACTFL National Conference on Professional Priorities, Boston, Mass.

Suarez, Y. L. 1978. Bilingualism in Mexico. *GURT 29,* ed. by J. Alatis, 202-13. Washington, D.C.: Georgetown University Press.

Suchman, J. R. 1962. *The elementary school training program in scientific inquiry.* Urbana, Ill.: University of Illinois Press.

Svalastoga, K., and P. Wolfe. 1969. A town in Danish borderland. *Studies in multilingualism,* ed. by N. Anderson, 26-44. Leiden: Brill.

Swain, M. 1972. *Bilingualism as a first language.* Unpub. Ph.D. thesis, University of California at Irvine.

Swain, M. 1974. French immersion programs across Canada: research findings. *The Canadian Modern Language Review* 31.117-29.

————. 1975. Writing skills of grade three French immersion pupils. *Working Papers on Bilingualism* 7.1-38.

————. 1978a. Home-school language switching. *Understanding second language learning: issues and approaches,* ed. by J. C. Richards, 238-51. Rowley, Mass.: Newbury House.

————. 1978b. Bilingual education for the English-Canadian. *Georgetown University Round Table on Language and Linguistics,* ed. by J. Alatis, 141-54. Washington, D.C.: Georgetown University Press.

————. 1980. *Immersion education: applicability for nonvernacular teaching to vernacular speakers.* Paper presented at Symposium on Standard Language Vernacular Relations and Bilingual Education. Racine, Wis., Nov.

————. 1981. Time and timing in bilingual education. *Language Learning.* In press.

Sweeney, W. O. 1975. The role of communications in the development process. *Teachers College Record* 76.597-604.

Swing, E. S. 1980. *Bilingualism and linguistic segregation in the schools of Brussels.* Quebec: International Center for Research on Bilingualism.

Sylvain, G. 1901. *Cric? Crac! Fables de la Fontaine racontées par un montagnard haitien et transcrites en vers créoles.* Paris: Atelier Haiteins.

Taiwo, C. O. 1976. The mother tongue as a means of promoting equal access to education in Nigeria: problems and solutions. *Linguistic documentation for developing countries, cases, problems, and solutions.* Paris: UNESCO.

Teitelbaum, H. 1976. *Testing biliguality in elementary school children.* Unpub. doctoral dissertation, University of New Mexico, Albuquerque.

Terrell, T. D. 1975a. Functional constraints on deletion of word final /s/ in Cuban Spanish. *Berkeley Linguistic Society 1.* Berkeley: University of California.

————. 1975b. Sobre la aspiración y la elisión de la /s/ implosiva y final en el español de Puerto Rico. *Nueva Revista de Filología Hispánica* 27.24-38.

————. 1977. A natural approach to the acquisition and learning of second languages. *Modern Language Journal* 59.325-36.

————. 1979a. Final s in Cuban Spanish. To appear in *Hispania.*

————. 1979b. Los efectos de la reestructuración fonémica de /s/ en el habla dominicana. To appear. *Proceedings of the 4th Symposium on Caribbean Dialectology.* Interamerican University Press.

————. 1980. *A natural approach to language teaching: an update.* Ms., Department of Spanish and Portuguese, University of California at Irvine.

Timm, L. A. 1975. Spanish-English code-switching: el porqué y how-not-to. *Romance Philology* 28.473-82.

————. 1978. Code-switching in war and peace. *Aspects of bilingualism,* ed. by M. Paradis, 302-15. Columbia, S.C.: Hornbeam Press.

Tinelli, H. 1974. Generative and creolization processes: nasality in Haitian Creole. *Lingua* 33.353-66.

Tiwari, B. N. 1966. *The Hindi language.* (in Hindi). Allahabad: Kitab Mahal.

Topping, D. M. 1975. A bilingual education program for Micronesia. *Linguistic Reporter* 17.5-6.

Torrance, E., J. Gowan, J. Wu, and N. Aliotti. 1970. Creative functioning of monolingual and bilingual children in Singapore. *Journal of Educational Psychology* 61.72-5.

Tough, J. 1977. *Development of meaning: talking to some purpose with young children.* London: Allen and Unwin.

Toukomaa, P., and T. Skutnabb-Kangas. 1977. *The intensive teaching of the mother tongue to migrant children of pre-school age.* Research Reports 26. Tampere: Department of Sociology and Social Psychology, University of Tampere, Finland.

Tremaine, R. 1975. *Syntax and Piagetian operational thought.* Washington, D.C.: Georgetown University Press.

Troike, R. C., and N. Modiano. 1975. *Proceedings of the first inter-American conference of bilingual education.* Washington, D.C.: Center for Applied Linguistics.

Trudgill, P. 1974. *Sociolinguistics.* Harmondsworth: Penguin.

_____. 1976-77. Creolization in reverse: reduction and simplification in the Albanian dialects of Greece. *Transactions of the Philological Society,* 32-50.

Trueba, H. T. 1979. Bilingual education models, types and designs. *Bilingual multicultural education and the professional: from theory to practice,* ed. by H. T. Treuba and C. Barnett-Mizrahi, 54-73. Rowley, Mass.: Newbury House.

_____, and C. Barnett-Mizrahi. 1979. *Bilingual multicultural education and the professional: from theory to practice.* Rowley, Mass.: Newbury House.

Tucker, G. R. 1975. The acquisition of knowledge by children educated bilingually. *Georgetown University Round Table on Languages and Linguistics,* ed. by D. P. Dato, 267-77. Washington, D.C.: Georgetown University Press.

_____. 1977. The linguistic perspective. *Bilingual education: current perspectives—linguistics,* 1-40. Arlington, Va.: Center for Applied Linguistics.

_____. 1980. Implications for U.S. bilingual education: evidence from Canadian research. *NCBE Focus,* no. 2.

Turner, P. R., ed. 1973. *Bilingualism in the southwest.* Tuscon: University of Arizona Press.

UNESCO. 1953. *The use of vernacular languages in education: monographs of fundamental education,* VIII. Paris: UNESCO.

_____. 1968. *Manpower aspects of educational planning: problems of the future.* Paris: International Institute for Educational Planning, UNESCO.

_____. 1977. *Meeting of experts on language teaching in a bi- or plurilingual and multi-cultural environment: final report* ED77/Conf.613/7. Paris: UNESCO.

Ulibarri, H. 1972. Bilingualism. *Foreign language education: an overview,* ed. by E. Birmaier. Skokie, Ill.: National Textbook Co.

Upshur, J. A. 1969. *'Test' is a four letter word.* Presented at the EPDA Institute, University of Illinois, Urbana, Illinois.

_____, and T. J. Homburg. 1980. *Some language test relations at successive ability levels.* Presented at the Second International Language Testing Symposium, Darmstadt, Germany. To appear in Oller (in press).

Urciuoli, B. 1980. *Social parameters of language contact.* Paper presented at the Conference on Spanish in the United States Setting. University of Illinois at Chicago Circle.

Valdés-Fallis, G. 1976. Social interaction and code-switching patterns: a case study of Spanish/English alternation. *Bilingualism in the bicentennial and beyond,* ed. by G. Keller, et al., 53-85. New York: Bilingual Press.

_____. 1978a. Code-switching among bilingual Mexican-American women: towards an understanding of sex-related language alternation. *International Journal of Sociology of Language* 17.65-71.

_____. 1978b. Code-switching as a deliberate verbal strategy: a microanalysis of direct and indirect requests among bilingual Chicano speakers. To appear. *Latino language and communicative behavior,* ed. by R. Durán. New Jersey: Ablex Publishing Company.

Valdman, A. 1975. The language situation in Haiti. *The Haitian potential,* ed. by V. Rubin and R. P. Schaedel, 61-82. New York: Teachers College Press.

_____. 1978. *Le créole: structure, statut et origine.* Paris: Klincksieck.

_____, ed. 1980. *Créole et enseignement primaire en Haiti.* Bloomington, Ind.: Creole Institute.

Vandezande, R. 1971. *Zwartboek van de Belgische taalwetgeving. Witboek van de subnationaliteit.* Brussels: Volksunie.

van Haegendoren, M. 1965. *The Flemish movement in Belgium.* Antwerp: Flemish Cultural Council.

van Nérum, C. J. 1838. *Essai sur l'instruction primaire et en particulier sur les écoles gratuites de Gand.* Ghent: Annoot-Braeckman.

Varo, C. 1971. *Consideraciones antropológicas y políticas en torno a la enseñanza del 'Spanglish' en Nueva York.* Río Piedras, Puerto Rico: Ediciones Librería Internacional.

Vieter, T. 1977. Sprachenrecht und Sprachenpolitik der Republik Malta. *Europa Ethnica* 3.123-32.

————. 1979. Das österreichische Volksgruppenrecht von 1976. *Ethnos* 18. Vienna: Braumüller.

Verdiere-de-Vits, M. 1971. *Organisation de l'enseignement en Belgique. Enseignement renove.* Unpub. ms.

Verdoodt, A. 1976. Les problèmes communautaires belges à la lumière des études d'opinion. *Courrier Hebdomadaire du CRISP* no. 742.12 novembre.

Verheyen, J. E. 1929. Le bilinguisme en Belgique. *Le bilinguisme et l'éducation,* travaux de la conference internationale tenue à Luxembourg du 2 au 5 avril 1928. Geneva: Bureau International d'Education.

Verlooy, J. B. C. 1938. *Verhandeling op d'onacht der moederlyke tael in de Nederlanden* (1788). Antwerp: De Sikkel. Trans. adapted from S. B. Clough, 1930. *A history of the Flemish movement in Belgium,* 17. New York: Richard R. Smith.

Vernet, P. 1980. *Techniques d'écriture du créole haitien.* Port-au-Prince: Centre de Linguistique Appliquée de Port-au-Prince.

Viletta, R. 1978. *Grundlagen des Sprachenrechts,* vol. I. Zurich: Schulthess Polygraphischer Verlag.

Volkhoff, M. 1944. *L'Expansion du néerlandais,* trad. J. Sepulchre. Brussels: Les Editions Lumière.

Voltaire, Y. 1980. Kréyòl pale, kréyòl konprann: kréyòl ékri, kréyòl pa konprann! *Bon Nouvèl* 150.19.

Vorish, Lillian, and Paul Rosier. 1978. Rock Point Community School: an example of a Navajo-English bilingual elementary school program. *TESOL Quarterly* 12.263-70.

Wald, B. 1974. Bilingualism. *Annual review of anthropology,* 301-21. Palo Alto, Cal.: Annual Review, Inc.

Wallman, S. 1972. Conceptual barriers to cross-cultural communication. *Cultural adaptation within modern Africa,* ed. by S. H. Irvine and J. T. Sanders, 35-47. New York: Teachers College Press.

Ward, F. C., ed. 1974. Education and development reconsidered. *The Bellagio Conference Papers.* New York: Praeger.

Warie, P. 1977. Some aspects of code-mixing in Thai. *Studies in the Linguistic Sciences* 7.21-40.

————. 1978. *Some sociolinguistic aspects of language contact in Thailand.* Unpub. Ph.D. thesis, University of Illinois, Urbana.

Weinreich, U. 1953. *Languages in contact: findings and problems.* The Hague: Mouton.

Weinstein, B. 1979. Language strategists: redefining political frontiers on the basis of linguistic choices. *World Politics* 31.346.

Wells, G. 1979. Describing children's linguistic development at home and at school. *British Education Research Journal* 5.75-89.

Wentz, J. 1977. *Some considerations in the development of syntactic description of code-switching.* Unpub. Ph.D. thesis, University of Illinois, Urbana.

Whinnom, K. 1971. Linguistic hybridization and the 'special case' of pidgins and creoles. *Pidginization and creolization of languages,* ed. by D. Hymes, 91-116. London: Cambridge University Press.

Widdowson, H. G. 1978. *Teaching language as communication.* London: Oxford University Press.

Wiesler, H. 1978. *La scolarisation en Haiti.* Port-au-Prince: Institut Haitien de Statistique.

Wilkins, D. A. 1978. *Notional syllabuses.* London: Oxford University Press.

Wilmars, D. 1966. *De psychologie van de franstalige in vlaanderen: de actergrond van de taalstrijd.* Antwerp: NV Standaard-Boekhandel.

Wingfield, R. 1966. *Haiti, a case study of an underdeveloped area.* Unpub. Ph.D. thesis, Louisiana State University.

Witkin, H., and D. Goodenough. 1977. Field dependence revisited. *Research Bulletin* 77.16. Princeton, N.J.: Educational Testing Service.

Witkin, H., C. Moore, D. Goodenough, and P. Cox. 1977. Field-dependent and field-independent cognitive styles and their educational implications. *Review of Educational Research* 47.1-64.

Wolfram, W. 1969. *A sociolinguistic study of Detroit Negro speech.* Washington, D.C.: Center for Applied Linguistics.

————. 1974. *Sociolinguistic aspects of assimilation.* Arlington, Va.: Center for Applied Linguistics.

Wright, D. 1978. The influence of intensive instruction upon the open exploration behavior of ninth grade students. *Journal of Research in Science Teaching* 15.535-41.

Yabar-Dextre, P. 1978. On the problem of choosing the language of instruction in a multi-lingual setting—the situation in Peru. *International Review of Education* 24.406-9.

Zentella, A. C. 1978. *Code-switching and interactions among Puerto Rican children.* Socio-linguistic Working Paper No. 50. Austin, Tx.: Southwest Educational Development Laboratory.

Zierer, E. 1977. *Second language teaching in a plurilingual context.* Paper presented at the UNESCO Meeting of Experts on Language and Teaching in a Bi- or Plurilingual and Multi-cultural Environment. Paris, December 19-23.

INDEX A
Languages and Language Communities

INDEX B
Authors and Subjects